IFIP Advances in Information and Communication Technology

476

Editor-in-Chief

Kai Rannenberg, Goethe University Frankfurt, Germany

IFIP – The International Federation for Information Processing

IFIP was founded in 1960 under the auspices of UNESCO, following the first World Computer Congress held in Paris the previous year. A federation for societies working in information processing, IFIP's aim is two-fold: to support information processing in the countries of its members and to encourage technology transfer to developing nations. As its mission statement clearly states:

> IFIP is the global non-profit federation of societies of ICT professionals that aims at achieving a worldwide professional and socially responsible development and application of information and communication technologies.

IFIP is a non-profit-making organization, run almost solely by 2500 volunteers. It operates through a number of technical committees and working groups, which organize events and publications. IFIP's events range from large international open conferences to working conferences and local seminars.

The flagship event is the IFIP World Computer Congress, at which both invited and contributed papers are presented. Contributed papers are rigorously refereed and the rejection rate is high.

As with the Congress, participation in the open conferences is open to all and papers may be invited or submitted. Again, submitted papers are stringently refereed.

The working conferences are structured differently. They are usually run by a working group and attendance is generally smaller and occasionally by invitation only. Their purpose is to create an atmosphere conducive to innovation and development. Refereeing is also rigorous and papers are subjected to extensive group discussion.

Publications arising from IFIP events vary. The papers presented at the IFIP World Computer Congress and at open conferences are published as conference proceedings, while the results of the working conferences are often published as collections of selected and edited papers.

IFIP distinguishes three types of institutional membership: Country Representative Members, Members at Large, and Associate Members. The type of organization that can apply for membership is a wide variety and includes national or international societies of individual computer scientists/ICT professionals, associations or federations of such societies, government institutions/government related organizations, national or international research institutes or consortia, universities, academies of sciences, companies, national or international associations or federations of companies.

More information about this series at http://www.springer.com/series/6102

David Aspinall · Jan Camenisch
Marit Hansen · Simone Fischer-Hübner
Charles Raab (Eds.)

Privacy and Identity Management

Time for a Revolution?

10th IFIP WG 9.2, 9.5, 9.6/11.7, 11.4, 11.6/SIG 9.2.2
International Summer School
Edinburgh, UK, August 16–21, 2015
Revised Selected Papers

 Springer

Editors

David Aspinall
University of Edinburgh
Edinburgh
UK

Jan Camenisch
IBM Research Zurich
Rueschlikon
Switzerland

Marit Hansen
Unabhängiges Landeszentrum für
  Datenschutz
Kiel
Germany

Simone Fischer-Hübner
Karlstad University
Karlstad
Sweden

Charles Raab
University of Edinburgh
Edinburgh
UK

ISSN 1868-4238   ISSN 1868-422X (electronic)
IFIP Advances in Information and Communication Technology
ISBN 978-3-319-41762-2   ISBN 978-3-319-41763-9   (eBook)
DOI 10.1007/978-3-319-41763-9

Library of Congress Control Number: 2016943443

Printed on acid-free paper

This Springer imprint is published by Springer Nature
The registered company is Springer International Publishing AG Switzerland

Preface

Over the last decade privacy has been increasingly eroded, and many efforts have been made to protect it. New and better privacy laws and regulations have been made, such as the European General Data Protection Regulation. Industry initiatives such as "Do Not Track" and better accountability have been launched. The research community on privacy and data protection has burgeoned, covering a wider range of technical, legal, and social disciplines. Many privacy-enhancing technologies (PETs) for user-controlled identity management and eIDs have gained in maturity, and the public at large is responding to privacy-related challenges.

Despite these positive signs, privacy remains highly vulnerable. Rapid technology developments and increasing interest in identities and other personal data from commercial and government sectors have fuelled increasing data collection to privacy's detriment, with little apparent financial advantage in its protection. Laws and regulation have been faltering for various reasons: weak and slow implementation, ineffective sanctions, and easy circumvention. Many laws aim at checkbox compliance rather than promoting the actual protection of human rights. Technology and processes have become so complex that not even experts – let alone end-users – can tell whether or not privacy is being protected; hence protective measures are inhibited. This makes it more difficult for user-controlled identity management to succeed in empowering users. Moreover, the Snowden revelations in 2013 made it clear that electronic infrastructures are very vulnerable, and protection mechanisms such as encryption are rarely used. Identity information of Internet and phone users is being collected and analyzed by intelligence services in the pursuit of national security. This is problematic not only for maintaining privacy and managing one's identities, but for the organization and structure of societies and economies in general. Against the hope that this message would be sufficiently clear to enable action to secure infrastructures, the crypto debate has instead re-surfaced, concerning whether users should be allowed to use proper encryption or not.

This raises questions about what is needed to increase privacy protection. Do we need a technological, social, or political revolution, or are we seeing a variety of evolutionary and piecemeal advances? Are the available legal, technical, organizational, economic, social, ethical, or psychological instruments effective? Do we need a transformation of our thinking and acting: a broad sociocultural movement based on personal initiative, not only for citizens to voice their opinions, but also to implement and maintain solutions as alternatives to those technical infrastructures that have been found wanting? These questions, as well as current research on privacy and identity management in general, were addressed at the 10th Annual IFIP (International Federation for Information Processing) Summer School on Privacy and Identity Management, which took place in Edinburgh, Scotland, August 16–21, 2015. The Summer School organization was a joint effort among IFIP Working Groups 9.2, 9.5, 9.6/11.7, 11.4, 11.6, and Special Interest Group 9.2.2, CRISP (Centre for Research into Information, Surveillance and Privacy), the University of Edinburgh School of Informatics and their Security and Privacy Research Group, and several European and national projects: A4Cloud, FutureID, PrismaCloud, PRISMS, and the Privacy-Forum. Sponsorship was received from these organizations and SICSA, the Scottish Informatics and Computer Science Alliance.

This Summer School series takes a holistic approach to society and technology and supports interdisciplinary exchange through keynote and plenary lectures, tutorials, workshops, and research paper presentations. Participants' contributions ranged across technical, legal, regulatory, socioeconomic, social, political, ethical, anthropological, philosophical, and psychological perspectives. The 2015 Summer School brought together some 75 researchers and practitioners from many disciplines, once again, including many young entrants to the field. They came to share their ideas, build up a collegial relationship with others, gain experience in making presentations, and have the chance to publish a paper through these resulting proceedings. Sessions were held on a range of topics: cloud computing, privacy-enhancing technologies, accountability, measuring privacy and understanding risks, the future of privacy and data protection regulation, the US privacy perspective, privacy and security, the PRISMS Decision System, engineering privacy, cryptography, surveillance, identity management, the European General Data Protection Regulation framework, communicating privacy issues to the general population, smart technologies, technology users' privacy preferences, sensitive applications, collaboration between humans and machines, and privacy and ethics.

Reflecting the theme of "Privacy and Identity Management: Time for a Revolution?", an evening audiovisual presentation was given by the composer Matthew Collings and digital designer Jules Rawlinson, based on their opera production, *A Requiem for Edward Snowden*, which was performed in the Edinburgh Festival Fringe. The opera addresses security, loss of faith, and personal sacrifice in a world where we are totally reliant on electronic communication and daily routines in which our privacy is routinely compromised. Collings and Rawlinson explained how they interpreted, interwove, and portrayed these themes as an audiovisual narrative incorporating electronic sound, acoustic instrumentation, and live visuals. The 2015 invited lectures were given by Gabriela Barrantes, Timothy Edgar, Lilian Edwards, Michael Friedewald, Mark Hartswood, Gerrit Hornung, Anja Lehmann, Melek Önen, and Angela Sasse, and a tutorial was given by Kami Vaniea. Many of the Summer School papers, covering a broad landscape of themes and topics, were revised and reviewed for publication in these proceedings, including the paper by Olha Drozd, which was judged to be the Summer School's best student paper.

We are grateful to the Program Committee, the many reviewers of abstracts and papers, those who advised authors on their revisions, the Principal of the University of Edinburgh, and the Head and staff of the School of Informatics at Edinburgh. All contributed in many ways to ensure the successful outcome of the Summer School.

Finally, we dedicate these proceedings to the memory of Caspar Bowden, our colleague, friend, and former participant in Summer Schools and other IFIP events. His final illness prevented him from accepting our invitation to give a prominent keynote lecture and, as before, attending and inspiring us in our common endeavor. Caspar died on the 9th of July, six weeks before the Summer School took place. He will be remembered as a highly knowledgeable expert and a tireless advocate for information privacy rights, and his loss is felt by so many across the world.

May 2016

David Aspinall
Jan Camenisch
Marit Hansen
Simone Fischer-Hübner
Charles Raab

Organization

Program Committee

David Aspinall	University of Edinburgh, UK
Michael Birnhack	Tel Aviv University, Israel
Franziska Boehm	University of Münster, Germany
Rainer Boehme	University of Münster, Germany
Katrin Borcea-Pfitzmann	Technische Universität Dresden, Germany
Jan Camenisch	IBM Research - Zurich, Switzerland
Colette Cuijpers	TILT - Tilburg University, The Netherlands
Josep Domingo-Ferrer	Universitat Rovira i Virgili, Spain
Changyu Dong	University of Strathclyde, UK
Carmen Fernández-Gago	University of Malaga, Spain
Simone Fischer-Hübner	Karlstad University, Sweden
Michael Friedewald	Fraunhofer Institute for Systems and Innovation Research, Germany
Lothar Fritsch	Karlstad University, Sweden
Anne Gerdes	University of Denmark, Denmark
Gloria Gonzalez Fuster	Vrije Universiteit Brussel (VUB), Research Group on Law Science Technology & Society (LSTS), Belgium
Marit Hansen	Unabhängiges Landeszentrum für Datenschutz Schleswig-Holstein, Germany
Mark Hartswood	University of Oxford, UK
Jaap-Henk Hoepman	Radboud University Nijmegen, The Netherlands
Els Kindt	K.U. Leuven, ICRI, Belgium
Eleni Kosta	TILT, Tilburg University, The Netherlands
David Kreps	University of Salford, UK
Anja Lehmann	IBM Research - Zurich, Switzerland
Joachim Meyer	Tel Aviv University, Israel
Monica Palmirani	CIRSFID, Italy
Siani Pearson	HP Labs, UK
Nadezhda Purtova	TILT, Tilburg University, The Netherlands
Charles Raab	University of Edinburgh, UK
Kai Rannenberg	Goethe University of Frankfurt, Germany
Kjetil Rommetveit	University of Bergen, Norway
Heiko Roßnagel	Fraunhofer IAO, Germany
Stefan Schiffner	ENISA, Greece
Daniel Slamanig	Graz University of Technology (IAIK), Austria
Sabine Trepte	Hohenheim University, Germany

Simone Van Der Hof	Leiden University, The Netherlands
Aimee van Wynsberghe	University of Twente, The Netherlands
Diane Whitehouse	The Castlegate Consultancy, UK
Erik Wästlund	Karlstad University, Sweden
Tal Zarsky	University of Haifa/NYU Law School, Israel
John Zic	CSIRO, Australia

Additional Reviewers

Blanco-Justicia, Alberto
Felici, Massimo
Hey, Tim
Ribes-González, Jordi

Contents

Modelling the Relationship Between Privacy and Security Perceptions and the Acceptance of Surveillance Practices

Michael Friedewald[1][(✉)], Marc van Lieshout[2], and Sven Rung[1]

[1] Fraunhofer Institute for Systems and Innovation Research ISI,
Breslauer Straße 48, 76139 Karlsruhe, Germany
{michael.friedewald,sven.rung}@isi.fraunhofer.de
[2] The Netherlands Organisation for Applied Science (TNO),
Strategy and Policy Department, P.O. Box 155, 2600 AD Delft, The Netherlands
Marc.vanLieshout@tno.nl

Abstract. The relationship between privacy and security is often but falsely understood as a zero-sum game, whereby more security can only be achieved by sacrifice of privacy. Since this has been proven as too simplistic this chapter explores what factors are influencing people's perceptions of privacy and security in the context of security-oriented surveillance practices. We are presenting a model showing that structural elements such as trust in the institutions that are implementing and operating surveillance systems are crucial for the acceptability while individual factors such as age, gender or region of living are less important than often assumed.

Keywords: Privacy · Public opinion · Security · Trade-off

1 Introduction

The relationship between privacy and security has often been understood as a zero-sum game, whereby any increase in security would inevitably mean a reduction in the privacy enjoyed by citizens. A typical incarnation of this thinking is the all-too-common argument: "If you have got nothing to hide you have got nothing to fear". This trade-off model has, however, been criticised because it approaches privacy and security in abstract terms and because it reduces public opinion to one specific attitude, which considers surveillance technologies to be useful in terms of security but potentially harmful in terms of privacy [23,25]. Whilst some people consider privacy and security as intrinsically intertwined conditions where the increase of one inevitably means the decrease of the other. There are also other views: There are those who are very sceptical about surveillance technologies and question whether their implementation can be considered beneficial in any way. Then there are people who do not consider monitoring technologies problematic at all and do not see their privacy threatened in any way by their proliferation. Finally there are those who doubt that surveillance technologies are effective enough in the prevention and detection of crime and terrorism to justify the infringement of privacy they cause [17].

Insight in the public understanding of security measures is important for decision makers in industry and politics who are often surprised about the negative public reactions showing that citizens are not willing to sacrifice their privacy for a bit more potential security. On the back of this the PRISMS project aimed to answer inter alia the question: When there is no simple trade-off between privacy and security perceptions, what then are the main factors that affect the perception and finally acceptance of specific security technologies, of specific security contexts and of specific security-related surveillance practices?

The PRISMS project has approached this question by conducting a large-scale survey of European citizens. In [12] we have shown that privacy and security attitudes of European citizens are largely independent from one another. Now we are exploring what factors are influencing citizens' perception towards surveillance-based security practices. This is, however, not simply a matter of gathering data from a public opinion survey, as such questions have intricate conceptual, methodological and empirical dimensions. Citizens are influenced by a multitude of factors. For example, privacy and security may be experienced differently in different political and socio-cultural contexts. In this chapter, however, our focus will be on the survey results, not their interpretation from different disciplinary perspectives.

2   Theoretical Approach

Researchers investigating the relationship between privacy and security have to deal with the so-called privacy paradox [8]: It is well known that while European citizens are concerned about how the government and private sector collect data about citizens and consumers, these same citizens seem happy to freely give up personal and private information when they use the Internet. This "paradox" is not really paradoxical but represents a typical value-action gap, which has been observed in other fields as well [12].[1]

2.1   Social Facts

Measuring privacy and security perceptions thus has to deal with problems similar to ecopsychology at the beginning of the environmental movement in the 1970s: What is the relationship between general values and concrete (environmental) concerns and how do they translate into individual behaviour? In PRISMS we have been inspired by the "theory of planned behaviour" (TPB) that suggests that if people evaluate the suggested behaviour as positive (attitude), and if they think their significant others want them to perform the behaviour (subjective norm), this results in a higher intention and they are more likely to behave in a certain way (Fig. 1).

---

[1] E.g. in the context of environmentalism consumers often state a high importance of environmental protection that is not reflected in their actual behaviour [16].

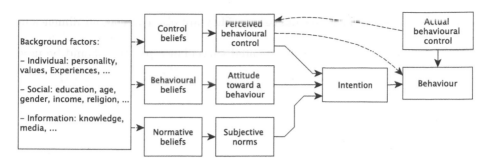

Fig. 1. Model of "planned behaviour" [1, p. 194]

TBP is a positivist approach as it assumes that there are rules structuring the way people think and these "social facts", as Emile Durkheim has been calling them, can be verified by scientific observation and experimentation [9]. We assume that privacy and security perceptions of human being are such social facts and that they can be explained by other attributes (variables) on an aggregated level. We are aware of the fact that this assumption has been criticised by other epistemological perspectives such as critical school, cultural studies and STS, which are highlighting that attitudes and values may be situationally determined rather than stable dispositions and that a number of context factors may limit individual choice [7]. On the other hand a high correlation of attitudes and subjective norms to behavioural intention, and subsequently to behaviour, has been confirmed in many studies [1].

2.2 Operationalisation of Central Concepts

As a consequence the PRISMS survey comprises of questions exploring respondents' perceptions of privacy and security issues as well as values questions including political views, attitudes to rights and perceptions of technology. For the operationalisation of the central concepts we rely on the privacy typology by Finn et al. [10] and a security typology by Lagazio [18], each distinguishing seven different dimensions. These typologies could be used to design batteries of questions to address the wide spectrum of meanings of privacy and security.

To address this ambiguity and context dependence of the central concepts the PRISMS survey is working with so called vignettes that are used when survey respondents may understand survey questions in different ways, due to the abstractness of the presented concepts (privacy, security), their complexity (security technologies and practices) and because they come from different cultures. Vignettes translate theoretical definitions of complicated concepts in presenting hypothetical situations and asking respondents questions to reveal their perceptions and values [22]. We have developed eight different vignettes (very short narratives of 50 to 100 words) presenting different types of security situations and surveillance technologies.[2] They are also covering all dimensions of privacy and security. For each of the vignettes citizens were asked if they think that the respective security-oriented surveillance practice should be used ("acceptance") and to what extend these practices threaten people's rights and freedoms ("intrusiveness").

2.3   Questionnaire and Variables

For our research question we have modified and extended the general TBP model (see Fig. 2) that includes demographic and structural factors and already suggests some interrelationships between the model elements, [cf. 4, 20, 24, for similar attempts].

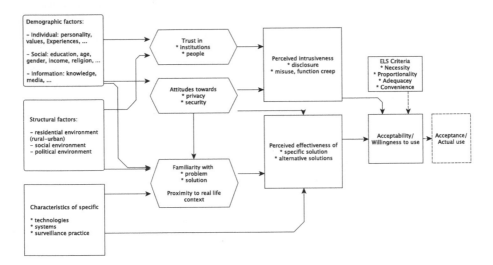

Fig. 2. Suggested relationships between variables explaining privacy and security perceptions and acceptance of security practices

The questionnaire used for the fieldwork thus did not only ask for an assessment of the central concepts privacy and security and of the acceptability and perceived intrusiveness of different security oriented surveillance practices but also those variables needed for the model:

Individual characteristics: Age, gender, education, political orientation, geographic area (country, region), employment status, trust in people, attitude

---

[2] The vignettes depicted situations of (1) foreign government (NSA type) surveillance, (2) school access by biometrics, (3) usage of smart meter data, (4) monitoring of terrorist website visits, (5) speed control in neighbourhoods by automatic number plate recognition (ANPR), (6) selling of Internet Service Provider (ISP) data, (7) use of DNA databases by police and (8) smart video surveillance of crowds.

towards the benefits and risks of science and technology, member of a minority (self assessment)

Experience, behaviour: Intensity of Internet use, experience with privacy invasions, experience with privacy preserving measures, perceived intrusiveness of security practice

Knowledge: Privacy and data protection knowledge

Interim target variables: Trust in institutions, security perceptions, privacy perceptions

Final target variable: Vignette acceptance

2.4   Fieldwork

Fieldwork took place between February and June 2014. The survey company Ipsos MORI conducted around 1,000 30-min phone interviews in all EU member states except Croatia (27,195 in total) amongst a representative sample (based on age, gender, work status and region) within each country. For economic reasons each interviewee was presented only four randomly selected vignettes, resulting in approx. 13,600 responses for each vignette (500 per country).[3]

3   Empirical Results

3.1   Concept and Methodology

Structural equation modelling (SEM) is a method used to study the relationship among multiple outcomes involving latent variables. In this respect SEM is similar to the regression models that were used to test if linear correlations exist between the different variables. However, SEM allows to estimate and test direct and indirect effects in a more complex system of regression equations and verify (or falsify) theories about the absence of relationships among latent variables [15]. For instance, for the development of the SEM we tested the direct influence of demographics variables such as age on the constructs such as privacy and security perceptions and on the acceptance of the vignettes but also the indirect influence of the demographic variable on the acceptance via the constructs.

The main task in the development of a SEM is to reduce the large number of possible connections between the variables by deleting connections that do not show a statistically significant impact on the target variable. This is done iteratively until a number of benchmarks indicate a good model fit.[4]

---

[3] The full questionnaire, technical details of the fieldwork and detailed analyses of the survey can be found in [13].

[4] For estimating fit and coefficients we have used the asymptotic distribution free (ADF) function for SEM. The main advantage of ADF is that it does not require multivariate normality. The estimation of the parameter is done by minimizing the discrepancy between the empirical covariance matrix, and a covariance matrix implied by the model [5].

The model explores the relationship between the different variables to explain which variables influence the acceptance or rejection of surveillance based security practices as outlined in the scenarios. On the highest level the model does no longer distinguish between the vignettes, neither between virtual and physical forms of surveillance nor between public and private operators. Even with these generalisations or simplifications the resulting model is rather complex; it includes 17 variables with more than 40 significant correlations. However, the coefficient of determination R^2, that indicates that the fraction by which the variance of the errors is smaller than the variance of the dependent variable. In our case the target variable "acceptance of surveillance oriented security measure" shows $R^2 = 0.484$, which means that almost half of the variability can be explained though the other variables in the model. This is a good value comparable to similar studies such as [4] or [24].

Due to the complexity of the model it will be presented in four parts or sub-models to single out important influence factors. Three of the sub-models focus on the main constructs (security perceptions, privacy perceptions and trust in institutions) while the last one discusses the "acceptance of security practices" as the target variable. The data used for the model can be found in Table 1.

The nodes in the following diagrams are representing those (influencing) variables that have a significant influence on the other (target) variable ("acceptance of a concrete security practice"). Elliptic nodes represent general demographics variables such as age, gender or education. Rectangular boxes stand for variables that are closely related to the context of surveillance and security practices. These include knowledge about data protection rights, experiences with privacy invasions etc. Hexagonal nodes stand for the main constructs that are also important mediating variables. The trapezoidal nodes finally stand for the target variable(s).[5] The coefficients listed in the second column of Table 1 can also be found next to the edges.

3.2   Factors Influencing "Security Concerns"

Figure 3 shows the influences that constitute citizens' personal security perception (in the context of surveillance oriented security practices). In contrast to the other constructs the security perception is strongly influenced by a number of factors.

Experience with prior privacy infringements has a strong positive effect on the security perception – this is in line with the notion that privacy and security are not perceived as competing values, but that privacy is rather seen as an element of security. On the other hand there are three factors that have a negative influence on the security perception. The higher the education the less worried citizens are about their security. The other negative influence factors are related to trust. The more people trust their fellow citizens and in particular institution the less their security concerns. Apart from these strong influence factors, age,

---

[5] For reasons of simplicity and readability we are not using the normal notation in the following SEM path diagrams. Error terms are not displayed either.

gender and rural-urban classification have a weaker influence on the formation of security perceptions.

Security perceptions in turn have a strong influence on privacy perception (in concrete security contexts!) and finally on the target variables.

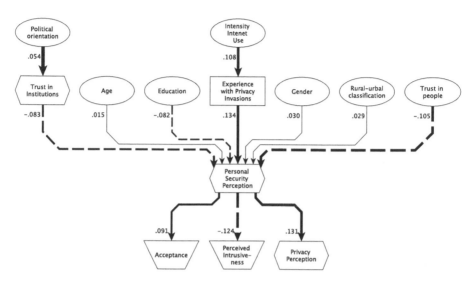

Fig. 3. Sub-model for security concerns. Dotted lines = negative influence, solid lines = positive influence, thickness of the line = strength of the influence

3.3 Factors Influencing "Privacy Concerns"

The influence factors on privacy perceptions as the second important construct is shown in Fig. 4. Privacy perception is constituted from a large number of influence factors without very dominant ones. The rather strong influence of the personal security perception was already mentioned before. Experience with privacy infringements and with privacy protecting measures (privacy activism) have a similarly strong influence on privacy perceptions. Minor influence factors include trust, political orientation and privacy knowledge. The educational level is having a relatively strong indirect influence moderated by trust and intensity of Internet use. In summary the formation of privacy perceptions depends on experience in the context where surveillance takes place and on general knowledge. These two elements help citizens to comprehend the complexity and rationale of surveillance measure and to assess the possibilities of safeguards.

Privacy perceptions are the most important influence factor for citizens' acceptance or rejection of concrete surveillance oriented security measures either directly or indirectly via the assessment of the intrusiveness.

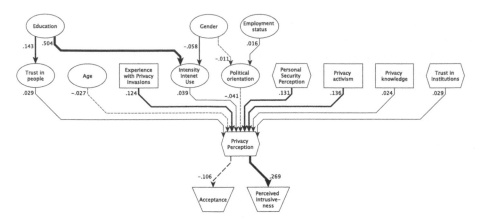

Fig. 4. Sub-model for privacy concerns. Dotted lines = negative influence, solid lines = positive influence, thickness of the line = strength of the influence

3.4 Factors Influencing "Trust in Institutions"

As already mentioned before trust in institutions is another important moderating factor in citizens' assessment of security technologies and practices. Figure 5 shows how the trust construct is influenced by other factors. The most dominant influence is the other dimension of trust, the trust in persons which shows to be highly correlated with trust in institutions. Other more important factors include a person's political orientation, where more conservative (right-winged) persons have a higher trust in institutions such as state agencies, companies and the press. On the other hand trust – in concrete surveillance/security situations – is also influenced by experiences that citizens have had. People who found their privacy invaded are less trusting towards institutions in general. The direct influence of education, gender and rural-urban classification is less important on the formation of trust in institutions. Blinkert has pointed out that this is related to the "relative structural effectiveness", which he defines as a combination of the effectiveness of the state's monopoly on legitimate use of force and the extent of social welfare and distributive justice, that varies greatly between countries and regions [4].

Trust in institutions has no immediate influence on the acceptance of a specific security measure but plays a strong role for people's assessment if such a measure is intrusive, i.e. if it threatens or protects people's fundamental rights. It also has minor effects on the perception of personal security and the perception of privacy, which in turn have a strong effect on acceptance.

3.5 Factors Influencing Acceptance of Surveillance-Oriented Security Technologies

Figure 6 finally shows which variables and constructs influence European citizens' acceptance or rejection of security practices. The most striking result is that the

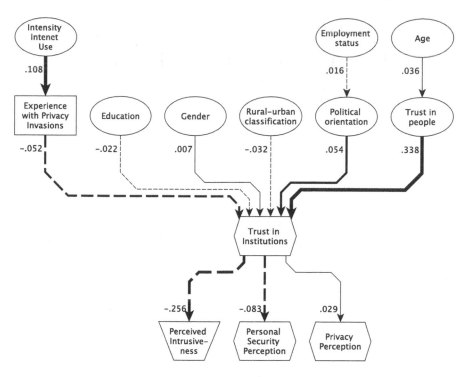

Fig. 5. Sub-model for citizens' trust in institutions. Dotted lines = negative influence, solid lines = positive influence, thickness of the line = strength of the influence

perceived impact of the practice on citizens' rights (here called intrusiveness) is the most critical factor for their acceptance or rejection that itself is strongly influenced by trust in institutions. Privacy and security perceptions follow as the next important factors, however, with a much smaller coefficient. Apart from these three factors most of the other variables play a direct or indirect role, but with a rather small contribution. The only new demographic variable that has a significant (but still small) influence on acceptance is the general attitude towards science and technology where people with a more positive assessment of their benefit have a greater acceptance.

3.6   The Full Picture

The combination of these sub-models does not only show the impacts described before but also the indirect and cumulative effects. Figure 7 is giving a comprehensive picture of the different factors influencing people's perceptions of privacy and security in the context of concrete applications of surveillance based security technologies. In this picture each of the variables (boxes) also includes the share that it contributes to the manifestation of the target variable. The higher this contribution, the bigger the size of the respective node.

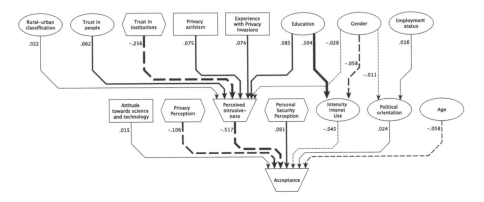

Fig. 6. Sub-model for acceptance of surveillance-oriented security technologies. Dotted lines = negative influence, solid lines = positive influence, thickness of the line = strength of the influence

Apart from the importance of the perceived intrusiveness, trust in institutions and the general perception of privacy and personal security that have already been discussed play a significant role in the acceptance of security oriented surveillance practices. The picture also gives a better impression of the relevance of different personal characteristics.

Among the individual characteristics education plays the most important role: the higher the education level the lower the acceptance of security technology. The influence of education is moderated mainly over three channels: (1) More educated people have a higher level of trust with an influence on the perception of intrusiveness; (2) more educated people usually use the Internet more intensively and have thus more experiences with the possibilities of online surveillance and (3) more educated people have less worries about their personal security.

The other influential personal characteristic is political orientation: More conservative people have a higher level of trust in institutions, also those operating surveillance oriented security technology and thus tend to accept them to a higher degree than more left-winged persons.

Noteworthy is also that age is playing a significant role in the model; the influence, however, on acceptance of surveillance based security technologies is small.

4   Discussion of Results

Our analysis of the questions that aimed to measure European citizens' attitudes towards specific examples of surveillance technologies and practices has the following main results:

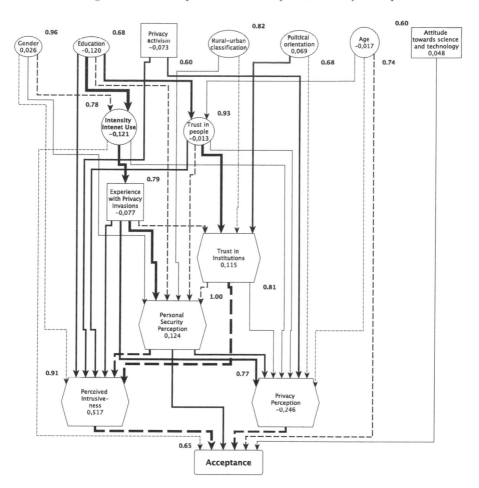

Fig. 7. Model of factors influencing acceptance of SOSTs (simplified). Dotted lines = negative influence, solid lines = positive influence, thickness of the line = strength of the influence, size of nodes = overall influence of a factor on acceptance

Trust in the operating institution is the essential factor for the acceptability of a security practice. The important role of trust, in people, in institutions as well as in the whole societal environment, is regularly confirmed in surveys [4,11,14].

The SurPRISE project, for instance, confirmed clearly that "the more people trust scientific and political institutions ... the more acceptable a technology would be." In their explanatory model institutional trust is the strongest positive influence factor for acceptability of surveillance oriented security technologies [24, p. 135f.].

The PACT project on the other side stresses the strong impact that distrust has on the likelihood that citizens reject a given security measure [21, p. v].

Table 1. Structural equation model data. Estimation Method = ADF; Number of obs = 12,196; Discrepancy = 0.1244

Target variable ← Influencing variables	Coef.	Std. err.	z	P>|z|*	95% Confidence Interval**	
Perceived Intrusiveness ←						
Personal Security Perception	0.125	0.013	9,450	0.000	0.099	0.151
Trust in Institutions	0.257	0.015	17,420	0.000	0.228	0.286
Intensity Internet Use	-0.074	0.009	-7,910	0.000	-0.093	-0.056
Trust in people	-0.062	0.011	-5,430	0.000	-0.085	-0.040
Privacy Perception	-0.269	0.011	-25,220	0.000	-0.290	-0.248
Political orientation	0.053	0.010	5,350	0.000	0.034	0.072
Privacy activism	-0.076	0.010	-7,290	0.000	-0.096	-0.055
Experience with Privacy Invasions	-0.074	0.011	-6,480	0.000	-0.097	-0.052
Education	-0.086	0.011	-7,520	0.000	-0.108	-0.064
Age	-0.061	0.009	-6,790	0.000	-0.078	-0.043
Rural-urban classification	-0.023	0.008	-2,920	0.004	-0.038	-0.007
Gender	0.028	0.005	5,940	0.000	0.019	0.037
Attitude towards science and technology	0.063	0.008	7,480	0.000	0.047	0.080
cons	0.602	0.017	36,130	0.000	0.569	0.635
Acceptance ←						
Perceived Intrusiveness	0.518	0.006	89,060	0.000	0.506	0.529
Personal Security Perception	0.092	0.008	11,350	0.000	0.076	0.108
Intensity Internet Use	-0.045	0.005	-9,010	0.000	-0.055	-0.035
Political orientation	0.025	0.006	3,850	0.000	0.012	0.037
Privacy Perception	-0.107	0.007	-15,100	0.000	-0.121	-0.093
Age	-0.058	0.006	-10,510	0.000	-0.069	-0.048
Attitude towards science and technology	0.015	0.005	2,890	0.004	0.005	0.026
cons	0.320	0.009	33,800	0.000	0.301	0.338

continued on next page

Table 1. (*Continued*)

Target variable ← Influencing variables	Coef.	Std. err.	z	P>|z|*	95% Confidence Interval**	
Personal Security Perception ←						
Trust in people	-0.106	0.009	-11,840	0.000	-0.123	-0.088
Trust in Institutions	-0.083	0.012	-7,150	0.000	-0.106	-0.060
Experience with Privacy Invasions	0.135	0.008	16,800	0.000	0.119	0.150
Education	-0.083	0.008	-10,770	0.000	-0.098	-0.068
Age	0.015	0.005	2,870	0.004	0.005	0.026
Rural-urban classification	0.029	0.006	5,230	0.000	0.018	0.040
Gender	0.031	0.003	9,170	0.000	0.024	0.037
_cons	0.376	0.009	44,150	0.000	0.359	0.393
Intensity Internet Use ←						
Education	0.504	0.013	40,220	0.000	0.480	0.529
Age	-0.534	0.009	-57,600	0.000	-0.552	-0.516
Gender	-0.058	0.005	-10,700	0.000	-0.069	-0.048
_cons	0.778	0.009	83,430	0.000	0.760	0.797
Political orientation ←						
Employment status	0.017	0.006	2,800	0.005	0.005	0.028
Gender	-0.012	0.004	-2,720	0.007	-0.021	-0.003
_cons	0.511	0.005	98,230	0.000	0.500	0.521
Trust in people ←						
Education	0.144	0.009	15,210	0.000	0.125	0.163
Age	0.037	0.007	5,310	0.000	0.023	0.050
_cons	0.425	0.007	58,640	0.000	0.411	0.439
Privacy Perception ←						
Personal Security Perception	0.131	0.011	12,120	0.000	0.110	0.153
Trust in Institutions	0.029	0.013	2,330	0.020	0.005	0.054

continued on next page

Table 1. (*Continued*)

Target variable ← Influencing variables	Coef.	Std. err.	z	P>|z|*	95% Confidence Interval**	
Intensity Internet Use	0.040	0.007	5,660	0.000	0.026	0.054
Trust in people	0.029	0.010	2,960	0.003	0.010	0.048
Political orientation	-0.041	0.009	-4,730	0.000	-0.058	-0.024
Privacy activism	0.137	0.008	16,410	0.000	0.120	0.153
Experience with Privacy Invasions	0.125	0.009	13,570	0.000	0.107	0.143
Age	-0.027	0.007	-3,710	0.000	-0.042	-0.013
Privacy knowledge	0.024	0.007	3,260	0.001	0.010	0.039
_cons	0.397	0.014	29,170	0.000	0.370	0.424
Privacy activism ←						
Intensity Internet Use	0.266	0.005	50,330	0.000	0.255	0.276
Experience with Privacy Invasions	0.253	0.010	24,300	0.000	0.232	0.273
_cons	0.105	0.004	24,950	0.000	0.097	0.113
Trust in Institutions ←						
Trust in people	0.338	0.007	47,770	0.000	0.324	0.352
Political orientation	0.055	0.007	7,830	0.000	0.041	0.068
Experience with Privacy Invasions	-0.053	0.007	-7,980	0.000	-0.066	-0.040
Education	-0.022	0.007	-3,440	0.001	-0.035	-0.010
Rural-urban classification	-0.033	0.005	-6,680	0.000	-0.042	-0.023
Gender	0.008	0.003	2,740	0.006	0.002	0.014
_cons	0.364	0.007	52,560	0.000	0.350	0.378
Experience with Privacy Invasions ←						
Intensity Internet Use	0.109	0.006	19,480	0.000	0.098	0.120
_cons	0.080	0.005	16,700	0.000	0.071	0.089

* A z-score is a measure of how many standard deviations below or above the population mean a raw score is. The value of the test P > |z| indicates the probability that the z-score is random. Zero values in this test indicate that the influence of the factor is not random, i.e. it has a significant influence. It does not give evidence about the strength of the influence.
** The true value of coefficient can be found with a 95% probability in the range given by the 95% Confidence Interval.

Finally also a recent Eurobarometer study on Europeans' attitudes towards security found that institutions' respect for fundamental rights and freedoms is a strongly impacting the perception of security [26, p. 15f.].

Transparency or openness has a positive effect on the willingness of citizens to accept security practices. This can be understood on different levels:

- Citizens tend to accept security practices when they are convinced that a security measure is necessary, proportionate and effective.
- People are more easily convinced when a security practice is embedded in a context that citizens are familiar with and where they understand who is surveying whom and how.
- As a result the surveillance activity should not be covert but perceivable for the citizen and communicated in a responsible way by the operator.
- Understanding and acceptance is also a question of proper knowledge and education - though not only in one way. While education contributes to understanding technicalities and complexities of a security practices it also drives critical reflections. The SurPRISE project also confirmed most of these observations [24, p. 154f.].
- Current security practices, however, often do not seem to take this lesson seriously. In a Eurobarometer survey a majority of European citizens said they think that the security technologies and practices in the fight against terrorism and crime have restricted their rights and freedoms, which then is negatively impacting citizens' trust [26, p. 45ff.].

All these factors also involve an inherent risk for manipulation, since a security practice can be designed to create false trust among citizens to be accepted [3].

On the downside our empirical results also showed that many citizens do not care about surveillance that does not negatively affect them personally but only others. The SuPRISE project similarly concludes that "the more participants perceive SOSTs to be targeted at others rather than themselves, the more likely they are to find a SOST more acceptable" [24, p. 138].

5   Conclusions

For the design and introduction of security measures it is useful to consider some of the main socio-demographic determinants for acceptance of these measures, since poorly-designed measures can consume significant resources without achieving either security or privacy while others can increase security at the expense of privacy. However, since there is no natural trade-off between privacy and security, carefully designed solutions can benefit both privacy and security.

Law enforcement and government officials often heavily weight security. On the other hand we have shown in our analysis of the vignettes that citizens' opinions on security measures vary, and are influenced by some crucial factors.

Apart from trust in the operating agency or company we could observe mainly four different types of reactions [6]:

1. Citizens may consider a measure as useless to enhance security, and at the same time invasive for their privacy. Such a situation has to be absolutely avoided.
2. Citizens may consider a measure useless to enhance security but with no risk for their privacy.
3. Citizens may consider a measure as useful in terms of security, but privacy invasive.
4. Finally, citizens may consider a measure both useful to increase security and with no risk for their privacy.

However, citizen perceptions do not (always) have to reflect the real effectiveness of a security measure and its real impact on privacy. Considering the importance of trust for the acceptability and acceptance the responsible parties should aim to reconcile the perceived and real impacts. Potential for conflicts can be mainly found at the border between reaction types 2 and 3 when citizens fear an invasion of their privacy or perceive a technology as ineffective. Citizens' reactions are mostly based upon perceptions rather than rational fact-based assessments. As we have shown before these are influenced by a multitude of factors. Trust in institutions is one, the perceived self-interest is another, the measure being overt or covert a potential third. These three elements should be taken into account in the design of new security technologies and in specific security investments. For these cases PRISMS has developed a participatory and discursive technique that can help decision-makers in industry, public authorities and politics to implement security measures that raise fewer concerns in the population and are thus more acceptable along the lines stated in many policy documents [2, 19].

Acknowledgement. This work was carried out in the project "PRISMS: Privacy and Security Mirrors" co-funded from the European Union's Seventh Framework Programme for research, technological development and demonstration under grant agreement 285399. For more information see: http://prismsproject.eu.

References

1. Ajzen, I., Fishbein, M.: The influence of attitudes on behavior. In: Albarracin, D., et al. (eds.) The Handbook of Attitudes, pp. 173–221. Erlbaum, Mahwah (2005)
2. Barnard-Wills, D.: Security, privacy and surveillance in european policy documents. International Data Priv. Law **3**(3), 170–180 (2013)
3. Barnard-Wills, D., et al.: Possible dual use of the decision support system. PRISMS Deliverable 10.3, June 2015
4. Blinkert, B.: Unsicherheitsbefindlichkeit als 'sozialer Tatbestand'. Kriminalitätsfurcht und die Wahrnehmung von Sicherheit und Unsicherheit in Europa. In: Erkundungen zur Zivilgesellschaft, pp. 119–146. Lit-Verlag, Münster (2013)

5. Browne, M.W.: Asymptotically distribution-free methods for the analysis of covariance structures. Br. J. Math. Stat. Psychol. **37**(1), 62–83 (1984)
6. Conti, G., et al.: Deconstructing the relationship between privacy and security. IEEE Technol. Soc. Mag. **33**(2), 28–30 (2014)
7. Cook, A.J., et al.: Taking a position: a reinterpretation of the theory of planned behaviour. J. Theory Soc. Behav. **35**(2), 143–154 (2005)
8. Dienlin, T., Trepte, S.: Is the privacy paradox a relic of the past? An in-depth analysis of privacy attitudes and privacy behaviors. Eur. J. Soc. Psychol. **45**, 285–297 (2015)
9. Durkheim, E.: The Rules of Sociological Method [1895]. Trans. by Lakes, S. The Free Press, New York et al. (1982)
10. Finn, R.L., et al.: Seven types of privacy. In: Gutwirth, S., et al. (eds.) European Data Protection: Coming of Age, pp. 3–32. Springer, Dordrecht (2013)
11. Fox, S., et al.: Trust and privacy online: Why Americans want to rewrite the rules. Washington, D.C.: Pew Internet & American Life Project, August 2001. http://www.pewinternet.org/files/old-media//Files/Reports/2000/PIP_Trust_Privacy_Report.pdf
12. Friedewald, M., van Lieshout, M., Rung, S., Ooms, M., Ypma, J.: Privacy and security perceptions of european citizens: a test of the trade-off model. In: Camenisch, J., Fischer-Hübner, S., Hansen, M. (eds.) Privacy and Identity 2014. IFIP AICT, vol. 457, pp. 39–53. Springer, Heidelberg (2015)
13. Friedewald, M., et al.: Report on the analysis of the PRISMS survey. PRISMS Deliverable 10.1. PRISMS project, October 2015. http://prismsproject.eu
14. Hummelsheim, D.: Subjektive Unsicherheit Lebenszufriedenheit in Deutschland: Empirische Ergebnisse einer repräsentativen Bevölkerungsbefragung. In: Zoche, P., et al. (ed.) Sichere Zeiten? Gesellschaftliche Dimensionen der Sicherheitsforschung, pp. 67–89. Lit Verlag, Münster (2015)
15. Kaplan, D.: Structural Equation Modeling: Foundations and Extensions. SAGE, Thousand Oaks (2000)
16. Kollmuss, A., Agyeman, J.: Mind the Gap: why do people act environmentally and what are the barriers to pro-environmental behavior? Environ. Educ. Res. **8**(3), 239–260 (2002)
17. Kreissl, R., et al.: Surveillance: preventing and detecting crime and terrorism. In: Wright, D., Kreissl, R. (eds.) Surveillance in Europe, pp. 150–210. Routledge, London (2015)
18. Lagazio, M.: The evolution of the concept of security. Thinker **43**(9), 36–43 (2012)
19. van Lieshout, M., et al.: The PRISMS Decision Support System. PRISMS Deliverable 11.3, July 2015. http://prismsproject.eu
20. Morton, A.: Measuring inherent privacy concern and desire for privacy: a pilot survey study of an instrument to measure dispositional privacy concern. In: Proceedings of the 2013 ASE/IEEE International Conference on Social Computing, 8–14 September 2013, pp. 468–477. IEEE Computer Society, Washington, D.C. (2013)
21. Patil, S., et al.: Public Perception of Security and Privacy: Results ofthe comprehensive analysis of PACT's pan-European Survey. PACT Deliverable 4.2. RAND Corporation, June 2014. http://www.rand.org/content/dam/rand/pubs/research_reports/RR700/RR704/RAND_RR704.pdf

22. Pavlov, A.: Application of the vignette approach to analyzing cross-cultural incompatibilities in attitudes to privacy of personal data and security checks at airports. In: Zureik, E., et al. (eds.) Surveillance, Privacy, and the Globalization of Personal Information: International Comparisons, pp. 31–45. McGill-Queen's University Press, Montreal (2010)

23. Pavone, V., Degli Esposti, S.: Public assessment of new surveillance-oriented security technologies: beyond the trade-off between privacy and security. Public Underst. Sci. **21**(5), 556–572 (2012)

24. Pavone, V., et al.: Key factors affecting public acceptance and acceptability of SOSTs. SurPRISE Deliverable 2.4. SurPRISE project, January 2015. http://surprise-project.eu/wp-content/uploads/2015/02/SurPRISE-D24-Key-Factors-affecting-public-acceptance-and-acceptability-of-SOSTs-c.pdf

25. Solove, D.J.: Understanding Privacy. Harvard University Press, Cambridge (2008)

26. TNS Opinion & Social, Europeans' attitudes towards Security, Special Eurobarometer 432. doi:10.2837/41650. http://ec.europa.eu/public_opinion/archives/ebs/ebs_432_en.pdf

The US Privacy Strategy

Timothy Edgar[✉]

Watson Institute for International and Public Affairs,
Brown University, 111 Thayer St., Providence, RI 02912, USA
timothy_edgar@brown.edu

Abstract. The hopes of privacy advocates that US president Barack Obama would implement digital privacy reforms have been largely dashed by revelations of extensive US government surveillance. Such revelations have added an acute sense of urgency among ordinary people to the debate over privacy, surveillance, and technology. Unfortunately, despite the existence of innovative cryptographic techniques to protect privacy, US policymakers have so far not taken advantage of them to enable signals intelligence collection in more privacy-protective ways. The problem is not limited to controversial surveillance programs. A once-promising US strategy for online identity, the National Strategy for Trusted Identities in Cyberspace (NSTIC), may also fall short on privacy because of a failure to use available privacy-protecting tools. There is no excuse of such ignorance of the cryptographic state of the art. There is a critical need for greater awareness of privacy-enhancing technologies among policymakers.

Keywords: Privacy · Surveillance · NSA · Privacy-enhancing technologies · Signals intelligence · Online identity

1 Introduction

This paper tells a tale of two privacy debates – a debate about surveillance, and a debate about online identity. The first debate concerns government access to data, and is related directly to the NSA surveillance programs disclosed in the past few years. The second largely concerns the practices of companies, not governments, as the private sector works to establish a new system of online authentication. Nevertheless, company misuse of personal information, no less than NSA spying, has raised widespread concerns among the public [1].

I participated in both the surveillance and the online identity debates while I served in the Obama White House as a privacy advisor. In both cases, we were aware of potentially groundbreaking technologies that could help us achieve our goals without sacrificing privacy. Nevertheless, we did not manage to make use of them. Unfortunately, little has changed: the hard work of implementing privacy-preserving technologies has barely begun.

Published by Springer International Publishing Switzerland 2016. All Rights Reserved
D. Aspinall et al. (Eds.): Privacy and Identity 2015, IFIP AICT 476, pp. 19–29, 2016.
DOI: 10.1007/978-3-319-41763-9_2

2   Time for a Revolution – Or a Requiem?

The title of this year's IFIP summer school – "time for a revolution?" – is a fitting one. The world continues to grapple with the fallout from revelations that began in June 2013 of extensive surveillance by the United States National Security Agency and allied intelligence services. Although Edward Snowden, a contractor for the NSA, disclosed government surveillance programs, the debate he began has sparked a broader global conversation about digital privacy. Ordinary people have become acutely aware of privacy as a value that is in the process of being lost. Only a revolution, it seems, can reverse the process.

At the IFIP summer school venue in Edinburgh, the theme of privacy resonated well beyond dry conversations of academics in the fields of law, policy and technology. Surveillance, privacy, and a loss of trust were the themes of an evocative audiovisual performance at the Edinburgh festival, a work of music and visual art by Matthew Collings and Jules Rawlinson that explored these issues on an emotional level. The performance struck a deep chord.

The title of Collings' and Rawlinson's work, "A Requiem for Edward Snowden", captures a deep distrust of the US government and especially of its intelligence agencies. Explaining the title, Matthew Collings described his view that Snowden would not survive his break with the NSA. "I was convinced that he would shortly be dead", Collings said. Collings also explained that he conceived of his "requiem" in a broader sense. "The death of the excitement of the internet" was a theme of the piece, Collings explained. "It's about the death of privacy, too" [2].

Edward Snowden, of course, remains alive, although on the run. Perhaps the same may be said of privacy. While the causes for diminished privacy are numerous, one culprit is the ignorance of lawmakers, policymakers and business leaders. While they should know better, they continue to insist that we trade privacy for security and convenience. Many people are willing to accept the argument that we have no choice but to sacrifice privacy for other important values only because they are not aware of privacy-enhancing technologies. These technologies may mitigate such trade-offs – if we choose to deploy them.

3   From "Yes, We Can" to "Yes, We Scan"

The election campaign of Barack Obama in 2008 raised expectations in the United States and around the world for a season of progressive change. Perhaps the mood was captured best in the iconic poster created by artist Shepard Fairey, featuring a stencil portrait of Obama, shaded in red, white and blue. Obama gazes thoughtfully into the distance. Below, there is the single word: "Hope". Other versions featured Obama's campaign slogan: "Yes, we can!" [3].

As Barack Obama took office in 2009, privacy and civil liberties advocates had some reason to be optimistic. During his campaign, then-Senator Obama faulted President George W. Bush for excessive claims of executive power in the "war on terrorism". In remarks on the campaign trail, Obama denounced the NSA's "warrantless wiretapping" program, authorized by Bush shortly after September 11, for exceeding

Bush's constitutional authority. He promised that, if elected, he would ask his legal team to review NSA surveillance programs and would reverse excessive executive orders "with the stroke of a pen" [4].

While the stage seemed to be set for a major shift on issues of surveillance and privacy, careful observers noticed nuances in Obama's remarks that were lost on much of the general public. On the campaign trail, Obama did not echo his supporters in denouncing the USA PATRIOT Act, the much-maligned law that broadened surveillance powers. Instead, Obama reserved his sharpest criticism for the way in which Bush had authorized surveillance programs, not for the programs themselves.

Charlie Savage, a national security reporter for The New York Times, notes that Obama consistently advocated a "rule of law" critique rather than a civil liberties critique when discussing national security. Obama argued that the Bush administration's approach was a threat to the separation of powers between the executive, legislative, and judicial branches outlined in the U.S. Constitution, upsetting its system of checks and balances. Obama did not voice nearly as strong an opinion on whether Bush policies violated the individual rights guaranteed in the Bill of Rights [5, pp. 50–55].

What was lost on many Obama supporters was the fact that the "rule of law" critique had become less relevant as the Bush presidency was coming to a close. Bush's second term in office was marked by an effort to normalize counterterrorism powers. Bush administration lawyers had already stepped back from some of the maximalist positions that they had advanced in the early days after September 11. The NSA surveillance programs that Bush created in his first term by executive order were now authorized by orders of the Foreign Intelligence Surveillance Court.

Obama was briefed on these programs shortly after he took office. He learned they were no longer based on a theory that the president, as Commander-in-Chief, could override the will of Congress and bypass the federal courts in order to conduct surveillance of the enemy in a time of "war on terrorism". Instead, NSA surveillance programs were now firmly grounded in federal law, as interpreted by the surveillance court. The court had accepted the expansive interpretations that national security lawyers had urged to bring Bush's unilateral surveillance programs under the court's purview. As a result, Obama chose to continue these NSA programs without substantial change.

Obama turned his attention to a broader privacy agenda. The major items were strengthening consumer privacy and addressing the growing problem of cybersecurity. The privacy issues associated with cybersecurity monitoring were complex and difficult. Obama was the first U.S. president to devote a major address entirely to the subject of cybersecurity. In 2009, he announced an ambitious plan to strengthen security for government and critical infrastructure networks. As part of that plan, he ordered a new initiative to facilitate the development of a system of online identity management, led by the private sector, that would include significant privacy safeguards [6].

In Obama's cybersecurity address, he also announced that he would appoint a privacy and civil liberties official to the White House National Security Staff, serving its new Cybersecurity Directorate. I was chosen to fill that position. Obama's decision to create my position reflected how important privacy issues had become in national security policy. While the National Security Council had long employed a small staff to address human rights issues, I became the first privacy official to serve on the NSC staff.

In June 2013, the Obama administration was blindsided by an avalanche of unauthorized disclosures of NSA surveillance programs. Edward Snowden, a young NSA contractor then living in Hawaii, had absconded with a trove of highly classified documents detailing the United States government's aggressive world-wide signals intelligence collection operations. Snowden leaked his documents to Glenn Greenwald, Laura Poitras, and other journalists. Over a series of months, stretching into years, the public was treated to a series of alarming revelations of global surveillance operations.

For many of Obama's progressive supporters, already dismayed by his continuation of Bush counterterrorism policies, the revelations were a shocking breach of trust. A parody of the Shepard Fairey "Hope" poster captures the sense of betrayal. Obama's portrait is modified to show him as an eavesdropper. He is outfitted with headphones, and the slogan underneath the portrait mocks his promise of change: "Yes, we scan", it reads. Fairey himself shares the dismay. In an interview in May 2015, Fairey said that Obama had not lived up to the famous image he had created for him. "I mean, drones and domestic spying are the last things I would have thought" Obama would support, he said [7, 8].

The government confirmed many of the surveillance programs that Snowden leaked. The programs that have occasioned the greatest debate in the United States involve programs of domestic collection. They include bulk collection of telephone metadata under section 215 of the USA PATRIOT Act and collection of Internet and other communications content under section 702 of FISA, where the data is inside the United States but the direct targets are foreign. These programs involve oversight by the Foreign Intelligence Surveillance Court.

Other controversial programs include surveillance of foreign leaders, bulk collection of foreign communications and data, and NSA's efforts to undermine global communications security. These programs fall outside the Foreign Intelligence Surveillance Act. They are authorized by Executive Order 12,333, and are subject to looser oversight rules enforced entirely within the Executive Branch. They do not require oversight by any court.

The intelligence community's initial reaction to the Snowden revelations was based on the way it had responded to similar controversies in the past. Intelligence officials denounced Snowden for betraying government secrets, and defended surveillance programs by pointing to protections for the privacy of American citizens and residents – "United States persons", in the jargon of intelligence oversight rules. U.S. person information was protected, officials said, in all intelligence activities. For those programs subject to the oversight of the surveillance court, the rules were even stricter.

The strategy fell flat. According to opinion polls, a majority of Americans viewed Edward Snowden more as a whistleblower than a traitor. They did not trust the NSA's assurances that their data was protected by privacy rules. Congress was up in arms about bulk collection of telephone metadata. The backlash surprised an intelligence community that had become accustomed, ever since the attacks of 9/11, to receiving the benefit of the doubt when it came to programs said to be necessary to fight terrorism.

The reaction of the international community also put the Obama administration under considerable pressure. German chancellor Angela Merkel was deeply offended to learn that her communications had been a target of NSA spying, and the German public shared her outrage. Brazilian president Dilma Rousseff was also angry when she found out the NSA had monitored her communications. Brazil organized an international conference on Internet governance, and raised awkward questions about U.S. dominance of the Internet's physical and economic infrastructure. Other friendly countries were likewise demanding explanations.

The administration also found itself under pressure from the technology industry. In late December 2013, executives from major technology companies, including Apple's Tim Cook, Yahoo's Marissa Mayer, and Google's Eric Schmidt, met with President Obama at the White House to press their concerns about NSA surveillance. The intelligence community's standard defense – our surveillance is directed at foreigners and we have rules to protect "U.S. person" information – was not addressing industry's concerns. If anything, the argument was counterproductive, as it implied that the privacy of foreign citizens did not count for anything. American technology companies were facing a real danger of lost business abroad. Estimates of lost business ranged from \$35 billion to \$180 billion, according to industry groups [9, 10].

4   Obama's Surveillance Reforms

The harsh reaction to the Snowden revelations made surveillance reform an imperative for the Obama administration. Obama's first step was to order his Director of National Intelligence, James Clapper, to increase the transparency of intelligence programs. Clapper had become infamous in the days after the revelations had begun in June 2013 for his denial at a public Congressional hearing that the NSA had records belonging to "millions or tens of millions of Americans". Clapper believed his answer was, in his words, "the least untruthful" statement he was able to give at the time, while preserving the secrecy of the NSA's programs.

Now, Clapper was put in charge of a drive to inform the public about how the NSA worked. He used a popular microblogging platform, "tumblr", to launch "IC on the Record", disseminating thousands of pages of declassified documents detailing the rules about how the NSA programs work. They included scores of once-secret surveillance court opinions. By the fall of 2013, one transparency advocate, Steve Aftergood, marveled, "Already we've seen a more extensive disclosure of classified information about current intelligence programs than we've seen for at least 40 years, and maybe ever." By March 2014, Obama's transparency reforms had resulted in the authorized disclosure of more than twice as many previously classified documents as Snowden had leaked [11, 12].

Advocates remained skeptical that the transparency reforms would last, viewing the initiative merely as a tactic to fight back against the Snowden leaks. Still, the intelligence community also put in place more permanent policies. They include an annual "transparency report" detailing the number of targets affected by orders of the Foreign Intelligence Surveillance Court. Previously, only the number of orders was released – a relatively meaningless number, given new legal authorities that allowed one order to cover tens of thousands of targets. The intelligence community also created an implementation plan to institutionalize its newfound commitment to transparency.

Obama's reforms went further than increased transparency. Obama also enhanced intelligence oversight to protect the privacy rights of foreigners. Presidential Policy Directive 28 (PPD-28), issued in January 2014, extends for the first time the mechanisms that the intelligence community uses to protect "U.S. person" information explicitly to protect information belonging to anyone, anywhere in the world. While the substance of the rules is relatively modest, the concept is revolutionary [13].

Retention and minimization limits that once applied only to U.S. persons now apply to all "personal information". Other protections have been codified as well. Signals intelligence cannot be used to disadvantage anyone, anywhere in the world, on the basis of race, gender, sexual orientation, or religion. The rules now explicitly prohibit such misuse of intelligence information – for example, by blackmailing a foreign leader who is gay.

PPD-28 also places limits on "bulk collection of signals intelligence". Bulk collection is not prohibited, but it is limited to six specific national security threats. The NSA may no longer collect signals intelligence in bulk unless it is to protect against espionage, international terrorism, proliferation of weapons of mass destruction, cybersecurity threats, threats to U.S. or allied military forces, or transnational crime. Broader foreign affairs objectives may now be achieved only through targeted intelligence collection.

Congress has also taken action to reform surveillance. In June 2015, section 215 of the USA PATRIOT Act was set to expire. As we have seen, it was an expansive interpretation of section 215 that was the legal authority for bulk collection of telephone metadata. The bulk collection legal theory was under fire. Although the Foreign Intelligence Surveillance Court continued to issue orders under section 215, civil liberties groups had challenged bulk collection in other federal courts. In a major blow to the government, the United States Court of Appeals for the Second Circuit ruled in May 2015 that bulk collection was not authorized by section 215 [14].

The Obama administration and a majority of both houses of Congress had negotiated an alternative to bulk collection, which was enacted shortly after section 215 expired. The principal sponsors of the reform bill, Senator Patrick Leahy (D-VT) and Representative James Sensenbrenner (R-WI), had been the original sponsors of the USA PATRIOT Act of 2001. Leahy and Sensenbrenner were responsible for that law's extravagantly Orwellian name, which is an acronym for the "Uniting and Strengthening America by Providing Appropriate Tools Required to Intercept and Obstruct Terrorism Act". Leahy and Sensenbrenner gave their bill to reform surveillance a similarly extravagant name, albeit one that leans in favor of civil liberties. The law that ended bulk collection is the USA FREEDOM Act of 2015, which stands for the "Uniting and Strengthening America by Fulfilling Rights and Ending Eavesdropping, Dragnet-collection and Online Monitoring Act".

The USA FREEDOM Act extended the expiring provisions of the USA PATRIOT Act, including section 215, for another four years, while prohibiting its use for bulk collection. The USA FREEDOM Act replaces bulk collection with a system under which telephone metadata will remain with the companies, but is subject to rapid queries by NSA analysts. NSA analysts must use a "specific selection term" to retrieve data; much of the debate over the bill concerned the breadth of this definition.

Congress also enacted reforms to the Foreign Intelligence Surveillance Court. Congress required the court to issue declassified versions of significant opinions – such as opinions that would interpret "specific selection term". Congress also created a mechanism for the court to appoint a "special advocate" – a lawyer with a top security clearance who could potentially challenge government lawyers before the court.

5 Using Technology to Protect Privacy: A Missed Opportunity?

The debate over surveillance reform in the United States has largely been a debate about law, usually among lawyers. Does section 215 of the USA PATRIOT Act authorize bulk collection? Is it constitutional? What should be rules for surveillance of foreign targets under section 702 of the Foreign Intelligence Surveillance Act? Is section 702 constitutional? The assumption is that a more refined set of legal rules can better calibrate societal trade-offs between privacy and security.

In the legal debate, privacy is often on the defensive. Of course, civil libertarians argue for legal rules that restrict collection, retention and use of personal information as a bulwark against abuse. Nevertheless, the public is likely to discount such arguments if it is sufficiently fearful of terrorism, reasoning that preventing attacks may be worth some risk of privacy abuse.

Technology offers an opportunity to reframe the debate. Some of the trade-offs that the policy debate takes for granted have increasingly become obsolete. Advances in cryptography over the past decade now provide new alternatives to mass surveillance programs. Cryptography often gives us the opportunity to "have our cake and eat it too", according to Anna Lysyanskaya, a computer scientist at Brown University. She argues that, "at least in theory", we can "gain the benefits of the digital age without sacrificing privacy". The argument for privacy is far stronger if there are practical alternatives that meet government's legitimate objectives [15].

In PPD-28, President Obama tasked the Director of National Intelligence with providing a report "assessing the feasibility of creating software that would allow the [intelligence community] more easily to conduct targeted information acquisition rather than bulk collection". It was a hopeful sign. An organization within the DNI's office, the Intelligence Advanced Research Projects Activity (IARPA), had funded substantial research in the areas of cryptography that could be helpful in preserving the privacy of data. The DNI, in turn, assigned the task of writing the report to the National Academy of Sciences (NAS).

The NAS report was something of a disappointment. While it recommended new software "to more effectively target collection and to control the usage of collected data", it discounted the more ambitious goal of replacing bulk collection altogether.

For one thing, the report noted, unless information is collected in bulk, there was no guarantee that data about past events would be available when needed; the database owner might not retain it. No cryptographic technique can recreate data that no longer exists. Cryptography also requires more computational power than collection and analysis of the bulk data in unencrypted form, i.e., "in the clear" [16, pp. 9–10].

The report concluded that "there is no software technique that will fully substitute for bulk collection; there is no technological magic."

While the report's conclusion was valid, its tone sent the wrong message. The disparaging use of the term "magic" was especially unfortunate, as advanced cryptographic techniques can produce results that, to the non-specialist, seem precisely like magic! One example is private information retrieval. Imagine that one party, such as the NSA, would like to retrieve information from a large database held by another party, such as a cloud computing provider, under section 702 of FISA. Without private information retrieval, the NSA must either trust the provider with its highly classified list of selectors, or the provider must trust the NSA with unrestricted access to its database or provide it with a complete copy. Private information retrieval uses cryptography to allow the NSA to search the company's database without the company learning the NSA's query, but with complete confidence that only data matching those selectors will be provided to the NSA.

Similarly, bulk collection of metadata could benefit from the use of secure two-party and multiparty computation. Under the USA FREEDOM Act, the NSA may no longer use section 215 of the USA PATRIOT Act to obtain in bulk all telephone metadata maintained by the telephone companies. Under the new law, those bulk records will remain with the companies. The NSA, however, may rapidly query metadata about people in communication with its targets and also about people in communication with those people – out to two "hops". It would seem the NSA's only choice is to trust the telephone companies with its target list so they can retrieve the information, hopefully without leaking classified information.

If that trust turns out to be misplaced, would the NSA's only solution be to ask Congress to restore bulk collection so it can go back to doing this for itself? Secure multiparty computation provides an alternative. It would permit the NSA to find the records that it needs by posing an encrypted question to an encrypted database maintained by the telephone companies. The NSA would learn nothing about data that it did not need. The telephone companies would learn nothing about the NSA's queries.

Using such techniques would provide at least some of the benefits of bulk collection, without the cost to privacy. They are only effective if they can be made efficient and can work on a large scale. As early as 2008, there was a demonstration of large scale, real-world use of secure multiparty computation that permitted participants in the Danish sugar-beet market to agree on a pricing scheme. In 2014, computer scientists proposed a scalable system using secure two-party computation, "Blind Seer", that could be deployed by an agency like the NSA with little cost to efficiency. [17] IARPA funded the research on "Blind Seer".

The government has known about privacy enhancing technologies for many years – as we have seen, it funded much of the research that has made the use of such techniques practical. Policymakers, however, continue to be largely unaware of the ways in which technology can mitigate trade-offs that may otherwise appear to be unavoidable. The debate over bulk collection and mass surveillance since 2013 has, unfortunately, so far been marked by a missed opportunity to "have our cake and eat it too".

6 Online Identity

Surveillance is not the only problem in which ignorance of technology is potentially dangerous to privacy. In Obama's cybersecurity address of 2009, he announced that he would propose an ambitious strategy to facilitate a more secure and effective system of online identity management. We worked on the strategy for two years. In 2011, the White House released its "National Strategy for Trusted Identities in Cyberspace" (NSTIC), a plan to create a secure "identity ecosystem", led by the private sector. A major goal of the NSTIC initiative is to move away from passwords to more reliable forms of identity management, allowing people to engage in transactions that requires higher levels of identity assurance [18].

The Commerce Department has taken the lead on implementing NSTIC, launching a dialogue with companies and other stakeholders. NSTIC has significant privacy implications. A system of online identity could pose a real threat to privacy, especially if it permits companies or the government more easily to link together all of a user's individual Internet activities and transactions.

NSTIC contains ambitious privacy goals. NSTIC calls for "privacy-enhancing technical standards" that "minimize the transmission of unnecessary information", allowing transactions that are "anonymous, anonymous with validated attributes, pseudonymous, and uniquely identified." The drafters of NSTIC were aware of the work on "anonymous credentials" by Jan Camenisch and Anna Lysyanskaya and other computer scientists. Anonymous credentials employ zero-knowledge proofs to allow the holder of a credential to validate the attributes that another party needs to complete a transaction online without revealing anything more (see e.g. [19]; an excellent non-technical explanation can be found in [20]).

While NSTIC did not proscribe a specific technical solution, fully realizing its privacy goals would require the use of anonymous credentials. The alternative is to trust an "identity provider" to validate online transactions. Initial NSTIC pilots, however, appear to be following the "trusted third party" model. One start-up, "ID.me", touts itself as a "trusted intermediary" for verifying identity. The founders of ID.me are featured on the government's NSTIC website meeting with President Obama. Even if third parties such as ID.me have excellent privacy policies, consumers are being asked to trust yet another entity with their private information [21, 22].

As with surveillance reform, the implementation of the Obama administration's online privacy strategy has so far missed an opportunity to make use of an innovative technology that could enhance privacy. Instead, policymakers and businesses are insisting on trade-offs that we do not have to make.

7 Ignorance of Technology Is no Excuse!

Ignorantia juris non excusat. "Ignorance of the law excuses not" is an ancient principle that prevents the guilty from escaping the consequences of flouting society's laws. The law has proven to be a less-than-ideal guardian of our privacy. A contributing factor to the failure of law and policy has been the ignorance of lawmakers and policymakers about innovative privacy-enhancing technologies. If we want to preserve our privacy, we must adopt a new principle – ignorance of technology is no excuse!

While the reasons for such ignorance are not entirely clear, the most likely explanation may be the loose and inconsistent rules that have allowed, at least in the United States, broad public and private sector use of large databases containing personal information without technical safeguards. If the use of privacy-enhancing technologies is regarded not as a necessary precondition for the use of such data, but only as a matter of academic interest, there is little reason for policymakers to become familiar with them. Compounding the problem, even informed and motivated policymakers may not know what questions to ask. Many privacy-enhancing technologies offer capabilities that are not obvious and may appear like magic to non-specialists.

The time has come for privacy-minded academics and advocates to evangelize on behalf of the benefits of privacy-enhancing technologies to a much broader audience. Privacy advocacy should move away from bemoaning the death of privacy towards offering a vision that breathes life into privacy.

As the performance of a "Requiem for Edward Snowden" was able to capture in image and music, we are at a crucial moment – a moment that calls for a revolution in privacy. If we fail to take stronger steps to accelerate real-world deployment of innovative solutions for preserving privacy, its legacy may best be celebrated by a singing a requiem for privacy – whatever the fate of the former NSA contractor hiding out in Moscow.

References

1. Cox, A.M.: Who should we fear more with our data: the government or companies? The Guardian, 20 Jan 2014 (2014). http://www.theguardian.com/commentisfree/2014/jan/20/obama-nsa-reform-companies-spying-data. Accessed 11 Feb 2016
2. Pollock, D.: How Edward Snowden inspired a musical vision of the future. The Scotsman, 20 Aug 2015 (2015). http://www.scotsman.com/lifestyle/culture/music/how-edward-snowden-inspired-a-musical-vision-of-the-future-1-3863946. Accessed 8 Feb 2016
3. Barton, L.: Hope – the image that is already an American classic. The Guardian, 9 Nov 2009 (2009) http://www.theguardian.com/artanddesign/2008/nov/10/barackobama-usa. Accessed 20 Feb 2016
4. Remarks by senator Barack Obama in Lancaster, Pennsylvania. CNN, 31 March 2008 (2008). https://www.youtube.com/watch?v=AzgNf9iZ2Bo. Accessed 11 Feb 2016
5. Savage, C.: Power Wars: Inside Obama's Post-9/11 Presidency. Little, Brown and Company (2015)
6. Remarks by the president on securing our nation's cyber infrastructure, 29 May 2009 (2009) https://www.whitehouse.gov/video/President-Obama-on-Cybersecurity#transcript. Accessed 20 Feb 2016
7. Patches, M.: Shepard fairey on the future of political art and whether Obama lived up to his "hope" poster. Esquire, 28 May 2015 (2015). http://www.esquire.com/news-politics/interviews/a35288/shepard-fairey-street-art-obama-hope-poster/. Accessed 20 Feb 2016

8. Jauregui, A.: Yes we scan: shepard fairey likes Obama NSA parodies, "Pleased" with subversive symbolism. Huffington Post, 23 June 2013 (2013). http://www.huffingtonpost.com/2013/06/28/yes-we-scan-shepard-fairey-obama-nsa_n_3517213.html. Accessed 20 Feb 2016

9. Rushe, D., Lewis, P.: Tech firms push back against White House efforts to divert NSA meeting. The Guardian, 17 Dec 2013 (2013). http://www.theguardian.com/world/2013/dec/17/tech-firms-obama-meeting-nsa-surveillance. Accessed 21 Feb 2016

10. Miller, C.C.: Revelations of N.S.A. spying cost U.S. tech companies. N.Y. TIMES, 21 March 2014 (2014). http://www.nytimes.com/2014/03/22/business/fallout-from-snowden-hurting-bottom-line-of-tech-companies.html. Accessed 21 Feb 2016

11. Aftergood, S.: ODNI rethinks secrecy and openness in intelligence, federation of American scientists. Secrecy News (blog), 20 March 2014 (2014). https://fas.org/blogs/secrecy/2014/03/litt-transparency/. Accessed 21 Feb 2016

12. Johnson, C.: Snowden's leaks lead to more disclosure from feds. NPR Morning Edition, 11 Oct 2013 (2013). http://www.npr.org/2013/10/11/231899987/snowdens-leaks-lead-to-more-disclosure-from-feds. Accessed 21 Feb 2016

13. Presidential Policy Directive – Signals Intelligence Activities (Presidential Policy Directive 28/PPD-28), 17 Jan 2014 (2014). https://www.whitehouse.gov/the-press-office/2014/01/17/presidential-policy-directive-signals-intelligence-activities. Accessed 21 Feb 2016

14. American Civil Liberties Union v. Clapper, No. 14-42-cv (2nd Cir. 7 May 2015)

15. Lysyanskaya, A.: Cryptography is the future. In: Rotenberg, M., Horwitz, J., Scott, J. (eds.): Privacy in the Modern Age: The Search for Solutions, pp. 112–118. The New Press (2015)

16. National Research Council: Bulk Collection of Signals Intelligence: Technical Options. The National Academies Press (2015)

17. Pappas, V., et al.: Blind seer: a scalable private DBMS. In: 2014 IEEE Symposium on Security and Privacy, pp. 359–374 (2014)

18. The White House; National Strategy for Trusted Identities in Cyberspace, April 2011 (2011). http://www.whitehouse.gov/sites/default/files/rss_viewer/NSTICstrategy_041511.pdf. Accessed 21 Feb 2016

19. Camenisch, J.L., Lysyanskaya, A.: An efficient system for non-transferable anonymous credentials with optional anonymity revocation. In: Pfitzmann, B. (ed.) EUROCRYPT 2001. LNCS, vol. 2045, pp. 93–118. Springer, Heidelberg (2001)

20. Lysyanskaya, A.: Cryptography: how to keep your secrets safe. Scientific American, Sept 2008 (2008). http://www.scientificamerican.com/article/cryptography-how-to-keep-your-secrets-safe/

21. www.nstic.gov/nistc/. Accessed 21 Feb 2016

22. ID.me Digital Credentials Now Accepted Across Government Websites. Business Wire, 3 Dec 2014 (2014). http://www.businesswire.com/news/home/20141203006149/en/ID.me-Digital-Credentials-Accepted-Government-Websites#.VSbEimZygTX. Accessed 21 Feb 2016

SmartSociety: Collaboration Between Humans and Machines, Promises and Perils

Mark Hartswood[(✉)] and Marina Jirotka

Department of Computer Science, Oxford University, Oxford, UK
{mark.hartswood,marina.jirotka}@cs.ox.ac.uk

Abstract. As the European Union (EU) funded SmartSociety project aims to create a toolset for rapidly and systematically engineering collective intelligence systems to support daily living, it simultaneously wants to ameliorate the risks to individuals of participating in these types of hyper-connected digital systems. This paper reports on a panel session at the close at of the 2015 IFIP summer school that reflected upon a keynote speech covering SmartSociety concepts, technologies and ethical dilemmas. The panel session was conceived as a consultative exercise as part of the ongoing Responsible Research and Innovation (RRI) approach embedded within the SmartSociety project. In this chapter we present an analysis of the panel session discussion, which touched on several key issues, including the relationships between technology and society, what we should expect from a 'SmartSociety', barriers and horizons in managing ethical issues, and brokerage as a methodological approach to weaving multiple perspectives into design.

Keywords: SmartSociety · Responsible Research and Innovation · Panel session · Techno-social visions · Brokerage

1 Introduction

SmartSociety[1] is a 4 year EU funded project that is at the forefront of how digital technologies are transforming our lives. SmartSociety builds on existing trends towards increasingly closely coupled systems of people, devices, data and algorithms designed to guide people in their everyday activities. SmartSociety aims to leverage collectives of people and machines to provide Smart City services in ways that satisfy individual goals while simultaneously tackling societal challenges such as sustainability. It welcomes the increasing interconnectedness of our physical and digital existences to support new ways for people to collectively solve problems by connecting them to remote pools of expertise and resources possessed by participating humans and machines [1].

SmartSociety aims to assist people in their everyday activities, while using the collective intelligence of the system as a whole to protect and preserve our shared resources. A traffic system enabled by SmartSociety would give advice to individuals on how to speedily complete their journey, while at the same time influencing overall flows of traffic to minimize pollution, reduce congestion, and reduce the impact of

---

[1] http://www.smart-society-project.eu/.

© IFIP International Federation for Information Processing 2016
Published by Springer International Publishing Switzerland 2016. All Rights Reserved
D. Aspinall et al. (Eds.): Privacy and Identity 2015, IFIP AICT 476, pp. 30–48, 2016.
DOI: 10.1007/978-3-319-41763-9_3

traffic incidents. Similarly, a SmartSociety tourism solution would utilize local knowledge to provide a customized experience for the individual user while at the same time smoothing the impact of tourism on the local infrastructure.

A SmartSociety keynote speech and panel session were included as part of the 2015 IFIP Summer School on Privacy and Identity Management[2] with the aim of presenting the project's vision and eliciting feedback from the privacy community concerning privacy and other ethical challenges that the project faces. This approach of engagement forms part of the Responsible Research and Innovation agenda within SmartSociety, where issues pertaining to privacy and other social values are addressed as an integral part of realizing the project's goals. The panel session was recorded and transcribed so as the consortium could benefit fully from the discussion. An analysis of this transcript forms the main contribution of this chapter.

In this chapter we briefly introduce the emerging paradigm of Responsible Research and Innovation, and how this is being realized within SmartSociety. We recap some of the themes of SmartSociety that were featured in the keynote presentation under the rubric of the 'Promises and Perils' of a SmartSociety. Finally, we present an analysis of the panel session discussion, which touched on several key issues, including the relationships between technology and society, what we should expect from a 'SmartSociety', barriers and horizons in managing ethical issues, and brokerage as a methodological approach to weaving multiple perspectives into design.

2 Responsible Research and Innovation in SmartSociety

Responsible Research and Innovation (RRI) seeks to open up innovation processes so that they incorporate a broader range of perspectives of the techno-social futures that innovation may bring about. RRI aims to achieve this by coordinating a varied range of multi-level activities[3] undertaken by multiple actors at multiple points with the research /innovation lifecycles towards ensuring the outcomes of research and innovation are 'socially acceptable' and 'socially beneficial'. These may include traditional ethics processes, risk assessments and foresight procedures, as well as more innovative activities tailored to specific domains or research streams that emphasize multi-stakeholder involvement [2].

RRI has been incorporated into funding bodies' research agendas. For the EU it is an integral part of the H2020 programme both as standalone actions as well as being integrated within other research themes[4]. In the UK, the Engineering and Physics Sciences Research Council (EPSRC) expects (but does not mandate) that RRI activities be built into research processes, offering the AREA[5] framework as guidance for

---

[2] http://www.ifip-summerschool.org/.

[3] E.g. in the planning, conduct and dissemination of research; during the formulation of research programmes and by policy makers in anticipating the regulatory requirements of innovation emerging from research.

[4] http://ec.europa.eu/programmes/horizon2020/en/h2020-section/responsible-research-innovation.

[5] The AREA acronym stands for: Anticipate, Reflect, Engage and Act. https://www.epsrc.ac.uk/research/framework/area/.

researchers wishing to pursue an RRI approach. While the stances of the EU and UK differ in detail, they both place considerable emphasis on consultation and engagement across a broad range of publics as a central pillar of RRI.

An obvious quandary for RRI is how to decide which outcomes are actually socially beneficial - especially since innovation events themselves tend to alter our values and perspectives as a basis for judgment. Two proposals for solving this problem have been proposed. The first, promoted by von Schomberg, is to envisage RRI as encoding existing values enshrined within national or international charters, such as the European Union treaty, as providing "normative anchor points" for shared values such as the right to privacy, enhancing sustainability, promoting equality and so on [3]. The second is less prescriptive of specific values and focuses instead on opening up spaces for reflection and dialogue where processes of value formation (including elements of consensus and conflict) can be played out [4]. Our approach draws on both of these proposals by following Brey [5] in framing issues in relation to values of democracy, fairness, autonomy and privacy. At the same time we treat each of these categories as a 'discursive space' where the implications of a SmartSociety for a given social values can be explored. This blended approach works especially well, since there is actually no single version of, for example, democracy and democratic values. Instead, many versions of democracy, democratic structures, processes and values are possible in different combinations that each has varying implications for participation and governance. Thus we may agree that democracy is important, but if we do so this is only a starting point for a more detailed conversation about what shape of democracy might be desirable or effective within Smart Societies.

To give a schematic overview of RRI, the following shows elements of RRI which have been proposed within the various sources cited above:

- [Upstream] Starting early in the research and innovation process.
- Anticipating the transformations and impacts of new products and processes.
- Giving a voice to multiple publics and stakeholders to explore the consequences of research and its desirability.
- [Midstream] Being responsive to the dialogue.
- Adjusting the trajectory of research.
- [Downstream] Creating the right policy and regulatory environment for the technology to emerge into.

Responsible Research and Innovation (RRI) was built in as an integral feature of the SmartSociety. The premise was that existing SmartSociety-like systems are often ad hoc and not as powerful as they could be, or else organized and powerful, yet poorly adaptive and often seemingly socially irresponsible. Examples include the emergent and entrenched asymmetries in power over personal data obtained though use of digital services such as Google and Facebook [6]. SmartSociety aims to improve this situation by creating the tools to build more powerful systems that have considerations of ethics and social values 'built in'.

We have developed a dedicated RRI procedure for SmartSociety that we are currently writing up for a separate publication. In essence, this process has four steps (1) Case studies and consultations to tease out issues with existing SmartSociety-type applications; (2) Synthesis of issues relevant to individual technical work-packages within the SmartSociety into a series of challenge documents that lays out the case study context and outlines the challenge; (3) Facilitating the technical work-package to respond to the challenge and (4) Structuring the responses into a series of project wide design guidelines and operating procedures. The IFIP Summer School keynote speech and workshop reported here forms part of step 1 in the above process. That is to say it has been a means of consulting the privacy research community about the ethics, privacy and social values challenges posed by SmartSociety. In the following section we spell out our consultation approach in greater detail.

3 Consultation Approach

Part of the RRI process within SmartSociety has been to undertake a series of con-sultative exercises with stakeholders in a variety of domains to create a tapestry of varied perspectives on the SmartSociety vision and possible consequences of SmartSociety technologies. The aim has not been to undertake a systematic and exhaustive consultation – mainly because SmartSociety technologies and ideas are still forming and still quite fluid, and may be applied across a diverse range of application areas – but rather to enrich the project with a series of external perspectives that may not otherwise feature endogenously.

In the closing sessions of the 2015 IFIP Summer School on Privacy and Identity Management, we were given an opportunity to present to the members of the privacy community represented at the workshop one version of the SmartSociety vision, and to elicit feedback from that community.

The following format was used. A keynote speech was given by the RRI researcher which covered the following topics: (a) An overview of SmartSociety; (b) an overview of RRI. This included the screening of a video created as part of an earlier project (FRRIICT) that demonstrates the issues for RRI of innovating in ICT[6]; (c) the SmartSociety vision as portrayed by a cartoon movie of imagined participants in a SmartSociety using SmartSociety services; and (d) a presentation of some of the pre-sumed ethical and societal issues posed by the SmartSociety vision, which were framed in terms of 'the perils and promises' of a SmartSociety.

After a short break, the presentation was followed by a panel session in which panelists gave their response to the presentation, and thereafter addressed questions raised by members of the audience. Prior to the event, the consent of panelists and the audience was obtained to audio-record the panel session discussion. An analysis of the recording forms the basis of this chapter, which will be also used internally within SmartSociety to raise social values and ethics related issues posed by the panel and the audience.

The four members of the panel consisted of (a) the leader of the one of the SmartSociety technical WPs; (b) a Social Scientist and Policy consultant; (c) a computer scientist and privacy advocate and (d) one of the co-authors of the SmartSociety proposal.

---

[6] https://www.youtube.com/channel/UCKITrA6PaVRkTsfdJtVP41w.

4   The Promise and Perils of a SmartSociety[7]

SmartSociety builds on seven technical work-packages each supplying a socio-technical component that contributes an important capability in order to realize a SmartSociety system as a functioning whole. These are:

- **Provenance and Trust** Provenance is a data trail that supports audit. Trust mechanisms include reputations systems such as those commonly found on internet platforms.
- **Sensor fusion** Sensors in the environment, or worn by the user, are interpreted by computers to give computers access to a high-level description of what is happening within a SmartSociety system.
- **Peer profiles** Data stores for information about people who are participating in a SmartSociety system.
- **Social Orchestration and algorithms** Providing the mechanisms by which SmartSociety tasks are composed and the algorithms that support the activities of the participating collectives.
- **Incentives** How to deliver incentives within a SmartSociety system to make participating more attractive and to direct the actions of the collective.
- **Programming framework** To give the application programmer pro-gramming constructs that apply directly to social entities such as col-lectives.
- **Platform** The infrastructure that ties the technical elements of a SmartSociety system into a cohesive whole.

Many familiar social web platforms, or cyber-social systems, such as Amazon or Uber (a controversial Ride Sharing platform), already include the key SmartSociety elements of reputation, incentives, algorithms and collectives etc. The SmartSociety vision is to provide better engineered components so that 'application developers' can rapidly build these classes of systems at will. Two advances unique to SmartSociety assist the engineering approach. One is the abstraction and modularization of key social web functionalities – e.g. reputation (e.g. ratings and reviews), incentives (e.g. badges and other rewards), embedded sensor systems (such as those present in phones and Google Glass) and user profiles. The second comprises three new technologies for combining the above components into new types of application. The first is a 'social orchestrator', that allows the specification and enactment of social activities such as negotiation. The second is a 'programming framework', which includes programming primitives that can be used to invoke collectives of people and/or machines and to give them the resources they need to undertake some task. The third is a platform that knits all of the above elements together.

---

[7] This section draws on a presentation authored by the following members of the SmartSociety consortium which is used with their permission. Michael Rovatsos (University of Edinburgh), Daniele Moirandi (U-Hopper), Vincenzo Maltese (University of Trento), Ronald Ronald Chenu-Abente (University of Trento), Alethia Hume (University of Trento).

In the SmartSociety keynote given at the IFIP workshop, the SmartSociety concept was demonstrated via a video[8] that was created within the project to show off a vision for the 'Ride Share' system called 'Smart Share'. Smart Share is an early demonstrator of SmartSociety capabilities, and ties together aspects of peer profiling, algorithms, reputation to enable collective sharing of individually owned resources – namely spare capacity in cars. Algorithms find matches between those wishing to travel. Peer profiles assert preferences to assist making a match. Reputation systems help establish trust. Incentives and 'gamification' mechanisms, such as 'badges', are used to encourage involvement.

The keynote was adapted from a talk given at the ICT Days meeting in Trento in 2014[9]. The aim, on that occasion, was also to be provocative and to spur discussion of the ethical issues relating to SmartSociety-like systems. The slides used for ICT Days were actually authored by technologists within the project, who were responding to their own interest in stimulating debate around ethical concerns.

The slides, aiming to be provocative, outlined the 'promises' and 'perils' of a future envisioned by SmartSociety. They achieved this by framing a series of utopias and dystopias – juxtaposing various promises of the SmartSociety project with various perils. One example is the promise of collective intelligence to solve previously unsolvable problems, versus the peril of assimilation within a collective where autonomy is erased through totalizing mechanisms of automated influence. The slides employed illustrations and imagery from popular culture that play on such fears and dystopian possibilities, including, for example, a reference to the Star Trek entity 'The Borg', which assimilates individuals into its 'hive mind' collective with the slogan "Resistance is futile".

Table 1. Privacy and governance

Promise	Peril
Control over personal data Being able to specify who can access data and for what purposes	*Useless information* Incomplete and unrepresentative collective data sets because of opt-outs
Anonymity Privacy enhancing technologies may provide various ways of acting anonymously, but accountably within a system	*Unmanageable complexity* Leading to increased technical, organizational (e.g. trusted third parties) and social complexity
Controlling disease Collective pooling of data may be of huge social benefit	*All-knowing state* Amassed data also has a huge surveillance potential and people may experience temptations to use it beyond its original purposes

---

[8] https://www.youtube.com/watch?v=SAhWCaCsXrA.

[9] http://2015.ictdays.it/en.

The polarity of promise and peril was used as an alliterative device to high-light some of the issues, and should not be read as a perspective literally held by the slides authors' on each of the issues raised. Tables 1, 2, 3 and 4 below showed the various promises and perils juxtaposed within the presentation.

Table 2. Augmented but self-determined users

Promise	Peril
Augmented users Benefiting from bodily monitoring and worn sensors	*Amplified data flows* New flows of personal data streaming out of any conceivable situation
Context-based services Providing advice based upon an interpretation of what a person is doing	*Invasive or intrusive* Misreading the context and interrupting at inopportune moments
Proactively Acting on a person's behalf in helpful ways	*Wrong data interpretation* Computers making mistakes that put people at a disadvantage

Table 3. Embedded algorithms

Promise	Peril
Man-machine collaboration Benefiting from machine intelligence that can check countless options	*Manipulation* 'Silently' embedding agency and interests that shape a person's actions or capacity to act
Personalization Knowing a person well enough to give him/her what s/he wants	*Surveillance* Knowing a person too well and acting inappropriately on that knowledge
Collective Intelligence Benefiting from the wisdom of the crowd	*Humans as cheap labor* Exploiting the cloud and undermining traditional labor rights

Table 4. Collective People-Machine Intelligence

Promise	Peril
Better health and care Critical mass for rare diseases or improved coordination of professional and informal care	*Facebook replacing your social life* Virtual venues impoverishing the physicality of conventional activities
Smarter use of natural resources (energy, water) Better management of the commons via collective management	*A terawatt of power to win Jeopardy* Increasing energy consumption of pervasive ICT infrastructures
Knowledge economy Greater independence and control over work	*Job destruction, eSlavery* Erosion of careers and deterioration of working conditions

5 Interpretative Approach

An anonymized transcript was made of the workshop recording as the basis for the analysis. A thematic analysis approach was used whereby emergent themes were identified and iteratively refined [7]. In addition, anonymized excerpts from the panel members' statements were presented in a data session involving wider members of the research group so as to elicit further interpretations of the material. The workshop approach is close to a focus group format where insights emerge discursively through the interplay of perspectives and experiences of the participants, yet it differs in that there are elements of performance and staging, and an interrogative style, which are typically absent from focus groups. The analysis undertaken resembles a continuation of this process, picking out the emergent themes, but also intertwining further perspectives available to the researchers who have the benefit of a lengthier reflection unavailable to the panelists who responded on the spot. Hopefully it is clear in the discussion below where the researcher's voice is more prominent. Hopefully, too, this voice is not perceived as being critical of participants or their views, but rather as taking those views as starting points for further deliberation. Inevitably, since the authors have a background in computer science, sociology and anthropology, as well as being deeply embedded within SmartSociety project as RRI researchers, their perspective on the issues raised in this chapter will reflect the perspectives, experiences and agendas of these *a priori* commitments.

6 Issues Raised: Managing Ethical Issues and Social Hazards of a SmartSociety

This section details the issues raised by the panelists and the questions addressed to the panel by the workshop audience.

6.1 Panel Members' Responses

Our four panelists included two men and two women. Female pronouns are used throughout this chapter to help hide panelist's identities. Distinct themes can be attributed to each of the panelists' responses. Panelist Tech (leader of a SmartSociety technical workpackage) raised the difficulty of providing guarantees that the interests of users are respected in SmartSociety-like systems. Panelist SocSci (a social scientist and policy consultant) drew attention to the ever-present dialogue around humans' ambivalent relationship to technology. Panelist PrivAdv (a computer scientist advocating the importance of privacy) raised fundamental questions over what the vision for a 'SmartSociety' might be. Finally, panelist SmartSoc (one of the original authors of the SmartSociety proposal) provided a context for SmartSociety's capacity to solve increasingly urgent social and economic problem around care. Therefore, two of the panelists were closely associated with the SmartSociety project, whereas the other two were not.

Below we consider each of these contributions in more detail.

Panelist Tech. Tech drew attention to the way that computer systems have a social effect, opening up a thread of discussion in this paper about the different ways that technology may stand in relation to social processes:

> "What we have seen in the [SmartSociety] project is that constantly there are – there's a tension – between what you try and do with technology – because basically you want as much data – and you want to manipulate... you want to determine the outcome of social interactions with machine support so that you can introduce more intelligence into the system and help optimize – let's say help solve the travel problem in a city. And on the other hand, of course, you have the privacy concerns – more than just privacy, I think it's also accountability, transparency and governance – because what we've seen in our project is that all these algorithms essentially [they] all introduce biases."

In the first part of the above quote - technology is conceived as an instrument to bring about certain social outcomes that are desired by the sponsor of the technology (perhaps tackling what are more broadly agreed concerns). The second part of the quote acknowledges that, at the same time, technology carries social dangers through unwanted side effects, which necessitate regulation and oversight. The dilemma outlined is that of wanting to use technology to do helpful things but, at the same time, introducing all sorts of new complexities, some of which have negative implications.

> "And the question is, which of these irresistible services and temptations that the data world offers are you going to turn down – which social processes are you going to stay out of – what is the price you pay for that – socially"

Yet, building the appropriate values and safeguards into the system is hard, especially since people may be complicit in bringing about harmful side-effects, as it can be very difficult to resist data-based services and the social web, and the costs of opting out of these solutions may be high.

A first reading of these quotes suggests that they are describing a technology-led process directed by a technical elite that frames societal problems and enacts a vision of how computers can help. But we have to acknowledge that technologists are society members too (!) and bring their life-perspectives to bear and enact values that have currency and are shared more broadly in society, even if they may only be partially representative of the wider population. That is to say, RRI researchers should not make a knee-jerk assumption that the values held by technologists may not be more broadly shared. On the other hand, an RRI approach would advocate consultative processes to widen the perspectives that are drawn upon in creating new techno-social visions.

A second possibility is to read within these quotes an implicit distinction between technology on the one hand (which is prior to, and acts upon, society), and society on the other (which has to respond, or resist, or cope with technology). But this distinction is also hard to sustain because the technology itself emerges from existing ideas that form part of the cultural zeitgeist. This presumed distinction between technology / society turned up a number of times within the workshop dialogue and represents an important theme in this chapter.

Panelist SocSci. SocSci pointed out that becoming reconciled to technology has been an ever-present issue for humankind. She applauded the interdisciplinary approach within SmartSociety, and saw as valuable the internal dialogues that have been initiated in the project.

> "We too [referring to the organization which she is affiliated] have worked with, if you want, instruments or approaches that have ranged from use of theatre, media, games, and have particularly placed an emphasis on dialogue – I'm think-ing about the 'Court of Ethics' which is a wonderful piece of drama, a play around robotics. This dialogue, about technology and society is as old as we are as human beings and I mean that as many ten thousands of years old … I'm pretty sure there might have been debates about the perils of fire versus the warmth and the cooking benefits that it could bring – it wouldn't have surprised me if there were not a debate and dialogue as long ago as that."

It is patently true that such an ongoing dialogue exists, and has existed across various epochs, as well as being enacted at different levels and locations throughout society, and through different cultural forms (including theatre, as indicated above). Dialogue is also a hugely important component of RRI as well as being a vital mechanism by which cultures anticipate and come to terms with new techno-social eras.

We can extend SocSci's contribution to consider several further facets to dialogue that are important. One is that the presence of dialogue is not by itself a guarantor of beneficial outcomes, with much depending on how any given dialogue is geared into political processes. Another is that what is at stake, and what dialogues are possible and effective in any given historical epoch, may vary considerably. Habermas, for example, identified the coffee house culture of the Enlightenment as leading to the emergence of a 'public sphere', which had not existed in such a cohesive and egalitarian fashion prior to that moment in time [8]. A third is the hegemonic aspects of dialogue that determine the legitimacy of content, participants and venues within particular dialogical spheres. Fourth and finally, there is an issue of the implied separation between "technology and society" which carries over from the previous panelist, Tech. We might want to keep in mind how technology itself underpins and transforms dialogic possibilities, with the social web as an example of this.

Panelist PrivAdv. This panelist questioned more fundamentally the presumptions underpinning the concept of a SmartSociety, and posited an alternative set of values and meanings that may be attached to being 'Smart'. Do our technologies that promote convenience make us Smarter – or does 'Smartness' come instead from a focus on empowerment, education, participation in decisions and the capacity to opt out of the presumed benefits of digital living? Actually, the smartness of society may be reduced through technology, but improved through education and thoughtfulness:

> "So Smart is a buzzword, coming from SmartCards, SmartCars, Smart-Everything, and usually what used to be intelligent, or networked, or computer-aided or -supported – but what really is needed I think is a SmartSociety – smart people, educated people – and people who don't have to rely on technology."

> "So is SmartSociety now really something that is [heading?] to educated people who can join the discourse about SmartSociety, for example, who are better off than before, but not only

because of convenience but also [because] of participating in decisions but also opting out, or refraining from cooperating with others?"

Interestingly, when these views were further discussed within our research group (as part of this analysis), then opinion was divided between those who were more sympathetic to the panelist's position, and those who more wholeheartedly embraced the role of technology to help people to collectively share resources and solve problems. Those viewing the SmartSociety ambition in a positive light also rejected commonly suggested negative trajectories, such as job erosion or loss of autonomy. Discussion around the SmartSociety vision evidently contributes to a broader debate over how, collectively, we identify and wish to tackle contemporary social problems, and what forms of living we aspire to. Thus the panelist provides a helpful challenge to SmartSociety and asserts values that SmartSociety represents less well. This question of what values the SmartSociety project upholds is another recurrent one within this paper.

This panelist, picking up on the project's focus on SmartCities, also identified presumed values within the SmartSociety project about what is desirable about participating in city life – for example, that everyone should be enthusiastically sociable in every situation:

"So I come from (place) and we are said to be very stubborn. I think that (place) should be the same. (It's not, I don't know.). Where it is, for many people, fully ok to live on your island and not to interact with so many people. Those who you are choosing to interact with, they are your really good friends really. So it takes a longer time, but then you choose, these are my small group of people I want to interact with, and not I'm choosing from a big list of people who want to talk about Jazz all the time in the car. Although it might be my interest to meet people at some part of the time, but not this is perhaps (the) first thing (that I wish to do). I don't think that (people from place) and others here are anti-social and don't want to socialize – it's more that there should also be the opportunity not be part of a SmartSociety which forces you to play according to those rules."

Our interpretation of these comments is that PrivAdv is not referring to the privacy aspects of being sociable *per se*, but rather the presumption (visible from the keynote presentation) within SmartSociety solutions that sociability is always a desirable quality. One concrete way these comments have been figured into the project is within a 'tourism scenario' that is under development as part of demonstration of SmartSociety ideas and technologies. We have pointed out that tourists are a diverse group with some wishing to solitary, as opposed to sociable, experiences. These perspectives have also contributed to internal debates within the project concerning diversity, and in particular how far SmartSociety systems can cater for diverse sensibilities.

This panelist questioned the how Smart Society may interfere with the autonomy of its participants by the sorts mechanisms proposed to shape the behavior of participants towards global objectives:

"for example, that I can go through Edinburgh without having a navigation that not only tells me where – what's the quickest way, but also, which already anticipates I where I am going or that I should go – or where I get the best vouchers for the 100th ride or so – so the incentives – the persuasion – in a direction where many people probably want to take it don't think that this may be manipulation – so not personalization but manipulation. And if you think about the interests and incentives of the stakeholders – big companies – their incentive has to be to maximize the money they make out of that. This is the reason for their existence. If they don't think about that, but only about how to empower people – smart people – making people Smart - that would be a different story – however, that's not the task of the company"

Usefully she highlights the importance of ownership of a SmartSociety application, and how ownership plays a strong role in dictating whose interests it ultimately serves, and how the mechanisms of the platform may be the (perhaps silent) bearers of those interests. These comments have assisted us to develop a framework where we interpret hybrid systems (i.e. ones involving people and machines) by analyzing of how interests are represented and balanced within the system.

Panelist SmartSoc. This panelist re-grounded SmartSociety by proposing the serious role of counter-balancing the effect in the West of ever rising demands upon already overstretched care and medical systems. She suggested that SmartSociety-inspired approaches could increase the capacity of care systems by supporting local collectives of lay and professional carers, whilst simultaneously delivering improved outcomes for patients. Moreover, she contends that privacy and ethical issues are more easily solved when contained within local communities, but presumes that data can be contained at this level:

> "So, for example, in Sweden at the moment there are some hospitals where people with kidney disease – they go in, and they self-dialyze. They go in and they connect themselves up to the machines, and the dialysis work gets done when they want it to rather than when the hospital system wants it to. What we see when that happens is there is a huge amount of sharing of information be-cause there's a local context – the collective around self-dialysis – where the sharing of information, and the information adapts and changes to the circum-stances. What you also see is a huge reduction in cost to the hospital – 50 % less money needs spent on doing that dialysis – and the number of infections goes down – the number of infections and errors is much smaller in the self-dialysis community than in the professionally dialyzed community."

> "And for me, at any rate, when I start talking about the big story of privacy, for example, and data protection and so on – I think top-down is just foolish. Particularly for these kinds of situation. You have to do it bottom-up. And these things can be built in from the bottom. And we have to understand, actually, a much more radical notion of what privacy by design is because actually the governance model, the local governance model, for how that information is interpreted and understood, has to be built into the development process – has to be built into the developer culture and the user culture, and those two overlap, and are built in from the bottom."

In the second quote the panelist is alluding to how 'top-down governance', such as via the application of privacy laws, still somehow fails to protect people in how their data is used by large institutions such as governments and corporations. The 'bottom-up' model that is advocated instead posits community ownership and the co-design of technologies to secure data locally within these 'data communities'.

However, this is an artful re-framing of the SmartSociety vision that circumvents some of the issues raised or hinted at by prior speakers. In this version of a SmartSociety, factors previously seen as matters of preference and privilege (deciding to be sociable or not; having time and resources to be a tourist) are replaced in this new context by matters characterized by hard choices and necessity. By positioning SmartSociety within would generally be considered a worthy application context, and as solving a serious societal problem, it becomes much harder to formulate a critique. One way of regaining a critical stance is to point at how technological approaches to dealing with issues of care and caring often focus too narrowly on the mechanics of care, as opposed to the emotional, spiritual or social needs of a dependent person, e.g. [9].

This panelist 'solved' some of the ethical and privacy concerns posed within a SmartSociety by including elements of co-production, and elements of community and individual control over personal data. Although this seems like an important strategy, it perhaps has the disadvantage that it repositions SmartSociety further away from the grander vision contained within the project's original grant proposal – which actually does propose 'internet-scale' systems. Perhaps many of the difficulties attached to SmartSociety arise because of the scale of the systems involved. While co-production, and minimizing scale and scope, render the issues more manageable, in doing so does the original SmartSociety vision remain intact?

6.2   Questions to the Panel

Following the panelists' responses roughly eight questions were put to the panel by audience members. Instead of going through each question sequentially, as we have done for the panelists' individual contributions, this section pulls out some recurrent themes that were identified in the questions and the panelists' responses.

In the main, questions focused less on SmartSociety and its facets, but more on general issues around ICT that have a social impact, and the difficulties inherent in tackling these issues. In the following sections we consider the problems the audience and panelists described with identifying and understanding issues and solutions, anticipating the problems that new technologies may bring about, and in embedding known solutions into policy processes. We then explore how one panelist's suggestion of brokerage provides a possible solution to these issues.

Horizons and Barriers.   On several occasions discussion referred to several types of horizons and barriers that were perceived to constrain how the ethical social issues raised by SmartSociety may be addressed. 'Horizons' is taken to mean some limit to appreciation or perception form a given perspective – such as how far into the future a person can see, or how far their knowledge extends. One such horizon related to limits to our understanding:

> "What happens where the functions of a SmartSociety [are] so complex they are beyond the comprehension of most people? People are 'not smart enough' to make sense of the complex systems in which they are enmeshed."

> "I think we have a fairly poor understanding of the informal processes that go on in these communities - and turning them into something that we can actively support with technology..." [Responding to an audience asking about horizontal processes that connect disparate communities.]

The first quote above (from an audience member) expresses a concern that people may not understand the technical systems in which they participate, implying that the future may be only comprehensible to a small number of technical elites. The second quote (from a technologist) expresses the reciprocal concern that technologists themselves may lack knowledge of social processes from the perspective of being able to develop technologies to support those processes. Taken together, these statements raise the specter of technology proceeding without a full social understanding to create something that members of society themselves cannot comprehend. These concerns resonate with the earlier theme of a supposed separation between technology and society. Yet we know that technology and society are not separate in the ways that some of the panelists may have been construed as implying. As new socio-technical systems emerge from a given socio-technical milieu, then both technologists and non-technologists will already have some grasp of each other's perspective, even if initially these shared perspectives may be limited. While horizons may exist at specific moments, over time, and through processes of social learning, the technology and its deeper historical roots or distant locales of production often become even more comprehensible, either through experience, education, through voluntary disclosure, or via processes of investigation and revelation. Similarly, there are very well established design approaches for opening up understandings of social processes and feeding them into system development, which are able to extend the designers' horizon of how certain social processes function.

Another is horizon is the future and our ability to anticipate outcomes:

"Lawmakers are in a much more difficult position … because this is information technology and it applies to all kinds of applications - it's very difficult for them to anticipate the consequences."

"Basically the changes we propose with big data and these kinds of analytics, say, in the long run, they will change society tremendously and we currently we cannot really anticipate how."

These statements express the paradox that in controlling the negative aspects of the techno-social we must act on what is essentially an unknowable future. This resembles Collingridge's dilemma that indicate at which point we are most in control and able to shape a technology, is precisely the point where we lack information about its consequences (see [10] for a discussion of Collingridge). However, the RRI literature draws a distinction between the possibility of anticipating, as opposed to the intractability of prediction, and how anticipation and prediction may be conflated [11]. Thus, it may be hard (if not impossible) to predict precisely what future data and analytics will actually herald, but relatively easy to imagine (anticipate) alternative techno-social futures that involve them.

Perhaps these epistemological and temporal horizons, which are perceived to limit how ethical and privacy issues may be addressed, have little to do with absence of the necessary skills and knowledge from society as a whole. Locally, hazards and potential remedies may be well understood, but also this knowledge may be compartmentalized and hard to assimilate into new settings. Indeed, another barrier alluded to during the panel session relates precisely to this difficulty of embedding values and safeguards into processes and systems:

"So even to get to the point where - the next stage - where you have to frame a procurement so that it is privacy-enhancing - well, how do you do that when you have no expertise about privacy-enhancing in people who are writing the procurement document and there are no products which can meet things that you might want to make mandatory requirements?"

"So at the moment we are very far away from actually being able to say we can provide guarantees and safeguard that people are being treated fairly, and equitably, and that the values they care about are reflected in those systems."

Barriers to assimilation were also identified in relation to political processes that were perceived as failing to ensure the appropriate policy and governance environment for emerging technologies:

"– it's a debate that's a social debate – and what I've seen of this debate so far hasn't been very well informed when politicians are involved." ... "[politicians at a Smart City event] agreed on the common vision that having real-time data on every citizen and everything that is going on, and everything that every citizen wants, is for them the perfect democracy."

"..but usually – politicians for example, ... they have not (inaudible words?) been helpful in the last time [i.e. in recent times] – they also want to stay in the position – they may do something for long effect but very often it's more – well – that – they decide what is good for people and not that the people are part of that."

An interesting question concerns how far these barriers and horizons represent hard, global constraints, and how much they are real, but only within a certain framing or context. Any given 'knowledge horizon' may only be local, and even seemingly 'hard' barriers, such as influencing policy makers, may be more tractable (for some) than the quotes above suggest. For example, the panel session discussion took an interesting turn when an audience member familiar with the lobbying process showed how this particular barrier could be overcome.

Brokerage. One audience member contrasted 'top down', 'bottom up' approaches with the idea of influencing a project "middle-sideways" through the process of brokerage:

"About creating brokerage between different kinds of lateral developments ... and disseminating learning about good and bad approaches and so forth. That's a very creative role of brokerage."

In a sense this statement provides an answer to some of the issues identified as barriers and horizons above. To overcome barriers, or to extend horizons, one needs new knowledge, expertise, processes and routines. Often the relevant experience already exists, but is hard to access. Brokerage plays the role of connecting otherwise compartmentalized knowledge, and creating supportive circumstances for knowledge to flow and be assimilated into a new locale. In many ways brokerage is a key activity within RRI. It was actually part of what was happening in the panel session itself as the session created a space for reflection and cross-fertilization between people with different kinds of experience and expertise.

Brokerage was demonstrated by this specific audience member as she (in asking her question) directed SmartSociety's attention to the SWAMI project[10] that had previously considered ethical issues in relation to ambient Intelligence – a precursor of SmartSociety technologies. Another panel member recommended the work of Henry

---

[10] http://is.jrc.ec.europa.eu/pages/TFS/SWAMI.html.

Mintzberg (e.g. [12]), who's approach from the field of management science resonates with the brokerage approach.

Brokerage is visible in these simple acts of recommending and sharing references to reports or academic papers. The recommendation is as important as the actual reference, as a key challenge for brokerage includes establishing trust and relevance because of the vast array of perspectives available for people to draw upon.

The audience member recommending the brokerage approach did so in response to a point made in the keynote presentation that SmartSociety aims to address ethical issues by designing components in ways that avoid unethical outcomes. Brokerage was suggested as an alternative to this 'prior ethical design' as it was seen as better supporting elements of 'creativity' and 'spontaneity' that may be lacking in either 'top down' or 'bottom up' design approaches. Again, this resonates with ideas within RRI of the importance of engagement - with publics and other stakeholders - not only to encourage new lines of influence in technology formation, but also to foster the creativity that comes from the cross-fertilization of perspectives.

Influencing Politicians as an Example of Brokerage. Following several (mainly negative) comments about how politicians are unapproachable and how they fail to understand important techno-social issues, one audience member was moved to declare her own expertise in liaising with and informing politicians:

> "You need to understand what politicians do when they work - and when can you influence them and with what can you influence them. Basically they don't respond well to ethical issues because they ask you "who should do what"? Because that's the kind of things they can demand in their political arena. So you have to really translate also those issues about who should do what, and then what is the role of the governance in making the person do that. Timing is extremely important, so a politician, or at least a member of parliament, usually can only talk about things when it's on the political agenda."

This audience member is evidently a skilled mediator on the topic of 'ethical concerns' and politicians. She offered a very different perspective to the exasperation expressed towards the political process documented in earlier quotes. Her contribution demystifies how political influence may be achieved, in particular, by revealing the rather mundane series of practical steps and pragmatic considerations involved in it. It is also another example of brokerage in action, where the venue /mechanism of the summer school panel session itself created opportunities for opening up otherwise compartmentalized knowledge.

7 Conclusions

SmartSociety carries with it its own vision, which is continuously undergoing evolution and redefinition to take on shapes and directions that are not always aligned across all project partners. This is a healthy state of affairs for a large, complex, cutting-edge research project. Indeed, the Summer School panel session made a significant contribution to further exploring what a SmartSociety might aim to be.

Various versions of the SmartSociety vision were on show during the keynote talk, panel session and in the questions and answers that followed. Summer School attendees saw SmartSociety as part of digitally enhanced everyday living, as a solution to profound social problems, as being smarter through less engagement with technology, and more through learning and thoughtfulness. They saw the grand, all-encompassing, societal level vision shine through the keynote presentation, as well as a more low-key reimagining of a localized community-level SmartSociety in the reply by one of the panelists. Whilst this contestation and exploration of the SmartSociety vision has positive aspects, there are downsides too, especially if the vision is so fluid that it proves always to be slippery and impossible to pin down. Indeed, the SmartSociety system itself has a chameleon-like ability to fit within practically any application context and, as it shifts between domains, the complexion of relevant values changes too. This leads to another problem whereby it becomes easy for advocates of SmartSociety to evade any given critique by giving it a new guise within an alternative setting. Also, different values come into play depending on scale and the application area, and repositioning SmartSociety solutions to operate over a smaller scale diffuses many of the ethical issues posed when it is articulated in terms of its grander ambitions. These observations suggest that, on the one hand, it could be easy for the SmartSociety project to deflect various ethical concerns by deftly repositioning itself but, on the other, that it is genuinely hard to pin down the complexities of values attached to the various guises of SmartSociety.

One way forward may be to explore actively how the SmartSociety vision fits within the field of existing and already deeply considered visions and critiques of techno-social futures. These may include ones that are more naturally allied to the SmartSociety vision, such as 'Social Physics' [13], and others that may be more oppositional, such as Morozov's critique of 'Technological Solutionism' [14]. As part of this process, it would be useful to strive to articulate the possible combinations of values that may attach to SmartSociety in its different guises, to discover on which occasions they are complementary and able to co-exist, and when they are actually antagonistic or truly mutually exclusive. These measures may help the consortium to articulate SmartSociety values in a clearer, more contextualized way, as well as to stimulate reflection upon and refine which values it ultimately wishes the SmartSociety system to uphold.

There were several moments in the workshop discussion where arguments hinged around a distinction between technology and society, such as where technology may be seen as coming to the aid of societal problems, with society needing to respond to unwanted side-effects. Such issues were often couched in terms of barriers or horizons. While these are real and limiting in each individual case, their relative severity seems also to depend on the situation or context in which they are experienced. For example, one audience member, steeped in the mechanisms underpinning political processes, hardly felt this to be a barrier at all, whilst others experienced the political world as frustrating and troubling.

A key contribution came from an audience member who highlighted an important role for brokerage. Brokerage involves creating networks of connections and flows of experience and expertise between otherwise discrete and compartmentalized communities to stimulate creativity and gain answers to issues where approaches already exist[11]. Brokerage resonates strongly with the processes involved in RRI, which also seek to draw multiple perspectives into innovation processes. Brokerage may be a way of positioning RRI as a source of creativity and an enabler of innovation, as opposed to the perception that RRI sometimes attracts of seeking to constrain and regulate. If we shift our perspective from thinking of technology and society as being separate entities (where society has to cope with more and more varied technologies) and instead consider the direction of travel as towards weaving ever more dense techno-socio hybrids, then to manage these trends effectively perhaps we do need processes similar to brokerage that help synthesize trans-disciplinary perspectives.

Finally, it is worth reflecting on the value of the panel session as a venue for stimulating debate. One aspect to highlight is that the discussion typically did not dwell on the implications of the core features of SmartSociety itself – such as algorithms, incentives, collective intelligence and so on, but rather focused on higher-level issues relating to the SmartSociety vision and the complexities of addressing ethical concerns more generally. Whilst these were useful discussions to have, in a future staging of the panel session we would consider adjusting the approach and reiterating key questions from the initial keynote to refocus any discussion around those core elements.

Overall, we believe that holding this workshop session was a valuable experience, both to enrich the summer school and to assist with the reflective process within SmartSociety project itself. We are grateful to the panelists and the summer school attendees for consenting to participate, and for their highly insightful and stimulating contributions.

Acknowledgements. This work was supported by EU FP7 FET SmartSociety project (http://www.smart-society-project.eu/) under the Grant agreement n.600854.

References

1. Miorandi, D., Maltese, V., Rovatsos, M., Nijholt, A., Stewart, J. (eds.): Social Collective Intelligence: Combining the Powers of Humans and Machines to Build a Smarter Society. Springer, New York (2015)
2. Stahl, B.C., Eden, G., Jirotka, M., Coeckelbergh, M.: From computer ethics to responsible research and innovation in ICT: the transition of reference discourses informing ethics-related research in information systems. Inf. Manag. **51**(6), 810–818 (2014)
3. von Schomberg, R.: A vision of responsible innovation. In: Owen, R., Heintz, M., Bessant, J. (eds.) Responsible Innovation. John Wiley, London (2013)
4. Owen, R., Macnaghten, P., Stilgoe, J.: Responsible research and innovation: from science in society to science for society, with society. Sci. Public Policy **39**(6), 751–760 (2012)
5. Brey, P.: Values in technology and disclosive computer ethics. In: Floridi, L. (ed.) The Cambridge Handbook of Information and Computer Ethics. Cambridge University Press, Cambridge (2009)
6. Lanier, J.: Who Owns the Future?. Simon and Schuster, New York (2014)

---

[11] Interestingly enough, brokerage could be couched in SmartSociety parlance as 'leveraging diversity in a collective social intelligence to create enriched hybrid perspectives'.

7. Guest, G.: Applied Thematic Analysis. SAGE Publications, Inc., California (2012)
8. Habermas, J.: The Structural Transformation of the Public Sphere: An Inquiry into a Category of Bourgeois Society. MIT press, Cambridge (1991)
9. Thieme, A., Vines, J., Wallace, J., Clarke, R.E., Slovák, P., McCarthy, J., Mas-simi, M., Grimes Parker, A.: Enabling empathy in health and care: design methods and challenges. In: CHI '14 Extended Abstracts on Human Factors in Computing Systems (CHI EA'14), pp. 139–142. ACM, New York (1985)
10. Croy, M.J.: Collingridge and the control of educational computer technology. Techné Res. Philos. Technol. 1(3/4), 107–115 (1996)
11. Guston, D.H.: Understanding 'anticipatory governance'. Soc. Stud. Sci. 44(2), 218–242 (2014)
12. Mintzberg, H., Waters, J.A.: Of strategies, deliberate and emergent. Strateg. Manag. J. 6(3), 257–272 (1985)
13. Pentland, A.: Social Physics: How Good Ideas Spread-The Lessons from a New Science. Penguin, London (2014)
14. Morozov, E.: To Save Everything, Click Here: The Folly Of Technological Solutionism. PublicAffairs, New York (2014)

An Experience with a De-identifying Task to Inform About Privacy Issues

Luis Gustavo Esquivel-Quirós[✉] and E. Gabriela Barrantes

Universidad de Costa Rica, San José, Costa Rica
luis.esquivel@ucr.ac.cr, gabriela.barrantes@ecci.ucr.ac.cr

Abstract. People tend to value their privacy, but are usually unaware about the extent to which their personal information is exposed through ordinary data available online. In this paper we describe an experience in which a group of students worked to identify a group of people from partial data that had been stripped of any direct identifiers, such as name or identification number. The students were successful in the assigned task, and as an indirect consequence, there was an increase of interest in the topic of privacy. With the partial evidence collected from this case, we argue that a hands-on, exercise-solving approach could be adapted to communicate privacy issues more effectively.

Keywords: Privacy concerns · De-identification · Re-identification · Education

1 Introduction

Information is constantly flowing from most of our electronic devices. We generate all kinds of information: social, geographical, financial, and many others. If the information refers to an individual, and if it is intentionally or unintentionally published, it might expose sensitive information which the individual might wish to, and possibly has the right to, keep private. This issue has been raised everywhere, but we were interested in the situation in Costa Rica; a small country with an educated population, and relatively high information and communication technology (ICT) penetration [6]. For years, it has produced and exported software, and international software and hardware companies now have part of their operations in our country [1].

Privacy issues have developed at different paces depending on the country. Costa Rica had a slow start in legislation and general awareness about privacy. Until recently, there were no specific privacy laws, and instead privacy breaches were dealt mostly by the Constitutional Court, using *Habeas Data*, which is a constitutional court action available in some countries, used to protect the rights of an individual over its own data, and in some ways analogous to the more commonly-known *Habeas Corpus* [5].

In 2011, the first privacy-specific law was approved, the *"Ley de Protección de la Persona frente al tratamiento de sus datos personales"* [8], and in 2013 the

Published by Springer International Publishing Switzerland 2016. All Rights Reserved
D. Aspinall et al. (Eds.): Privacy and Identity 2015, IFIP AICT 476, pp. 49–60, 2016.
DOI: 10.1007/978-3-319-41763-9_4

regulations for the law were published [4]. The law also created PRODHAB, a regulatory agency (*"Agencia de Protección de Datos de los Habitantes"*) which started operations in 2013 [2,8].

Costa Rica has experienced scandals due to breaches in privacy, including some very prominent ones in recent years that received wide media coverage. For example, there was the case of Keylor Navas, a relatively famous national soccer player, in which it came to light that his family in Costa Rica was the subject of more than 20 frivolous consults at the hands of employees of the Organization for Judiciary Research (OIJ) [13]. The case started in October 2014, and caused a public outcry that ended up in an inquiry by a Legislative Assembly commission [23]. The commission reached its conclusion in May 2015 [15], but by November 2015 it had disappeared from the public view, without significant consequences.

However, even with the new law, the PRODHAB, the press coverage of privacy breach scandals, and the general level of education, people in Costa Rica seem mostly unaware or indifferent to privacy issues, as could be inferred from the press coverage of such cases. Each time a given person suffers a privacy breach, there is enough public outrage to keep it in the news for some time, but it is mostly forgotten soon after. We believe that this reflects a cognitive dissonance between beliefs about privacy and actual attitudes about data online. This phenomenon has been well documented in other countries, and is referred to as the *"Privacy Paradox"* [18].

A different privacy issue also present in Costa Rica has to do with the general lack of understanding of the complex interactions among different pieces of data that could link seemingly "sanitized" data to sensitive information about the individual. For example, some of the recent rulings of the Constitutional Court show that judges consider privacy important, but are not aware that the data being authorized for release could be used to put individuals in danger [12]. This so-called "re-identification" threat is also a well-documented reality, with most documented cases dealing with data published in the United States ([9,16,24]).

Given all of the above, it was important for us to test directly what the situation was in Costa Rica. More specifically, we wanted to determine how easy (or difficult) it would be for a non-expert to re-identify local individuals. Therefore, we decided to run a limited re-identification exercise with a group of educated, but non-expert participants. We also restricted it to "young" people (under 35 years of age), as there is evidence indicating that the privacy paradox is an issue in this group [14]. However, after running the task we realized that it had an unexpected outcome regardless of how easy it was for the participants to identify the local individuals, so we decided to report our findings from the re-identification task as evidence for a possible educational strategy to raise awareness about privacy issues.

In Sects. 2 and 3 we define basic privacy and data protection concepts, respectively. In Sect. 4 we present the methodology used. Section 5 presents our results and their analysis. Section 6 summarizes our findings, and Sect. 7 proposes future directions for this work.

2 Privacy

The concept of "privacy" has no single, clear and definite meaning, and varies widely between different cultures. This concept is discussed in philosophy, politics, law, sociology, anthropology, psychology, and other areas. The difference between the public and the private have been recognized in some form in most societies, albeit there is no general agreement about the meaning, the limits, and the application of these limits (legal framework) [8,11,21].

Following Daniel Solove [22], privacy can be generically conceptualized as a barrier that people can hold to provide themselves with some relief from different sorts of social friction, which will allow them to function as a member of a society without being overwhelmed by the multiple pressures it imposes.

A definition for privacy that is relevant for information privacy was given by Alan Westin [25]: *"Privacy is the claim of individuals, groups, or institutions to determine for themselves when, how, and to what extent information about them is communicated to others."*

William Parent [17] defines privacy as the condition of not having undocumented and unauthorized personal information in possession of other parties. His position is that there is a privacy loss when others acquire personal information about an individual without his or her authorization. Personal information is defined by Parent as any information about facts that the person chooses to not reveal about him or herself. In this view, personal information becomes "documented" only if it becomes public with the authorization or actions of the individual.

The concept is in fact very dependent upon the context [22] wich makes raising awareness about issues related to it complicated, which might explain why conciousness about privacy in the general population remains an elusive goal.

3 Identification, De-identification and Re-identification

For terminology only, we will follow the decisions about data privacy definitions stated in the Internal Report 8053 of the National Institute of Standards and Technology of the United States [10]. In particular, we will **not** use the term "anonymization", and "personal information" will refer to any information from an individual, but "identifying information" would be the subset of personal information that could be used to identify that individual. The definition recognizes that personal data from which all identifying information has been removed, sometimes can be traced back to the individual.

A **de-identification** process concerns itself with stripping identifying information from personal information. The purpose is usually to decrease the risk of sensitive data about the individual being associated back to him or her. A process used to defeat de-identification is called **re-identification**. Such a process attempts to link data back to its originator. There are many possible strategies to accomplish this task [9].

4   Methodology

Given that the focus of our main exercise was to probe the ease of re-identification in our environment, the methodology focused on re-identification details. Most of the post-exercise written questions were oriented in that direction, and individual concerns about privacy were not directly referenced. For the purpose of this paper, we relied on items that provided indirect indications about the participants' concerns about privacy, and the oral responses of the participants during the interactions with the experimenters.

Subsection 4.1 describes the design of the re-identification exercise that was to be carried out by the participants in the study. Subsection 4.2 deals with the details of the exercise execution. Subsection 4.3 presents the indicators taken from the questionnaire used by the participants to qualify the exercise.

4.1   Exercise Design

The design of the re-identification exercise required choosing the following:

1. A base dataset;
2. The de-identified subsets; and
3. A group of individuals who will execute the exercise.

The choices taken are described below.

Choosing the Base Dataset. The exercise required the participants to re-identify a group of people, given some weakly de-identified data. Therefore, the first challenge was to define this group. The requirements for the base dataset were the following:

1. We had to be able to find enough publicly available information about them
2. They had to be somehow "interesting" for the participants in the exercise
3. They had to be relatively public figures so we would not infringe any local privacy laws
4. We needed a relatively large number of individuals (more than 20) to be able to choose different combinations among them

Some possibilities included local politicians, entertainment personalities, fairy tale characters, and sports figures. We ended up choosing local football (soccer) players, given the World Cup excitement, and the importance of football in Costa Rica. More specifically, we choose all the players that were called in a single selection summons, which gave us a total of 30 players.

We collected the following publicly-available information about the players:

- Local ID number (*Cédula de identidad*)
- Complete name
- Birth date
- Marital status
- Number of children
- Province were registered to vote
- Current club

Choosing the De-identified Subsets. After collecting the base dataset, we had to define the subsets of de-identified data that would be given to study participants to re-identify. We defined two subsets for the exercise, to test if restricting the amount of de-identified information would make a difference in the re-identification efficacy. The first subset was comprised of data from three queries on the base dataset, and no further data was provided during the exercise. The definition of the queries follows:

- Birth year, age, place of birth, province where registered to vote, for all 30 players
- Marital status and number of children, but only for married players
- Number of children and current club, but only if the current club was local.

The second de-identified subset was potentially different for each participant. No data was given outright, but a participant could request from the experimenters up to three queries from the base dataset, with the following rules:

- In the first query, a participant could request all the data in a non-direct ID column (for example, column "number of children", but not "Local ID number"). The student could specify the column by name, but could only pick one, two or three columns.
- In the second query, a participant could request at most two columns, but only 50 % of the data for that column was given (data for 15 randomly chosen players).
- In the third query, the participant could request only one attribute, and again, only 50 % of the data would be returned.

Choosing the Participants. We needed as participants a group of young people who were not very familiar with either computer security or privacy issues. We had the generous cooperation of the students and the professor in the FS408 Thermodynamics class, at the end of 2013. This is a second-year course in the curriculum of the Bachelor Degree in Physics at the Universidad de Costa Rica.

None of the students in the group had previous, specialized experience in security, data mining, or protection of data privacy, and they were all Physics majors. There were 49 participating students. They were naturally divided into two attendance modalities: 34 in-class and 15 remote students. We used this natural division to test two different types of query.

The participants were mostly male given that the student population for the Physics major at the Universidad de Costa Rica presents a marked gender imbalance, as it can be seen in Table 1. However, both the group and each of the subgroups were very homogeneous in age. The youngest student was 19, and the oldest 29 at the time. Table 2 summarizes the age distribution of the participants in the exercise.

Table 1. Summary of gender distribution of participants.

Population	Male	Female	Total population
In-person	26	8	34
Remote	14	1	15
Whole group	40	9	49

Table 2. Summary of age distribution of participants.

Population	Average	Stand. Dev	Median	Mode
In-person	21,21	1,49	21	20
Remote	23,07	3,13	22	21
Whole group	21,78	2,27	21	20

4.2   Execution

The full class had to attend a brief presentation on general privacy issues. This presentation included basic concepts on privacy protection, and legal consequences of information published online, showing local and international examples ([3,19]). We showed them examples of potential dangers such as identity theft, and misuse of sensible information. After the talk, all students had to participate in a group activity where they re-identified characters in a fairy tale, with a subsequent discussion of methods and results. During both activities, they were allowed to ask questions, make suggestions and offer opinions.

The next step was to explain the rules of the identification exercise, but before that, an explanation was given about the possible uses of the data to be collected, and the possibility of opting-out. Those students who were willing to participate had to complete and sign informed consent forms.

There was a small reward associated to the completion of the exercise. If the student demonstrated serious effort towards the re-identification, and answered a question about the entropy of the data, the completed exercise counted as an extra quiz. The actual re-identification success did not count towards the grade.

Afterwards, all students were given their respective instruments, which included the de-identified datasets, and a questionnaire to be completed after the exercise. They were given a week to complete it. In-class students were given the fixed dataset and remote students had to generate their own using the rules explained in Sect. 4. The goal was to identify (obtain the names) of the largest number of players. As mentioned in Sect. 4, the reason that different datasets were used for each group is that originally the exercise was meant to compile information about the ease of re-identification in Costa Rica.

The answers to the exercise were collected a week after it was handed out. The experimenters had a brief discussion session with the students at that point. The students in the remote modality had the responsibility to be present if there was an evaluation activity, so all of them attended the class in the first week, but most of them were not present for the discussion on the second week.

4.3 Questionnaire and Analysis Strategy

The questionnaire that the students had to complete after completing the re-identification exercise, contained nine items, divided into three closed, and six open-text questions. The questions were oriented to determine the difficulty of the re-identification task. Because the written instrument was not explicitly designed to measure levels of concern about privacy, we used the answers to the following items as proxies for concern:

- **Perception about the exercise:** This was a single-choice question. It stated: *"In which category would you assign this exercise?"*. It had four possibilities: "challenging", "interesting", "normal" and "boring".
- **Guess about the correct number of re-identifications:** The answer to this question required a number from 0 to 30. The question was: "How many people did you re-identify?".

5 Results and Analysis

We will start by presenting the efficacy of the actual re-identification performed by the students (Subsect. 5.1). Next we show the perceptions about the exercise itself (Subsect. 5.2) which is the closest to a direct indicator of a change in concern about privacy. We then analyze the self-reported perception of accuracy (Subsect. 5.3) as an indicator of learning. Attitudes during the in-class interactions are described in Subsect. 5.4. Finally, in Subsect. 5.5 there is a brief discussion of the results.

5.1 Success in Re-identification

The students were quite successful finding who the players were. All participants completed the exercise, and turned it in on time. As explained in Sect. 4, being able to correctly identify the players was not being graded in itself. Even so, a large percentage of students (90 % for the in-class and 93.3 % for the remote groups) identified correctly more than 96 % (29 or 30) of the de-identified players. The student who identified the smallest number of players, "only" managed to identify 16 of them, although he claimed to know next to nothing about football.

In fact, students were so effective in the re-identification, that they *corrected* one player's birth date, on which we inadvertently had introduced a mistake when collecting the information.

Figure 1 presents the normalized frequency histograms for the number of correctly re-identified players.

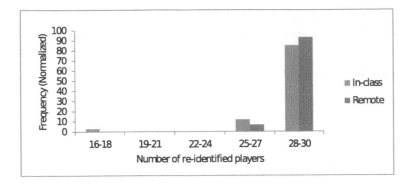

Fig. 1. Frequency (normalized) of correctly re-identified players. (Color figure online)

5.2 Perceptions About the Exercise

The ratings given by the students to the exercise are summarized in Table 3. Given the unconcerned attitudes revealed during the first week activities (see Subsect. 5.4), the change to consider the exercise as mostly "interesting" (67.7 and 73.3 % for in-class and remote students, respectively), constitute a clear indicator of a growing concern. Note that the exercise itself belongs to a discipline different from the group's major, so it is unlikely that the rating reveals a disciplinary issue.

Table 3. Exercise ratings

Rating	In-class	Remote
Challenging	1 (2.9 %)	0 (0 %)
Interesting	23 (67.7 %)	11 (73.3 %)
Normal	6 (17.6 %)	3 (20 %)
Boring	4 (11.8 %)	1 (6.7 %)

5.3 Efficacy Perception

When students had to complete the questionnaire, they still did not know if their re-identifications were correct. We asked them to guess how many players they had identified correctly. Table 4 compares their self-evaluated accuracy with the reality of how many players they had identified correctly. It turns out that their guesses are quite close to reality, which indicates that they had really understood the underlying processes. This result, combined with the fact that 48 out of 49 students identified 25 or more of the 30 players with no previous knowledge about re-identification techniques, shows that this is not a difficult process with common tools and data available today online.

Table 4. Self-evaluation of success in re-identification

Population	Real		Guessed	
	Average	Stand. Dev.	Average	Stand. Dev.
In-person	28,82	2,64	29,29	2,39
Remote	29,4	1,06	28,6	5,15
Whole group	29	2,28	29,08	3,43

5.4 Attitude Change: The In-class Interaction

We describe the subjective assessment of the authors about students' attitudes before and after the exercise.

In the first session, after our talk, most students agreed that they cared about their privacy, but considered that it was not at risk because of the information publicly available about them. Some even offered details on people they knew whose identity was stolen, but the general feeling was that it was something that happened to other people, and that they were safe. Even after running the mini-exercise of re-identifying characters in a fairy tale, their concern did not increase, as they claimed that it was "too easy".

A week later, after completing the exercise, the authors met with the students to pick up the answers and have a group discussion about the results. The mood of the group was more guarded, and some of the students expressed apprehension about their data online, and some of them explained that they did not realize that it was "so easy" to find a trove of information about people.

5.5 Discussion

The indicators used suggest that there may be an attitude change about privacy after executing the re-identification exercise, which was engineered to be relatively easy (it was weakly de-identified). Interestingly enough, it made no difference whether students received a pre-made group of de-identified data, or could devise queries by themselves. We thus believe that the most valuable part of the experience was the exercise itself, because it was hands-on [20].

The talk itself, which warned about what the students later discovered through the exercise, had no measurable effect, so it was surprising when some of the previously sceptic students expressed concern about privacy in the after-exercise discussion. Although we are just describing a single case, our results are consistent with constructivist literature in education [7].

We believe that the most valuable insight is that the task described, being very easy, but definitely practical, could be adapted to raise the privacy awareness of almost any person by executing a re-identification exercise.

We cannot say at this time whether any attitude changes will be maintained, which would be interesting to investigate in the future.

6 Conclusions

We presented a case where a group of students showed an attitude change about privacy issues after completing a hands-on re-identification exercise.

Almost all students (48 out of 49) were able to re-identify 25 players or more, even though they were not trained for the process, confirming the assumption that it is not very complex.

During the first session, students were not particularly interested in the exercise. After the students finished the re-identification process, some of them expressed more concern for their privacy in the post-exercise session. From the answers in the questionnaire, we know they were interested, which is in itself an attitude change. We argue that the interest about the exercise reflects an internal process that led to the greater concern expressed by some in the second session, which potentially suggests an attitude change about privacy.

The ease of resolution, plus the increased interest, points us in the direction that similar exercises could be used to raise awareness about privacy in the general population.

7 Future Work

We intend to test the results of the case presented with a larger, more diverse sample. However, the delivery described (talk, synthetic re-identification exercise, re-identification exercise with real individuals), is relatively expensive. We expect to eventually develop automated, online versions of similar exercises, which would allow us to reach a larger public.

Acknowledgments. This work was done for research project 834-B4-150 at Universidad de Costa Rica (UCR), the Research Center in Information and Communication Technologies (CITIC) and the Department of Computer Science (ECCI). Funding was also received from the Ministry of Science and Technology of Costa Rica (MICITT) and the National Council for Scientific and Technological research (CONICIT). Special thanks to Professor Hugo Solis, his FS0408 students, and the Physics Department at UCR.

References

1. Costa Rica líder en Latinoamérica en exportación de software — Cámara de Tecnologías de Información y Comunicación de Costa Rica (CAMTIC). http://www.camtic.org/hagamos-clic/costa-rica-lider-en-latinoamerica-en-exportacion-de-software/
2. PRODHAB — Agencia de Protección de Datos de los Habitantes. http://www.prodhab.go.cr/. Accessed 30 Nov 2015
3. Twitter sued over Hardy tweet. http://www.smh.com.au/technology/technology-news/twitter-sued-over-hardy-tweet-20120216-1tbxz.html

4. Reglamento a la Ley de protección de la persona frente al tratamiento de sus datos personales (2013). https://www.tse.go.cr/pdf/normativa/reglamentoley-proteccionpersona.pdf
5. Avendaño, A.: Protección de datos en el gobierno digital. In: Ciberseguridad en Costa Rica, pp. 349–356. Programa Sociedad de la Información y el Conocimiento, PROSIC. Universidad de Costa Rica, San José, October 2010. http://www.prosic.ucr.ac.cr/sites/default/files/documentos/ciberseguridad_en_costa_rica.pdf
6. Bolaños, R.: Acceso y uso de las tic en la administració pública, empresas y hogares. In: Informe Anual 2014. Programa Sociedad de la Información y el Conocimiento, PROSIC, pp. 123–156. Universidad de Costa Rica, San José (2014). http://www.prosic.ucr.ac.cr/sites/default/files/documentos/cap4_3.pdf
7. Bransford, J.D., Schwartz, D.L.: Rethinking transfer: a simple proposal with multiple implications. In: Review of Research in Education, pp. 61–100. American Educatonal Research Association, Washington, DC (1999)
8. Rica, C., Legislativa, A.: Ley de protección de la persona frente al tratamiento de sus datos personales (2011). http://www.tse.go.cr/pdf/normativa/leydeproteccion-delapersona.pdf
9. El Emam, K., Jonker, E., Arbuckle, L., Malin, B.: A systematic review of re-identification attacks on health data. PloS one **6**(12), e28071 (2011). http://dx.plos.org/10.1371/journal.pone.0028071
10. Garfinkel, S.L.: NISTIR 8053. de-identification of personal information. Technical report, National Institute of Standards and Technology, Gaithersburg, MD, USA, october 2015
11. Gopalan, R., Antón, A., Doyle, J.: UCON LEGAL. In: Proceedings of the 2nd ACM SIGHIT Symposium on International Health Informatics - IHI 2012, p. 227, No. 111. ACM, New York, January 2012. http://dl.acm.org/citation.cfm?id=2110363.2110391
12. Herrera, M.: Sala IV: Salario de los empleados del Estado es un dato público (2014). http://www.nacion.com/nacional/sala-iv/Sala-IV-Salario-empleados-publico_0_1404459700.html
13. MARCA.com: Keylor Navas spied on by the Costa Rican police. Marca (2014). http://www.marca.com/en/2014/10/29/en/football/real_madrid/1414591431.html
14. Marwick, A.E., Murgia-Diaz, D., Palfrey, J.G.: Youth, Privacy and Reputation (Literature Review) (2010). http://papers.ssrn.com/abstract=1588163
15. Mata, E.: Congreso señala débil protección de datos en el OIJ (2015). http://www.nacion.com/nacional/politica/Congreso-achaca-debil-proteccion-OIJ_0_1487051331.html
16. Narayanan, A., Shmatikov, V.: Robust De-anonymization of Large Sparse Datasets. In: 2008 IEEE Symposium on Security and Privacy (sp 2008), pp. 111–125. IEEE, May 2008. http://ieeexplore.ieee.org/lpdocs/epic03/wrapper.htm?arnumber=4531148
17. Parent, W.A.: Ethical issues in the use of computers. In: Privacy, Morality, and the Law, pp. 201–215. Wadsworth Publ. Co., Belmont (1985)
18. Preibusch, S.: Guide to measuring privacy concern: review of survey and observational instruments. Int. J. Hum. Comput. Stud. **71**(12), 1133–1143 (2013). http://www.sciencedirect.com/science/article/pii/S1071581913001183
19. Rhodes, M.G., Somvichian, W., Wong, K.C.: Google-Motion-to-Dismiss-061313. Technical report. Attorneys for Defendant GOOGLE INC. (2013)

20. Schneider, B., Wallace, J., Blikstein, P., Pea, R.: Preparing for future learning with a tangible user interface: the case of neuroscience. IEEE Trans. Learn. Technol. **6**(2), 117–129 (2013). http://dx.doi.org/10.1109/TLT.2013.15
21. Shklovski, I., Vertesi, J.: "un-googling" publications: the ethics and problems of anonymization. In: CHI 2013 Extended Abstracts on Human Factors in Computing Systems, pp. 2169–2178. CHI EA 2013. ACM, New York (2013). http://doi.acm.org/10.1145/2468356.2468737
22. Solove, D.J.: A taxonomy of privacy. Univ. Pennsylvania Law Rev. **154**(3), 477–560 (2006). http://www.jstor.org/stable/40041279, https://www.law.upenn.edu/journals/lawreview/articles/volume154/issue3/Solove154U.Pa.L.Rev.477(2006).pdf
23. Soto, J.: Diputados crearn comisin para investigar espionaje en el OIJ contra Keylor Navas. La Nación (2014). http://www.crhoy.com/diputados-crearan-comision-para-investigar-espionaje-en-el-oij-contra-keylor-navas/
24. Sweeney, L.: Uniqueness of Simple Demographics in the U.S. Population, LIDAP-WP4 (2000)
25. Westin, A.: Privacy and Freedom. Bodley Head, London (1970)

A4Cloud Workshop: Accountability in the Cloud

Carmen Fernandez-Gago[1]([✉]), Siani Pearson[2], Michela D'Errico[2],
Rehab Alnemr[2], Tobias Pulls[3], and Anderson Santana de Oliveira[4]

[1] Network, Information and Computer Security Lab,
University of Malaga, 29071 Malaga, Spain
`mcgago@lcc.uma.es`
[2] Hewlett Packard Labs, Bristol, UK
{`siani.pearson,michela.derrico,rehab.alnemr`}`@hpe.com`
[3] Karlstad University, Karlstad, Sweden
`tobias.pulls@kau.se`
[4] SAP Labs France, Mougins, France
`anderson.santana.de.oliveira@sap.com`

Abstract. As cloud computing becomes a widely used technology, it is
essential to provide mechanisms and tools that enable trust about how
personal data is dealt with by cloud providers. The Cloud Accountability (A4Cloud) project tries to solve the problem of ensuring trust in the
cloud by providing tools that support the process of achieving accountability. In this paper we will concentrate on some specific tools that were
demonstrated and discussed during the A4Cloud workshop held in association with the IFIP Privacy Summer School in Edinburgh in 2015. In
particular, we will describe tools that facilitate the appropriate choice
of a cloud provider such as the Cloud Offerings Advisory Tool (COAT)
and the Data Protection Impact Assessment Tool (DPIAT), tools that
are in charge of controlling the data of the users such as the Data Track
(DT) tool, and tools that help specify and enforce accountability related
policies by using the Accountability-Primelife Policy Language (A-PPL)
and an associated enforcement engine.

Keywords: Accountability · Tools · Control tools · Facilitating tools

1 Introduction

Cloud computing technology is becoming more and more popular and it is being
widely used by companies and users nowadays. However, there are still some

---

This work has been partially funded by the European Commission through the
FP7/2007-2013 project A4Cloud under grant agreement number 317550. The first
author is supported by the Ministery of Economy of Spain through the Young
Researchers Programme: project PRECISE (TIN2014-54427-JIN). The authors
would like to thank Saul Formoso for taking notes during the workshop and all
the members of A4Cloud involved in the development of the tools.

Published by Springer International Publishing Switzerland 2016. All Rights Reserved
D. Aspinall et al. (Eds.): Privacy and Identity 2015, IFIP AICT 476, pp. 61–78, 2016.
DOI: 10.1007/978-3-319-41763-9_5

concerns about security and how personal data is dealt with by cloud providers. There should be mechanisms and tools in place that help users to have trust in the cloud. The goal of the A4Cloud project [1] is to provide tools and mechanisms that help achieve *accountability* for cloud providers, including demonstration that they are accountable, and helping users to know whether the cloud provider of their choice is accountable. Accountability consists of defining governance to comply in a responsible manner with internal and external criteria, ensuring implementation of appropriate actions, explaining and justifying those actions and remedying any failure to act properly [2]. The approach followed by A4Cloud is interdisciplinary and includes legal and regulatory, socio-economic and technical aspects.

This paper describes the outcomes of the workshop held during the IFIP summer school 2015 on the topic of accountability for data protection in the cloud. At the time of this workshop some of the A4Cloud prototypes were in a mature enough state to be demonstrated. We chose different kinds of such prototypes to be shown at the workshop. The chosen tools offered complementary functionalities that will be also described in this paper. On the one hand, we concentrated on the Cloud Offering Advisory Tool (COAT) and Data Protection Impact Assessment Tool (DPIAT) that facilitate users in finding and assessing a suitable cloud provider that may fulfill their needs. On the other hand, we also considered tools that aid users having control over their data, such as the Data Track (DT) tool or the Accountability-PrimeLife Policy Language (A-PPL), that is the reference language for representation of accountability policies. These policies can be defined by using the Data Protection Policies Tool (DPPT) and enforced by the associated engine.

The structure of the paper is as follows. Section 2 provides an overview of the A4Cloud project, whereas the following sections provide insights on specific tools demonstrated within the workshop. Section 3 describes tools for facilitating users' choice of providers: in particular, COAT and DPIAT. Section 4 describes some control and transparency tools, namely DPPT and A-PPL Engine. The feedback given by the participants in the workshop is analysed in Sect. 5. Finally, Sect. 6 concludes the paper.

2   Overview of the Accountability Project

The goal of the A4Cloud project is to provide an increased basis for trustworthiness in cloud computing by devising methods and tools, through which cloud stakeholders can be made accountable for the privacy and confidentiality of personal data held in the cloud. These methods and tools combine risk analysis, policy enforcement, monitoring and compliance auditing. They will contribute to the governance of cloud activities, providing transparency and assisting legal, regulatory and socio-economic policy enforcement. The A4Cloud tools are grouped into different categories depending on their functionality or their intended usage. They are classified as follows [3]:

- *Preventive tools* are those that aid mitigation of the consequences of any unau-
  thorised action. These tools include assessing risk, selection of providers or
  identification of appropriate policies to mitigate the risks. These tools are the
  Data Protection Impact Assessment Tool (DPIAT), Cloud Offerings Advisory
  Tool (COAT), Accountability Lab (AccLab), the Data Protection Policies Tool
  (DPPT), Accountable Primelife Policy Engine (A-PPL Engine) and Assertion
  Tool (AT).
- *Detective tools* are those that monitor for and detect policy violations. The cor-
  responding A4Cloud tools are the Audit Agent System (AAS), Data Transfer
  Monitoring Tool (DTMT), Data Track (DT) and Transparency Log (TL).
- *Corrective tools* are those designed to mitigate the consequences of any inci-
  dent occuring. They are the Incident Management (IMT) and the Remediation
  Tool (RT).

Among the preventive tools we are going to concentrate in this paper on those
designed for facilitating the choice of a cloud provider. They are DPIAT and
COAT. We will be also concentrating on the definition of policies and enforcement and will pay special attention to the DPPT tool to define policies and
A-PPL engine to enforce and handle policies specified in A-PPL and created by
DPPT. Among the detective tools we consider in this paper the DT tool. This
tool can be classified as a Data Subject Control tool that provides controls for
the management and protection of the personal data of the users.

For the scope of this work no corrective tools were included in the workshop
as they were not mature enough to be demonstrated.

3   Tools for Facilitating Choice

3.1   COAT

The Cloud Offerings Advisory Tool (COAT) is a cloud brokerage tool that facilitates evaluation of cloud offerings and contract terms with the goal of enabling
more educated decision making about which service and service provider to
select. It allows potential cloud customers – with a focus on end users and Small
and Medium Sized Enterprises (SMEs) – to make informed choices about data
protection, privacy, compliance and governance, based upon making the cloud
contracts more transparent to these cloud customers. This type of tool is useful for a number of reasons: reading and interpreting terms and conditions in
cloud service offers can be challenging, and indeed non legal experts cannot easily make out the differences between contracts relating to cloud offerings. SMEs
and individuals in particular do not typically have enough technical and financial resources to assess cloud offers in this way. However, there is no current
brokering service that focuses on the user's data protection requirements.

A number of related factors vary across cloud providers, and are reflected in
the contracts. For example, security measures (including the type of encryption
and key management solution), processing locations (that determine which law
applies), data protection roles (which reflect the capacity of the cloud service

provider acting in relation to the personal data), data deletion procedures, notification about changes to terms and conditions, the ways in which subcontracting to a third party is allowed, notification in the event of a security breach involving the customer's data, notification when law enforcement requests a customer's data, the period during which the CSP keeps a customer's data after service termination, and so on. The tool highlights these differences, and explains to the user what implications this might have. The focus of the tool is on providing feedback and advice related to properties that reflect compliance with regulatory obligations rather than providing feedback on qualitative performance aspects (such as availability), although potentially the tool could be integrated with other tools that offer the latter.

From the cloud customer point of view, the tool aims to ease the comparison of alternative cloud offerings, and provide greater transparency and guidance when considering which provider to use. From the cloud service provider point of view, the tool can provide benefits in terms of decreasing the complexity for customers when choosing a cloud provider, highlighting the unique criteria in the cloud service provider's offer, increasing market exposure, and ultimately matching cloud demands with their offerings.

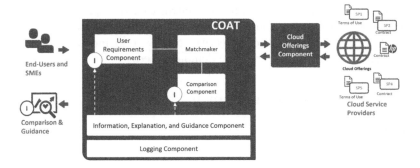

Fig. 1. COAT high level architecture

The overall system is depicted in Fig. 1, in which a Web User Interface enables interaction with the target users. During this interaction, potential cloud customers can provide as input to the graphical interface a collection of answers to a questionnaire (that can change according to the inputs already provided), but most of this information is optional and need not be provided although the interactions help guide the users as to their needs and provide a more targeted output. Such information includes the data location, the roles involved in the scenario to be built on the cloud, contact details of those responsible for defining the purpose of use for the involved data, contextual information about the environment setting and the user needs and requirements. Other knowledge used by the system includes the cloud service offerings in structured form, models of cloud contracts and points of attention and reputation information with respect to the agents involved in the offering process. During this process of interaction, guidance is provided on privacy and security aspects to pay attention to when comparing the terms of cloud service offerings. The outcome of COAT is an immediate and dynamically changeable feedback panel that includes an overview of compatible service offerings matching the user requirements and links to further information and analysis. A familiar store-type interface is used to reduce complexity and improve usability. See Fig. 2 for an example, which shows the questionnaire on the left hand side, the results on the right hand side and an example of advice that is provided in a dynamic way as the user considers the answer to individual questions. The matching is based on data protection requirements, and transparency is improved about what exactly the service providers are offering from a data protection perspective and how those choices might impact the potential cloud customer.

Fig. 2. Example COAT screenshot

Ongoing research involves usage of ontologies for more sophisticated reasoning and linkage to PLA terms, and usage of maturity and reputational models to optimise ordering of the outputs. For further information about the system, see [4].

3.2 DPIAT

The Data Protection Impact Assessment Tool (DPIAT) is a decision support tool focusing on assessment of the risks associated with the proposed usage of cloud computing, involving personal and/or confidential data. It assesses the proposed use of cloud services, helping users to understand, assess, and select CSPs that offer acceptable standards in terms of data protection. The tool is tailored to satisfy the needs of SMEs that intend to process personal data in the cloud; it guides them through the impact assessment and educates them about personal data protection risks, taking into account specific cloud risk scenarios. The approach is based on legal and socio-economic analysis of privacy issues for cloud deployments and takes into consideration the new requirements put forward in the proposed European Union (EU) General Data Protection Regulation (GDPR) [5], which introduces a new obligation on data controllers and/or processors to carry out a Data Protection Impact Assessment prior to risky processing operations (although the requirements differ slightly across the various drafts of the Regulation).

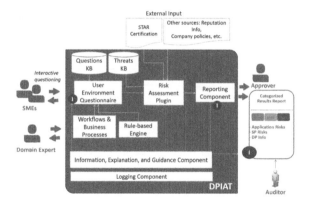

Fig. 3. The high level approach of the data protection impact assessment tool

Figure 3 shows the high level approach of DPIAT. The assessment is based on input about the business context gathered within successive questionnaires for an initial screening and for a full screening for a given project, combined with risk assessment of cloud offerings [6] based upon information generated voluntarily by CSPs, and collected from the CSA Security, Trust and Assurance Registry (STAR) [7]. The output of the first phase of the DPIAT reflects advice about whether to proceed to the second phase of assessment. The second phase questionnaire contains a set of 50 questions. An example of part of this input questionnaire, which is responsive to the questions asked in the sense that the next questions to be asked depend partly upon previous answers, is given in Fig. 4, which also illustrates how guidance related to the particular answers selected is provided dynamically during the process of answering the questions.

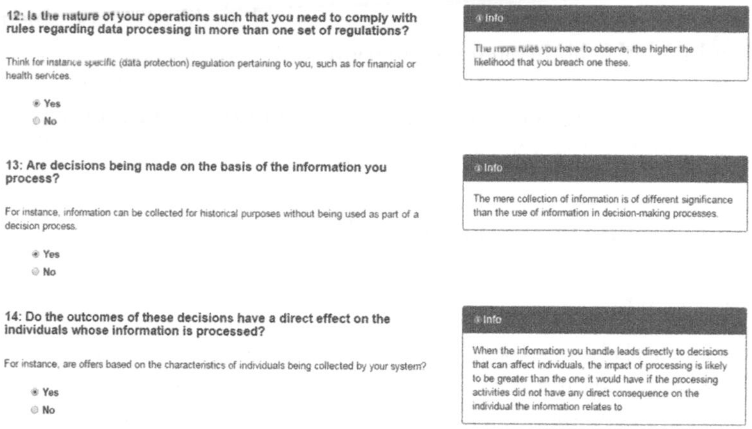
12: Is the nature of your operations such that you need to comply with rules regarding data processing in more than one set of regulations?
Think for instance specific (data protection) regulation pertaining to you, such as for financial or health services.
Yes
No
Info
The more rules you have to observe, the higher the likelihood that you breach one these.
13: Are decisions being made on the basis of the information you process?
For instance, information can be collected for historical purposes without being used as part of a decision process.
Yes
No
Info
The mere collection of information is of different significance than the use of information in decision-making processes.
14: Do the outcomes of these decisions have a direct effect on the individuals whose information is processed?
For instance, are offers based on the characteristics of individuals being collected by your system?
Yes
No
Info
When the information you handle leads directly to decisions that can affect individuals, the impact of processing is likely to be greater than the one it would have if the processing activities did not have any direct consequence on the individual the information relates to

Fig. 4. Example section of DPIAT full screening questionnaire

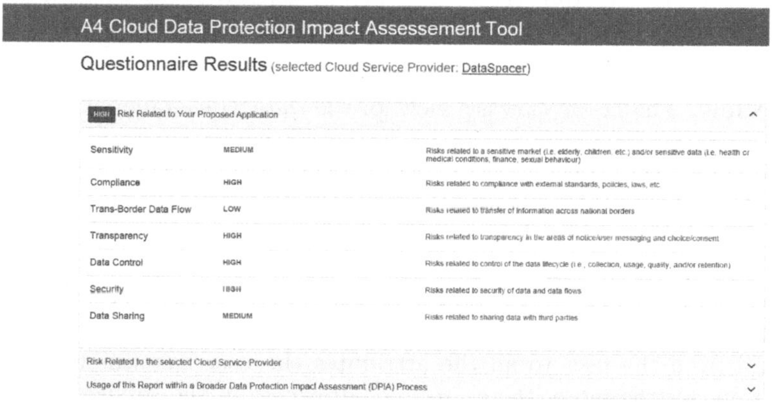
A4 Cloud Data Protection Impact Assessement Tool
Questionnaire Results (selected Cloud Service Provider: DataSpacer)
HIGH Risk Related to Your Proposed Application
Sensitivity MEDIUM Risks related to a sensitive market (i.e. elderly, children, etc.) and/or sensitive data (i.e. health or medical conditions, finance, sexual behaviour)
Compliance HIGH Risks related to compliance with external standards, policies, laws, etc
Trans-Border Data Flow LOW Risks related to transfer of information across national borders
Transparency HIGH Risks related to transparency in the areas of notice/user messaging and choice/consent
Data Control HIGH Risks related to control of the data lifecycle (i.e., collection, usage, quality, and/or retention)
Security HIGH Risks related to security of data and data flows
Data Sharing MEDIUM Risks related to sharing data with third parties
Risk Related to the selected Cloud Service Provider
Usage of this Report within a Broader Data Protection Impact Assessment (DPIA) Process

Fig. 5. Example DPIAT report, with first section expanded

The output of this phase is a report that includes: the data protection risk profile, assistance in deciding whether to proceed or not, and the context of usage of this tool within a wider DPIA process. Amongst other things, the tool is able to demonstrate the effectiveness and appropriateness of the implemented practices of a cloud provider helping him to target resources in the most efficient manner to reduce risks. The report from this phase contains three sections. The first, project-based risk assessment, is based on the answers to the questionnaire and contains the risk level associated with: sensitivity, compliance, transborder data flow, transparency, data control, security, and data sharing. An example is shown in Fig. 5. The focus here is on assessment of potential harm to individuals and society, which is not typically part of a classic organisational risk assessment process. The second part of the report displays risks associated with the security controls used by the selected CSP. It contains the 35 ENISA risk categories [8] with their associated quantitative and qualitative assessments. The last section highlights additional information that the user needs to know related to requirements associated with GDPR article 33 [5]. The system also logs the offered advice and the user's decision for accountability purposes. For further information about the system, including a full list of questions, see [9].

4 Control and Transparency Tools

4.1 Data Track

The Data Track (DT) is a tool that enables data subjects to get an overview of what information they have disclosed to online services [10]. DT provides several different views on the disclosed data – each view tailored to help data subjects answer different questions – and enables the data subject to exercise some control over the data stored on the service's side. Data disclosures are collected by DT with the help of compatible service providers. Next, we present one of the views followed by what type of control DT provides for compatible service providers.

Trace View. The Trace View is a view for the Data Track tailored for answering the question "What information about me have I sent to which online services?". Figure 6 shows the Trace View. In the middle of the view there is a picture representing the user him- or her-self. At the top of the view are *attributes*: each attribute has a *type* (like e-email or username) and one or more *values* (like "alice@example.com" or "bob"). At the bottom of the view are *services* like Spotify or Facebook. The view is called the Trace View because when the user clicks on a service there is a trace (line) drawn from the service to the user, and from the user to all the attributes the user has sent to the service in question. Furthermore, there are lines drawn from the service to any other *downstream* services used by the service provider to provide the service. In Fig. 6, Spotify is as an example using Visa (presumably to accept creditcard payments for subscriptions).

Exercising Control. For compatible services, the Data Track enables the user to request access to, correction of, or deletion of their personal data stored remotely at services. In A4Cloud, a DT-compatible service is provided by the A-PPL Engine (presented in Sect. 4.2). Outside A4Cloud, the vast majority of conventional services do not provide data subjects with online APIs to excercise control over their personal data.

4.2 Privacy Policy Definition and Enforcement

Implementation of privacy policies can be thought of as a two phase process, as shown in Fig. 7. Tasks carried out in the first phase have the objective to formally specify the policies that describe the different aspects of the practices related

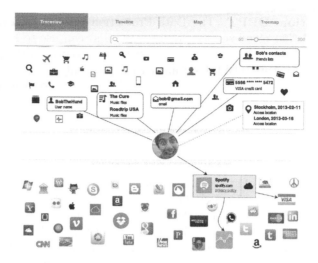

Fig. 6. The trace view of the data track.

to the cloud service provision. During this phase different types of artifacts are designed and produced. For privacy policy statements that can be technically enforced by means of software tools, appropriate technical representation of the statements need to be generated. The specific language for the technical representation of the policies is tied to specific components tasked with the policy enforcement. The A4Cloud Project has designed (i) a language, called A-PPL, whose expression capabilities address the need for accountability related policies; (ii) an engine, the A-PPL Engine, which is able to translate into actions policies specified in A-PPL. During the second phase of the policy implementation process, policies are technically enforced by the engine, which also provide features, such as logging and notifications, that contribute to building an accountable enforcement environment. In the following subsections we will describe the tools used in the policy definition and the policy enforcement phases, respectively DPPT and the A-PPL Engine, along with the artifacts produced and used.

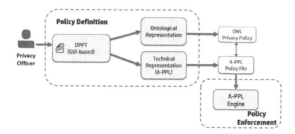

Fig. 7. Privacy policy definition and enforcement

Policy Definition: DPPT. The Data Protection Policies Tool (DPPT) is a GUI-based tool that cloud service providers (CSPs) can use to specify privacy policy statements to produce two different artifacts: an ontological representation of the policy statements (OWL file); an A-PPL (basically, an xml-based) policy file, that contains a representation in A-PPL of the policy statements that need to be enforced through the A-PPL Engine. The OWL Privacy Policy is linked to the A-PPL policy, in that a subset of the statements will have a corresponding A-PPL policy element.

The DPPT GUI, shown in Fig. 8, presents a set of data protection aspects, organised in graphical panes. For each data protection aspect the CSP's privacy officer can specify a set of statements. When all the choices have been made, an A-PPL policy file can be created. The creation of the different policy elements involves using the data provided through the GUI to customise an appropriate policy element template. In order to bind a privacy policy statement with an A-PPL element template we have carried out an analysis of A-PPL Engine capabilities and mapped those to the data protection statements that can be fulfilled by enforcing that A-PPL element. The different A-PPL elements produced as a result of the templates customisation are then composed according to A-PPL schema to create a valid A-PPL policy file. Once created, the policy can be sent to the A-PPL Engine by clicking the button "Send to Engine". The result of the action is that the policy is stored by the A-PPL Engine, which is then ready to enforce them. We clarify that the actual enforcement will be done once data subjects' personal data will be stored and bound to the policy. This is done at service registration phase, when data subjects are asked to provide data in order to start using the cloud service.

In the following, we will provide details about the options that can be selected to create a set of enforceable privacy policy elements.

Data Processing. A CSP can specify the personal data elements that the service will process. In our A4Cloud reference scenario, the privacy officer will select data items belonging to two different personal data categories: "User Account" and "Health Data". "User account" includes typical elements such as email address, username. "Health Data" refers to data elements that are processed by CSPs providing health statistics services. Examples of this category are blood pressure, blood sugar level, heart rate. Personal data categories are bound to ontological classes that describe them as belonging to specific data sensitivity categories. For example, the "Health Data" class is classified as "Sensitive Data", according to the definition of sensitive in EU privacy laws [11]. The set of data items selected will be referenced in other policy statements to specify additional policies that apply to them.

CSPs need also to specify for how long data will be kept. This can be done by providing the time period value through the GUI. The A-PPL element generated for this statement will enable the engine to automatically manage the deletion of data.

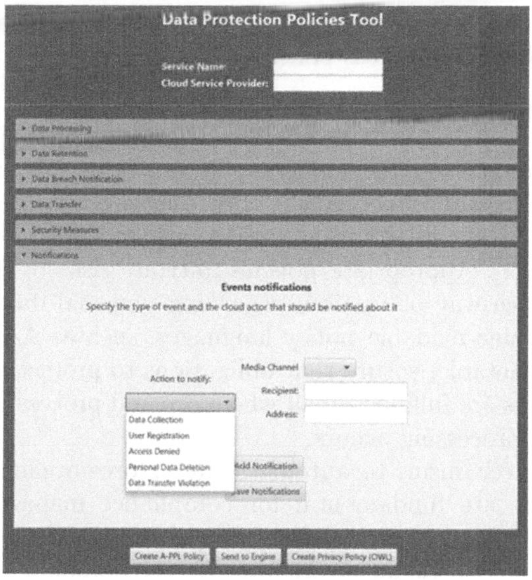

Fig. 8. DPPT GUI: configuration of notification sending

Notification. *Notification* is an essential element of accountability and should be used by CSPs to notify (within a predefined timeframe) about relevant events related to data processing operations. Depending on the types of events that can be captured by the components deployed for audit and monitoring purposes, sending of notifications can be automated. DPPT GUI allows the provider to configure the A-PPL Engine for notifications sending. The GUI presents a set of options for the type of events, which reflect the capabilities of the audit and monitoring tools developed within A4Cloud. Examples of event types are: data personal data deletion, data transfer policy violation, access denied. Specific type of events that affect personal data, such as data leakage or data loss, assume particular relevance and are specified in a separate section of the GUI. The information required to be provided for the generation of the corresponding A-PPL policy element includes: the type of event to notify about, the relevant stakeholder identifier to be notified, the communication channel (basically e-mail or post), the address and the timeframe.

Control Rights. Access rights (read, write, delete, update) need to be granted to different actors over different sets of personal data items. The GUI allows the provider to create different access rules for each actor that needs to process personal data collected from data subjects. Data Subjects need to be given access to their own personal data, therefore the CSP should create a specific rule that specifies that a given data subject can access her own data to perform all the available operations. The creation of the A-PPL policy elements for enforcement of access control requires the CSP to provide information such as the set of personal data, the identifier of the actor that should be given access, its role (relevant if the underlying access control system is role-based) and the access rights to grant.

Policy Enforcement: A-PPL Engine. Organizational cloud customers usually assume the role of data controller, thus they are held accountable for the way cloud services respond to many regulations, including the EU Data Protection Directive [11]. Appropriate policies mitigate risks to data protection as they clarify in which way obligations regarding personal data are carried out. In particular, machine-readable policy languages, such as A-PPL [12,13] make organizations accountable, ensure that obligations to protect personal data and data subjects' rights are fulfilled by all who store and process the data, irrespective of where that processing occurs.

In the cloud, mechanisms to automatically enforce organizational and data governance policies are fundamental for compliance management. Using the A4Cloud policy enforcement tools, cloud providers can offer more transparency about the data handling. As far as assurance is given about the deployment and configuration of the tools, which in general can be achieved with independent audits, the policy enforcement will happen in a predictable manner, satisfying the data controller needs and obligations, but also as determined by the data controller, giving back control to the (cloud) data subject. The enforcement engine works in cooperation with further A4Cloud tools to reinforce the assurance about the correct policy execution.

A-PPL Engine High Level Architecture. The A-PPL engine has been created as an extension of the PPL engine in order to enforce the new A-PPL language policies. The first step was to extend the PPL XML schema with the new obligations defined in A-PPL. Many PPL engine functionalities have been simplified since the notion of sticky policy is no longer used.

The new A-PPL engine is a simplified version of the PPL engine. Many PPL engine functionalities have been removed since they are no longer needed in A-PPL: the matching engine is no longer used since the notions of sticky policy and data handling preferences do not exist in the A-PPL language.

A new module called **Policy Administration Point (PAP)** is responsible for storing, updating and deleting PIIs and their policies in the database.

The access control is performed in the Policy Decision point (PDP) module which uses the Heras XACML engine [14] exactly the way it was implemented in PPL. The usage control is enforced in the obligation handler module which includes the event and action handlers sub-modules.

The Policy Enforcement Point (PEP) is the main module of the engine, which enforces the A-PPL policy of a PII when access is requested to it. For this reason, it communicates with the frontend of the engine (ppl-rest module) as well as the PDP and obligation handler.

Upon storing the PII, the engine receives also an A-PPL policy that contains the rules and obligations related to how that piece of personal data has to be handled. For this reason, PII and their associated policy are represented in A-PPLE with the *<PIIType>* element, which has the following attributes:

- *owner*: Denotes the owner of the PIIs
- *attributeName*: It is the name of the PII element.
- *attributeValue*: The value of the PII element
- *policySetOrPolicy*: One or more "sticky" policies describing the access and usage control rights for this PII.
- *creationDate*: The creation date of PII.
- *modificationDate*: The modification date of PII.

When PII is retrieved from the engine, the policy associated with this personal data is analysed by the **Policy Decision Point (PDP)** that takes into account access and usage control rules.

In addition, obligations related to the personal data handling are executed when certain events occur inside the engine. The **Obligation Handler** component is responsible for analysing these A-PPL obligations (pairs of triggers and actions).

All actions happening inside A-PPLE are logged by a central component called **Logging Handler**. It stores the log entries related to decisions and actions (e.g. ActionLog) concerning the PIIs stored inside the engine.

We can see in Fig. 9, that A-PPLE adopts a two-layer high-level architecture so that isolation between the engine components and data is performed: The core elements responsible for the policy enforcement functionalities reside in the Business layer. The Persistence layer consists of the PII Store and the Policy Repository where PIIs and the associated sticky policies are stored as well as the Logs produced by the Logging Handler component. Access to the persistence layer is achieved through a Persistence Handler component, which abstracts the underlying location and storage data model to the above business layer functions [15].

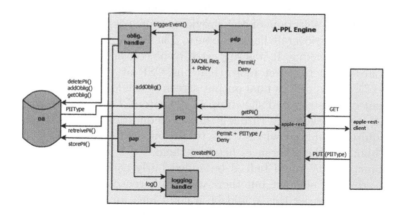

Fig. 9. A-PPL engine architecture

5   Discussion

In this section we will describe how we structure the workshop and the feed-back and questions that we received from the audience. Firstly, we introduced a general overview of the A4Cloud project in order to give the audience a general view on it. Then, the group was split into four different subgroups of four or five people each. Each of these subgroups approached specific booths for each of the tools (there was a shared booth for DPIAT and COAT), where a member of A4Cloud explained their corresponding tool. They introduced the group to their main features and showed how the tools work in practice. The presentation was interactive and anyone could ask questions at any time.

5.1   DT

Since the nature of the DT tool is mainly how data is dealt with, some concerns were related to mainly how it is stored or visualised, or how to input the infor-mation into the tool. The audience was also concerned about the resolution of conflicts or the evaluation of this tool as well as about monitoring aspects. These aspects led to the question of how this tool improves the accountability of the service provider. In general, attendees viewed the tool as an interesting one for auditing companies.

They also pointed out that security aspects should be considered in order to move forward. For the sake of usability, it was mentioned that it would be interesting if the DT tool worked in a mobile environment.

5.2   DPIAT

The comments and concerns raised by the audience with respect to the DPIAT are manifold. They relate to different aspects such as the selection of providers, how risk is considered and how the rating and the evaluation are performed.

Concerning the selection of the providers, some issues arose with respect to the way that the overall flags compute. The main question is whether the algorithm needs tweaking. It was suggested to be convenient for the user if there would be an option to select more than one CSP at the beginning (perhaps, up to three?). Then, on the final output screen it would be a good idea to have the different options selected shown up in the second band of output. This way the user does not have to go through the whole questionnaire each time if they were not quite sure about which CSPs to use but had a good idea. This would also help highlight the differences between them.

This functionality could indeed be added fairly easily to allow comparison of several providers at once, but there was a difference of opinion amongst the attendees as to whether this would be a good idea, or appropriate for typical contexts in which the tool might be used. Also, it would be interesting to clarify in which category governments fall as they could also be users of the tool.

Attendees' concerns about risk were related to how it is presented for users to understand it. The distinction between the risks to data subjects (the core of a DPIA), and those related to a more classic organisational risk assessment (on the proposed service provider) should be clear. Also, the attendees suggested that the colour code and used signs for the DPIAT overall output, e.g. a high risk should show up as red, not green (this seemed due to a glitch with the system on the day). It was noted that risk mitigation is missing and also other factors that might be relevant for assessing risk, e.g. who owns the key?

There was a difference in opinion about how helpful an overall rating would be for the first section. Perhaps, the consensus was that it would be helpful indeed for decision making, but one would have to be very careful how that was done. It is important that there would be some explanation about what this overall rating would mean, and what the implications would be. It was highly stressed by the more mature researchers and experts that it should be clear how the user should interpret the findings, and what it meant for them in terms of what they should do next, etc.

It was advised to check whether or not the very high and extremely high, etc. of the second part were indeed the same bands (and associated meaning) as those used in the first part - it seemed that there might be a mismatch with different terms being used.

Perhaps it needed to be clearer how DPIAT should be used in the context of an overall DPIA process, and how things like consultation of stakeholders fit in. We do have some information on this, but it still seems not so clear about what else must be done, and when and how often the DPIAT tool could be used. Questions raised related to how and who assess cloud providers. An important issue is also time consuming for running the tools. It would be very interesting to run all the tools at once.

The major concern that attendees had was that there was no justification of why the results were given, or explanation of how the results were obtained, or way of the user or a third party to check the verification of the process used to obtain these results. One aspect of dealing with this is that an explanation of how the results were obtained should be added within the tool in a way that it could be accessed by a user exactly, even if the particular chain of processing leading to that particular result might not be exposable in other words, to be able to click to see how it was done, and provide more evidence about that. Which results from the system can be relied on, and why? There should be more explanation about how the risk was obtained, to what extent probability and impact are taken into account, etc., and whether that differs across the different sections of output. In what way is the output to be regarded as a proof for interpretation and used by the user, and in what way could it be provided as a proof for a data protection authority? The legal implications are different. What is the outcome of the result (single answer, guidelines, etc.)? What is it useful for?

5.3   COAT

Some options in the answers given seem very odd, e.g. in the encryption options there should be a distinction made between data at rest and during transit, and also the types of weaker and stronger encryption should be brought out more accurately. We had already realised this and updated the questionnaire offline, although that was not yet reflected within the demo version. Instead of just having the option of Europe in some of the questions, there should be the possibility (by another question popping up to bring up certain countries if Europe were selected) to allow more specific selection of countries (i.e. local is not enough, it may need to be local and Belgium, or whatever). This is necessary for various reasons (legal and user preferences).

There were also issues relating to what we have been showing for some time in this same demo versus our proposed improvements that were not yet reflected within it, such as more sophisticated ordering of results, display of certification/seals, etc. Questions from the audience were related to the use of standards, in the sense of how everything related to the tool would be documented.

Concerning legal regulations it was pointed out that different regulations depending on the countries should be taken into account.

5.4   A-PPL

One of the first questions that arose from the audience was why the A-PPL language was chosen. If the reason is a question of scalability this seems to be a good reason. The way requirements are dealt with is also another of the questions: are all the requirements translated into the policy? The A-PPL tool is based on the existence of a privacy officer. We have to check what is going to be done in the case where there is not such an officer, as it could be the case for example of SMEs.

6   Conclusion and Future Work

In this paper we have described the tools and the feedback provided by attendees during the A4Cloud workshop held at the IFIP summer school 2015. The A4Cloud project tackles the problem of providing accountability from an interdisciplinary perspective involving technical, legal and socio-economic aspects. A4Cloud provides a set of tools and mechanisms for the different stakeholders involved in the cloud for achieving accountability. Thus, in this paper, we have concentrated on tools for facilitating choice (COAT and DPIAT) and tools for offering control (DT, DPPT and A-PPL Engine). At the time of the workshop all these tool prototypes were in a mature enough state to be demonstrated. Therefore, the attendees could have a very good idea of how they could be used by users or providers.

The feedback from this workshop is being taken into account as the tool prototypes are further modified. Many of the issues raised have already been addressed within improved versions of the tools. We are carrying out further validation of the tools, for example, within a wearables scenario, as well as their socio-economic impact assessment.

References

1. A4Cloud: The Cloud Accountability Project. http://www.a4cloud.eu/
2. Catteddu, D., Felici, M., Hogben, G., Holcroft, A., Kosta, E., Leenes, R., Millard, C., Niezen, M., Nuñez, D., Papanikolaou, N., et al.: Towards a model of accountability for cloud computing services. In: Pre-Proceedings of International Workshop on Trustworthiness, Accountability and Forensics in the Cloud (TAFC) (2013)
3. Pearson, S., Wainwright, N.: An interdisciplinary approach to accountability for future internet service provision. Proc. IJTMCC 1, 52–72 (2013)
4. Alnemr, R., Pearson, S., Leenes, R., Mhungu, R.: Coat: cloud offerings advisory tool. In: IEEE 6th International Conference on Cloud Computing Technology and Science, CloudCom 2014, Singapore, 15–18 December 2014
5. EU Parliament and EU Council: Proposal for a regulation of the European parliament and of the council on the protection of individuals with regard to the processing of personal data and on the free movement of such data (general data protection regulation) (2012)
6. Cayirci, E., Garaga, A., de Oliveira, A.S., Roudier, Y.: A cloud adoption risk assessment model. In: IEEE Utility and Cloud Computing (UCC), pp. 908–913 (2014)
7. Cloud Security Alliance: Security, Trust & Assurance Registry (STAR). https://cloudsecurityalliance.org/star/
8. ENISA: Cloud computing - benefits, risks and recommendations for information security (2009)
9. Alnemr, R., et al.: A data protection impact assessment methodology for cloud. In: Berendt, B., Engel, T., Ikonomou, D., Le Métayer, D., Schiffner, S. (eds.) APF 2015. LNCS, vol. 9484, pp. 60–92. Springer, Heidelberg (2016). doi:10.1007/978-3-319-31456-3_4
10. Angulo, J., Fischer-Hübner, S., Pulls, T., Wästlund, E.: Usable transparency with the data track: a tool for visualizing data disclosures. In: Begole, B., Kim, J., Inkpen, K., Woo, W. (eds.) Proceedings of the 33rd Annual ACM Conference Extended Abstracts on Human Factors in Computing Systems, CHI 2015 Extended Abstracts, pp. 1803–1808, Seoul, Republic of Korea. ACM, 18–23 April 2015
11. European Parliament, the Council of the European Union: Directive 95/46/EC of the European Parliament and of the Council of 24 October 1995 on the protection of individuals with regard to the processing of personal data and on the free movement of such data (1995). http://ec.europa.eu/justice/policies/privacy/docs/95-46-ce/dir1995-46_part1_en.pdf
12. Azraoui, M., Elkhiyaoui, K., Önen, M., Bernsmed, K., De Oliveira, A.S., Sendor, J.: A-PPL: an accountability policy language. In: Garcia-Alfaro, J., Herrera-Joancomartí, J., Lupu, E., Posegga, J., Aldini, A., Martinelli, F., Suri, N. (eds.) DPM/SETOP/QASA 2014. LNCS, vol. 8872, pp. 319–326. Springer, Heidelberg (2015)

13. Benghabrit, W., Grall, H., Royer, J.C., Sellami, M., Azraoui, M., Elkhiyaoui, K., Önen, M., de Oliveira, A.S., Bernsmed, K.: A cloud accountability policy representation framework. In: Helfert, M., Desprez, F., Ferguson, D., Leymann, F., Muñoz, V.M. (eds.) CLOSER 2014 - Proceedings of the 4th International Conference on Cloud Computing and Services Science, pp. 489–498. SciTePress, Barcelona, 3–5 April 2014

14. HERAS AF team: HERAS AF (Holistic Enterprise-Ready Application Security Architecture Framework). http://herasaf.org/

15. Garaga, A., de Oliveira, A.S., Sendor, J., Azraoui, M., Elkhiyaoui, K., Molva, R., Cherrueau, R.A., Douence, R., Grall, H., Royer, J.C., Sellami, M., Südholt, M., Bernsmed, K.: D:C-4.1: policy representation framework. Technical report D:C-4.1, Accountability for Cloud and Future Internet Services - A4Cloud Project (2013)

Signatures for Privacy, Trust and Accountability in the Cloud: Applications and Requirements

Alaa Alaqra[1], Simone Fischer-Hübner[1(✉)], Thomas Groß[2],
Thomas Lorünser[3], and Daniel Slamanig[4]

[1] Karlstad University, Karlstad, Sweden
simofihu@kau.se
[2] Newcastle University, Newcastle, UK
[3] Austrian Institute of Technology, Seibersdorf, Austria
[4] Graz University of Technology, Graz, Austria

Abstract. This paper summarises the results of a workshop at the IFIP Summer School 2015 introducing the EU Horizon 2020 project PRIS-MACLOUD, that is, Privacy and Security Maintaining Services in the Cloud. The contributions of this summary are three-fold. Firstly, it provides an overview to the PRISMACLOUD cryptographic tools and use-case scenarios that were presented as part of this workshop. Secondly, it distills the discussion results of parallel focus groups. Thirdly, it summarises a "Deep Dive on Crypto" session that offered technical information on the new tools. Overall, the workshop aimed a outlining application scenarios and eliciting end-user requirements for PRISMACLOUD.

Keywords: Privacy · Cloud computing · Functional signatures · Malleable signatures · Graph signatures · Anonymous credentials · User requirements

1 Introduction

Cloud computing is a very promising direction within ICT, but the practical adoption of cloud computing technologies may be greatly hindered by the lack of adequate technical controls to enforce the privacy of data and users in this outsourcing scenario. Solving this issues is especially challenging due to some fundamental properties of cloud computing such as being an open platform, its anytime and anywhere accessibility, as well as the intrinsic multi-tenancy, which introduce new security and privacy threats. In general, cloud computing is typically an outsourcing model and if the associated threats are not addressed adequately it leads to a tremendous risk for cloud users and their data. Thus, it is widely accepted that outsourcing of data and computations to third party cloud infrastructure requires various challenging security and privacy issues to be solved in order to gain users' trust. Besides the evident privacy and confidentiality issues associated with outsourced personal data and other type of confidential

© IFIP International Federation for Information Processing 2016
Published by Springer International Publishing Switzerland 2016. All Rights Reserved
D. Aspinall et al. (Eds.): Privacy and Identity 2015, IFIP AICT 476, pp. 79–96, 2016.
DOI: 10.1007/978-3-319-41763-9_6

data (e.g., business secrets), which are a quite well understood albeit unsolved problem, this new computing paradigm introduces additional problems related to authenticity, verifiability and accountability. Basically, the question is how we can ensure that the cloud *works* as it is intended or claimed to do and how can the cloud be held accountable if deviations occur. Thereby, one may not only be concerned with the data itself, but also with processes (tasks/workflows) running in the cloud and processing the data. Moreover, such concerns may also be related to the used infrastructure itself.

Enforcing authenticity, verifiability and accountability for cloud based data processing by means of cryptography is one core topic within the recently started EU Horizon 2020 project PRISMACLOUD[1] on Privacy and Security Maintaining Services in the Cloud [11]. Its general goal is the research and development of tools and methodologies to strengthen the security, privacy and accountability for cloud based services, i.e., to make them more trustworthy. The main results will be showcased in different use-cases from the three application domains e-Health, e-Government and Smart Cities, which typically deal with sensitive data of citizens. To maximize the impact of the project results another focus of PRISMACLOUD is on the usability of developed solutions. Therefore, we are studying how users perceive such technologies if used within cloud based services, and elicit end user and human-computer interaction (HCI) requirements and guidelines for usable cryptography and protocols for the cloud. The aim is to design services which provide adequate security features but at the same time respect the users' needs in order to guarantee for the best acceptance of security technologies. The users should be able to understand and perceive the increased security and privacy they have when interacting with an augmented system while not being confronted with obstacles complicating their real tasks.

At the IFIP Summer School 2015 (Edinburgh, August 2015), the PRISMACLOUD project has organised a workshop comprising a series of parallel focus group sessions on the first day and a second-day "Deep Dive on Cryptography" workshop session. The motivation behind organizing this workshop related to the PRISMACLOUD project was as follows. Firstly, it was our intention to benefit from the knowledge of experts (from different domains) participating at the summer school in order to gather feedback, criticism and input on very early descriptions of the use-cases within PRISMACLOUD and to elicit end user and HCI requirements. Secondly, it was our aim to bring the attention of the audience to the cryptographic tools that are used and further developed within PRISMACLOUD. In particular, to attract interest from other researchers to also conduct research in this important field as well as interest from other security and privacy related research projects and researchers to cooperate with PRISMACLOUD. This paper summarises the content and discussion results of this workshop.

Outline. The remainder of this paper is structured as follows: In the next section, the cryptographic tools for the use-cases within PRISMACLOUD will be introduced. Section 3 briefly presents preliminary use-case scenarios in the areas of e-Health, e-Government and Smart Cities that are currently elaborated in

---

[1] https://prismacloud.eu.

PRISMACLOUD and helped explaining the ideas in the workshop and served as a basis for our focus group discussions. Section 4 presents the discussion results including the elicited end user and HCI requirements of five parallel focus groups that were part of the workshop. Section 5 will then summarise the results of the discussion on the second day on graph signatures and topology certification (as they have not been covered in the presented use-cases). Section 6 is finally rounding up this paper with overall conclusions.

2   Cryptographic Tools

Securing data over its life cycle in the cloud by means of cryptography is extremely challenging yet appealing to prevent many of provider related threats. This is due to the fact, that today widely used cryptography is designed to protect the confidentiality and authenticity of data in a very stringent way, i.e., without allowing for any modification. However, in the cloud setting it is important to support controlled altering and sharing of data in an agile way in order not to lose the benefits of cloud computing for cryptographically protected data. A very descriptive example is cloud storage. If we simply encrypt the data before uploading to the cloud we are protected from all major threats but completely lose the possibility to share or process the data, hence, we have to resign from almost all additional benefits of cloud computing for the sake of security. The same is true for authenticity protected data by means of signatures, every alteration of the data would immediately render the signature invalid, no matter how small it may be.

In PRISMACLOUD we focus on the research and development of efficient cryptographic methods tailored to fit the needs of cloud computing and allow for controlled modification and sharing of data without giving up on the end-to-end security paradigm. We carefully selected technologies which have the potential to better protect the security of data during their stay in the cloud in a more agile way than currently possible. Subsequently, we briefly introduce some cryptographic tools that (a) are used within the use-cases presented and discussed in the workshop and (b) that have been presented throughout the second technical part of the workshop. Some of them do not appear in the use-cases that have been selected for the workshop and focus groups at the first workshop day. In particular, we will briefly present the concept of distributed cloud storage, different variants of signature schemes with special properties and the concept of (attribute-based) anonymous credentials.

Distributed Cloud Storage. Protecting the privacy, integrity and availability of stored data in the public cloud setting while at the same time allowing them to be shared in dynamic groups is a challenging problem. Currently, most cloud storage services store the data either unencrypted or apply encryption in a way that the keys remain under complete control of the cloud service provider. Hence, the data is susceptible to insider attacks and curious providers. In PRISMACLOUD we follow a distributed systems approach and apply the cloud-of-clouds paradigm to increase availability and robustness. Here, the information is split into a number of shares [12], of which any subset of a fixed number allows the reconstruction of the original data. This approach is keyless and removes many obstacles in the area of usability and group key management [10]. Additionally it is capable to provide long-term security and everlasting privacy, which is very interesting for archiving of sensitive data. The confidentiality of data is guaranteed independently of the adversarial power and future developments, i.e., the rise of quantum computers. However, this assumption only holds as long as the majority of nodes in the cryptographic storage network have not been compromised. This assumption is different from conventional approaches and was a matter of discussion in the workshop.

Malleable and Functional Signatures. Malleable signatures are digital signatures that have some well-defined malleability property. This means, that signed data can be changed in a controlled way without invalidating the corresponding signature. In the following we will only very loosely discuss the two classes of malleable signatures that are of interest for the use-cases presented during the workshop. Firstly, malleable signatures that treat the signed message as structured data and allow to modify (e.g., black-out) well-defined parts of such a signed message. Such schemes, depending on their properties, i.e., who is allowed to perform the modifications, are modifications visible, etc., are denoted redactable [9,13] or sanitizable [1] signature schemes. The prime application of such a scheme is publishing a redacted version of a previously signed document where all sensitive information have been removed from the document without invalidating the original signature and thus the evidence for the authenticity of the document (cf. Fig. 1).

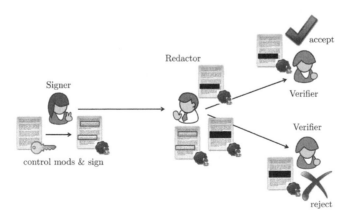

Fig. 1. Malleable signatures for document redaction.

Another class of schemes that usually treats messages as numeric data and targets on computing on signed data are called homomorphic signature schemes [6]. Basically, this means that there exists a public operation on signatures that carries over to the signed messages, e.g., one can compute the sum of single signed messages and derive a valid signature from the corresponding messages without requiring the secret signing key (cf. Fig. 2). These schemes (and their practical efficiency) thereby greatly differ in the supported class of computations, e.g., linear functions, polynomial functions of some higher but fixed degree or arbitrary computations (fully homomorphic signature schemes).

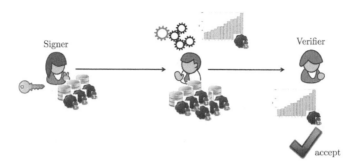

Fig. 2. Malleable signatures for numeric computations.

Functional signatures [4] allow to delegate signature generation for message meeting certain conditions to other parties, who can then compute signatures for a certain functionality on behalf of the original signer. Prime examples are proxy-signatures [3] for delegating signing capabilities and their application to certify computations on data (verifiable computations). Within PRISMACLOUD we want to study the application of aforementioned types of signature schemes to add verifiability features to data processing in the cloud in terms of end-to-end authenticity as well as verifiability of computations.

Graph Signatures. Graph signatures [8] are a new primitive we investigate within PRISMACLOUD, which makes it possible that two parties engage in an interactive protocol to issue a signature on a graph. The resulting signature enables a prover to convince a verifier that the signed graph fulfils certain security properties (e.g., isolation or connectedness) without disclosing the blueprint of the graph itself. The foundational scheme for graph signatures [8] works on arbitrary undirected graphs. It encodes the graph data structure into a Camenisch-Lysyanskaya signature, making it accessible to zero-knowledge proofs of knowledge. The method for this is a form of Gödel numbering, that is, of representing data uniquely as products of prime numbers. This technique makes it possible that subsequent cryptographic proofs can argue over vertices, edges and labels. Within PRISMACLOUD we develop and optimize the use of graph signatures for practical use in virtualized infrastructures. Their application allows an auditor to analyse the configuration of a cloud, and to issue a signature on its topology (or a sequence of signatures on dynamically changing topologies) [7]. The signature encodes the topology as a graph in a special way, such that the cloud provider can prove high-level security properties such as isolation of tenants to verifiers. Furthermore, we will bridge between cloud security assurance and verification methodology and certification. We do this by establishing a framework that issues signatures and proves security properties based on standard graph models of cloud topologies and security goals stated in formal language, such that the virtualization assurance language VALID [2].

Anonymous Credentials. Anonymous credentials (often denoted Privacy ABCs or simply ABCs) [5] are an important privacy-enhancing cryptographic tool that can be used to realize a privacy-friendly authentication mechanisms. In particular, it allows users to obtain credentials (that may contain various attributes of users) from some organization such that can later use them for authentication without the organization being able to track them. Moreover, if a user presents the credential more than once, these presentations cannot be linked together (unless special care is taken to allow such a mechanism). Finally, they allow data minimization. This means that the user does not need to reveal all the attributes encoded into a credential, but can selectively decide which attributes to show. Typically ABCs also allow a user to only prove that certain attributes satisfy some relation without revealing anything beyond, i.e., to demonstrate that the credential holder is older than some required threshold without revealing the birth date. In cloud based applications and services, the user's privacy is enormously endangered, since tracking user's data and behaviour is easily possible. Consequently, within PRISMACLOUD we focus on bringing ABCs into practical application and also on improving their applicability.

3   Use-Case Scenarios

In the introductory workshop presentation, the following four use-case scenarios were presented to illustrate the use of the cryptographic tools of the project. The E-Health scenarios (a) and (b) use malleable signatures, the E-Government scenario is based on distributed cloud storage and the Smart Cities scenario involves anonymous credentials.

(a) **E-Health: blood test.** Consider a case where a patient goes to the doctor for a routine check-up and takes an extensive blood test. The blood test is taken by the doctor's nurse and the results are uploaded to a cloud portal and are digitally signed by the nurse. The doctor has access to the complete blood test results. Later, the patient visits a dietitian, who requires few specific fields of the blood test. The patient doesn't want to reveal all fields from the extensive blood test. So the patient selects the mandatory fields from the extensive blood test for the dietitian to see and redacts ("blacks-out") the other fields.

Alternative case: Consider a case where the patient goes to the doctor for a routine check-up and takes an extensive blood test. The blood test results and diagnosis report are uploaded to a cloud portal and are digitally signed by the doctor. The doctor has access to the complete blood test results. However, the patient wants a second opinion from another doctor regarding her results. The patient doesn't want to reveal the diagnosis fields from the report. So the patient selects the blood test results for the second doctor while redacting ("blacking-out") the diagnosis field.

(b) **E-Health: smart phone monitor application.** Consider a case, where a patient has a smart phone training application that uses the sensors on the phone/wearable device to monitor and collect personal data of the patient. The patient would like to share only a statistical summary of activity progress information of the data collected by the application with her personal trainer without revealing sensitive medical data values.

(c) **E-Government: disaster files recovery.** For disaster recovery and backup purposes, IT providers of governmental institutions split their databases into multiple parts (shares) that are stored at independent cloud providers. Consider a case where a disaster occurs, and there is a risk of a potential data loss. To reconstruct data, only a predefined subset of shares stored at different cloud providers would be required, e.g., 4 shares out of 7.

(d) **Smart Cities: handicap parking.** Consider a case where handicapped citizens are required to use either their regular phones or smart phones to validate themselves in order for them to park at the handicap parking spot. Parking reservations are then stored centrally in the cloud for constantly monitoring the load of parking reservations. When using a regular phone, a control station by the parking will be used to authorize the parking using an SMS. When using a smart phone, the parking app would use the NFC badge (digital identification) and GPS location for authorization. With a privacy-enhanced solution based on a mobile phone based on an anonymous credentials-equipped mobile phone, the users could secretly authorise themselves for being eligible for this service without leaking any other information.

4 Day 1- Focus Groups Discussions

In the following subsections, we present a description of the workshop process. We give first an overview of the focus groups and then further details of the discussions and results per group in terms of the elicited requirements.

4.1 Workshop Format

A workshop in the form of expert focus group discussions was conducted on the first day with summer school participants who can be considered as experts in the field of privacy and security. The use-case scenarios in the areas of e-Health, e-Government, and Smart Cities developed in PRISMACLOUD and briefly presented above in Sect. 3, were used in the workshop in order to give a context for the use of the project's cryptographic tools. The aim of the focus group discussions was to discuss use-case scenarios, to explore end user and HCI challenges of the scenarios and further elicit requirements in regards to usability, trust, and privacy.

The workshop consisted of informative and interactive parts. In total 25 participants with different research levels and backgrounds formed 5 interdisciplinary focus groups, coming mainly from Europe and Asia. The informative part consisted of a brief introduction to PRISMACLOUD, the three use-case scenarios, and a technical overview of signatures schemes covering malleable and functional signatures and other PRISMACLOUD crypto tools in preparations of the focus group tasks and discussions. Each group had a moderator (the authors of this paper) who guided the group through tasks, brainstorming activities, discussions, and feedback throughout the interactive sessions.

The interactive session consisted of three parts: (a) An introduction to the workshops agenda, materials, group forming, and group members' introductions. (b) Selection of use-case scenarios to be discussed by that focus group and discussion of related cryptographic tools, and further the implications and features of those functions in regards to usability, privacy, and trust. (c) Requirements elicitation of cryptographic tools from part (b) to enhance usability, privacy, and trust in the cloud. For the brainstorming discussions, participants wrote short notes on opportunities and concerns that they see in regard to the selected case scenarios on post-it notes that were stuck on poster.

Results from the focus group sessions were documented as summaries by the moderator of each group. The summaries below followed the basic structure of:

A. Group participants
B. Use-case scenario
C. Key points of the discussion
D. Elicited requirements

4.2   Focus Groups

The participants varied in formation of the 5 focus groups. For instance, one group consisted of only security and privacy PhD students group (FG1), others included a mix of security and privacy researchers with of participants with backgrounds in cryptography (FG2, FG3, FG4), cognitive science (FG2) and legal practice (FG5). For the use-case selection, the e-Health use-case scenario was chosen by FG1, FG3, and FG5, Smart Cities use-case was chosen by FG2, and FG4 discussed all. It was noted that the 5 focus groups have focused on different aspects of the scenario (which was expected), and the resulting requirements have reflected on these diverse focuses. All groups discussed the scenarios cryptographic aspects, however the focus was on control, privacy, and trust (FG1), functions, applications, and usability (FG2), rules and policies (FG3), cryptographic tools (FG4), as well as data types and legal rights (FG5), which is to be seen in the following subsections.

Focus Group No. 1

(A) Group participants: The group consisted of 4 Computer Science PhD students doing research in IT Security & Privacy. A Computer Security professor and PRISMACLOUD project member acted as the workshop leader.

(B) Use-case scenario: As a scenario, the presented e-Health scenario on the redaction of blood test parameters in medical files stored in the cloud via malleable signatures was chosen and not further modified.

(C) Key points of the discussion: It was discussed that malleable signatures can in this case enhance privacy, as they give the data subject/redactor more control over what information to disclose to the verifier and what data she would like to redact. Hence, it allows the data subjects to enforce data minimization. At the same time, the barrier for patients to exercise control may be lower if they can do it electronically and thus directly, instead of having to request signed redacted data offline (e.g. via mail). Patients may also put more trust into the health care provider, if they get options to control their data. Also, trust by the verifier can be enhanced, as the malleable signature guarantees that also the redacted document remains authentic.

However, increased patient control may also put extra burden and responsibility on the users. Moreover, it can also be debated whether patients should really have full electronic access to their medical dossiers, as they may not always be able to interpret all details and consequences correctly. From the patients? perspective, they may not feel competent enough to do redactions themselves. For example, if they redact too much information, it may endanger their safety. They may therefore want to delegate this task to a trusted third party. However, accountability for the redaction may in this case be at stake.

As for redaction, doctors or nurses must be trusted to make competent decisions in regard to the amount of information that can be redacted by different patients considering both the patient's privacy and safety. If the redactor cannot be authenticated (i.e., in technical terms: the redaction operation is "unkeyed"), the verifier may lack trust in the redaction, e.g. may not be sure that really only information that was not needed in a certain context was redacted by authorized persons. Moreover, the patient may repudiate. If it is possible that the doctor can do the redaction and later claim that the patient did so, this may create privacy and trust issues.

If the signer who is in charge of sampling the blood test creates a malleable signature on the blood test that authorizing the patient concerned to do redactions on his blood test, then the identity of the patient may leak to the signer. However, for privacy reasons it is the practice that blood tests should be submitted anonymously.

It may affect trust if the verifiers cannot distinguish the cases when data has been redacted from documents or not. Also, privacy may be affected if the fact that information has been redacted (i.e. that the patient chose to hide certain medical values) cannot be hidden.

(D) Elicited requirements: The following list includes a number of requirements for enhancing privacy, trust and usability that were jointly suggested by the workshop participants:

- R1A. It must be possible for the patient to delegate redactions to a specialist that he trusts; In this case, the delegate must be accountable for his actions.

- R1B. The redactor should be accountable (i.e., the redaction operation should be a "keyed" operation).
- R1C. Even if the redactor can be made accountable, there should be a possibility that the redactor can be anonymous or pseudonymous to the signer (so that the anonymity of blood tests can be guaranteed).
- R1D. In dependence of the case, the redaction should be "visible" or "invisible" to the verifiers, i.e. in some cases the very fact that data was redacted should be hidden.
- R1E. Usable guidelines and support are needed for informing users about how much information is advisable to redact taking both privacy and patient safety criteria into consideration.
- R1F. The user interface should be based on suitable metaphors and HCI concepts and complementing tutorials for illustrating how the system works for promoting user trust in the claimed functionality of malleable signatures.
- R1G. The definition of fields that can be redacted should follow the data minimisation principle while considering the patient's safety. Doctor and nurses need guidelines and support on how to define redactable fields while following these principles.

Focus Group No. 2

(A) Group participants: The 5 participants of this group were 3 from computer privacy and security and 2 from cognitive science background. One issue regarding the mixture of the participants was related to their different levels of experience, which have hindered some discussion flows and interactivity, i.e. the two more senior researchers and practitioners in computer privacy and security were more dominant in the discussion due to their knowledge and expertise. An HCI Computer Security PhD. candidate and PRISMACLOUD project member acted as the workshop leader.

(B) Use-case scenario: When choosing the use-case, participants questioned the reason behind choosing a specific scenario and applicability of any chosen scenario. There was a discussion on how plausible the scenario is, and whether the scope is too narrow. Eventually, smart city and handicap parking was chosen as a preliminary case scenario.

(C) Key points of the discussion: The group started the discussion with the scenarios' functions. A main concern was raised on whether there is a need to use the cloud at all for this use-case scenario and when verifying credentials in the cloud which hardware and software to be considered from the users' side, in this case the discussion focused on the smart mobile phone. A debate arouse regarding whether the cryptographic tools are useful, it concluded with a suggestion to use attribute-based signatures to sign GPS coordinates as a claim of a handicapped person on a specific parking spot. Inspection measures versus linkability problem was brought up as there was a discussion on what is required to be considered and done in regards to this tradeoff, i.e., there is a need for inspection means, however linkability can't be avoided.

Some concern came up whether the application might give a false sense of privacy, where users might not be aware of the extent of data they are exposing. On the other hand, sabotaging users launching denial of service (DoS) and distributed denial of service attacks by anonymously reserving all parking places were discussed. Fraud and fault issues were addressed, and the discussion on how users can still lend out the handicap privileges despite the applications' main functions.

Finally, participants discussed usability issues with the app in comparison to the handicap card. The latter requires no effort on the behalf of the user, whereas the first is more demanding, i.e., credentials: there is a need for certain devices, and a level of understanding by the handicap users to get the application to work and show that the parking is authorized.

(D) Elicited requirements:

- R2A. Trust requirements for the users: need of evaluators and transparency.
- R2B. Each user must possess a credential that is securely stored on a mobile device, and a provably correct anonymous credentials protocol and implementation (validation + verification).
- R2C. Important to protect the verifiers' availability and integrity (no corruption or coercion).
- R2D. Payment requirement, even a little in order to mitigate DoS.
- R2E. Revocation should be possible; temporary impaired/handicapped people (doctors/physicians can issue revocation).
- R2F. Fraud inspection means are needed.
- R2G. Usability: Less credentials to handle for easy decision making and less interferences with driving.
- R2H. Suitable user interfaces and tutorials so that users can be aware of the systems functions and limitations.
- R2I. Mobile application needs to be generic, for usability and appeal.

Focus Group No. 3

(A) Group participants: The 5 group members consisted of a senior researcher in applied cryptography, a researcher and 2 PhD students in privacy and security related work within computing science, and a research engineer on privacy policies specification and their enforcement within a cloud computing environment. A technical Computer Security senior researcher and PRISMACLOUD project member acted as the workshop leader.

(B) Use-case scenario: In this group, the e-Health scenario was chosen, and the discussion focused on the application of malleable signature schemes.

(C) Key points of the discussion: In particular, the discussion was about "blacking out fields" from medical data. In the beginning, there were some issues that needed clarification by the moderator (as there were questions from the participants which were only answered in the second part of the workshop). Afterwords,

the discussion identified positive aspects of applying such schemes, e.g., more efficient processes (less interaction steps are required) and no longer requiring the signer if we want to give away authentic data to another party (offline feature). Nevertheless, the focus was more on the related problems and thus focused on what one would need to do in order to make such schemes applicable in practice.

It was identified that it is very important to specify redaction rules of how signed messages/documents are allowed to be redacted/modified. Thereby, it could be problematic if redacted versions of a document would be used in various different areas (e.g., e-Health and outside e-Health) - as this makes it hard to specify in which context which redaction is allowed. This could then lead to a redacted document that could be misused in the respective other area. Technically, one could counter this problem by using redaction policies (i.e., using a formal specification language to exactly specify what is allowed) and it should clearly (formally) define what is allowed to do in which context (it seems, however, that this is a highly non-trivial task). Policies could also support users (signers as well as redactors) to eliminate human errors and make such redaction tools easier to handle. Another problem that was identified in context of users is that users (signers) may not be able to comprehend what data to "mark" as being redactable. Consequently, it seems that for practical applications there is an inevitable need for policy and software support tool.

(D) Elicited requirements:

- R3A. Important to specify redaction rules of how signed messages/documents are allowed to be redacted/modified.
- R3B. Need for redaction policies (i.e., using a formal specification language to specify what is allowed) and it should clearly define what is allowed in which context.
- R3C. Practical applications' strong need for policies and software support tools.

Focus Group No. 4

(A) Group participants: The group consisted of (1) an associate professor of privacy enhancing protocols and privacy by design, (2) a principal research scientist in the Security and Cloud Research Lab with a focus on privacy enhancing technologies, accountability and the cloud, (3) a research engineer involved in developing a monitoring framework for cloud assurance and accountability, and (4) a PhD student working on data pseudonymization and anonymization. A technical Computer Security senior researcher and PRISMACLOUD project member acted as the workshop leader.

(B) Use-case scenario: In general, the group attempted to analyze all scenarios, but discussion got caught up on signatures. It started with detailed explanation of redactable signatures and the health use-case. The use of malleable signatures and verifiable computation in the blood test use-case was then discussed.

(C) Key points of the discussion: The discussion was focused on the tools. First the redactable signatures were introduced and explained by the moderator, the group understood the features and also the need for redaction in some situations, e.g. anonymous data sharing in health care applications, although they doubted the feature of anonymity, because inferences can be made by learning meta-data. There are maybe better or additional means necessary like anonymiza-tion/pseudonymization to provide protection against re-identification. It was also a questions to which extent this features could be limited to third parties and selectively delegated. Another concern regarding the redactability was, if it was really deleted. This comment was also referring to the problem of re-identification. One participant questioned the use of malleable signatures, and claimed that the concept is very close to ABC which even provide unlinkabil-ity and most of the features of redactable signatures cloud be implemented by the use of ABCs. He was interested in the advantage of redactable signatures compared to ABCs.

In the discussion of malleable signatures and verifiable computation, confi-dentiality was pointed out to be a more critical issue than authenticity. There was doubt about the use-case and participants thought the introduction of a trusted third party is dangerous. A concern regarding the danger of the third party adding not the right values to influence the result to their own favor, and that this scenario only makes sense if the final signature can also be used to verify that the right values have been included in the computation.

Reasons why ABC is necessary and what can be done with it were discussed. There was a concern regarding the smart city use-case with the electronic version of the disable batch. The fear was that it is still possible to link GPS or other metadata to anonymous credentials, e.g., license plate.

In the case of distributed storage, participants saw an opportunity to further compute data in such a setting which would be another advantage of such a system. However, they would like to see good technical arguments to make sure that they don't collaborate, because otherwise they would not fully trust this assumption to be true in many situations.

(D) Elicited requirements

- R4A. Different scenarios for redactor roles are needed; if redactor=user, then use ABCs.
- R4B. Need for proactive measures for introducing redactable fields.
- R4C. Address the need for third parties, and improve means for trusting them (confidentiality).
- R4D. Need for additional means to protect against re-identification and aid anonymization and pseudo anonymization.
- R4E. Need for good technical arguments for trusting distributed storage sys-tems.
- R4F. Need to address scalability, what if many fields should be redactable.

Focus Group No. 5

(A) Group participants: Five participants from computer security (2), privacy (1) and legal (2) background. The different backgrounds made for an interesting and inspiring discussion with multiple angles covered. The discussion was fruitful, albeit straying from the initial agenda. A technical Computer Security senior researcher and PRISMACLOUD project member acted as the workshop leader.

(B) Use-case scenario: The discussion gravitated around finding scenarios for case studies, yet touched upon general principles. The scenario became the catalyst of the discussion, which yielded further considerations in multiple topics. As scenario, the group proposed e-Health as general area and specifically a fitness app that stores the data in the cloud. The question was raised what data is shared or stored locally on the user's device.

(C) Key points of the discussion: A core topic discussed by the group is the data types that need consideration in such a scenario, where the group named the following types:

- Medical data,
- Personal identifiable data,
- Location data,
- Time data (history over time), and
- Metadata (data about data).

The group raised the question about derivative data, i.e., data derived from the user's primary data, e.g., information learned and stored in Machine Learning Models. The question of ownership arises for the ownership and the user's rights with respect to that data. How could cryptography offer a chain of custody for such derivative data?

The group considered the overall risk of the scenario. Here, the opinion was voiced that having data stored in the cloud is equivalent to a risk. Further, it was raised whether the data should be stored in the cloud at all, and whether the benefits thereof make up for the risk. Further the group questioned the aggregation of data over time. What can parties learn from the user's cloud-stored data over the user's lifetime? Poignantly put, the question was asked "Will I get problems in 10 years time?" With respect to the data types mentioned before, the question was asked whether generally, there is too much data shared.

The primary question asked how cryptography can increase the trust in the system. To gain efficient solutions, the group advocated a "trust-but-verify" approach, which entails that one trusts parties optimistically, yet verifies that they are well behaved. This trust required that data processing goes beyond informed consent.

The group voiced the opinion that the legal system has an important role to play to ensure the privacy of the overall solution. Poignantly, this was put as "Court counters Curiosity". Furthermore, the question was raised whether it should be a human right to have access to cryptography. This discussion is in the context of privacy being supported by human rights and constitutions. Cryptography is a means to ensure privacy protection.

(D) Elicited requirements: The group discussed requirements on the system vis–vis of requirements on cryptographic primitives.

- R5A. Simplicity and enhanced user experience.
- R5B. Restrictions on retention of the primary data as well as on the retention of derived data.
- R5C. Use of sticky policies (privacy policies attached, sticking, to the data) that enable a cross-system tracking of privacy policies, obligations and purpose-binding made. The sticky policies should be enforced by cryptography.
- R5D. Strong purpose-binding throughout, that is, it is specified and enforced what purpose data can be used for. Purpose-binding could be enforced by encryption, e.g., attribute-based encryption with purpose credentials as attributes.
- R5E. Need for misuse detection.

As cryptography requirements, the group advocated

- R5F. Encryption of data at rest as minimal requirement, with the key stored on a user's device.
- R5G. Malleable signatures should be used to allow the discovery of misbehaviour.
- R5H. The cryptographic primitives employed should yield evidence.

5 Day 2- Deep Dive on Cryptography: Graph Signatures and Topology Certification

This section summarises the content and discussion for the second day "Deep Dive on Cryptography" workshop on graph signatures and topology certification, as this concept was not covered by the use-cases presented in the workshop. The objective of this second day workshop was in contrast to the first day focus groups not primarily the elicitation of requirements, but rather in addition to giving a short tutorial, the discussion of further possible application scenarios. The workshop contribution set the state illustrating that graphs are indeed a common data structure in computer science, naming examples of

- Social network graphs for a Blackhat organisation,
- Causality graphs (structured occurrence nets) for criminal investigations, and
- Topology graphs of virtualised infrastructures.

It was observed that often in these cases the integrity data substrate and the derived graph is not guaranteed and that the graphs contain confidential or sensitive information. Hence, there is a tension between integrity and confidentiality requirements.

Concretely, these conflicting requirements were illustrated for multi-tenant virtualised infrastructures, in which tenants seek to gain security assurance on the infrastructure while infrastructure providers (and other tenants) want to keep the blueprint of their infrastructure confidential. This problem is aggravated as a tenant's sub-system can be impacted by configuration changes elsewhere in the infrastructure. For instance, a misconfigured VLAN identifier elsewhere could lead to other tenants getting access to a tenant's private network, causing an isolation breach.

Naturally, tenants have little reason to trust the provider's assertions of the secure configuration of the entire infrastructure. They would require evidence for the security assurance based on an independent trust root. Hence, we introduce an auditor as third party, who inspects the low-level configuration of the infrastructure, derives a graph representation, and signs this representation. The signature is done in such a way that the provider can subsequently prove to the tenants that security properties they require are fulfilled. For instance, a tenant A could require that no other tenant has access to A's resources.

A more elaborate version of this scenario was presented in [7]. Figure 3 depicts the system model for the topology certification. The auditor continuously inspects the low-level configuration and issues multiple signatures for defined time instances. The provider receives all these signatures together with diff-logs on the graph representation. Henceforth, the provider is enables to prove that security properties on the topology are fulfilled for times asked about by the tenants.

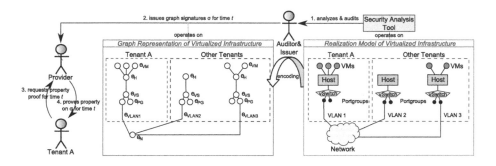

Fig. 3. System model of the topology certification proposal (from [7]).

It was pointed out that the graph signature primitive is generic, as it makes it possible to establish a signature on a graph independent of the question subsequently asked about the graph. The scheme is also expressive, as it can encode statements from arbitrary **NP**-languages.

The audience made observations that the graph signature scheme could be used for a variety of scenarios. One proposal made was that graph signatures could be used to prove that the surveillance and investigation of a secret agency has only infiltrated people with k degrees of distance in the social network graph

of a designated target, based on a selector. Legal oversight requires such organisations to limit their investigations to a low number of hops from the designated
selector. Previously, it was impossible to verify claims that the secret service
agency has been compliant with the regulations. However, an independent auditor could derive a social network graph representation on surveillance requests
and issue a graph signature, which would in turn enable the secret service agency
to prove in zero-knowledge that it was compliant.

6 Conclusions

The workshop took advantage of diverse discussions that happened in the focus
groups and workshop sessions for eliciting requirements for PRISMACLOUD.
Experts, coming from different areas and working backgrounds, have discussed
opportunities and challenges in regards to enhancing privacy and trust in the
cloud throughout the selected use-case scenarios discussions. It was concluded
that the main notions to ensure trust are accountability, transparency, verification and authentication. There is a clear need for means, such as crypto tools,
for enhancing users' privacy and control especially when dealing in different data
types, such as (explicitly and implicitly) disclosed and derived data, in the cloud.
Specific considerations are needed for PRISMACLOUD, such as for redaction rules
and policies which need to be clearly stated, e.g., in regard to the competence of
the redactor and to the awareness of responsibilities associated with redaction,
and delegation policies; i.e., delegations of redactions to a third party/specialist
needs to fulfil trust requirements set by guidelines, policies, and laws. Privacy
enhancing means by cryptography need usable guidelines and suitable interfaces
and metaphors to communicate privacy incentives and risks to the users and
ensure that a certain level of awareness is reached when using these means. Support from the legal perspective is necessary, e.g. by enforcing the encryption
of users' data in the cloud as a requirement for privacy or, as one focus group
discussed, even by establishing a human right to access cryptography.

Acknowledgements. The authors have received funding from the the European
Union's Horizon 2020 research and innovation programme under grant agreement No
644962 (PRISMACLOUD project). A special thanks to the workshop participants for their
input.

References

1. Ateniese, G., Chou, D.H., de Medeiros, B., Tsudik, G.: Sanitizable signatures. In:
   di Vimercati, S.C., Syverson, P.F., Gollmann, D. (eds.) ESORICS 2005. LNCS,
   vol. 3679, pp. 159–177. Springer, Heidelberg (2005)
2. Bleikertz, S., Groß, T.: A virtualization assurance language for isolation and
   deployment. In: POLICY. IEEE, June 2011
3. Boldyreva, A., Palacio, A., Warinschi, B.: Secure proxy signature schemes for delegation of signing rights. J. Cryptology **25**(1), 57–115 (2012)

4. Boyle, E., Goldwasser, S., Ivan, I.: Functional signatures and pseudorandom functions. In: Krawczyk, H. (ed.) PKC 2014. LNCS, vol. 8383, pp. 501–519. Springer, Heidelberg (2014)
5. Camenisch, J.: Concepts around privacy-preserving attribute-based credentials - making authentication with anonymous credentials practical. In: Hansen, M., Hoepman, J.-H., Leenes, R., Whitehouse, D. (eds.) Privacy and Identity Management for Emerging Services and Technologies. IFIP Advances in Information and Communication Technology, vol. 421, pp. 53–63. Springer, Heidelberg (2014)
6. Catalano, D.: Homomorphic signatures and message authentication codes. In: Abdalla, M., De Prisco, R. (eds.) SCN 2014. LNCS, vol. 8642, pp. 514–519. Springer, Heidelberg (2014)
7. Groß, T.: Efficient certification and zero-knowledge proofs of knowledge on infrastructure topology graphs. In: Proceedings of the 6th edition of the ACM Workshop on Cloud Computing Security (CCSW 2014). pp. 69–80. ACM (2014)
8. Groß, T.: Signatures and efficient proofs on committed graphs and NP-statements. In: Böhme, R., Okamoto, T. (eds.) FC 2015. LNCS, vol. 8975, pp. 293–314. Springer, Heidelberg (2015)
9. Johnson, R., Molnar, D., Song, D., Wagner, D.: Homomorphic signature schemes. In: Preneel, B. (ed.) CT-RSA 2002. LNCS, vol. 2271, pp. 244–262. Springer, Heidelberg (2002)
10. Lorüenser, T., Happe, A., Slamanig, D.: ARCHISTAR: Towards Secure and Robust Cloud Based Data Sharing. In: IEEE 7th CloudCom 2015, IEEE, Vancouver, November 30–3 December (2015)
11. Lorünser, T., Rodriguez, C.B., Demirel, D., Fischer-Hübner, S., Groß, T., Länger, T., des Noes, M., Pöhls, H.C., Rozenberg, B., Slamanig, D.: Towards a new paradigm for privacy and security in cloud services. In: Cleary, F., Felici, M. (eds.) Cyber Security and Privacy. Communications in Computer and Information Science, vol. 530, pp. 14–25. Springer, Heidelberg (2015). doi:10.1007/978-3-319-25360-2_2
12. Shamir, A.: How to share a secret. Commun. ACM **22**(11), 612–613 (1979)
13. Steinfeld, R., Bull, L., Zheng, Y.: Content extraction signatures. In: Kim, K. (ed.) ICISC 2001. LNCS, vol. 2288, pp. 285–304. Springer, Heidelberg (2002)

Report on the Workshop on Assessing the Maturity of Privacy Enhancing Technologies

Marit Hansen[1]([✉]), Jaap-Henk Hoepman[2], Meiko Jensen[1], and Stefan Schiffner[3]

[1] Unabhängiges Landeszentrum für Datenschutz, Kiel, Germany
marit.hansen@privacyresearch.eu, meiko.jensen@rub.de
[2] Radboud University, Nijmegen, The Netherlands
jhh@cs.ru.nl
[3] European Union Agency for Network and Information Security (ENISA),
Heraklion/Athens, Greece
Stefan.Schiffner@enisa.europa.eu

Abstract. Privacy enhancing technologies (PETs) are regarded as an important building block for implementing privacy guarantees. However, the maturity of different PETs varies and is not easy to determine. In this paper, we present an assessment framework that allows to compare the maturity of PETs. This framework combines two rating scales: one for technology readiness and one for privacy enhancement quality. The assessment methodology has been tested in two experiments, one of them being conducted at the 2015 IFIP Summer School on Privacy and Identity Management with junior and senior researchers. We describe the first experiment and how we gathered feedback on our assessment methodology in an interactive workshop. The results were used to refine and improve the assessment framework.

Keywords: Privacy · Data protection · Privacy enhancing technologies · (PETs) · PET readiness · PET maturity · Maturity assessment · Technology readiness

1 Introduction

Privacy enhancing technologies (PETs) have been demanded by various stakeholders as an important building block for maintaining and improving privacy guarantees in an increasingly computerised world: John Borking and Charles Raab regard PETs as "a promising aid to achieve basic privacy norms in lawful data processing" [4]. Ann Cavoukian points out that PETs "embody fundamental privacy principles by minimising personal data use, maximising data security, and empowering individuals" and stresses that "PETs can be engineered directly into the design of information technologies, architectures and systems" [5].

In 2007 the European Commission stated in a Memo: "The Commission expects that wider use of PETs would improve the protection of privacy as well as help fulfil the data protection rules. The use of PETs would be complementary

© IFIP International Federation for Information Processing 2016
Published by Springer International Publishing Switzerland 2016. All Rights Reserved
D. Aspinall et al. (Eds.): Privacy and Identity 2015, IFIP AICT 476, pp. 97–110, 2016.
DOI: 10.1007/978-3-319-41763-9_7

to the existing legal framework and enforcement mechanisms." [8]. However, today's adoption of PETs in practice is low. In the information security realm catalogues of tools, algorithms, and methods exist that support data controllers and developers in choosing the appropriate measures to protect their assets. For privacy and data protection, this work has not been done, yet. A first step can be seen in a report on Privacy and Data Protection by Design published by the European Union Agency for Network and Information Security (ENISA) [7], which gives an overview on today's landscape concerning privacy engineering. While the report identifies different maturity levels of PETs, it does not provide criteria on how to assess the individual maturity. All the same, the European General Data Protection Regulation [3] will demand data protection by design (Art. 23 General Data Protection Regulation) which will encompass the usage of PETs.

For this purpose, data controllers and data processors as well as supervisory authorities will have to decide which PETs are considered state-of-the-art and have to be taken into account when designing, implementing, or operating an information system. Also, standardisation bodies, funding organisations, or policy makers may be interested in knowing about the maturity of a PET. This was the starting point for our work on developing a methodology that can provide comparable information on the maturity of different PETs.

We decided not to limit our view on technology readiness levels as introduced by NASA for arbitrary technologies [12], because we are convinced that a mere assessment of technology readiness may result in a misleading outcome for privacy technologies if the quality for privacy protection is neglected. Therefore, we aim at assessing individual results for technology readiness and privacy enhancement quality as a second dimension that are combined into an overall PET maturity score.

In a workshop at the IFIP Summer School on Privacy and Identity Management 2015 we presented our interim results and conducted a preliminary evaluation of our methodology with the audience to receive early feedback. This paper describes our approach, the interaction with the audience, and lessons learnt. A final version of the overall results has been published as an ENISA report [10].

The remainder of the text is organised as follows: After we have briefly introduced related work such as technology readiness levels in Sect. 2, we present our framework developed for assessing PET maturity, cf. Sect. 3. The following Sect. 4 describes the evaluation performed during the IFIP Summer School and its results. Finally, Sect. 5 summarises our findings.

2   Related Work

The National Aeronautics and Space Administration (NASA) uses the Technology Readiness Levels (TRL) scale, that ranges from 1 to 9 [12]. For the NASA TRL scale guidance reports and TRL Calculators are provided to help gathering the necessary information. The European Commission uses nine Technology

Readiness Levels in its funding programme Horizon 2020 [9] that are comparable to the NASA TRL scale:

- TRL 1: basic principles observed
- TRL 2: technology concept formulated
- TRL 3: experimental proof of concept
- TRL 4: technology validated in lab
- TRL 5: technology validated in relevant environment (industrially relevant environment in the case of key enabling technologies)
- TRL 6: technology demonstrated in relevant environment (industrially relevant environment in the case of key enabling technologies)
- TRL 7: system prototype demonstration in operational environment
- TRL 8: system complete and qualified
- TRL 9: actual system proven in operational environment (competitive manufacturing in the case of key enabling technologies; or in space)

Many aspects of the TRL approach have been critically discussed over the last decades, in particular by pointing out limitations and needs for a multidimensional approach [13]. Improvements of the process have been proposed for the TRL assessment process [15]. In particular it has been pointed out that assessing 'readiness' without regarding 'quality' is of limited value, e.g. [16]. For PET assessment it is questionable whether readiness scores are meaningful without knowledge about the privacy enhancement quality: a wide adoption of a PET with a high readiness score, but unsatisfying protection may prevent the development and deployment of better solutions.

Many privacy researchers are working on determining selective privacy properties of information and communications technologies which shows the current need for expert knowledge in the assessment process. For an overview on relevant criteria we took into account standards related to security properties and quality assessment methodologies, such as ISO/IEC 27004 [1], NIST Special Publication 800-55 [6], Control Objectives for Information and Related Technology (COBIT) [11], and the recently released ISO/IEC standard 25010 on Systems and Software Quality Requirements and Evaluation (SQuaRE) [2].

3 The Assessment Framework

In this section, we present a four-step assessment process and define the scale for readiness as well as the scale for quality. We also point out how the assessment should take place and how the individual results are combined to express the maturity of a PET.

3.1 The Assessment Process

The assessment process consists of four steps (see Fig. 1) that are performed by the person responsible for the assessment: the *assessor*.

Fig. 1. Overview of the PET maturity assessment process

First, the assessor properly defines the *Target of Assessment* (ToA), i.e. the PET in focus. Without clarity on the PET to be assessed, its scope, its boundaries, and its interfaces a meaningful assessment is not possible. Different versions of a PET usually have to be assessed separately, e.g. if the running code still lacks some privacy functionality that is conceptualised for a future version.

Second, the assessor creates a board of experts whose opinions will be used as input in the assessment process. The experts should be familiar with the domain of application the PET is assessed and/or with privacy engineering. We believe that at least five experts should be involved if possible. Different expert boards likely will have differing results. While reproducibility of the assessment cannot be guaranteed (and exact reproducibility is highly unlikely), the process should be transparent for maximum comprehensibility.

Third, the assessor gathers measurable indicators as well as asks for the expert opinions by means of dedicated forms, consisting of both a scale-based assessment and a detailed opinion comment part.

Fourth, the assessor combines the separate results—a *Readiness Score* and a *Quality Assessment*—into the final *PET Maturity Level*. Further, the assessor compiles the Assessment Report from the collected input as well as the documentation and logging processes.

The involvement of the experts and the combination of their opinions and measurable indicators both for readiness and quality evaluation is illustrated in Fig. 2.

The following subsections describe the scales for readiness and quality as well as criteria for their assessment.

3.2 A Scale for Readiness

The intuitive understanding of readiness denotes whether a PET can be considered state-of-the-art, i.e., it can be deployed in practice at a large scale, or

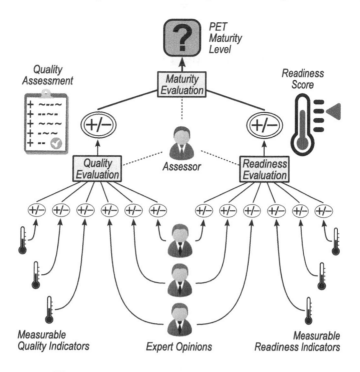

Fig. 2. PET maturity assessment methodology

whether effort, i.e. time and money, is needed to achieve this goal. On this basis we define the following levels, see also [10].

idea: Lowest level of readiness. The PET has been proposed as an idea in an informal fashion, e.g. written as a blog post, discussed at a conference, described in a white paper or technical report.

research: The PET is a serious object of rigorous scientific study. At least one, preferably more, academic papers have been published in the scientific literature, discussing the PET in detail and at least arguing its correctness and security and privacy properties.

proof-of-concept: The PET has been implemented, and can be tested for certain properties, such as computational complexity, protection properties, etc. "Running code" is available. No actual application of the PET in practice, involving real users, exists. Not all features are implemented.

pilot: The PET is or has recently been used in practice in at least a small scale pilot application with real users. The scope of application and the user base may have been restricted, e.g. to power users, students, etc.

product: The highest readiness level. The PET has been incorporated in one or more generally available products that have been or are being used in practice by a significant number of users. The user group is not a priori restricted by the developers.

outdated: The PET is not used anymore, e.g., because the need for the PET has faded, because it is depending on another technology that is not maintained anymore, or because there are better PETs that have superseded that PET.

Note that over its lifetime a PET may have different readiness levels, depending on its evolution. Also, there are transition phases where mixed levels could be appropriate, e.g. a readiness level of pilot/product for a PET that is currently being beta-tested as a (commercial) general purpose product after having been used in some pilots.

Threshold indicators can help determining the readiness level:

idea→research: This threshold indicator is met if there exists at least one scientific publication that focuses on the ToA.

research→proof-of-concept: This threshold indicator is met if there exists at least one working implementation (e.g. laboratory prototype, open source project, proof of existing code, or similar, that compiles and executes, and implements the ToA).

proof-of-concept→pilot: This threshold indicator is met if there exists at least one real-world utilisation of the ToA, with non-laboratory users, performed in a real-world application context.

pilot→product: This threshold indicator is met if there exists at least one product available in a business market, or in a context in which the utilisation of the ToA happens in a real-world business context with transfer of value.

product→outdated: This threshold indicator is met if (1) the only technology that allows for utilising the ToA gets obsolete or ceases to exist, or (2) a devastating quality problem of the ToA was revealed, which cannot be fixed.

3.3 A Scale for Quality

The following characteristics for PET quality have been developed from the ISO/IEC system and software quality models standard ISO 25010 [2] with several adjustments. For more information see [10].

Protection: Protection should be understood as the degree of protection offered (in terms of for example unlinkability, transparency, and/or intervenability) to prevent privacy infringements while allowing access and normal functionality for authorised agents. Also depends on the type of threats and attacks against which the PET offers protection.

Trust assumptions: Trust assumptions are characterised by the technical components and/or human or institutional agents that need to be trusted, and the nature and extent of trust that must assumed in order to use the PET. The more components or agents need to be trusted, the lower the score. For example, whether the system assumes an honest but curious adversary, whether the system is based on a non-standard cryptographic assumption, whether it relies on a trusted third party, or whether a trusted hardware component is used. Standard assumptions, for instance that the software and hardware need to be trusted, are out of scope. Note that trust assumptions can also be legal, i.e. a juridical process is a critical part of the protection offered, or organisational, i.e. the protection offered depends on procedural safeguards.

Side effects: Side effects are the extent to which the PET introduces undesirable side effects. These effects include increased organisational overhead due to key management, increased use of bandwidth (without performance impact) due to cover traffic, etc. Assessing side effects depends on the composability, i.e. how easy it is to compose the PET with other components without negatively influencing these components, and on the number and severity of these side effects themselves.

Reliability: Reliability is the degree to which a system or component performs specified functions under specified conditions for a specified period of time. It is measured in terms of fault tolerance and recoverability, as well as in terms of the number of vulnerabilities discovered.

Performance efficiency: Performance efficiency is the performance relative to the amount of resources used under stated conditions. It is measured in terms of resource use, i.e., storage, computational power, and bandwidth and speed, i.e., latency and throughput.

Operability: Operability is the degree to which the product has attributes that enable it to be understood, and easily integrated into a larger system by a system developer. It is measured in terms of appropriateness, recognisability, learnability, technical accessibility, and compliance.

Maintainability: Maintainability is the degree of effectiveness and efficiency with which the product can be modified or adapted to underlying changes in the overall system architecture. It is measured in terms of modularity, reusability, analysability, changeability, modification stability, and testability. Open source software typically scores high on this characteristic. Also, systems that have an active developer community, or that have official support, score high.

Transferability: Transferability is the degree to which a system or component can be effectively and efficiently transferred from one hardware, software or other operational or usage environment to another. It is measured in terms of portability and adaptability.

Scope: The scope refers to the number of different application domains the PET is applied in or is applicable to.

The quality characteristics cannot be automatically assessed in a meaningful way. Instead, expert knowledge is necessary. However, several soft indicators can support the experts:

Protection (1) documented protection levels and properties.

Trust assumptions (1) documented trust assumptions. (2) described adversarial model. (3) legal measures. (4) organisational measures.

Side effects (1) documentation on known side effects.

Reliability (1) availability of stress test reports. (2) the number of unsuccessful or successful penetration tests. (3) number of vulnerabilities discovered.

Performance efficiency (1) benchmarks or performance figures for storage, computational power, bandwidth, latency and throughput.

Operability See maintainability.

Maintainability (1) whether the system is modular in design. (2) whether test suits exist. (3) whether the ToA is open source. (4) availability, extent and detail of documentation. (5) whether an active developer community exists.

Transferability (1) list of different software and/or hardware platforms the ToA has been ported to. (2) evidence regarding the amount of work needed to port the ToA. (3) whether the ToA uses general purpose programming languages and build environments, and standard libraries. (4) availability and detail of instructions to port the ToA to other platforms.

Scope (1) list of application domains the ToA is known to be applicable to. (2) number of different products serving different markets that use the ToA.

For the quality assessment the experts assign for each of these nine characteristics a score in the following five-value range:

| $--$ (very poor) | $-$ (poor) | 0 (satisfactory) | $+$ (good) | $++$ (very good) |

The experts are asked to assign an overarching total quality score on the same scale. The standard calculation would be to combine the nine individual scores with different weights:

– The characteristics *protection* and *trust assumptions* have a factor 3 weight.
– The characteristics *side effects*, *reliability* and *performance efficiency* are calculated with factor 2.
– For the remaining characteristics, i.e. *operability*, *maintainability*, *transferability*, and *scope* factor 1 is used.

By this way of calculation, the importance of *protection* and *trust assumptions* for PET quality is clearly emphasised.

3.4   Combining Readiness and Quality to Express Maturity

For combining the information on readiness and quality on the maturity of a PET, we propose to communicate the overall scale in the following way, putting the quality score into superscript:

$$\text{readiness}^{\text{quality}}$$

For instance, a PET maturity level of $\texttt{pilot}^+$ denotes readiness level $\texttt{pilot}$ and quality $+$. Figure 3 contains all possible combinations.

4   Evaluation

During the work on PET maturity, we discussed our interim results with several people from the privacy engineering domain. In addition, we conducted two evaluations: one evaluation strictly following the four-step process with roles of

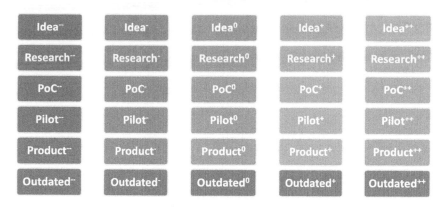

Fig. 3. Overview of possible PET maturity level values

the assessor and experts under rather controlled conditions that took part in autumn 2015, and previously another less formal experiment for gathering early feedback. This second evaluation experiment was conducted during the 2015 IFIP Summer School with the participants who were willing to contribute. Both evaluations are described in [10] where it is also pointed out that further work has to be invested for assessing a wide range of PETs.

4.1 2015 IFIP Summer School Experiment

In August 2015, the IFIP Summer School on Privacy and Identity Management took place in Edinburgh. All attendees were invited to participate in the evaluation. The audience consisted of both experienced scientists on privacy engineering or privacy requirements and Ph.D. students from the disciplines of law, computer science, or social sciences. A workshop on "Assessing PET Maturity" was held on Wednesday, 19th of August, 2015. Prior to this workshop, all participants were asked to fill out a questionnaire for assessing a specific PET. Note that no precautions were taken to avoid double submissions or to prevent exchange of opinions between participants. The different readiness scales and privacy enhancement quality characteristics (see Sects. 3.2 and 3.3) were explained to the participants in two pages of introductory text as part of the questionnaire.

As Target of Assessment the tool for anonymising Internet communication *TOR – The Onion Router* was chosen because most of the Summer School attendees had probably at least heard about that PET or had gathered some practical experience. For simplicity reasons, we did not give more information on the Target of Assessment than "The Onion Router (TOR)" (see Fig. 4).

The questionnaire was filled in by 14 attendees. Most of them took less than 20 min for filling in the questionnaire, only one person needed significantly more time. During the workshop with several more people who had not filled in the questionnaire, the results of the evaluation were presented and discussed.

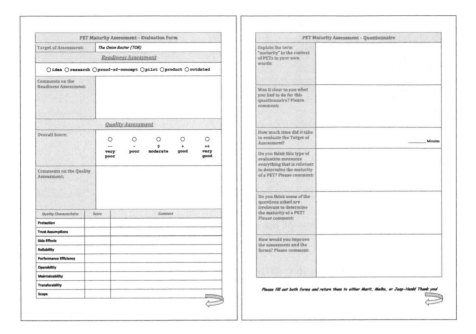

Fig. 4. Questionnaire for evaluating TOR

4.2   Evaluation Results

Looking at the definitions in the readiness scale, most participants thought that for TOR the readiness level of `product` would be appropriate (see Fig. 5). Two participants were in favour of `pilot`, one person considered TOR as `outdated`. In the discussion at the workshop most people agreed on the readiness level `product`. In the debate it was scrutinised whether a valid business model is necessary for the assessment `product` and how the attacks by the National Security Agency, as reported in the files from Edward Snowden's NSA revelations (e.g. for TOR [14]), would influence the evaluation.

In the quality assessment, the differences were bigger (see Fig. 6): One participant attested poor quality (−), the others regarded TOR's quality as good (+). One participant did not vote at all. In such a situation, the detailed comments would have to be discussed among the experts, as it is known in reviewers' discussions on the quality of an academic paper. Also, it makes sense to document the reasoning so that it becomes clear which sources have been used by the experts, how reliable they may be, and whether their judgement focuses on specific usage contexts.

It is also interesting to look in more detail into the differing assessment results for each quality characteristic (see Fig. 7). Obviously the participants had different views on several aspects regarding TOR. The characteristic *protection* was not regarded as poor or very poor by any participant. In the discussion it turned out that in particular the characteristic *side effects* were understood

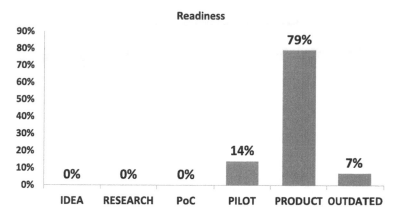

Fig. 5. Readiness assessment of TOR

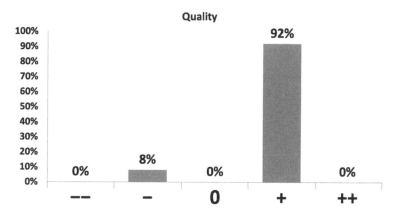

Fig. 6. Quality assessment of TOR

differently by the participants. Variations in assessments for *operability*, *maintainability*, and *transferability* can be explained by different practical experience with the tool.

Despite all differences in the detailed assessment, almost all participants agreed both on readiness and quality, resulting into a PET maturity level of product[+].

The experiment's results were used to prepare a controlled small-scale study for another PET maturity assessment where the roles of the assessor and experts were clearly assigned, the experts were chosen on the basis of their knowledge, it was enough time for an evaluation, the experts met in a phone call to discuss their individual results, and the procedure was well documented (see [10]). This following evaluation of our PET maturity assessment methodology focused on the adequacy, ease of use, effectiveness, and effort required to evaluate a PET.

Fig. 7. Quality characteristics assessment of TOR (Color figure online)

Both experiments showed that the methodology is easy to use for experts, but probably not for non-experts. Also the lack of practical experience can be a problem when being asked to score characteristics related to operation of a PET. The separation between readiness and quality scores was acknowledged by the participants in the experiments. It was also evident that a fully automatic assessment on the basis of easily collectable and measurable indicators would not yield reliable results. Therefore the combination with an assessment by human experts was regarded as a necessity for a meaningful outcome.

Since the experts' opinions play an important role, the exact results may not be reproducible with other groups of experts. The tasks of the assessor, especially the choice of experts, the definition of the Target of Assessment, and the consolidation of the individual results, have to be exercised with due diligence.

The methodology should be further investigated with a larger number of PET assessments and an evaluation of the documented assessment processes. We believe that the consistent application to a set of different PETs will elicit the usefulness of the methodology.

5   Conclusions

The assessment of privacy enhancing technologies will become increasingly important as soon as the European General Data Protection Regulation has come into force. However, this is not an easy endeavor. In particular the direct application of the Technology Readiness Level scale could lead to misunderstanding if the privacy enhancement quality is ignored in the assessment.

We have proposed a framework for assessing both PET readiness and PET quality properties that can be combined into a PET maturity score. For this, we use input measurable indicators as well as human experts who are involved in the assessment process in a way comparable to scientific reviewers. In preparation of a controlled experiment that strictly followed the proposed process (see [10]) we used the opportunity of the interdisciplinary IFIP Summer School on Privacy and Identity Management to test the developed questionnaires and gather feedback from the participants.

We hope that the developed methodology will be used for assessing the maturity for PETs with varying complexity. Our vision is an easily accessible repository with PETs and their assessment results where readiness and quality can be discussed, where input for further improvements can be collected, and where researchers and developers can contribute to advance the state-of-the-art. This could boost the deployment of PETs by system developers and designers, the demands from data controllers and data processors, and the integration in the checking and consulting activities of the supervisory authorities competent for privacy and data protection.

Acknowledgments. Part of this work was supported by the European Commission, FP7 ICT programme, under contract no. 318424 (FutureID project). S. Schiffner is currently employed by ENISA; the views presented in this paper are those of the authors and do not necessarily reflect those of ENISA. The work documented in this paper is part of ENISA's ongoing efforts to foster the uptake of privacy-enhancing technologies in Europe.

References

1. ISO/IEC 27004: Information technology - Security techniques - Information security management - Measurement (2009)
2. ISO/IEC 25010: Systems and software engineering - Systems and software quality requirements and evaluation (SQuaRE) - System and software quality models (2011)
3. European Parliament legislative resolution of 12 March 2014 on the proposal for a regulation of the European Parliament and of the Council on the protection of individuals with regard to the processing of personal data and on the free movement of such data (General Data Protection Regulation) (COM(2012) 0011 - C7-0025/2012 - 2012/0011(COD)) (2014). http://www.europarl.europa.eu/sides/getDoc.do?type=TA&language=EN&reference=P7-TA-2014-0212
4. Borking, J.J., Raab, C.D.: Laws, PETs and other technologies for privacy protection. J. Inf. Law Technol. (JILT) **1**(1), 1–14 (2001). http://www2.warwick.ac.uk/fac/soc/law/elj/jilt/2001_1/borking
5. Cavoukian, A.: Privacy Protection Measures and Technologies in Business Organizations: Aspects and Standards, chap. Privacy by Design: Origins, Meanings, and Prospects for Assuring Privacy and Trust in the Information Era, pp. 170–208. IGI Global (2012)
6. Chew, E., Swanson, M., Stine, K., Bartol, N., Brown, A., Robinson, W.: Performance Measurement Guide for Information Security. NIST Special Publication 800–55 Revision 1 (2008). http://csrc.nist.gov/publications/nistpubs/800-55-Rev1/SP800-55-rev1.pdf

7. Danezis, G., Domingo-Ferrer, J., Hansen, M., Hoepman, J.H., Le Métayer, D., Tirtea, R., Schiffner, S.: Privacy and Data Protection by Design - from policy to engineering. Technical report, ENISA (2014). http://www.enisa.europa.eu/activities/identity-and-trust/library/deliverables/privacy-and-data-protection-by-design/at_download/fullReport

8. European Commission: Privacy Enhancing Technologies (PETs) - the existing legal framework. MEMO/07/159, May 2007. http://europa.eu/rapid/press-release_MEMO-07-159_en.htm

9. European Commission: Horizon 2020 - Work Programme 2014–2015, Annex G. Technology readiness levels (TRL). European Commission Decision C (2014) 4995 of 22. Technical report (2014), July 2014. http://ec.europa.eu/research/participants/data/ref/h2020/wp/2014_2015/annexes/h2020-wp1415-annex-g-trl_en.pdf

10. Hansen, M., Hoepman, J.H., Jensen, M., Schiffner, S.: Readiness Analysis for the Adoption and Evolution of Privacy Enhancing Technologies: Methodology, Pilot Assessment, and Continuity Plan. Technical report, ENISA (2015). https://www.enisa.europa.eu/activities/identity-and-trust/library/deliverables/pets

11. ISACA: COBIT 5 for Information Security (2012). http://www.isaca.org

12. Mankins, J.C.: Technology readiness assessments: a retrospective. Acta Astronaut. **65**, 1216–1223 (2009)

13. Nolte, W.L.: Did I Ever Tell You About the Whale? Or Measuring Technology Maturity. Information Age Publishing, Charlotte (2008)

14. NSA: Tor Stinks - presentation slides as part of Edward Snowden's NSA revelations, June 2012. https://cryptome.org/2013/10/nsa-tor-stinks.pdf

15. Olechowski, A.L., Eppinger, S.D., Joglekar, N.: Technology Readiness Levels at 40: A Study of State-of-the-Art Use, Challenges, and Opportunities. MIT Sloan Research Paper No. 5127–15. Technical report, MIT (2015). http://dx.doi.org/10.2139/ssrn.2588524

16. Smith, J.D.: An alternative to technology readiness levels for non-developmental item (NDI) software. In: Proceedings of the 38th Annual Hawaii International Conference on System Sciences - HICSS 2005 (2005)

Smart Technologies – Workshop on Challenges and Trends for Privacy in a Hyper-connected World

Andreas Baur-Ahrens[1], Felix Bieker[2], Michael Friedewald[3(✉)],
Christian Geminn[4], Marit Hansen[2], Murat Karaboga[3],
and Hannah Obersteller[2]

[1] International Centre for Ethics in the Sciences and Humanities,
University of Tübingen, Tübingen, Germany
a.baur-ahrens@uni-tuebingen.de
[2] Unabhängiges Landeszentrum für Datenschutz Schleswig-Holstein,
Kiel, Germany
{fbieker,marit.hansen,
hobersteller}@datenschutzzentrum.de
[3] Fraunhofer Institute for Systems and Innovation Research ISI,
Karlsruhe, Germany
{michael.friedewald,murat.karaboga}@isi.fraunhofer.de
[4] Research Center for Information System Design, Kassel University,
Kassel, Germany
c.geminn@uni-kassel.de

Abstract. In this workshop we addressed what it means to live in a smart world with particular regard to privacy. Together with the audience, we discussed the impacts of smart devices on individuals and society. The workshop was therefore interdisciplinary by design and brought together different perspectives including technology, data protection and law, ethics and regulation. In four presentations, a range of issues, trends and challenges stemming from smart devices in general and smart cars in particular – as one example of an emerging and extensive smart technology – were raised. In the discussion, it became clear that privacy and its implementation are at the core of the relationship between users on the one side and smart appliances as well as the technical systems and companies behind them on the other and that there is an ongoing need to broaden the understanding of privacy in the direction of a social and collective value.

Keywords: Data protection · Ethics · Internet of things · Regulation · Smart cars · Privacy · Smart devices

1 Introduction

Smart devices are invading more and more aspects of our everyday lives. They can assist their owners while driving, while working out, while shopping and in the context of many other activities. Whereas first generation devices often lacked the refinement necessary

D. Aspinall et al. (Eds.): Privacy and Identity 2015, IFIP AICT 476, pp. 111–128, 2016.
DOI: 10.1007/978-3-319-41763-9_8

for immediate economic success, they still acted as a window into the future by demonstrating the seemingly endless possibilities of a "smart world". Today, some smart devices and systems are already well established, for instance those that are concerned with assisted driving, whereas others, like smart glasses, remain experimental.

At this stage of the technological development of smart appliances, it is worthwhile and necessary to have a thorough look at the effects and challenges that the technology poses to privacy. Coming from different professional and academic disciplines, we therefore provided four perspectives on smart devices in order to make an interdisciplinary contribution to their assessment.

(1) While some smart technologies, like smart cars, are comparatively new to the market and are still under development, the general challenges for privacy resulting from connection and interaction are not new at all. From a technical perspective, the question arises as to whether and how we can learn from experiences with internet and smart phone usage concerning data traces, profiling of users and a lack of transparency to foster a privacy-enhancing design of smart cars and their infrastructure.

(2) From a legal perspective, the increasing quantity and quality of smart devices and appliances is foremost a challenge to the right to respect for private and family life as well as the right to protection of personal data as established in the Charter of Fundamental Rights of the European Union. Furthermore, national constitutional rights like Germany's right to informational self-determination come into play.

(3) From an ethical point of view, a world where decisions are increasingly influenced – or even made – by smart and data gathering devices raises an array of questions. For instance, which opportunities for action do we value as crucial for human beings and how much control do we hand over to technologies and technical systems? One way of addressing these questions is to look at the structural and diffuse power relations that govern the field. This is not only related to the power of smart technologies themselves, but also to the power of social actors enhanced by smart devices and the power of concepts, e.g. "efficiency" that might oppose values like individual privacy. A broad concept of power can help to evaluate the impact of a world of smart appliances.

(4) The challenges that smart devices entail for privacy in modern societies necessitate solutions that are aimed at providing a reasonable balance between the interests of users, state actors and economic players and on a more generic level between socially desirable and unacceptable technological developments. With reference to the aforementioned legal and ethical perspectives, a political science point of view dealt with the question, which particular regulatory measures are taken into consideration in order to shape the digital future in a socially appropriate and sustainable manner.

Thus, the workshop was structured in a way that allowed for discussion and questions after the first half and at the end of the workshop. Therefore the first two presentations were focused on smart cars as one particular example of an emerging and potentially highly intrusive smart technology and examined them from both a technological and a legal perspective. The two following presentations also formed a unit.

Here, we took a step back and emphasised on the ethical and regulatory issues of smart devices in general. In the concluding discussion, which was open to the floor, an interdisciplinary reflection took place.

2   Workshop Content

The workshop began with a short introduction by the organisers, giving a broad overview of the topic, including more general challenges and trends resulting from current technological developments in the field of smart devices. In the following, we summarise the input given in the presentations:

2.1   Privacy Risks for Smart Car Users – Lessons Learned from Internet and Smart Phone Usage

The workshop started with a presentation on the challenges for privacy arising from technology itself. It was aimed at giving the audience a basic understanding of the kind of data that is collected by a smart device, of data flows, as well as possibilities of tracking and profiling the user. In order to give a comprehensive example with great practical relevance, the presentation focussed on the privacy risks posed by smart cars, [1, 2], which also allowed the elaboration of the economic exploitation of user profiles by private companies.

Focusing on the technical background and consequences for the user who is faced with smart devices, and thereby outlining the issues from a technical and data protection perspective, the presentation also served as a general introduction to the issues raised in the following talks. The starting point was a comparison of the rapidly advancing technologies behind smart cars with – already well-established – smart phones. It was argued that – from a technical point of view – the same data protection issues were present. Consequently, now that the number of smart cars is increasing and a strategy for handling upcoming issues has to be found, it is advisable to take a look back to earlier developments and learn from shortcomings, close gaps, and thereby create a framework which allows us to benefit from the technical progress, but which also respects the rights of individuals. Here, three main aspects have to be considered: Internet and telecommunications are used for functionalities provided in the car, information from and about the car is not only processed locally, but also in the external communication networks or even in data clouds, and finally, the car and its components have to be regarded as network nodes.

Smart cars, – every single component which makes the car a smart one – gather manifold kinds of data from manifold sources. Most of it is to be considered as personal data and as such falls under data protection legislation. The data is collected by several sensors, is transmitted with different techniques and is potentially stored and exploited in multiple ways. In smart cars, the following data concerning the vehicle is accumulated and accessible via the OBD-II-port ("On-Board Diagnostic System") in particular: the Unique Mobile Device Identifiers all mobile devices have, the numbers of SIM cards used for transfer of data needed for instance for voice controlled components (such as navigation assistance), MAC addresses of those network components needed to connect with WiFi hotspots, Bluetooth identifiers as far as Bluetooth is employed to connect for instance a smart phone with the car, RFID identifiers as they are needed for key remote controls. Whenever the respective devices or on board components communicate with the external world, this data is also transferred. Furthermore, information on the device setting (e.g. language) is communicated. This "phenomenon" is not new, but very similar to the functioning of internet browsers.

In addition to these issues already known from former technological achievements, smart cars are equipped with multiple sensors, which measure the status of mechanical car components. This means that, for example, data on tire pressure, the state of engine and gears, as well as brake performance is collected and error messages are stored. Also, in most modern cars GPS transmitters are installed. They make it possible to collect data on the exact position of a car, the direction it is going, and generally deliver more precise results than what can be achieved by tracking the vehicle via speed mobile radio cells and WiFi hotspots [3]. Besides car data, data directly related to the driver and/or passengers is collected: The driver has to create a user account first in order to make use of the smart components of the car. For this purpose, personal data like name and address must be indicated. The smart car is able to store different preferred settings (from side mirrors to infotainment) for different drivers. Biometric data may be used to identify the driver as authorised to drive the car. Finally, some systems monitor and analyse driver medical data (e.g. heartbeat or eye movement) in order, for example, to detect signs of fatigue.

All this data is collected and can be extracted from the smart car. Yet, another parallel to former technological developments is that many business models to use this data in a meaningful way already exist or are under development. Car insurance companies that offer insurance policies following the 'pay-as-you-drive' model are just one example. This means that all relevant data from the car is analysed by the insurance company and an individual insurance rate is calculated accordingly.

Another example is the "expansion" of big mobile phone or IT companies into the automobile sector (mainly with the goal of integrating their system software into the car and facilitating a connection to their mobile devices) [4]. Just like internet user data, driver data can be analysed to offer more personalised and more specific services – like personalised maps or navigation services – which are able to take into account personal habits of the driver. This means, for instance, that the driver can choose not to drive routes which pass casinos or ex-partners' homes. All this data needs to be transferred to the service providers. This creates "usage patterns" just as they are known from internet usage. Data footprints allow the identification and tracking of the driver. Furthermore, due to the enormous volume of data that is collected, and of course for practical reasons, smart car data is often stored in the cloud. This raises the question of how it can be guaranteed that data is only used for the purpose it was collected, not merged or aggregated beyond this dedication and not accessed by an arbitrary amount of parties. As shown above, this driver data is potentially even a different quality of personal data as it brings together personal data on habits and activities, internet usage and health (e.g. control of eye movement) and therefore – especially in combination with personal settings – can be used to create very precise profiles of drivers. This makes the question of secure storage and access to those profiles even more delicate. Of course, these issues are well known from established online services. With respect to the developing market of smart cars, a repetition of history should be avoided.

Research on data-minimising techniques and methods for use in smart cars is ongoing. But although interesting approaches, such as a frequent change of pseudonyms have been put forward, they are not yet "market-ready" [5].

2.2 Smart Cars as Challenges for Data Protection

The second presentation dealt with the challenges that smart cars pose to data protection law. As demonstrated above, smart or connected vehicles introduce technologies that were previously predominantly associated with smartphones and big data analysis into the traffic arena ([6], pp. 201 et seq.). Motor vehicles have always been considered to be symbols of freedom and independence and as such they hold special meaning for society as a whole. In the Seventies, Germany's largest automobile club, ADAC, created the slogan "Freie Fahrt für freie Bürger" which loosely translates to "Free driving for free citizens" as a reaction to an initiative to limit the maximum speed on German motorways. The slogan has been exploited for numerous agendas since then, but its ongoing popularity still highlights people's association of driving with freedom.

Cars in particular are seen as private spaces and despite the many windows and the need for adherence to traffic regulations, for social interaction and for cooperation with other drivers, most drivers seem to have high expectations of privacy when travelling in their cars.[1] As shown in the first presentation, the technical capabilities of smart cars allow for the collection of massive amounts of highly detailed personal data which can be compiled to create profiles regarding driving, usage, communication, movement, behaviour and relationships. These profiles can in turn be used to predict future actions. Thus, smart cars may not adhere to the expectation of privacy and freedom that cars are usually associated with.

Cars and driving affect – and are affected by – a number of basic rights; foremost those that guarantee mobility like Art. 45 I of the Charter of Fundamental Rights of the European Union (CFR, 2012/C 326/02), those that are concerned with life and integrity of the person like Art. 2 I and 3 I CFR, and those concerned with property like Art. 17 I CFR ([8], pp. 353 et seq.). However, mobility and safety are also prerequisites, means and requirements, for instance for the freedom to choose an occupation and the right to engage in work (Art. 15 CFR), as well as the freedom to conduct a business (Art. 16 CFR). Furthermore, cars can be the subject of research and thus of Art. 13 CFR. Interconnectedness means that even more basic rights come into play; particularly the right to respect for private life and communications (Art. 7 CFR) and the right to protection of personal data (Art. 8 CFR) ([8], p. 354). We have to ensure that smart cars are designed in a way that aids in the exercise of these rights and does not hinder them ([9], pp. 391 et seq.).

---

[1] For a detailed explanation of the concept of a car as a "private-in-public place" see [7].

The function of the law in general and of data protection law in particular in relation to smart cars is to secure freedom, responsibility and trust ([8], p. 357). The risks of use and abuse are determined by the sensitivity of the collected data, the value of the data, and the manner and duration of data storage. Not too long ago, the extent to which cars were connected did not exceed the use of clunky car phones. The data collected by a smart car equipped with cameras, microphones and all kinds of sensors however will tell a lot about the status of the car, the behaviour of the driver, and much more. It is thus not difficult to imagine that numerous people and entities will be affected by and may want to have access to that data: drivers, passengers, owners, renters, vehicle fleet management, manufacturers, suppliers, insurances, repair shops, towing services, emergency services, service providers, police, secret services, people involved in accidents, courts, government agencies, advertisers, market research companies and more (cf. [8], pp. 355 et seq.; [10], p. 247). Some of the aforementioned may even be able to force access to the data. There can be a multitude of reasons for wanting such data: diagnosis, maintenance, evidence, insurance claims, to collect toll, infotainment, pay as you drive insurance models, geolocation, development of future car models, product liabilities, contractual liabilities etc.

The data collected by the sensors of a connected car is personal data, if the data relates to an identified or identifiable natural person (for more details see [11], pp. 373 et seq.). At least the owner of the car will usually be identifiable. The classification as personal data remains intact, even if the reference is false, for instance because another person is actually driving. The purpose of the collection will not always be clear or may change at a later point in time, especially in the context of autonomous driving.

So who should be allowed to have access to data collected by a connected vehicle and under which conditions? Many manufacturers have a very clear opinion: The data is ours to use as we please. This is consistent with efforts to deprive car owners of the ability to perform maintenance and repairs. Future car owners may have a lot less control and authority over their cars than car owners today; going so far as to having to face their own cars as witnesses in a court case against them – figuratively speaking.[2] Drivers become more and more transparent, while it becomes less transparent who has control over data, what the possibilities for control are, what data is actually collected and what is done with that data. This is intensified by the fact that in many countries telecommunications data retention laws are in place which means that any communication data to and from a connected car via internet or mobile telephony will be retained as well.

In the context of connected cars' data collection, processing and storage are generally based on the data subject's consent. One notable exception and an example of data processing based on a legal obligation is the emergency call or short eCall system which will become mandatory in all new cars sold from April 2018 onwards [59]. The eCall system is a dormant system meaning that data is shared only in the event of an accident. The system sends a predefined data set to a public safety answering point (PSAP) and automatically enables voice communication with the emergency telephone

---

[2] This could be a violation of 'nemo tenetur se ipsum accusare' ([12], p. 85).

number 112.[3] This means that – among other things – devices like a positioning system and a hands-free speakerphone has to be integrated into every car.

When it comes to consent, drivers are confronted with non-negotiable terms and conditions by the manufacturers. Furthermore, third party applications will usually be offered which will come with their own sets of terms and conditions. All of these have to be brought to the attention of relevant persons. However, it cannot be expected that these persons will actually go through these documents as is the case with many other applications. Due to the fact that users are frequently confronted with lengthy terms and conditions, mostly via the screens of desktop computers or mobile devices, and that most users never experience any consequences as a result of accepting, many get used to simply accepting them without giving the matter much thought or even any thought at all. This is further complicated by the fact that software and hardware updates may add new capabilities, requiring new consent. Consent becomes formalism instead of being an expression of private autonomy and self-determination with regard to the collection of personal data. On top of this, the requirement for consent is that it must be informed consent, whereas in reality, data subjects do not know which data is ultimately collected and processed, or by whom ([11], pp. 376 et seq.).

A review of connected car privacy policies and terms of service, conducted by the British Columbia Freedom of Information and Privacy Association, indicates that many are in violation of data protection laws. The report states that there is a "lack of consent and forced agreement to unnecessary and arguably inappropriate uses such as marketing" and that standards such as 'openness, accountability, individual access and limiting collection, retention, use and disclosure of customer data' are not met ([14], p. 6).

In November 2014, members of the *Alliance of Automobile Manufacturers* and the *Association of Global Automakers* (both are U.S. trade groups) signed a commitment containing "Consumer Privacy Protection Principles" [15]. However, the principles set forth in the commitment offer a lower standard of data protection than that is already in place in the European Union and cannot serve as guidelines for the discussion in Europe.[4]

Another issue in the context of connected driving lies in the fact that it may not be possible for the data controller to identify whose data are processed. The owner of a car may have given consent, but what about passengers and other people driving the vehicle? Do they all have to be registered and give consent? The data of the holder of a pay-as-you-drive insurance policy may be processed based on the contract between him or her and the insurance company. If a different person drives the car, that data may not be processed on the basis of the insurance contract, since he or she is not a contracting party. So that person would have to somehow give consent, since the processing of his or her data is an infringement of a fundamental right. And what about the following example: The 2016 Chevrolet Malibu will offer a "Teen Driver System" that will provide parents with a "report card" containing statistics such as maximum speed and

---

[3] The eCall system is furthermore open to the implementation of additional telematics services, which also raises concerns regarding data protection and data security [13].

[4] Nevertheless pleading for a vertical solution see [16].

distance driven [17]. This example illustrates the potential to control others that comes with all the sensors built into connected cars.

Traffic infrastructure is also digitised. Examples for this are road toll systems, which use cameras to capture license plates and then check via a centralised database whether or not the toll was paid for the vehicle registered under a captured license plate. Similar systems are used by police during manhunts and as an investigative measure, but are also used by private entities, for instance at parking lots – to determine parking duration. This means that cars that are not connected, not smart, may also leave a data trail.

In summary, the emergence of smart and connected vehicles raises the following legal questions: How can we enable drivers to make informed decisions regarding any data collected by a smart vehicle? How can we ensure transparency? Is the current concept of consent up to the task? In addition to these pressing challenges, there is the issue of cyber security (for an overview see [18]). Weaknesses in sophisticated systems integrated into smart vehicles could potentially be used to deliberately cause accidents.[5] Thieves and stalkers could also prey on such weaknesses. All in all, data security in connected cars is not just a matter of privacy, but also of security breaches which may result in loss of property, serious bodily harm and even death.

Moreover, calls for back doors for electronic communication systems have been heard all over Europe and the U.S. in recent times.[6] Do we want to allow police officers to remotely access such systems, for instance to extract data in order to reconstruct where the driver went at what time, to create movement profiles? To allow them to use the microphones used by the eCall system for audio surveillance? Or maybe even to disable a car during a chase by activating the brakes? Already, U.S. car hire companies use GPS to track the movement of "subprime" borrowers and outfit cars with devices to remotely disable the ignition in cases of non-payment (so-called "starter interrupt devices") [20].

The future of connected driving, an industry of particular importance to many European nations, hinges on finding solutions to these pressing challenges.

2.3   An Ethical Perspective on the Power of Smart Devices

Following the two presentations on smart cars as a comprehensive example of the use of smart technologies, the second part of the workshop broadened scope in order to discuss the ethical and regulatory implications of smart devices in general. In the third presentation, the ethical issues of smart devices in general were highlighted in order to foster a discussion on (potential) consequences and challenges and to provoke critical thinking. Three exemplary illustrations for an ethical reflection were subsequently provided.

---

[5] On the significance of IT security in cars with particular regard to embedded security see [19].

[6] Perhaps most impactful has been a speech by UK Prime Minister David Cameron given on 12 January 2015.

Why Should We Talk about Ethics of Smart Devices? Ethics as a discipline is concerned with the preconditions and the evaluation of action. According to Hubig, ethical reasoning becomes necessary where 'there are specific characteristics of technology that shape the scope of possibilities to act' [21]. Ethical reasoning is important in order to avoid that technology determines the development of a society.

Before highlighting and discussing some examples of (prospective) smart devices with regard to ethics, a brief overview of some conceptualisations of power is provided in order to help in recognising and analysing power relations that affect the possibilities of humans to act. For this purpose, relational power approaches and especially a constitutive understanding of power are useful. Constitutive forms of power can be defined as 'internal relations of structural positions [...] that define what kinds of social beings actors are' as well as their 'social capacities and interests' [22]. Furthermore, there are forms of power that constitute 'all social subjects with various social powers through systems of knowledge and discursive practices of broad and general social scope' [22]. Constitutive power (re)produces social identities, practices and authorisations of meaning and action [23].

Technologies play a vital part in co-constitutive (i.e. mutually reproducing) power relations as they are more than only a neutral instrument or intermediate of power relations between individuals or institutions: technology has an effect on social relations (see [24, 25]). Following this understanding, smart devices are in a relationship with humans that has an impact on humans' scope for action, on identities and interests, and on (power) relations between individuals and between individuals and social institutions.

This perspective on the role of technology served as the background against which we looked at three different illustrations of smart devices. By searching for and questioning the (co-constitutive) power relations that are influenced by smart technology, we can by no means grasp all ethical issues of smart devices. However, we may enhance and structure our ethical reflection by highlighting effects of smart technologies on the scope of human action.

Reflection on Some Exemplary Illustrations. *Smart and Connected Cars.* The first case study picks up the example used in the previous presentations. By the introduction of a system of smart and connected cars, the character of cars and their meaning for society change. Whilst traditionally a symbol of individual liberty and of the widespread mobility – the ability to go independently wherever and whenever – smart and connected cars are much more defined by being only a small part of a greater network. It is the network and its social and economic significance that becomes the most important aspect; and cars as the network's small cogs enable its functioning. Thereby, the values of the infrastructure, of the vendors and the environment are being inscribed into cars and are represented by the smart functions of cars. Concepts such as "efficiency", "security" or "environmentalism" gain power and govern the field, subsequently also influencing and judging the behaviour of car drivers in their way. It may even become a problem if people resist using smart cars, as their behaviour can then be interpreted as antisocial resistance against the values at the core of the system. To name only one consequence: those who do not want to take part in a smart car system, but stick to old technology could be charged higher insurance fees [26]. Based on these deliberations, we can assume that the perspective on car traffic will change completely. The traffic system providers, vendors, and producers gain power over individuals by rendering certain behaviours appropriate or inappropriate.

Fitness Wearables. The second example looked at fitness wearables such as smart watches or sleep and lifestyle trackers. Perhaps the most important aspect of fitness wearables is their constant measuring and thereby the constant evaluation of the self. With these devices comes an idea of normality that is inscribed in the practices of comparison of the data the device collects with certain pre-given "normal" behaviours and average values.

The comparison to a certain normality inscribed and always shown by the wearable changes the self-perception of individuals and their relationship and behaviour towards society. On the one hand, if the normal and the evaluation of the self diverge, there is the feeling of being abnormal or even ill. On the other hand, the envisaged effects are self-optimisation towards a goal that is written into and represented by the device. The device does not force people to obey and follow certain ways of life, but by its ubiquitous comparison to a normatively desired "standard" and persuasive design it enacts forms of self-governance. 'Even if a system were designed to only make suggestions, it would still find itself treading a fine line between inspiration and frustration, between obliging helpfulness and pig-headed patronization' [27].

The illustration of fitness wearables shows that data and smart devices can have power over individuals. But only if the devices are used and accepted, which is where we can observe the co-constitutive character. They do not unfold power on their own.

At the same time one can conceive of this kind of smart device as having an empowering effect for humans by raising self-awareness. However, this self-awareness is based on, and influenced by, the assessment of the self which has been conducted by others.

Virtual Reality and Decision Making. In the last illustration, we drew on an even more general characteristic of smart devices. By using sensors measuring the environment, then calculating and processing the gathered raw data, interpreting it and eventually by visualising and evaluating the data, smart devices occupy a position between "reality" and individuals. Technology in these cases performs a mediating role and shows an enriched reality, as many things that sensors can detect in our environments are not detectable in this way by humans. Furthermore, this reality is constantly being interpreted and evaluated.

As a consequence, smart devices can lead to better informed decisions, as humans receive more information through technology than they could collect and process on their own. Then again, these decisions are of course highly influenced and biased by the functioning of the devices and the interpretations and processes that the engineers and developing companies have (unconsciously) built into their products. One has without a doubt to consider that there is not "one reality out there" that humans can eventually and objectively conceive. But in this case, we have to deal with a mediated "virtual" reality where a company is the middleman. Furthermore, by using information from smart devices as a basis for our everyday decisions, these decisions become increasingly dependent on the (correct) functioning of the smart devices. This leads to another question: if we base our decisions deliberately and unconsciously on a virtual reality enhanced by smart devices, who is ultimately responsible and to be held accountable for these decisions? Is it always the human being, or also the smart device, respectively its developers or retailers? Can the technology be held responsible only if the information provided is "wrong" – and what is wrong information? Or is it the relation itself – the socio-technological system – that is responsible? And what are the consequences thereof in practice?

The issue of accountability becomes even more significant when we look at autonomous decision-making by technology, e.g. when algorithms of smart technologies assess the risk to aviation security posed by individual air passengers. How can one assure that smart devices do not reproduce or reinforce discrimination or social sorting (see [28, 29])? And again, who is to be held responsible for these decisions that are taken by technology (see [30, 31])?

We may summarise from an ethical perspective that smart devices are becoming an important part in existing and emerging power relations and that this can lead to value conflicts such as efficiency vs. privacy. Power relations can evolve in several ways: Humans may be empowered by intelligent devices; they may also be in a more dependent power relation and thereby be governed by the concepts, functions and decisions of smart devices; and finally, humans may even self-govern themselves along the concepts and functions of smart devices.

2.4   Regulating a Hyper-connected World

For the final part of the workshop, we concluded with a general overview of the recent regulatory challenges that derive from a hyper-connected world. However, the discussion on the regulation of smart devices, which has been ongoing for some time now, is recently most prominently referred to under the heading 'Internet of Things' (IoT). Starting with a brief terminology and description of the privacy challenges posed by the IoT, the following section introduces the different traditions in data protection regulation on either side of the Atlantic and the most recent political debates in the US and the EU on the regulation of the IoT, as these two trading blocks are most likely to have a major impact on the emerging IoT market.

The Internet of Things as the Backbone of a Hyper-connected World. Early debates on the emergence of networked devices and information systems – which in their entirety are nowadays most commonly referred to as the *Internet of Things*[7] – date back to the early 1990s. Back then, the gradual miniaturisation of computers led to debates on *ubiquitous computing, pervasive computing* etc. [35]. During the 2000s, with *Radio Frequency Identification* (RFID), it became possible to address specific devices within a short distance sensor network and to let them communicate with other RFID-capable devices [36]. However, these technologies did not yet incorporate the

---

[7] Whereas the term smart device describes the concrete technical artefact, the term *Internet of Things* was coined by a presentation by Kevin Ashton in 1999 in order to describe the broader phenomenon of interconnected smart devices [32]. Highlighting the pervasive character of this development, the term *Internet of Everything* (IoE) [33] is also quite popular, while Weber [34] refers to it as the *Data of Things* respectively DoT.

internet. Instead, the notion of ubiquitous computing envisioned relatively autonomous devices, and the notion of RFID envisioned primarily local networks. Only with the advent of communication protocols such as *IEEE 802.15.4*, *6LoWPAN* or *CoAP* and by outsourcing processing power into the cloud, did the phenomenon which is today referred to as the Internet of Things, finally come to life.

Based on the promises of an increasingly connected world, a substantial change is predicted in at least five different markets. First, in the consumer market through fitness trackers, ambient assisted living systems, home automation and mobility services such as Uber or iDrive by BMW; second, in the production chain and logistics sector through the industrial internet; third, in the infrastructure sector through smart traffic, smart grids and smart meters; fourth, in the healthcare sector through the data provided by e.g. fitness trackers or networked insulin devices, and finally, in the agriculture industry ([37], pp. 20 et seq.).

The commercial sector, in particular, sees a big opportunity for innovation and further economic growth in the spread of connected technologies [38] and the extended usage of collected data through new data literacy behaviours and big data analyses. Although personal data is not relevant in all of the aforementioned markets, for a lot of devices, applications and services, the collection and use of personal data is crucial. Unlike previous data collecting technologies, through the IoT not only is more data, but also new kinds of data of any person within sensor range collected, as described in Sects. 2.1 and 2.2 [39].

The privacy challenges emerging from this development [34] lead to questions as to how to deal with the future development of the IoT and how to engage these challenges with regulatory measures. However, during the past decades, two quite different traditions in the governance of data protection and privacy emerged on both sides of the Atlantic which also shape the current debates on the regulation of the IoT.

Regulatory Traditions of Data Protection in the US and EU. The European approach to data protection regulation, which is often referred to as a comprehensive regime, relies – most prominently represented by the Data Protection Directive 95/46/EC and its successor, the Data Protection Regulation – on a set of formal rules, which are derived from fundamental rights and freedoms, and enforced across the public and private sectors through independent regulatory agencies. The US approach, however, is considered as a limited regime by only applying formal rules to the public sector while relying mainly on sectoral privacy laws, self-regulation and technology in the private sector and at the same time in large parts lacking an institutional monitoring and enforcement mechanism [40]. These regimes, however, need to be considered as the formal side of the governance of privacy. Besides these, due to the enormous speed of technological change, a major part of the regulation of privacy takes place at numerous global, regional and national levels of governance and involves a complex web of state-regulation, self-regulation and technology [41].

Regulatory Fora and Focus on Either Side of the Atlantic. To date, there are no laws or an overarching national strategy put forward by US Congress, dealing specifically with the IoT. Instead, at least two dozen separate federal agencies – ranging from the Federal Aviation Administration (FAA) to the National Highway Traffic Safety Administration (NHTSA), the Food and Drug Administration (FDA) and the

Department of Agriculture – and more than 30 different congressional committees deal with specific aspects of the IoT, usually publishing nothing more than non-binding statements. In the meantime, the Federal Trade Commission (FTC), which is the foremost authority on privacy issues, emerged as the government's regulatory body for the IoT, while the NHTSA and the FAA are both grappling with IoT related issues such as driverless cars and drones, respectively [42]. The hearings, round tables and working groups conducted by these authorities and committees usually follow a multi-stakeholder path and involve representatives from the technology industry, privacy groups and Congressional offices [43]. Although there is no concerted regulation strategy, the position of the US on the regulation of the IoT can be described as a rather passive "laissez-faire" approach that is extremely cautious not to stifle innovative business models that may emerge with the advent of the IoT. In this context, it is regularly pointed to the major influence of the industry on even the most minimal steps in the field of IoT regulation in order to explain the cautious attitude of Congress [44].

Both in the US and EU, a core component of efforts in dealing with the IoT relates to device and network security, most notably data security and breach notification. In the US, data security legislation is the lowest common denominator in regulatory matters on which many of the relevant stakeholders can give their assent [45] and also the one demand on which the FTC has shown itself to be intransigent [46]. Different government policies regarding data security and cybersecurity show the increased attention this topic has received in the past on a federal level. However, regarding data protection, including its principles of data minimisation, purpose limitation and the data subject's rights to information and consent, the picture differs considerably. While the FTC recommends data minimisation as one necessary step in order to achieve better data security and data protection, it still gives companies a lot of flexibility by proposing that they can decide not to collect data at all, to collect only the types of data necessary to the functioning of the product or the service being offered, to collect data that is less sensitive or to de-identify the data they collected. In the event that a company decides that none of these options work, the FTC recommends the company to seek consumers' consent for collecting additional, unexpected data [46]. The recommendations of the FTC led to a series of harsh criticism from industry and other governmental bodies [47, 48]. Regarding informed consent in the light of the emerging IoT sector, the FTC points out that notice and choice are particularly important when sensitive (e.g. health) data is collected and that informed choice remains practicable, although it is not considered important in every data collection. In contrast, both other governmental as well as industry representatives share the opinion that potential new uses of data, leading to societal and economic benefits, could be restricted by such measures and that a risk-based approach in dealing with the IoT should be favoured [42–44, 49, 50].

Contrary to the US approach and besides the various national strategies of EU Member States, the European Commission plays an active part in the formal regulation of the IoT [51]. This is mainly based on the notion that European industry – but also politics in its task of supporting economic development – largely overslept the development of the Internet during the 1990s and the spread of smart devices since the middle of the last decade and thus failed to keep up with US and Asian competitors in the microelectronics sector such as with personal computers, home entertainment and smart mobile telephony. As a result, the key idea behind the present activities of the European Commission is to not repeat the mistakes previously made and instead, to actively shape emerging IoT markets. In this respect, the work of the European Commission involves the establishment of several multi-stakeholder discussion groups and consultations – involving representatives from industry and privacy groups – that started around 2005. Initially, they focused on RFID, which finally led to an action plan, that was presented back in 2009 [52–54] and which has, since then, shaped the rather comprehensive IoT strategy of the EU.

At the moment, the EU General Data Protection Regulation (GDPR) and the creation of the Digital Single Market are considered as playing a major role in shaping the regulatory cornerstones of the future IoT regulation. Furthermore, a review of the ePrivacy Directive is scheduled for 2016 [55]. Within these efforts and in contrast to the US approach, the EU not only commits itself to foster the free flow of information but also to enhance data security and – regarding data protection and privacy – also to adhere 'to the highest standards of protection guaranteed by Articles 7 and 8 of the Charter of Fundamental Rights' ([55]; see also: [56]). Thus, in line with the opinion of the Article 29 Working Party, data minimisation, purpose limitation and the data subject's right to information and consent are still favoured in the sense of the Data Protection Directive [57]. Although the worst fears of privacy groups about the weakening of the principles of purpose limitation, information and consent by the Council of Ministers [58] appear rather unfounded in the face of the final text of the GDPR, only the future will tell, how these general principles will be applied, for example through Codes of Conduct, positions, guidance or decisions by DPAs, through court decisions or through an intervention by the European Data Protection Board (EDPB). In the bottom line, however, in all of the activities of the EU, is that there is a much greater focus on individual rights, data protection and the assessment of ethical problems in comparison to the US.

Especially in the context of a technology that is regarded as disruptive as the IoT sector currently is considered to be, proponents of the new technology usually urge governments not to stifle innovation and economic growth by hard legislation, whereas privacy advocates warn of the significant privacy risks of a hyper-connected world and call for legislative reform. Furthermore, different traditions in the understanding and governance of privacy shape current governmental action in IoT regulation. Particularly the principles of data minimisation, purpose limitation and informed consent will remain both in the US and – despite the agreement on the GDPR – in the EU subject of an ongoing debate on the regulation of the IoT. While the US favours a "laissez-faire" approach, the European Union has committed itself to establish more durable, technology neutral rules which enable the free flow of information while still being able to provide a high level of protection of fundamental rights. However, IoT regulation will most likely remain a current topic, as the evolution of the IoT will probably raise new privacy challenges.

3   Discussion and Concluding Thoughts

The broad (technical) overview of major challenges concerning smart cars in the first part of the workshop raised several questions from the audience, as well as remarks concerning their own – personal and research – experiences with smart cars. The (potential) accessibility of the data for official authorities – mainly the police – was viewed very critically. In fact, it was put forward that in the past police authorities have used traffic information collected and shared by customers of a large navigation device and service provider to place speeding cameras.

In the final discussion, we considered certain technologies more carefully, for instance smart devices that are used in health systems. It was stated that, although there is a lot of information and data gathered about the patient, it is, above all, the health company that produces and runs the smart device/system that is empowered by the vast amount of data gathered. A similar question was raised when discussing who is really empowered by the apps and technologies that are used to run Uber cars that have a disruptive effect.

We realised that privacy is primarily defined as an individual value and as such, it is often deemed subordinate to social values such as traffic security, efficiency or environmentalism. We reasoned therefore on the need to understand privacy as a social and collective value in a democratic society in order to compete and remain valid in the conflicts of values that simmer around smart technologies.

In summary, the workshop showed that smart devices are becoming an increasingly important part in our lives. They pose severe challenges to current legal systems and they demand regulation and technology design that ensures that the technological capabilities and business possibilities of smart devices are not the only driving forces, but instead that fundamental legal and ethical values are taken into account. We should keep in mind that privacy is foremost a fundamental right and has to be upheld in the face of technological advancement. This stems from the acknowledgement that it is an important societal value which affects the relationship, not only between humans, but also between humans, the technologies they use and the systems, companies and institutions behind them. The goal of the workshop, which was to look at the manifold societal challenges from a multitude of disciplinary perspectives in a condensed way, and to bring together these perspectives, has been achieved.

Acknowledgement. This work is partially funded by the German Ministry of Education and Research within the project "Forum Privacy and Self-determined Life in the Digital World". For more information see: https://www.forum-privatheit.de.

References

1. Hansen, M.: Das Netz im Auto & das Auto im Netz. Datenschutz und Datensicherheit **6** (2015), 367–371 (2015)
2. Hansen, M.: Zukunft von Datenschutz und Privatsphäre in einer mobilen Welt. Datenschutz und Datensicherheit **7**(2015), 435–439 (2015)

3. U.S. Government Accountability Office: In-Car Location-Based Services: Companies Are Taking Steps to Protect Privacy, but Some Risks May Not Be Clear to Consumers, GAO-14-81 (2013)
4. Kelly, T.: Consumers are in the Connected Car's Driver Seat in 2015, Wired, 28 Jan 2015 (2015). http://www.wired.com/2015/01/consumers-are-in-the-connected-cars-driver-seat-in-2015/. Accessed 24 Nov 2015
5. Troncoso, C., et al.: On the difficulty of achieving anonymity for vehicle-2-X communication. Comput. Netw. **55**(14), 3199–3210 (2011)
6. Weichert, T.: Datenschutz im Auto – Teil 1. Straßenverkehrsrecht, pp. 201–207 (2014)
7. Urry, J.: Inhabiting the car. Sociol. Rev. **54**(s1), 17–31 (2006)
8. Roßnagel, A.: Grundrechtsausgleich beim vernetzten Automobil. Datenschutz und Datensicherheit **6**(2015), 353–358 (2015)
9. Rieß, J., Greß, S.: Privacy by Design für Automobile auf der Datenautobahn. Datenschutz und Datensicherheit **6**(2015), 391–396 (2015)
10. Lüdemann, V.: Connected cars. Zeitschrift für Datenschutz **6**(2015), 247–254 (2015)
11. Buchner, B.: Datenschutz im vernetzten Automobil. Datenschutz und Datensicherheit **6** (2015), 372–377 (2015)
12. Mielchen, D.: Verrat durch den eigenen PKW – wie kann man sich schützen? Straßenverkehrsrecht, pp. 81–87 (2014)
13. Lüdemann, V., Sengstacken, C.: Lebensretter eCall: Türöffner für neue Telematik-Dienstleistungen. Recht der Datenverarbeitung, pp. 177–182 (2014)
14. British Columbia Freedom of Information and Privacy Association: The Connected Car: Who is in the Driver's Seat?. FIPA, Vancouver (2015)
15. Alliance of Automobile Manufacturers, Inc. and Association of Global Automakers, Inc.: Consumer Privacy Protection Principles, Privacy Principles for Vehicle Technologies and Services, Washington, D.C. (2014)
16. Sörup, T., Marquardt, S.: Datenschutz bei Connected Cars. Zeitschrift für Datenschutz **7** (2015), 310–314 (2015)
17. Chevrolet. http://www.chevrolet.com/2016-malibu/. Accessed 23 Nov 2015
18. Krauß, C., Waidner, M.: IT-Sicherheit und Datenschutz im vernetzten Fahrzeug. Datenschutz und Datensicherheit **6**(2015), 383–387 (2015)
19. Lemke, K., Paar, C., Wolf, M. (eds.): Embedded Security in Cars. Springer, Heidelberg (2006)
20. Corkery, M., Silver-Greenberg, J.: Miss a Payment? Good Luck Moving That Car. The New York Times, New York edition, 25 September 2014. A1
21. Hubig, C.: Die Kunst des Möglichen II. Ethik der Technik als provisorische Moral. Bielefeld, transcript (2007)
22. Barnett, M., Duvall, R.: Power in global governance. In: Barnett, M., Duvall, R. (eds.) Power in Global Governance, pp. 1–32. Cambridge University Press, Cambridge (2005)
23. Foucault, M.: Discipline and Punish: The Birth of the Prison. Penguin Books, London (1991/1977)
24. Latour, B.: Reassembling the Social. An Introduction to Actor-Network-Theory. Oxford University Press, Oxford (2005)
25. Acuto, M., Curtis, S. (eds.): Reassembling International Theory: Assemblage Thinking and International Relations. Palgrave Macmillan, Basingstoke (2014)
26. Morozov, E.: The rise of data and the death of politics. The Guardian (2014) http://www.theguardian.com/technology/2014/jul/20/rise-of-data-death-of-politics-evgeny-morozov-algorithmic-regulation. Accessed 17 Nov 2015

27. Bohn, J., Coroamă, V., Langheinrich, M., Mattern, F., Rohs, M.: Living in a world of smart everyday objects – Social, economic, and ethical implications. Hum. Ecol. Risk Assess. **10**(5), 763–785 (2004)
28. Gandy, O.H.: engaging rational discrimination: exploring reasons for placing regulatory constraints on decision support systems. Ethics Inf. Technol. **12**(1), 29–42 (2010)
29. Lyon, D. (ed.): Surveillance as Social Sorting: Privacy, Risk, and Digital Discrimination. Routledge, London/New York (2003)
30. Himma, K.E.: Artificial agency, consciousness, and the criteria for moral agency: what properties must an artificial agent have to be a moral agent? Ethics Inf. Technol. **11**, 19–29 (2009)
31. Johnson, D.G., Miller, K.W.: A dialogue on responsibility, moral agency, and IT systems Proceedings of the 2006 ACM symposium on Applied computing – SAC 2006, pp. 272–276. ACM Press (2006)
32. Ashton, K.: That 'Internet of Things' Thing. RFID J. (2009) http://www.rfidjournal.com/articles/view?4986. Accessed 19 Nov 2015
33. Bajarin, T.: The next big thing for tech: the internet of everything. In: Time (2014) http://time.com/539/the-next-big-thing-for-tech-the-internet-of-everything/. Accessed 19 Nov 2015
34. Weber, R.H.: The digital future – A challenge for privacy? Comput. Law Secur. Rev. **31**(2), 234–242 (2015)
35. Weiser, M.: The computer for the 21st century. Sci. Am. **265**(9), 66–75 (1991)
36. Fleisch, E., Mattern, F.: Das Internet der Dinge. Ubiquitous Computing und RFID in der Praxis: Visionen, Technologien, Anwendungen, Handlungsanleitungen. Springer, Berlin (2005)
37. Sprenger, F., Engemann, C.: Internet der Dinge: Über smarte Objekte, intelligente Umgebungen und die technische Durchdringung der Welt, Transcript Verlag, Bielefeld, pp. 7–58 (2015)
38. Gartner: Gartner says a Typical Family Home Could Contain More Than 500 Smart Devices by 2022. In: Gartner Press Release, 08 Sept 2014 (2014) https://www.gartner.com/newsroom/id/2839717. Accessed 19 Nov 2015
39. Swan, M.: Sensor Mania! The Internet of Things, wearable computing, objective metrics, and the quantified self 2.0. J. Sensor Actuator Netw. **1**(3), 217–253 (2012)
40. Newman, A.L.: The governance of privacy. In: Levi-Faur, D. (ed.): The Oxford Handbook of Governance, pp. 599–611. Oxford University Press, Oxford (2013)
41. Bennett, C.J., Raab, C.D.: The Governance of Privacy: Policy Instruments in Global Perspective, 2nd and updated edn. MIT Press, Cambridge (2006)
42. Samuelsohn, D.: What Washington really knows about the Internet of Things. A Politico investigation. In: Politico (2015). http://www.politico.com/agenda/story/2015/06/internet-of-things-caucus-legislation-regulation-000086. Accessed 19 Nov 2015
43. Politico Staff: The Internet of Things: What's Washington's Role? A politico working group report. In: Politico (2015) http://www.politico.com/agenda/story/2015/08/internet-of-things-mckinsey-working-group-000207. Accessed 19 Nov 2015
44. Romm, T.: Round 1 goes to the lobbyists: A barely there technology is already winning the influence battle in Washington. Here's how. In: Politico (2015) http://www.politico.com/agenda/story/2015/06/internet-of-things-government-lobbying-000097. Accessed 19 Nov 2015
45. Peppet, S.R.: Regulating the internet of things: First steps toward managing discrimination, privacy, security & consent. In: Texas Law Review (forthcoming, 2014)
46. Federal Trade Commission: Internet of Things. Privacy & Security in a Connected World. FTC Staff Report, January 2015

47. Gross, G.: FTC calls on IoT vendors to protect privacy. PCWorld (2015) http://www.pcworld.com/article/2876332/ftc-calls-on-iot-vendors-to-protect-privacy.html. Accessed 24 Nov 2015
48. Diallo, A.: Do smart devices need regulation? FTC examines Internet of Things, Forbes (2013). http://www.forbes.com/sites/amadoudiallo/2013/11/23/ftc-regulation-internet-of-things/. Accessed 24 Nov 2015
49. The White House: Big Data: Seizing opportunities, preserving values, May 2014
50. President's Council of Advisors on Science and Technology: Report to the President. Big Data and Privacy: A technological perspective, May 2014
51. Gabriel, P., Gaßner, K., Lange, S.: Das Internet der Dinge – Basis für die IKT-Infrastruktur von morgen. Anwendungen, Akteure und politische Handlungsfelder. Institut für Innovation und Technik. Feller, Berlin (2010)
52. European Commission: Radio Frequency Identification (RFID) in Europe: steps towards a policy framework. 15 March 2007, Com(2007) 96 final (2007)
53. European Commission: Internet of Things – An action plan for Europe. Brussels, 18 June 2009, COM(2009) 278 final (2009a)
54. European Commission: Commission recommendation of 12.5.2009 on the implementation of privacy and data protection principles in applications supported by radio-frequency identification. Brussels, 12 May 2009, C(2009) 3200 final (2009b)
55. European Commission: A Digital Single Market Strategy for Europe. SWD(2015) 100 final (2015)
56. European Commission: Digital Agenda: Commission consults on rules for wirelessly connected devices - the "Internet of Things". Press Release, 12 April 2012, IP/12/360 (2012)
57. Article 29 Data Protection Working Party (2014): Opinion 8/2014 on the on [sic] Recent Developments on the Internet of Things, 16 September 2014, 14/EN, WP 223
58. Järvinen, H. (2015): Privacy and Data Protection under threat from EU Council agreement. 15.06.2015, Press Release by European Digital Rights and Privacy International. https://edri.org/press-release-privacy-and-data-protection-under-threat-from-eu-council-agreement/. Accessed 19 Nov 2015
59. Regulation (EU) 2015/758 of the European Parliament and of the Council of 29 April 2015 concerning type-approval requirements for the deployment of the eCall in-vehicle system based on the 112 service and amending Directive 2007/46/EC. O.J. L 123, 19 May 2015

Privacy Pattern Catalogue: A Tool for Integrating Privacy Principles of ISO/IEC 29100 into the Software Development Process

Olha Drozd$^{(\boxtimes)}$

Vienna University of Economics and Business, Vienna, Austria
olha.drozd@wu.ac.at

Abstract. A proper integration of privacy patterns into a software development process enables development of reliable and privacy-friendly software products. While previous work has identified some loosely connected privacy patterns, there exists no comprehensive privacy pattern catalogue that is specifically designed for the application by software architects during the software development process. To address this gap an interactive online privacy pattern catalogue was developed using patterns obtained from interviews with privacy experts as well as from existing privacy patterns work. The catalogue classifies patterns according to the description of the privacy principles of the international standard ISO/IEC 29100:2011 (E) and is, therefore, internationally applicable.

Keywords: Privacy patterns · Privacy principles · ISO/IEC 29100:2011 (E) · Privacy by design · Privacy pattern catalogue

1 Introduction

Any software that processes personally identifiable information (i.e. any information that can be used to identify the natural person to whom such information relates, or is or might be directly or indirectly linked to that person [1]) should protect the privacy of data subjects. In order to develop qualitative privacy-friendly software, privacy should be integrated into software at early stages of the software development process. At the design stage of the software development cycle one can utilize the privacy patterns to facilitate privacy integration [2]. "A pattern is a piece of literature that describes a design problem and a general solution for the problem in a particular context [3]."

Some attempts were made to collect privacy patterns, but those collections were limited to a very specific context. For example, Hafiz concentrates on patterns for the design of anonymity systems [4]. The Privacy and Identity Management in Europe for Life pattern collection provides a list of human-computer interaction patterns [5]. The University of California (UC) Berkley School of Information's collection [6] broadens the application context of privacy patterns, but describes only 9 privacy patterns. PRIPARE project [7] presents the newest attempt to collect privacy patterns. However, their list of patterns is also limited. They added some new patterns but omitted some old ones that were mentioned in the previous work.

© IFIP International Federation for Information Processing 2016
Published by Springer International Publishing Switzerland 2016. All Rights Reserved
D. Aspinall et al. (Eds.): Privacy and Identity 2015, IFIP AICT 476, pp. 129–140, 2016.
DOI: 10.1007/978-3-319-41763-9_9

While reviewing the literature, no pattern classifications, catalogues or tools providing a structured approach to privacy pattern integration into the software development process in connection with the ISO (the International Organization for Standardization)/IEC (the International Electrotechnical Commission) 29100 standard were found. To fill this gap an interactive online privacy pattern catalogue was developed. This structured solution-oriented representation of patterns that collects numerous patterns in one place and allows end user to easily navigate through the catalogue, could convince companies to adopt privacy by design approach.

The target audience of the catalogue is software architects and software developers. The catalogue enables them to efficiently integrate the privacy principles of ISO/IEC 29100 into the software development process. The ISO/IEC 29100 privacy principles were selected because they comprehensively cover the domain of privacy requirements and because the standard is internationally applicable.

The paper is divided into 5 parts. The background part provides the background information on the design patterns and the ISO/IEC 29100 standard. The method section describes the structured-case method employed in this research project. The part following the methodology section explains the idea of the privacy pattern catalogue and describes its functionality. The discussion part provides an overview of the issues that appeared during the compilation of the catalogue and describes how those issues were addressed in the catalogue as well as how they might be solved in the future work. Finally, the conclusion summarizes the main points of the paper.

2   Background

Privacy by design aims to integrate privacy requirements into every stage of the software development process [2]. This paper addresses the problem of privacy integration at the design stage of the system development process by using design patterns as one of the main components of the catalogue. The descriptions of 11 privacy principles from the ISO/IEC 29100 standard were selected as the source of the privacy requirements.

2.1   Design Patterns

As it was mentioned before, privacy patterns may help to integrate privacy at the design stage of the software development process [2]. There exist many definitions of patterns. For instance, in building and architecture pattern describes an iterative problem in a specific environment and a reusable solution to it [8]. In software engineering "patterns codify reusable design expertise that provides time-proven solutions to commonly occurring software problems that arise in particular contexts and domains [9]." Another definition of the term pattern in software engineering field describes pattern as "a description of communicating objects and classes that are customized to solve a general design problem in a particular context [10]."

All the above-mentioned definitions suggest describing patterns in terms of problem description, solution to the problem and context where this problem occurs.

The existent lists of privacy patterns describe them in different ways. Hafiz provides a very detailed description of patterns and uses the following sections: intent, also know as, motivation, context, problem, forces, solution, design issues, consequences, known uses, related patterns [4]. PRIPARE project uses a similar approach in its description of privacy patterns. Every pattern here is described with the help of summary, problem, context, goals, motivating example, solution, constraints and consequences, known uses, tags, categories and technology readiness level [7]. Patterns collected at the UC Berkeley School of Information use a less detailed description template. The sections intent, context, problem, solution and examples are used in that project [6]. The template of the PrimeLife project contains the following sections: problem, solution, use when, how, why, related patterns [5]. The sections problem, solution and context seem to be a universal way to describe patterns because they are always present, in various formulations, in the definitions as well as in the pattern lists. That is why for the purpose of this research the patterns were explained with the help of those three sections. The consequences section was added to the description to provide a better understanding of the results after implementation of the pattern. This section proved to be useful in the above-described pattern lists as well.

For example, the pattern Data Track from the PrimeLife project is described in the catalogue as follows (Table 1): [5]

Table 1. Description of the data track pattern.

Section	Description
Problem	Users may lose an overview of what kind of data they disclosed to whom under which conditions
Solution	Provide an end-user transparency tool that provides the user with a detailed overview of all the user's personal data releases to communication partners
Context	Implement when personal data are released
Consequences	Easier recollection of where, when and under what conditions the user posted which data

2.2   ISO/IEC 29100 as the Source of the Privacy Requirements

The aim of the catalogue is to facilitate the integration of privacy requirements at the design stage of the software development process. There are a number of data protection laws that could be used as a requirement sources but they are often specific to every country and are, unfortunately, slightly outdated. For example, "Privacy Online: Fair Information Practices in the Electronic Marketplace" [11] is specific to the United States, "Organization of Economic Co-Operation and Development Guidelines on the Protection of Privacy and Transborder Flows of Personal Data" [12] is somewhat outdated, General Data Protection Regulation [13] covers only the European Union and still needs to be finalized.

The ISO/IEC 29100 standard was chosen as the source of the privacy requirements, as it is an international standard that "provides a high-level framework for the protection of personally identifiable information (PII) within information and communication technology (ICT) systems [1]." Moreover, the ISO/IEC 29100 standard was compiled to help, inter alia, architect, design and develop ICT systems or services in a privacy-friendly way [1]. In addition to the advantageous characteristics mentioned above, being international, this standard could be equally applied in different countries. It also comprehensively covers the domain of privacy requirements.

In the standard the requirements are presented in the form of 11 privacy principles: consent and choice; purpose legitimacy and specification; collection limitation; data minimization; use, retention and disclosure limitation; accuracy and quality; openness, transparency and notice; individual participation and access; accountability; information security; privacy compliance [1]. Each principle is then described in more detail with the help of the list of bullet points. Every bullet point explains, in the form of an instruction, what adhering to this or that principle means. For instance, to adhere to the collection limitation principle one should limit "the collection of PII to that which is within the bounds of applicable law and strictly necessary for the specified purpose(s) [1]." Other principles are explained in a similar way. The number of bullet points varies depending on the privacy principle.

The privacy principles of ISO/IEC 29100 and the instructions form the first and the second level of the catalogue hierarchy respectively. The third level of the catalogue is filled with the privacy patterns that help (directly or indirectly) to implement the corresponding privacy principle instruction (Fig. 1).

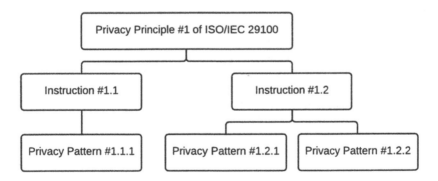

Fig. 1. Catalogue concept

3 Method

The catalogue was compiled by applying a structured-case methodological framework for building theory in information systems research [14]. The structured-case consists of 3 structural components, namely "the conceptual framework, the research cycle and the literature-based scrutiny of the theory built [14]." The general idea of the structured-case research method is shown in Fig. 2.

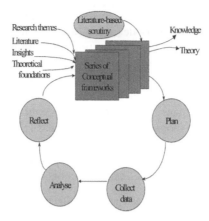

Fig. 2. The structured-case research method (Source: Carroll, J.M., Swatman, P.A.: Structured-case: a methodological framework for building theory in information systems research. Eur. J. Inf. Syst. 9, 235–242 (2000))

3.1 Conceptual Framework

According to Miles and Huberman, "a conceptual framework explains either graphically or in narrative form, the main things to be studied – the key factors, constructs or variables – and the presumed relationships among them [15]."

Figure 1 depicts the concept of the privacy pattern catalogue – the elements of the catalogue and the hierarchical relationship between them. The first list of privacy patterns for the conceptual framework was compiled from the reviewed privacy pattern literature. As it is allowed, or even welcomed, in structured-case methodology to update the framework if valuable knowledge is gained during the research process [14], new patterns were added and the description of some patterns was refined in the course of the project.

3.2 Research Cycle

Each research cycle was divided into four stages: plan, collect, analyse and reflect [14].

Plan. 11 interviews with privacy experts (PhD candidates, PhDs, professors and professionals in the field of data protection) from Austria, Germany, Greece, Ireland, Sweden and the USA were planned. The three main goals of those interviews were to classify the patterns according to the privacy principle instructions of ISO/IEC 29100, to expand the set of privacy patterns derived from the literature review and, if necessary, to update the description of patterns. To make the process of interviewing easier, the online questionnaire was developed. The questionnaire consisted of 55 privacy principle instructions and 28 privacy patterns with the descriptions. The patterns and their descriptions were derived from the literature review.

Each instruction of the privacy principle formed a separate question. For example, the consent and choice principle is described with the help of a bulleted list of 5 instructions [1]. Therefore, there were 5 questions concerning the consent and choice principle in the questionnaire. The privacy patterns were described in terms of what context they can be used in, what problem they solve, what solution they offer and what consequences should be expected after the implementation of the patterns. That is, in the same way as it was planned to describe the patterns in the catalogue. The description was shown upon mouseover on the 'i' icon. Figure 3 illustrates the cropped version of the first page of the questionnaire.

It was decided that the results of this research project would be presented in the form of the interactive online privacy pattern catalogue.

Collect. 11 interviews were conducted at the collection stage of the research cycle. The privacy experts were asked to choose patterns that, in their opinion, could implement the instructions of the privacy principles. They also chose what connection (direct or indirect) the pattern had to the privacy principle instruction. The interviewees were asked to explain their decisions briefly. The questionnaire also presented a possibility to add privacy patterns if the experts suggested patterns that were missing from the list. The interviewees also commented on the descriptions of patterns and on the questionnaire in general. The answers from the questionnaire were saved into the database and the experts' comments were recorded.

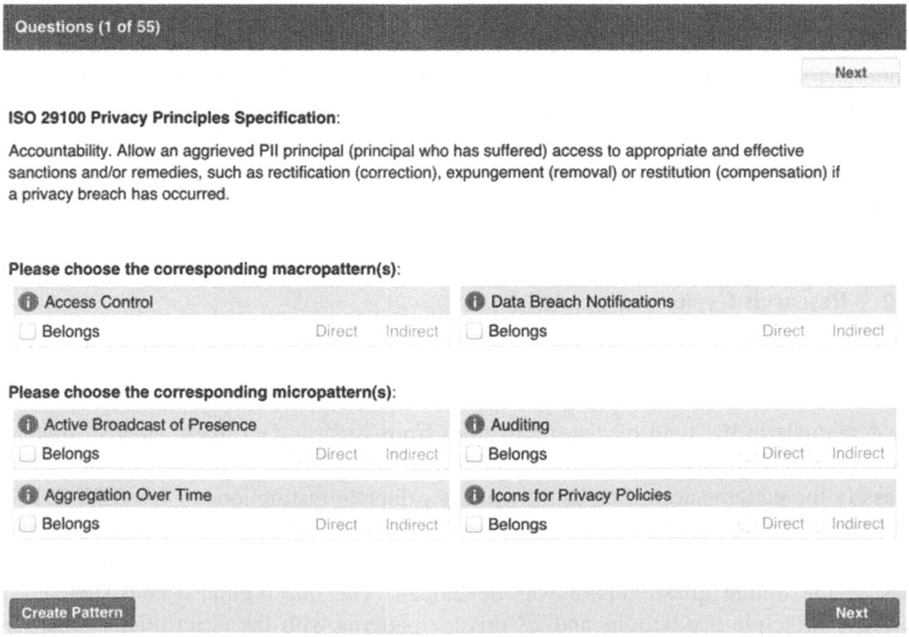

Fig. 3. The first page of the questionnaire (cropped version)

Analyse. The data from the database were organized into 55 bar charts. One of the bar graphs is shown in Fig. 4. The important comments and improvement suggestions from the recordings were transcribed and, if confirmed during the reflection stage, implemented for the next research cycle.

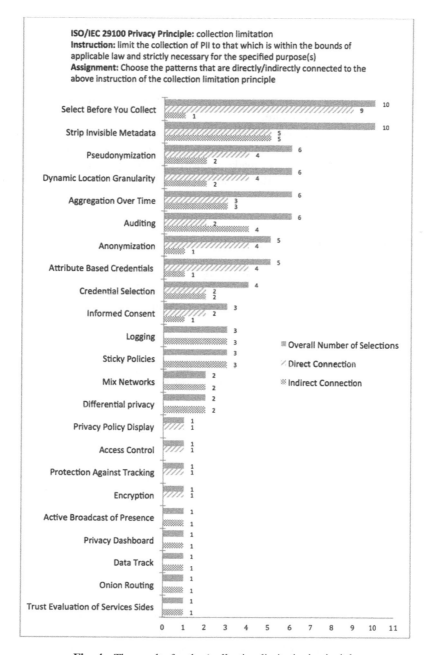

Fig. 4. The results for the 'collection limitation' principle

Reflect. The fellow researchers evaluated the results of the analysis and reflected on the interviewees' comments regarding the research process and the conceptual framework. The conceptual framework was updated with the new knowledge acquired at previous stages of the research cycle.

3.3   Theory Building

The research cycles were stopped at 11 interviews because the amount of new data, improvement suggestions and ideas received from the experts were low in the last interviews.

The last component of the structured-case methodology requires the results to be compared to the existent literature.

The findings were compared with the scarce literature on privacy patterns as well as with the technology descriptions suggested during interviews. To the best of my knowledge there were no attempts made to classify privacy patterns according to the privacy principles of ISO/IEC 29100, so no comparison was performed on the findings concerning this matter.

4   Privacy Pattern Catalogue

The interactive online privacy pattern catalogue (Fig. 5) [16] has been developed to present the results in a comprehensible and usable way. This online tool presents 40 privacy patterns in a structured way by grouping them according to the privacy principle instructions.

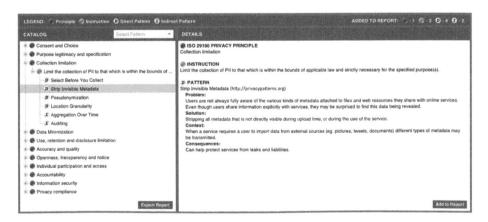

Fig. 5. The interactive privacy pattern catalogue

The catalogue could be useful for software architects and software developers in the projects where ISO/IEC 29100 certification is required. Depending on the status of the project, software architects can use the catalogue in both top-down and bottom-up directions. A top-down approach is used to identify which patterns implement a specific ISO/IEC 29100 privacy principle or instruction. A bottom-up approach provides the information on the ISO/IEC 29100 privacy principle and the corresponding instruction implemented by the chosen privacy pattern. Additionally, one can utilize the catalogue for the training purposes.

Two extra functionalities were integrated into the catalogue:

- Search by privacy pattern
- Export the report

The first feature gives a possibility to view what instructions and privacy principles are (to some extent) covered by the chosen privacy pattern.

The second feature could be very useful for the top-down approach. Because of the large amount of possible combinations, it could be difficult and time-consuming for a software architect to document the principles, instructions and patterns that are relevant to the project. To address this issue the system allows software architects to select required elements, stores all chosen items in a database through the whole selection process and offers a possibility to generate a report (Fig. 6) that contains all selected elements.

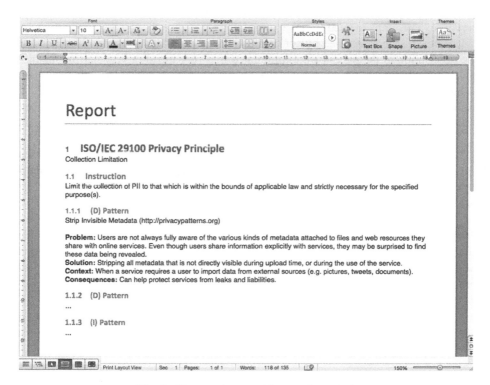

Fig. 6. Generated report (shortened version)

5 Discussion

While compiling the above-described catalogue a number of issues occurred.

Although the interviews are considered to be one of the powerful methods for gaining knowledge, there are some problems connected with this way of gathering information. In the case of this project the interviews lasted up to 4.5 h and the interviewees mentioned the problem of time pressure and the need to complete the questionnaire as quickly as possible. Indeed, the lack of time can cause two problems: either the information gathered will be incomplete or the interviewees will generate more input than they usually would do in the normal situation but the obtained information could be unreliable [17]. In order to examine how this issue might have influenced the results, the existent catalogue could be compared to the results obtained from the answers to the questionnaire that was filled out without time pressure.

The conceptual framework illustrates a clean tree structure of the catalogue. However, the privacy pattern instructions of the ISO/IEC 29100 overlap in some cases. This makes it possible that the same pattern could be assigned to different instructions. To mitigate this issue and to give a better overview of what instructions could be covered by one and the same pattern, the catalogue offers the 'search by privacy pattern' functionality. By using this functionality the user can obtain a summary of all the privacy principle instructions and corresponding privacy principles that are (to a certain extent) implemented by the chosen pattern.

Another issue mentioned by some interviewees was that sometimes the name and the description of the pattern were formulated in a very broad or very narrow manner. This may explain why abstract patterns appeared more often in the catalogue compared to the concrete ones. To partially solve this issue the comments from the interviews will be used to extend the catalogue by categorizing patterns into different dimensions and adding various angles of view in terms of context. This should bring even more structure to the pattern collection.

Additionally, the patterns could be described in more detail using more sections in the description template. One area that is currently under investigation is the compilation of a standardized template for privacy patterns. After the template is finalized the patterns in the catalogue should be updated according to it.

Another issue arises due to the fact that there are some privacy principle instructions, which do not have corresponding direct privacy patterns. This research project showed that "technical" patterns cover only a part of the ISO/IEC 29100 requirements. Some requirements could only be implemented by the organizational measures and processes. This means that the privacy patterns in the field of information technology governance should be identified and described.

The catalogue could also be extended by adding another hierarchy level (Fig. 7) to cater for privacy enhancing technologies (PETs) that would be assigned to the corresponding patterns.

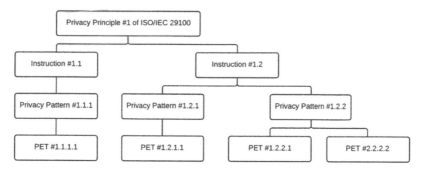

Fig. 7. Concept of an extended catalogue

6   Conclusion

This work presents an interactive online privacy pattern catalogue for software architects and software developers drawing both on a review of existing privacy patterns and on the interviews with privacy experts.

In the catalogue, privacy patterns are matched with the privacy principle instructions of the ISO/IEC 29100 standard, i.e. the users can view the list of patterns that implement a particular privacy principle instruction and read detailed information about those patterns. The users can also search by a particular pattern to see what privacy principles and their instructions could be implemented by that pattern. The catalogue provides a possibility to select patterns that are relevant to the project, from the software architect's point of view, and then automatically generate a report that presents all the selected items in a structured manner.

The process of privacy pattern classification showed that "technical" privacy patterns cover only a part of the privacy principle instructions of the ISO/IEC 29100 standard. As a result, the catalogue contains privacy principle requirements without corresponding direct privacy patterns. Those principle instructions could be implemented with the help of organizational processes.

References

1. International Standard ISO/IEC 29100:2011(E) Information technology — Security techniques — Privacy framework (2011)
2. Hoepman, J.: Privacy design strategies. arXiv Prepr. arXiv:1210.6621, p. 12 (2012)
3. Coplien, J.O.: Software Patterns. Lucent Technologies, Bell Labs Innovations, New York (1996)
4. Hafiz, M.: A collection of privacy design patterns. In: Proceedings of the 2006 Conference Pattern Languages Programs - PLoP 2006, vol. 1 (2006)
5. Fischer-Hübner, S., Köffel, C., Pettersson, J.-S., Wolkerstorfer, P., Graf, C., Holtz, L.E., König, U., Hedbom, H., Kellermann, B.: HCI Pattern Collection – Version 2. Priv. Identity Manag. Eur. Life. 61 (2010)
6. Privacy Patterns: http://www.privacypatterns.org. Accessed 14 July 2015

7. Privacypatterns.eu - Collecting Patterns for Better Privacy. https://privacypatterns.eu/. Accessed 14 July 2015
8. Alexander, C., Ishikawa, S., Silverstein, M.: A Pattern Language: Towns, Buildings, Construction (1977)
9. Schmidt, D.C., Buschmann, F.: Patterns, frameworks, and middleware: their synergistic relationships. In: Proceedings of the 25th International Conference on Software Engineering (2003)
10. Gamma, E., Helm, R., Johnson, R.E., Vlissides, J.: Design patterns: elements of reusable object-oriented software. Design **206**, 395 (1995)
11. Anthony, S.F., Thompson, M.W., Swindle, O., Leary, T.B.: Privacy online : fair information practices in the electronic marketplace a report to congress. Security (2000)
12. Organisation of Economic Co-Operation and Development: OECD guidelines governing the protection of privacy and transborder flows of personal data (1980)
13. Proposal for a Regulation of the European Parliament and of the Council on the protection of individuals with regard to the processing of personal data and on the free movement of such data (2012)
14. Carroll, J.M., Swatman, P.A.: Structured-case: a methodological framework for building theory in information systems research. Eur. J. Inf. Syst. **9**, 235–242 (2000)
15. Miles, M.B., Huberman, A.M.: Qualitative Data Analysis (1994)
16. Privacy Pattern Catalogue. privacypatterns.wu.ac.at. Accessed 01 Nov 2015
17. Myers, M.D., Newman, M.: The qualitative interview in IS research: examining the craft. Inf. Organ. **17**, 2–26 (2007)

Developing a Structured Metric to Measure Privacy Risk in Privacy Impact Assessments

Sushant Agarwal[(✉)]

Institute for Management Information Systems,
Vienna University of Economics and Business, Vienna, Austria
sagarwal@wu.ac.at

Abstract. Today's IT applications involving the processing of personal data of customers are becoming increasingly complex. This complexity drives the probability of privacy breaches. Considerable damage to a company's reputation and financial standing may ensue. Privacy Impact Assessments (PIAs) aim to systematically approach and reduce privacy risks caused by IT applications. Data protection authorities and the European Commission promote using PIAs in application design to help attaining 'privacy by design' right from the inception of a new IT application. To help companies developing IT applications with conducting PIAs, many open-source tools are available online (GS1 tool, iPIA tool, SPIA tool etc.). Although these tools are modular and well structured, they fail to provide a metric to comparing progress in the implementation of privacy controls. In general, most of the tools use qualitative scoring for privacy risk, through which the measurement of progress is difficult. To address these shortcomings of existing tools, this paper presents a structured scoring methodology for privacy risk. A three-step semi-quantitative approach is used to calculate a relative score, which enables the comparison of privacy risks between incremental versions of an IT application. This comparison enables the monitoring of progress and thus, makes PIAs more relevant for the companies.

Keywords: Privacy risk · Risk score · Privacy impact assessment

1 Introduction

Privacy risk is defined as the risk of harm originating through an intrusion into privacy [1]. Not only can privacy breaches lead to lawsuits damaging a company's reputation and finances, but also can hamper trust of customers and overall brand perception. A PIA enables a company to identify risks pertaining to privacy and helps in adhering to data protection laws. Privacy Impact Assessments (PIAs) are crucial for companies using IT applications that process personal data of customers and employees. The European Commission acknowledges importance of PIAs and the proposed data protection regulations mandate PIAs where sensitive data is processed [2]. Also, a lot of tools have been developed to conduct PIAs such as - GS1 tool [3], iPIA tool [4], SPIA tool [5] etc. to support and ease the process of these assessments.

Literature emphasizes that PIA should be considered as a continuous process, so that engineers and managers of a company can consider the possible privacy issues

D. Aspinall et al. (Eds.): Privacy and Identity 2015, IFIP AICT 476, pp. 141–155, 2016.
DOI: 10.1007/978-3-319-41763-9_10

through the complete IT development lifecycle to minimize the privacy risk [6, 7]. In most PIA reports, PIA results/outcomes are descriptive and long [8]. If PIA is to be considered as a continuous process then it's important to have a metric for comparison over time. Progress in terms of privacy risks should be easy to measure and monitor using PIA, which is currently difficult.

Though, in the field of security risk management, extensive research has been done to quantify risk. Many methodologies have been proposed to define a numeric risk metric: probability models [9], decision-tree models [10], and composite indices based on impact and likelihood [11, 12]. These models stand in sharp contrast to the qualitative definition of privacy risk in most PIA methodologies [3–5]. For example, even though GS1 has a predefined number for the risk based on likelihood and impact and also a user selectable score for control effectiveness, the end score is still qualitative [3]. In UK's ICO code of practice for conducting PIAs, a template has been proposed which lacks a metric to score the privacy risks or to measure the improvements [1]. Oetzel and Spiekermann (2013) consider qualitative metric - low, medium, high for scoring privacy risk in the proposed iPIA tool [4]. Though the process is modular and captures both customer's and company's point of view, score is unstructured and difficult to measure. Also the EU CEN standards for RFID PIAs focus on qualitative evaluation of threats based on financial factors [13]. Hence, as far as to my knowledge, a metric to provide guidance to score a PIA in measureable terms has not been provided in the current literature so far.

To fill this gap, this paper proposes a structured privacy score metric for the PIA process. In the field of risk management, two approaches are mainly used to compute the level of risk. On one hand, the qualitative approach considers assets, vulnerabilities and threats to estimate an approximate risk level (generally as low, medium or high) [15, 16]. On the other hand, the quantitative approach considers risk score numerically as the product of likelihood and impact [11]. Qualitative scoring is used when the level of risk is low and it's difficult to quantify risks. In contrast, quantitative scoring is used when ample information about risk is available and likelihood and impact can be quantified [17]. However, privacy risk levels can be high but at the same time it is difficult to quantify impact and likelihood [18]. Therefore, a semi-quantitative approach is considered for this paper as it combines both qualitative and quantitative approaches to estimate the risk score. Using this approach a relative risk scale is defined to represent the severity [19]. As the risk score obtained is relative, this cannot be used to compare two different applications. But, can be used to compare the different versions of the risk assessment for the same application. This semi-quantitative metric enables companies to better monitoring and tracking of privacy risks throughout a system's development lifecycle.

The remaining paper proceeds as follows: in Sect. 2, existing PIA methodologies are briefly described Sect. 3 proposes a new 3-step process of risk identification, modeling and quantitative evaluation. Section 4 illustrates the proposed methodology with a case study. Section 5 draws conclusions.

2 Current Practices for Privacy Risk

In the literature, many different methodologies [1, 4] and tools [3, 5] have been discussed (a good overview and evaluation of tools can be found in a paper by Wadhwa et al. [14]). Three PIA tools are discussed here focusing on their methodology for scoring privacy risk.

2.1 GS1 PIA Tool

To 'rapidly perform a comprehensive assessment of privacy risks of any new EPC/RFID implementation' [3], the not-for-profit organization GS1 developed an easy to use MS Excel based PIA tool focusing on RFID implementation. For privacy risk, the tool has predefined levels of likelihood and impact and allows variable scoring for the control effectiveness. Even though scores for likelihood and impact can be changed, the main emphasis is on the control effectiveness score (level of maturity of implemented control to tackle privacy risk). Table 1 shows the scoring logic and each variable is scored on a scale of 1–5. Based on the level of PIA required, there are 5 risk areas with a total of 5 questions each for controls. While likelihood and impact are scored for a risk area, control effectiveness is scored individually for each control (C1, C2, C3, C4, and C5). Risk score follows a semi-quantitative approach and is measured based on the following formula 1:

$$Risk = Impact \times Likelihood - (C1 + C2 + C3 + C4 + C5) \tag{1}$$

The methodology aims well at a numerical score to measure and monitor the privacy risks level. Also, scoring considers perspectives of both the data subject (usually the customer) and the organization (company). However, the criteria for scoring is broad and generalized i.e. not specific for privacy risks. For example, consider the following risk area – 'The data subject is unaware of the collection of personal data'. Criteria can be refined and narrowed down based on sensitivity, financial value of personal data for instance, to score the impact and likelihood for privacy risk score.

2.2 iPIA Tool

This tool has been developed at Institute for Management Information Systems, Vienna University [4]. It is an open source application written in PHP and JavaScript using jQuery UI. Similar to the GS1 tool, this tool also focuses on RFID applications. The process of assessment consists of 8 main parts and unlike other PIA tools, risk is not measured using impact and likelihood. Here, the degree of protection for each target is evaluated based on three demand categories: low, scored at 1; medium scored at 2; and high, scored 3. For this degree of protection there are two main dimensions split further into sub-categories. Based on this privacy target score, threats are then ranked in the subsequent steps. Table 2 shows the categories for the degree of protection for privacy target.

Table 1. Scoring technique used in GS1 PIA Tool

Score	Likelihood	Score	Impact	Score	Control effectiveness
5	It is very likely that this risk will occur in the organization	5	The impact to the data subject will be highly detrimental and cause residual effects to the organization.	5	Risk mitigation strategy or control process in place - proven highly effective in the previous 12 months
4	It is likely that this risk will occur in the organization	4	The impact to the data subject will be detrimental and cause residual effects to the organization.	4	Risk mitigation strategy or control process in place - proven effective in the past 6 months
3	This risk may occur in the organization	3	The impact to the data subject will be minor and cause some residual effects to the organization.	3	Risk mitigation strategy or control process in place - proven largely effective
2	It is unlikely that this risk will occur	2	There could be minor impact to the data subject with some residual effects to the organization.	2	Risk mitigation strategy or control process recently implemented - effectiveness is questionable or unknown
1	It is very unlikely that this risk will occur	1	There would be no impact to the data subject with no residual effects to the organization.	1	Risk mitigation strategy or control process is not in place or is under development

Instead of measuring the level of risk, this tool measures the level of protection required. The scoring is discrete and there is no overall score which makes it difficult to compare two different versions of a PIA report.

Table 2. Scoring technique used in iPIA Tool

Category	Subcategory	Score
Operator perspective	Impact on reputation and brand value	Low, Med, High
	Financial loss	
Consumer perspective	Social standing	
	Financial well being	
	Personal freedom	
Overall category		

2.3   SPIA Tool

Focused on both security and privacy, this tool has been developed by University of Pennsylvania [5]. Similar to GS1 tool this tool is also based on MS Excel spreadsheet. The tool has two risk scores for the pre-defined threat scenarios – (1) current state and

Table 3. Scoring technique in SPIA tool

Score	Probability	Score	Consequence
0	Threat does not apply to this application / database	0	Threat is not applicable to this application
1	The event would only occur under exceptional circumstances	1	Negligible impact on ability to plan and conduct business activities with minimal reduction in customer service, operational efficiency and staff morale. Very limited, or no financial/political impact
2	The event could occur at some time, but probably will not	2	Minor impact on ability to plan and conduct business activities with minimal reduction in customer service, operational efficiency and staff morale. Minimal financial or political impact.
3	The event should occur at some time	3	Medium impact on ability to plan and conduct business activities with a moderate reduction in customer service, operational efficiency and staff morale. Some financial or political impact is experienced.
4	The event will probably occur at some time	4	Major impact on ability to plan and conduct business activities with significant reduction in customer service, operational efficiency and staff morale. Considerable financial or political impact
5	The event is expected to occur in most circumstances	5	Comprehensive impact on ability to plan and conduct business activities with total disruption in customer service, operational efficiency and staff morale. Devastating financial or political impact

(2) future state. For both these states, level of probability and consequence are entered and risk score is calculated as the product of probability and consequence. Table 3 shows the categories for probability and consequence.

This tool has a larger scale as compared to other tools but scores are still ambiguous as it is difficult to objectify difference between the different levels. For instance, the probability as "(3) should occur at some time" and "(4) probably occur at some time" are quite similar. Also, scoring for consequences is highly influenced by security risk assessment making it difficult to gauge the privacy risk.

2.4   Summary

It can be concluded, based on these tools (summarized in Table 4), that scoring of privacy risks has not been well focused. The concept for scoring privacy risk has been adapted from IT security management literature [11]. This makes it difficult to score and increasing the ambiguity in the scoring. In other words, as the scoring criteria are generalized and not specific for privacy risk, it becomes difficult to assign a particular score for a privacy risk scenario. For example, likelihood is only based on the probability levels and lacks any criteria which changes the probability of a privacy breach like financial value, sensitivity of data, level of security of data etc.

Table 4. Pros and cons of the tools

Tool	Pros	Cons
GS1 Tool	Uses a semi-quantitative approach, considers control effectiveness to monitor the progress	Criteria for scoring is too generic
iPIA Tool	Considers operator and customer perspective separately	No risk score, protection demand is qualitative
SPIA Tool	Considers current and future state, aiming towards estimating the progress	Highly influenced by security risk assessment and scoring criteria are difficult to distinguish

3   A Proposed Methodology for Measuring Privacy Risk

The process of the proposed privacy risk scoring methodology involves three steps – (1) Risk Identification, (2) Risk Modeling (qualitative part) and (3) Risk Evaluation (quantitative part). First, in risk identification, scenarios for which risk is to be evaluated are considered. Second, in risk modeling step, qualitative modeling of the risk scenario is done so as to establish a relation between assets, vulnerabilities and threats. Third, in the risk evaluation step, a relative numerical score for the risk scenario is evaluated.

3.1 Risk Identification

This step involves identifying risk scenarios for the considered IT application. In this paper, risk scenarios are identified based on the EU data protection directive 95/46/EC [20] but can also be extended depending on the complexity of the application. These legal regulations also reflect company's perspective as following these regulations is one of the major considerations before deploying a new application. Risk scenarios are thus, the opposite cases of legal regulations as risk involved is doing something against the law. For instance, if the law states that the data should be used only for specified purpose, risk scenario would be - data is used for unspecified purpose i.e., worst-case scenario against a particular regulation (opposite of the regulation).

3.2 Risk Modeling

To analyze and score privacy risk, it is important to have a clear picture of the risk scenario involved. Therefore, this step deals with modeling risk scenarios qualitatively, which are identified in the previous step. It helps in understanding the complex risk scenario through abstraction. Hence, for scenario abstraction and for simplifying the scenario, CORAS diagrams are used for modeling. CORAS approach is a general approach for risk analysis and fits well with privacy risk scenarios. Qualitatively, the risk is defined as the potential for loss, damage or destruction of an asset as a result of a threat exploiting vulnerability. Figure 1 shows a generalized CORAS risk diagram. It starts with who all can expose the system to risk (which includes system design as well). Usually, the negligence of employees to handle the data properly or poor system design can lead to a privacy breach. Then, vulnerability, which is basically a weakness, is identified. This vulnerability can be exploited by a threat to depreciate the value of an asset. Then the threat corresponding to the vulnerability is determined which is simply the cause for unwanted incident. Similarly, unwanted incident is then classified which is the scenario when the vulnerability is exploited by the threat. Lastly, asset loss i.e. asset which is affected by the unwanted scenario is depicted in Fig. 1.

Fig. 1. Schematic of risk modeling using CORAS approach

Figure 2 shows an example of CORAS diagram for EU directive 95/46/EC article 6 about personal data being processed fairly and lawfully [20]. If privacy concerns are undermined then there is less chance of fair and lawful processing. Negligence of employees, mischief of a hacker as well as poor system design can initiate the threat. Vulnerability here is, thus, ignoring/not considering the regulations. As a result, the threat is usage of personal data against the law leading to an unwanted incident as either lawsuit(s) against the company or bad publicity in the media.

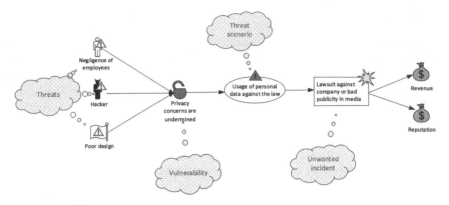

Fig. 2. Example of risk modeling using CORAS approach

3.3 Risk Evaluation

After defining the risk qualitatively, this section attempts at quantification of risk score for the modeled scenario. Similar to the IT security risk management approach [11], privacy risk is defined as the product of impact and likelihood explained in the subsequent sub-sections.

Impact. For assessing the impact Solove's taxonomy is used [21]. The taxonomy focuses on specific activities that may pose privacy problems rather than just the definitions of different aspects of privacy. Also it aims at activities that create privacy problems and that can upset the balance of social or institutional power in undesirable ways. This makes it easier to match and relate it to the risk diagrams. The taxonomy is split into four categories: (1) Information collection – related to collection of data, (2) Information processing – involves the way information is stored, manipulated and used, (3) Information dissemination – is about circulating and sharing the information, (4) Invasion – involves interference into people's private affairs. These four categories are subsequently split into further categories. Table 5 shows the different dimensions based on Solove's work. Some principles are not considered because they are not relevant for the scope of privacy risk involving customer-company relationship. For instance 'interrogation', which is various forms of questioning or probing for information, is highly unlikely in this scenario. Also, 'decisional interference' is excluded as it's related to government's incursion into the data subject's decisions regarding his/her private affairs.

Each risk scenario is considered and matched with different dimensions of impact. Then a simple sum of the categories applicable for the directive is calculated. This sum becomes the impact score for the risk scenario. For example, according to EU directive's article 6, collected data should be accurate. For this article, risk scenario would be the worst-case possibility i.e. very low data quality. Poor accuracy can lead to 'exclusion' as wrong information might devoid an individual from some offer [21, p. 521]. Similarly, it can also lead to 'breach of confidentiality' [21, p. 524] as an individual trusted the company and had high confidence while sharing personal data. It can also lead to 'distortion' [21, p. 546] as the personal information about the

Table 5. Dimensions for impact based on Solove's taxonomy

Category	Subcategory
Information Collection	Surveillance
Information processing	Aggregation
	Identification
	Insecurity
	Secondary Use
	Exclusion
Information Dissemination	Breach of confidentiality
	Disclosure
	Exposure
	Appropriation
	Distortion
	Increased Accessibility
Invasion	Intrusion

individual has low accuracy and wrong information would lead to distortion if used in some application. Therefore, three dimensions are valid for low data accuracy or low data quality. For scoring, simplistic harm benefit analysis is considered. All the different dimensions here are considered as harms and there are no benefits. So, the impact score is the net harm, which is the number of the affected dimensions, 3 in this example.

Likelihood. For measuring likelihood, Lipton's work on 'Mapping online privacy' is used [22]. This work focuses on privacy issues related to digital data. Unlike Solove's work, giving the methodology a broader view by incorporating online privacy of customers. It identifies 6 different dimensions of privacy – (1) Actors and relationships includes all those involved in a privacy incursion, (2) Conduct is about privacy threatening activities, (3) Motivations is simply about the motives for privacy threatening activities, (4) Harms and remedies includes all the harms and ways to redress those harms, (5) Nature of information is about the content of the information and (6) Format of information, which is about the format used to gather information online and disseminate it later. To estimate likelihood four of the six dimensions (i.e., all except 'conduct' and 'harms & remedies' which are similar to privacy risk and its consequences respectively) are used to measure likelihood.

The dimensions of likelihood are broadly classified in two categories – (1) Actors involved and (2) Data Characteristics. The data characteristics category incorporate the different dimensions of motivation, nature and format of information. Figure 3 shows the different dimensions of likelihood. Actors involved can be divided into 3 categories – First, the company, which involves both the employees and system design (also a strong passive actor in relation to the personal data). Second, 3rd parties which are involved in handling the personal data and third, other actors like competitors and hackers who also have interest in the collected personal data of the customers. Similarly, data characteristics is also divided into 3 categories – (1) Amount of data,

(2) Sensitivity of data, (3) Value of data involved. Amount of data is about the total rows and columns of the data. If more data is collected then the likelihood of privacy risk in general increases. Also, the value of data is about the monetary benefits of a privacy breach. If cost of an activity leading to privacy risk is low than the likelihood will be higher as vulnerability can be exploited easily without any substantial cost. Similar is the case with benefits obtained with that malicious activity, i.e., the higher the financial value of data, the higher is the likelihood of occurrence of similar activity. Additionally, a category regarding sensitivity of data is considered for measuring likelihood because financial value is not always higher for more sensitive data as it depends more on the context. For example, CEN standards define a higher asset value to an email address as compared to racial origin, which is actually a very sensitive data type. But, as maybe current scope of commercial exploitation is not that high for racial origin (as compared to email address), there is a higher commercial value for email addresses. Nevertheless, sensitive data is usually intimate for the customers and this gives a high motivation to the actors who have intentions of damaging the reputation of the firm collecting and disseminating the personal sensitive data.

4   A Case Study – Application to the Law

In this section a case study is presented to illustrate the proposed methodology. A fictitious restaurant with an online ordering and home delivery system is considered for the example. Customers can open restaurant's webpage, order food, pay it online and can get it delivered to their desired address.

According to article 6 of EU data protection directive – 'personal data of data-subjects must be adequate, relevant and not excessive in relation to the purposes for which they are collected and/or further processed' [20]. The risk scenario would therefore be collection of personal data inadequate, irrelevant and excessive for the purpose.

Figure 4 shows the modeled risk diagram for the scenario. Due to either negligence of employees, their lack of awareness or the poor design of the system can lead to scenarios where data collected is excessive of the purpose. Underlying vulnerability here is that before deploying a system or during its design the purpose of collected personal data fields is not checked or actively updated with the changes in the design. This vulnerability is leads to a threat, which is simply the excessive data collection (opposite scenario of the legal regulation). Then, unwanted scenario for this threat would be higher risk in securing and handling more data fields as compared to the case when limited data would have been collected. Also, according to article 10 of EU data protection directive [20], data subjects should be given the information regarding the purpose of data collection which would be difficult to provide as data collected is excessive to the purpose. Hence, it will lead to loss of reputation and trust of customers (data-subjects) for the company.

Let us assume that the restaurant collects the personal details as shown in Table 6. The purpose is to process an online order and deliver the food at the given address which requires last name to identify a person, address to deliver it and telephone number to notify when the delivery staff is at the given address.

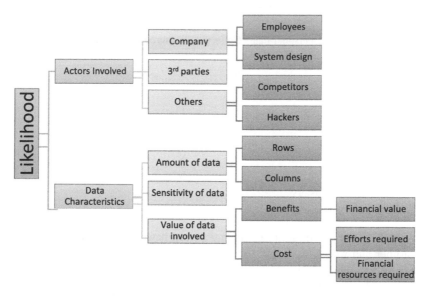

Fig. 3. Dimensions for measuring likelihood

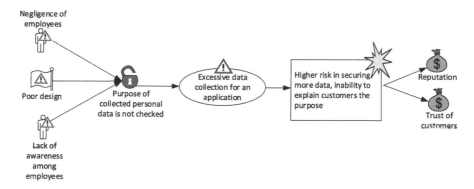

Fig. 4. CORAS diagram for the risk scenario

The next step is quantifying the impact and likelihood score. Using Solove's (2006) taxonomy, the impact dimensions are measured as shown in Table 6. If excessive data is collected then it can lead to increased surveillance with the help of excessive data fields that are collected. In the example, browsing history is a case of surveillance on customer's browsing habits. Similarly, it also leads to aggregation as a more comprehensive profile of the customers would be collected, which can also lead to identification. In general, customer would be roughly identified for the delivery using last name and address but the data collected would lead to exact identification. Also, more data leads to more insecurity and might tempt the restaurant for other secondary uses like sending marketing emails based on customer profile. Personal data of a customer can be also misused by an employee or a hacker to use his/her identity for a malicious

Table 6. Categories of personal data collected by the restaurant

Category of personal data	Collected	Required for the purpose?
First name	Y	N
Last name	Y	Y
Address	Y	Y
Telephone	Y	Y
Email	Y	N
Gender	Y	N
Birthday	Y	N
Order history	Y	N
Browsing history	Y	N

activity leading to appropriation. Company would have increased accessibility about the customer and would be in fact intruding in customer's personal life by collecting personal information, which is not required for the application. Therefore the impact score is quite high as 9/13 (Table 7).

The likelihood score would be subjective and more context dependent. For this scenario, the main actors are easily identifiable – system design and employees at the restaurant. Data characteristics score would depend on the quantity, financial value, and sensitivity of the collected data. Considering the fact that only the basic demographics like name, age, address and phone numbers are collected, the score would be 2/3. For sensitivity it would be 0. For amount of data the score can be set to 1 (out of 3) as not much data is collected. Value of data would be around 2 out of 3 as address, telephone numbers, browsing history etc. have high marketing value. In total, the score for likelihood would be 5/10 as shown in Table 8.

Table 7. Impact score for the example

Dimensions for impact	S U M	Surveillance	Aggregation	Identification	Insecurity	Secondary Use	Exclusion	Breach of confidentiality	Disclosure	Exposure	Appropriation	Distortion	Increased Accessibility	Intrusion
Excessive collection	**9**	Y	Y	Y	Y	Y	N	N	Y	N	Y	N	Y	Y

Hence, the risk score would be 8.75 out of 25 as shown in the Table 9. The scale has been adjusted such that the maximum risk score would be 25. The risk is then represented on a an impact-likelihood (probability) graph [11]. It can be observed from the graph in Fig. 5 that risk score lies in the escape/transfer region. Hence, it is required to escape the scenario by modifying the design of the system, which can be either done by an audit to confirm the use of all the data collected or by reducing the personal data which is being collected. Subsequently, in the later stages, likelihood can be decreased by improving the system design or securing the collected data (to increase the efforts required for unreasonable access). Similarly, impact would be reduced when limited data is collected for a predefined purpose as dimensions of intrusion, surveillance etc. would then not be valid.

Table 8. Estimating the likelihood

Dimensions	Score	Max
Actors involved	2	3
Amount of data	1	3
Sensitivity of data	0	1
Value of data	2	3
Total	**5**	**10**

Table 9. Calculating the risk score

	Score	Score out of 5
Impact	9/13	3.5
Likelihood	5/10	2.5
Risk score		**8.75/25**

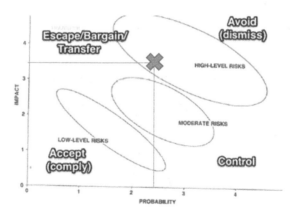

Fig. 5. Risk score on impact likelihood graph

5   Conclusions and Future Work

Following an IT security risk management approach, this paper proposes a structured privacy risk metric. The risk score enables measuring the progress made in minimizing privacy risk between the incremental development cycles in system development. Risk scenarios based on EU data protection directive 95/46/EC have been taken as an example to illustrate the process. These scenarios are modeled using CORAS diagrams for better understanding and abstraction. For quantification, risk is then broken down into impact and likelihood. The dimensions for likelihood focus on company's perspective by considering actors, financial value of data etc. and dimensions for impact based on Solove's taxonomy help in measuring the impact from the customer's point of view. In the end, a privacy risk score is obtained as the product of impact and likelihood.

The focus in previous sections has been to develop a structured metric for privacy risk score and scales for measuring impact and likelihood are not discussed in detail. 0 and 1 have been used for scoring the impact dimensions and all of them have the same weightage. However, impact dimensions can have different weightages based on the scenario. For example, consider a scenario where CCTV cameras are used in a store for surveillance. If cameras are around the changing rooms then it can lead to 'Exposure' of customers i.e. might reveal their nude body. In this scenario, weightage for 'Exposure' should be higher than 'Aggregation' of their purchase history. Hence, the future work would involve selecting suitable functions to aggregate impact dimensions along with assigning appropriate weightages to them. Additionally, the scoring metric would then be integrated in a PIA tool to benchmark it in a real-life scenario. It would be crucial to tackle the tradeoff between customizability and complexity. A rigorous and fully customizable risk scoring algorithm might lead a complex PIA process whereas, standardizing all the parameters might reduce the usefulness of the score. Hence, for a simple yet meaningful PIA, it is important that scoring process does not add a lot of complexity to the process.

References

1. Information Commissioner's Office UK: Conducting privacy impact assessments code of practice. 50 (2014)
2. European Commission: Proposal for protection of individuals with regard to the processing of personal data and on the free movement of such data. 0011 (2012)
3. GS1: GS1 EPC/RFID Privacy Impact Assessment Tool (2012)
4. Oetzel, M.C., Spiekermann, S.: A systematic methodology for privacy impact assessments: a design science approach. Eur. J. Inf. Syst. 23, 126–150 (2013)
5. University of Pennsylvania: Introduction to the SPIA Program. http://www.upenn.edu/computing/security/spia/spia_step_by_step.pdf
6. Spiekermann, S.: The RFID PIA – developed by industry, endorsed by regulators. In: Wright, D., Hert, P. (eds.) Privacy Impact Assessment, pp. 323–346. Springer, Netherlands (2012)
7. Wright, D., de Hert, P.: Privacy Impact Assessment. Springer, Berlin (2012)
8. PIAw@tch: Significant Privacy Impact Assessment Report accessible online. http://www.piawatch.eu/pia-report
9. Cheng, P.C., Rohatgi, P., Keser, C., Karger, P.A., Wagner, G.M., Reninger, A.S.: Fuzzy multi-level security: an experiment on quantified risk-adaptive access control. In: IEEE Symposium on Security and Privacy, SP 2007, pp. 222–230 (2007)

10. Sahinoglu, M.: Security meter: a practical decision-tree model to quantify risk. IEEE Secur. Priv. **3**, 18–24 (2005)
11. Vose, D.: Risk Analysis: A Quantitative Guide. John Wiley & Sons, Chichester (2008)
12. ISO: ISO/IEC 27005 Information technology - Security Techniques - Information security risk management. ISO/IEC (2008)
13. CEN: Information technology - RFID privacy impact assessment process (2014)
14. Wadhwa, K., Rodrigues, R.: Evaluating privacy impact assessments. Innov. Eur. J. Soc. Sci. Res. **26**(1–2), 1–20 (2013)
15. Yazar, Z.: A qualitative risk analysis and management tool–CRAMM. SANS InfoSec Read. Room White Pap. (2002)
16. Vellani, K.: Strategic Security Management: A Risk Assessment Guide for Decision Makers. Elsevier Science, New York (2006)
17. Stoneburner, G., Goguen, A., Feringa, A.: Risk management guide for information technology systems. NIST Spec. Publ. **800**, 800–830 (2002)
18. Data Security and Privacy Group Edelman: The costs, causes and consequences of privacy risk
19. Borghesi, A., Gaudenzi, B.: Risk Management: How to Assess, Transfer and Communicate Critical Risks. Springer Science & Business Media, Mailand (2012)
20. European Parliament: Directive 95/46/EC. Off. J. Eur. Communities. L 281/31 (1995)
21. Solove, D.: A taxonomy of privacy. Univ. PA. Law Rev. **154**, 477–560 (2006)
22. Lipton, J.D.: Mapping Online Privacy. Northwest. Univ. Law Rev. **104**, 477–515 (2010)

Accountability in the EU Data Protection Reform: Balancing Citizens' and Business' Rights

Lina Jasmontaite[(✉)] and Valerie Verdoodt

KU Leuven – Centre for IT and IP Law – iMinds, Leuven, Belgium
{lina.jasmontaite,valerie.verdoodt}@kuleuven.be

Abstract. The principle of accountability has been present in the field of data protection and privacy for several decades. Recently, accountability as a data protection principle gained fresh prominence with the revision of the data protection frameworks by the leading actors – the OECD, the Council of Europe, and the European Union. Anticipating the adoption of the General Data Protection Regulation, this contribution examines the positions of the EU legislative actors on Article 22 defining the responsibility of the data controller ("the general accountability article"). To date, there has been little agreement on the limitations of the newly introduced Article 22 and its practical implications for individuals and business. As such, this contribution analyses the debates that took place among the Council of the EU, the European Parliament and the European Commission throughout the negotiation process of General Data Protection Regulation. The contribution aims at providing new insights into the underpinning values and objectives of the accountability article.

Keywords: Accountability · Controllers · Data subjects · The General Data Protection Regulation · A risk-based approach · A rules-based approach · A principles-based approach · Processors

1   Introduction

In the field of data protection, the principle of accountability has been rather implicit and mostly referred to as the responsibility of data controllers for their data processing activities. In this respect, Article 22 on the responsibility of the controller ("the general accountability article") of the draft General Data Protection Regulation ("Regulation") was not revolutionary. Nevertheless, if adopted in its initial form as proposed by the EC, the general accountability article would have marked a new development within the EU data protection framework by introducing a non-exhaustive list of accountability measures for data controllers. Indeed, it would not only have required data controllers to develop policies addressing the management of personal data but also to implement measures allowing demonstration of compliance with the EU data protection framework. The initial draft Regulation foresaw five measures facilitating the implementation of the accountability principle in practice (see infra). As the EU data protection reform is almost completed, the final text of the general accountability article

Published by Springer International Publishing Switzerland 2016. All Rights Reserved
D. Aspinall et al. (Eds.): Privacy and Identity 2015, IFIP AICT 476, pp. 156–169, 2016.
DOI: 10.1007/978-3-319-41763-9_11

is known.[1] Accordingly, it is timely to analyse the past and current discussions on Article 22 to gain a better idea of the practical implications of this provision.

It seems that the amendments put forward by the European Parliament ("Parliament"), as well as the Council of the EU ("Council"), prevailed over the initial EC's approach. The Parliament and the Council suggested to delete the non-exhaustive list of accountability measures and leave only the general requirement for data controllers to "implement appropriate measures" and be able to demonstrate compliance with the legal framework (Council of the EU 2015). In view of the compromise text of the Regulation, we question the significance and the impact of Article 22 for EU citizens and business.

The aim of this paper is to examine the practical implications of the accountability measures for both business and citizens' rights. To achieve this objective, the contribution reflects on the origin and layout of the general accountability provision. Then, it reflects on the EU legislators' debates on the provision. In the subsequent sections, the paper compares and analyses the different views of the Commission, the Parliament and the Council on Article 22. The concluding part recognises that the issue of implementing accountability in practice is an intriguing one and needs to be further addressed in research analysing the attribution of responsibilities between controllers and processors.

2 Accountability in the Field of Data Protection and Privacy

To better understand the discussions on the accountability principle, one has to grasp the general obligations arising from accountability, such as reporting and explaining policies and actions taken with respect to one's business practices. The following sections go beyond the general premise that being accountable is being transparent and responsible to your stakeholders for your performance and conduct, and give a brief overview of accountability debates in the context of the EU data protection reform.

2.1 The Concept of Accountability

The concept of accountability is relevant for different sectors ranging from public administration and finance to data protection and ICT. Accordingly, accountability entails different meanings that are assigned to it by various scholars and organisations. A definition that has been widely recognised originates from the governance scholar, Bovens, defining accountability as both a virtue that entails "a normative concept, as a set of standards for the behaviour of actors, or as a desirable state of affairs" and as a mechanism "that involves an obligation to explain and justify conduct" (Bovens 2010).

---

[1] This contribution was initially drafted in November 2015. The text was revised in February 2016 and now includes references to the compromise text of political agreement, published by the Council of EU on the 28 January 2016. At the moment, it is estimated that the final text of the General Data Protection Regulation will be published in Official Journal in June 2016. Note that the numbering of the provisions and recitals may change in the final version of the General Data Protection Regulation.

An example of such a mechanism could be an obligation to demonstrate that the processing of personal data is in compliance with the EU data protection framework.

In the field of data protection and privacy, "accountability is [considered to be] a form of enhanced responsibility" (Bennett 2012). The actual recognition of the principle within EU data protection legislation marks a shift from a primarily reactive approach to a proactive one, according to certain scholars. As per Alhadeff, Van Alsenoy and Dumortier, accountability is "a proactive demonstration of an organization's capacity to comply has the potential of improving the current state of the art in two ways: (1) transparency and confidence for both regulators and data subjects, and (2) greater transparency of corporate practices" (Alhadeff et al. 2010). Indeed, the proposed accountability provision requires the controller to adopt policies and implement appropriate measures to ensure, and be able to demonstrate compliance with the data protection framework (EC 2012a). At the same time, it is suggested that "accountability instruments are ways to make the [EU] adequacy framework work more effectively" (Bennett 2010). In other words, the introduction of the accountability mechanism can be regarded as a remedy for the widely criticised EU adequacy framework, which prohibits personal data transfers to (third) countries that are not recognised by the Commission as having an "adequate" level of protection as under Directive 95/46/EC.

2.2   The Endless Debate: 'Who is Accountable'?

In Europe, discussions on the question 'who is accountable' in the field of data protection have been influenced by the European Convention for the Protection of Human Rights and Fundamental Freedoms ("Convention"). The European Court of Human Rights, while interpreting the Convention, has developed a doctrine of positive obligations in its case law (De Hert 2012). According to this doctrine, states have an obligation to take appropriate actions to ensure that citizens can exercise their rights without any constraints (De Hert 2012). In other words, governments are not only required to provide adequate legislation and policies, but they also need to ensure effective enforcement of legislative measures. Furthermore, this doctrine calls for a clear attribution and effective implementation of responsibilities of the actors involved. In the context of privacy and data protection, this means that governments are the main duty-bearers responsible for ensuring that both controllers and processors take an appropriate share of responsibility for the protection of data subjects' rights (De Hert 2012).

While the concept of a controller's accountability has been present ever since the adoption of the OECD Guidelines on the Protection of Privacy and Transborder Flows of Personal Data ("Guidelines"), this attribution of responsibility has become controversial because of the growing processors' influence over personal data processing operations (OECD 2013). Some legislators, in particular the Council of Europe, have been addressing this issue in their attempts to modernise the existing data protection frameworks. The Council of Europe seeks to introduce additional obligations for both processors and controllers in the revised Convention No. 108 (Council of Europe 2012). More specifically, the Council of Europe sees processors as active agents who have to take appropriate measures to implement data protection requirements (Article 8 bis).

At the moment, the discussions on the modernisation of the Convention No. 108 are still ongoing and the final text of the provision remains uncertain (CAHDATA 2014). Nevertheless, given the support of the Data Protection Authorities to the accountability principle, it is reasonable to expect that additional accountability obligations will be introduced for both controllers and processors (European Conference of Data Protection Authorities 2014).

Similar to the Council of Europe proposal, the Regulation provides input for the accountability debate and the attribution of responsibility between the agents engaged in the processing of personal data. According to Recital 62, one of the main objectives of the Regulation is to clarify the responsibilities of controllers and processors (EC 2012a). To achieve this, the general accountability article (Article 22) describes obligations for the controller to comply with the Regulation and to demonstrate compliance. The processor's obligations are clarified in Article 26, which is partly based on Article 17 (2) of the Data Protection Directive, but also implements new elements. For instance, processors should be regarded as joint controllers if they process data beyond the controller's instructions (EC Explanatory Memorandum 2012b). Other new obligations that would apply to both controllers and processors are the documentation obligation (Article 28) and the obligation to carry out a Data Protection Impact Assessment (DPIA). Furthermore, the Regulation would extend liability and the right to compensation of damages caused by processors (Article 77). Therefore, it seems that the concept of accountability in data protection goes beyond the controller's accountability foreseen in Article 22, forcing processors to take their share of responsibility for the protection of personal data.

At the same time, the debate on accountability essentially relates to the evolving role of national data protection authorities and data subjects. The latter are no longer seen as "merely passive objects who require protection of the law against exploitation" (EDPS 2015). Indeed, individuals actively engage in online services and generate content. Therefore, it is suggested that citizens should bear responsibility for their choices made in the online environment, similarly to the situation in the offline world, rather than merely being the ones to whom controllers and processors should be accountable (EDPS 2015).

3   Towards the EU Institutions' Agreement on Accountability

Now that the concept of accountability and the actors involved have been discussed, the following section of the paper focuses on the accountability debate within the EU data protection reform. The section firstly introduces the initial EC proposal for the accountability provision and then addresses the positions of the European Parliament and the Council of the EU.

3.1   The EC Rules-Based Approach: More Prescriptions yet no Remedy?

As indicated, the EC proposal for the General Data Protection Regulation introduced a non-exhaustive list of mechanisms to implement the accountability principle for controllers in Article 22. The first mechanism encompassed a documentation require-ment, according to which, controllers should keep relevant documentation of "all pro-cessing operations under its responsibility" (Article 28) (EC 2012a). The second mechanism included security obligations according to which controllers should take appropriate technical and organisational measures ensuring an adequate level of security of the processing operations (Article 30). The third mechanism required controllers to conduct a DPIA in situations where the processing may "present risks to the rights and freedoms of data subjects" (Article 33). The fourth mechanism included an obligation for controllers to obtain an authorisation from the DPA prior to the processing operations in cases where the DPIA is required or the DPA deems it to be necessary (Article 34). Lastly, the fifth mechanism addressed a designation of a data protection officer ("DPO") who would be responsible for the entity's compliance with the EU data protection framework (Article 35). It should be noted that while the draft Regulation published by the EC, listed the DPO appointment amongst the accountability measures, it would have been obligatory only in a limited number of situations.

With regard to the non-exhaustive list of accountability measures, it seems that the EC's position was shaped by the opinions of the Article 29 Data Protection Working Party ("Working Party"), which presents the views of the European national data protection authorities ("DPAs"). The Working Party has suggested to introduce the accountability principle in response to the EC's call for consultation on a comprehensive approach of the EU data protection framework (Article 29 Working Party, WP168). The European DPAs suggested that in order to be accountable, data controllers (depending on the nature of their data processing activities) should take both proactive and reactive measures (Article 29 Working Party, WP168). The following section discusses the positions of and the amendments to Article 22 proposed by the Parliament and the Council.

3.2   EU Legislators' Discussions During the Trilogue

The proposed Regulation, after being embroiled in the EU legislative process since January 2012, entered into the last stage of the first reading process – the trilogue – in 2015. While the Parliament decided on the proposed data protection package in March 2014, by approving amendments proposed by the LIBE Committee (European Par-liament 2014), the Council of the EU ("Council") struggled to reach a political agreement. After difficult deliberations, the Council adopted a common position on the proposal in June 2015. Having political agreements in both the Parliament and the Council allowed to proceed with further negotiations in the trilogue stage.

The amendments of the Parliament sought to clarify the responsibilities of con-trollers under Article 22. The Parliament specified that controllers should develop "appropriate policies and implement appropriate and demonstrable technical and organizational measures" (European Parliament 2014). In particular, the Parliament suggested to develop compliance measures that would take into consideration "the state of the art, the nature of personal data processing, the context, scope and purposes of the processing, the risks for the rights and freedoms of the data subjects and the type of the organization, both at the time of the determination of the means for processing and at the time of the processing itself" (European Parliament 2014). Aside from the amendments related to the proportionality principle, the Parliament followed up on the European Data Protection Supervisor's recommendation and introduced a requirement to review, and, if needed, update compliance policies every two years (European Parliament 2014). The Parliament also took into consideration recommendations of civil liberty groups and included a new obligation for publicly listed companies requiring to summarise the implemented accountability mechanisms in "any regular general reports of the activities" (European Parliament 2014).

The Council on the other hand introduced a risk-based approach according to which the controller, when implementing accountability mechanisms, would have to consider "the nature, scope, context and purposes of the processing as well as the likelihood and severity of risk for the rights and freedoms of individuals" (Council of the EU 2015 (June)). The contributions of delegations submitted in fall 2014 reveal that the Member States were considering the use of both "high risks" and "low risks", yet the concept of "high risks" prevailed (Council of the EU 2014 (September)). It can be observed that despite delegations representing Denmark, Germany, the Netherlands, Portugal, and the United Kingdom expressed doubts about the costs associated with the implementation of the accountability provision, the Member States reached a satisfactory agreement (Council of the EU 2014 (July)).

While there were many differences between the positions of the Parliament and the Council, there were also several similarities. Both the Parliament and the Council suggested to delete the non-exhaustive list of measures implementing the accountability principle from the final text of the Regulation (Council of the EU 2014 (August)). Furthermore, both EU institutions emphasised the need to reflect on the nature, context, scope and risk associated with the data processing when selecting accountability mechanisms. However, the Council's amendments to the article entailed a more business-friendly approach. The Council was striving for an accountability provision that would not be overly prescriptive and leave discretion to data controllers to select measures implementing the provision in practice.

4   Practical Implications of the General Accountability Article

After analysing the positions of the EU institutions, it is timely to reflect on the actual implications of the newly introduced Article 22 in practice. This section will first reflect on how accountability relates to the key principles of good governance, which are also embedded in the EU data protection framework. Second, it will further investigate the implications of the proposed general accountability article for data subjects and businesses, in light of the different positions of the EC and the Council. On the one hand, the EC advocated for a prescriptive, rules-based approach and included the non-exhaustive list of measures, which were supposed to be applicable to data controllers when processing personal data. On the other hand, the Council insisted on a risk-based approach (or a principle-based approach) with respect to the accountability principle. In particular, the Council suggested to correlate accountability measures with risks associated with a particular processing and to remove the list of accountability measures.

4.1   Good Governance Meets Data Protection

In general, good governance facilitates the implementation of the human rights' framework, and, as such, is relevant in the context of data protection where the fundamental rights to privacy and data protection are at stake. The Working Party has played an important role in providing guidance on how accountability in the context of data protection links to elements of good governance, such as transparency, proportionality and a risk-based approach. It could be argued that by introducing the accountability principle in the GDPR, the elements of good governance will be formally integrated in the EU data protection framework. Consequently, this may have a positive impact on the rights of data subjects and businesses.

Transparency - A First Step on the Path to Empowerment. First, the Working Party recognises a close link between accountability and the notion of transparency in its opinions (WP217). In particular, the Working Party considers transparency to be "an integral element of many accountability measures" (WP173). In the context of big data analytics, for instance, the Working Party lists transparency among the additional safeguards preventing undue impact on data subjects (WP203). Moreover, transparency is deemed to be a precondition for user empowerment, as it would allow data subjects to exercise their rights more effectively (WP203). To this end, the Working Party recommends data controllers to document the internal assessment conducted at the purpose specification stage (WP203). Such documentation would allow data controllers to demonstrate compliance with legal requirements, and additionally, could facilitate an easier demonstration of accountability. Accordingly, the Working Party has recognised that documentation could (in certain cases) facilitate the exercise of data subjects' rights and enforcement actions of national data protection authorities (WP217). Finally, being transparent vis-à-vis data processing practices can be a competitive advantage as it enhances user trust in online services.

Proportionality Calls for a Balanced Approach. Secondly, the Working Party has established a link between accountability and proportionality. For instance, if controllers opt for their legitimate interest as the ground legitimising the data processing (Article 7 (f) Directive 95/46/EC), controllers should perform a balancing test at the time of specifying the purposes of data collection. The balancing test would allow to determine whether the controller has a legitimate interest to undertake the foreseen data collection in a particular situation and whether that processing will not impinge on data subjects' rights (WP217). Moreover, the balancing test would allow to take into consideration the context and purposes of the processing as well as the risks in relation to the fundamental rights and freedoms of individuals.

Risk-Based Approach as an Integral Part of Accountability. Finally, at the core of good governance programmes lies the concept of "risk management", which includes the processes of identification, assessment, monitoring, mitigation and re-evaluation of risks. The Working Party has clarified that the core element of accountability in the data protection context is a risk based-approach (WP218). Specifically, the following provisions are developed with a risk based-approach in mind:

- the obligations of security (Article 30),
- the data protection impact assessment (Article 33),
- the data protection by design principle (Article 23),
- the obligation for documentation (Article 28), and
- the certification and codes of conduct (Articles 38 and 39).

The above listed provisions allow data controllers to select appropriate measures ensuring compliance with data protection rules. Furthermore, the provisions are based on the principle of proportionality and, as such, allow for business models, sectors and the particular risks associated with the processing of personal data to be taken into consideration. Developing measures on a case-by-case basis could ensure scalability of the accountability principle (WP173). In addition, the assessment and evaluation of the risks associated with the processing of personal data can enhance the practice of written policies and documentation. Therefore, it can be observed that the elements of good governance may benefit data subjects and businesses.

The following two sections of this paper will discuss the potential impact of the accountability measures as proposed by the Commission and the Council on data subjects and businesses.

4.2   Accountability Measures to Empower Individuals?

First of all, the potential impact of the proposed accountability article on data subjects' rights such as the right to access, the right to be informed and the right not to be subjected to automated processing in certain circumstances will be examined. It should be noted that Article 22 does not refer to data subjects' right per se. Data subjects' rights and controllers' obligations to respect these rights are specified in the third chapter of the Regulation.

The third chapter strengthens the existing data subjects' rights (e.g., right to access) and introduces new ones (e.g., right to data portability). Accordingly, it attains the core objective of the EU data protection reform, namely to empower data subjects. In particular, this objective is achieved by moving the primary responsibility for data protection enforcement from the individual (i.e., the data subject filing complaints with the DPA) to the organisation that processes personal data (i.e., the data controller) (Alhadeff et al. 2012). In other words, the initial aim of Article 22 was to move the EU data protection rules from a reactive or complaint-based approach to a proactive approach, where the controller has to:

(1) ensure compliance with the data protection framework;
(2) be able to demonstrate that the processing is performed in compliance with the data protection framework; and
(3) be able to verify that it has implemented mechanisms ensuring the effectiveness of the accountability measures (such verification should be carried out by independent internal or external auditors).

When considering the impact of the proactive approach on data subjects, it is worthwhile to reflect on the way data subjects could invoke the redress mechanism. In other words, how could data subjects ensure that controllers implement their accountability obligations? Should they bring complaints or requests directly to controllers or processors or should they rely on the actions of national data protection authorities? Under which conditions could individual data subjects or their representatives bring such claims? In practice, data subjects should bring complaints to their DPA, which then on behalf of a data subject would start an investigation or an enforcement action.

Documentation to Facilitate Accountable Storytelling: Honesty is the Best Policy. The EC emphasised the importance of formal procedures and listed documentation among the accountability measures (Article 28). Supporters of this rather prescriptive approach to accountability may argue that it could increase transparency of data controllers' and processors' data processing practices towards individuals and as such increase trust of individuals. In fact, European Digital Rights, an international non-profit association which brings together 33 privacy and civil rights organisations, even advocated a stronger provision which would include an obligation for data controllers and processors to publicly disclose a summary of the implemented accountability measures (EDRI 2012). While this suggestion was supported by the Parliament, it was erased during the trilogue phase.

Nevertheless, it is important to note that the act of documentation can be meaningful to the extent it is honest and truthful. Indeed, account giving should not be about persuasion and manipulation. As per Raab, accountability does not only entail "giving an account" but also challenging an account giver and asking for evidence in support of any claims (Raab 2012). Considering this point of view, the possibility to challenge controllers' and processors' policies and measures taken in a particular data processing operation can empower data subjects.

Data Protection Impact Assessment: The Representation of Data Subjects in the Decision-Making Process. Secondly, data subjects should be given a voice in the decision-making related to certain processing operations. Indeed, the EC text suggested that controllers and processors take data subjects' views into consideration when conducting DPIA for processing operations that entail "risks to the rights and freedoms of data subjects by virtue of their nature, their scope or their purposes" (EC 2012a). While scholars and practitioners generally agree on the DPIA's added value to the data protection framework (and in particular to data subjects' rights) the process of carrying out the DPIA entails several challenges (Wright et al. 2011). Some of these challenges were addressed in the Parliament's amendments introducing categories of information that need to be included in a DPIA and that could potentially enhance the level of transparency of the DPIA process. In particular, it was suggested to include the systematic description of personal data processed, the purposes of the operations, the assessment of the necessity and proportionality of the processing and the measures to mitigate the identified risks to individuals (Council of the EU 2015 (June)).

The Council, on the other hand has diluted the scope of an obligation to carry out a DPIA by limiting it only to controllers (Council of the EU 2015 (June)). As a result, many businesses that process personal data on behalf of the controller will be excluded from its application. Moreover, the Council followed a risk-based approach and suggested to only conduct a DPIA "where a type of processing [...] is likely to result in a high risk for the rights and freedoms of individuals" (Council of the EU 2015 (June)). Limiting the scope of the obligation would favour businesses rather than individuals, and as such it is not welcomed by privacy advocates.

Data Protection Officer: An Enabler of Data Subjects' Rights. Although Article 18 of Directive 95/46/EC already refers to a "Data Protection Officer" the mandatory appointment of a DPO would mean a new obligation for both controllers and processors in most of the EU Member States. The initial requirement, as proposed by the EC, for businesses with more than 250 employees to appoint such an officer was met with resistance (EUROCHAMBRES 2012). In particular, the new obligation triggered discussions on indicators of high risks of data processing activities among stakeholders (BEUC 2012). The Parliament took this debate further by suggesting that businesses should appoint a DPO where processing operations exceed "more than 5000 data subjects in any consecutive 12-month period" (European Parliament 2014). As far as this provision is concerned, it seems that the Council sided with businesses – it deleted the mandatory nature of the DPO. By doing so, the Council not only awarded data controllers (and processors) with more flexibility when it comes to appointing a DPO but also with a possibility to save on personnel costs. This being said, it should be noted that a DPO would be responsible for a company's compliance with the EU data protection framework and for handling data subjects' access requests. The latter point is often undermined, yet it is in the interest of data subjects that companies appoint a DPO – a contact person – who would essentially facilitate the exercise of individuals' rights to access, rectification and deletion of the collected personal data.

Prior Authorisation and Prior Consultation: Adding a Layer of Accountability. Getting rid of the prior notification requirement to the DPAs was one of the objectives of the EU data protection reform. Primarily this change was considered in the business context because it would allow cutting the costs of the administration and speed up the decision-making process of new processing operations. In fact, the prior notification requirement is not deemed to be a tool protecting data subjects' rights, but rather a way for a DPA to learn about the scale and scope of data processing operations in its jurisdiction. Accordingly, the purpose of prior authorisation or prior consultation is fundamentally different from the current prior notification to the DPA. Prior authorisation or consultation would be limited to situations where a DPIA would conclude that the processing operations pose high risks to data subjects' rights. In response to requests for a consultation, DPAs could issue recommendations on how to address and mitigate specific data protection risks. These recommendations could in turn foster the protection of data subjects' rights.

The Parliament supported such a measure, yet it suggested limiting it to situations where the controller and processor did not appoint a DPO, or where the DPO or DPIA would have concluded that such consultation is necessary. The Council amendments on the other hand wreck the rationale of Article 34 and the concept of prior checking as set forth in Article 20 of Directive 95/46/EC. The Council suggested making the consultation of the DPA mandatory only for the controllers (and not processors) "in the absence of measures to be taken by the controller to mitigate the risk" ( ). In practice, however, such a situation seems highly unlikely.

Data Security Requirements for Controllers and Processors: Secure Processing.
The draft Regulation listed the implementation of data security requirements among the accountability mechanisms for controllers in Article 22. However, Article 30 requires both controllers and processors to take appropriate technical and organisational measures that would ensure adequate security of personal data. Both the Parliament and the Council supported this provision and added that those measures should be proportional and take into consideration the state of the art of available technology. The Parliament further specified this obligation by requiring controllers and processors to have a security policy, which would "ensure the ongoing confidentiality, integrity, availability and resilience of systems and services processing personal data" (European Parliament 2014). It could be argued that this attribution of responsibilities between controllers and processors benefits both business and citizens. Indeed, the Regulation will force processors to step up and accept their share of responsibility for the implementation of accountability and the compliance with the data security requirements.

4.3   Accountability is a Burden for Business: In Need of Deep Pockets

While it is argued that the general accountability article will create a data protection culture within companies, it can be speculated that those prescriptive obligations would significantly increase the administrative burden and costs of compliance for businesses (BEUC 2012). For instance, the Dutch delegation to the Council of the EU has estimated that the obligatory documentation, the DPIA and the designation of a data protection officer would result in a significant (up to double) increase of compliance costs for businesses (Council of the EU 2014 (September)). Due to the potential increase of business costs, the proposed article was especially criticised by representatives of small and medium enterprises ("SMEs"). For example, the European Small Business Alliance ("ESBA"), an NGO representing the interests of SMEs, considered an obligation to conduct a DPIA appropriate only if the processing of data is part of the SME's core activity. It also pointed out that the appointment of a DPO would unrealistically burden newly set up SMEs.

Indeed, businesses will not be keen on implementing such obligations, unless there are strong incentives for doing so (e.g., a reduction of fines or limitation of their liability in case of a data breach). On several occasions, the Working Party examined the extent to which DPAs should take into consideration a data controller's implementation attempts when deciding on an appropriate sanction. As per the Working Party, merely implementing the principle does not imply compliance of a data controller with data protection legislation (WP173). In other words, the implementation of various accountability measures would not exempt data controllers or processors from law enforcement actions. At the same time, perhaps each national DPA could clarify its position on this matter.

5   Conclusion

This contribution has provided an overview of discussions surrounding the accountability principle as introduced in Article 22 of the General Data Protection Regulation. The chapter went beyond the mere description of the initial EC text and provided insights into the debates of the EU legislators on the accountability provision. As the final text of the General Data Protection is available, it can be concluded that the foreseen potential of the general accountability article has been significantly reduced. The final wording of Article 22 to some extent reiterates Article 30 governing issues related to the security of processing, whereas it was expected that the proposed provision would mark a shift from a reactive to proactive approach regarding the protection of personal data.

While the general accountability provision is limited to controllers, the EC (in its initial proposal) included processors in several of the articles specifying accountability measures (i.e., documentation, DPIA, prior authorisation or prior consultation of the supervisory authority, appointment of a DPO and security). The authors are inclined to believe that having formal legal accountability requirements for both processors and controllers would be an ideal situation. Indeed, only the clear attribution of responsibilities between the actors involved in data processing operations would have benefited the protection of a data subject's rights and freedoms. Other changes concerning Article 22 (i.e., deletion of the non-exhaustive list and removal of a requirement to "adopt policies") may have no significant impact on data subjects' rights or on business because the subsequent provisions in Chapter IV outlining obligations of controllers and processors further clarify accountability mechanisms.

Article 22 now entails a flexible, risk based-approach, which requires data controllers to implement appropriate organisational and technical measures and be able to demonstrate such measures. Considering the expectations and the final text of this provision, it can be suggested that the accountability principle, as formulated in the political agreement among the EU legislators, signifies the need to re-open a wider debate on the scope and meaning of accountability in the field of data protection.

Acknowledgments. This paper was made possible by the funding of the EU Seventh Framework Programme projects: the PARIS project (PrivAcy pReserving Infrastructure for Surveillance), grant no. 312504; the EPISECC project (Establish Pan-European information space to Enhance seCurity of Citizens), grant no. 607078; and the PREEMPTIVE project (Preventive Methodology and Tools to Protect Utilities), grant no. 607093. It also received funding from the IWT in the context of the SBO project on Security and Privacy for Online Social Networks (SPION) (www.spion.me), as well as the Flemish research institute iMinds (www.iminds.be).

References

Alhadeff, J., Van Alsenoy, B., Dumortier, J.: The accountability principle in data protection regulation: origin, development and future directions. In: Guagnin, D., Hempel, L., Ilten, C., Kroener, I., Neyland, D., Postigo, H. (eds.) Managing Privacy through Accountability. Springer (2012)

Article 29 Working Party Working Party, The Future of Privacy: Joint contribution to the Consultation of the European Commission on the legal framework for the fundamental right to protection of personal data (WP168)

Article 29 Data Protection Working Party, Opinion 3/2010 on the principle of accountability (WP173)

Article 29 Data Protection Working Party, Opinion 03/2013 on purpose limitation (WP203)

Article 29 Data Protection Working Party, Opinion 06/2014 on the Notion of legitimate interests of the data controller under Article 7 of Directive 95/46/EC (WP217)

Article 29 Data Protection Working Party, Statement on the role of a risk based approach in data protection legal frameworks (WP218)

Association of European Chambers of Commerce (EUROCHAMBRES), EC proposal for a General Data Protection Regulation (2012). http://www.eurochambres.eu/objects/1/Files/PositionPaperDataProtectionRegulation.pdf

BEUC the European Consumer Organisation (BEUC), Data Protection Proposal for a Regulation BEUC Position Paper (2012). https://epic.org/privacy/BEUC-Position-Paper.pdf

Bennett, C.: International Privacy Standards: Can Accountability Be Adequate? Privacy Laws and Business International, vol. 106 (2010)

Bennett, C.: The accountability approach to privacy and data protection: assumptions and caveats. In: Guagnin, D., Hempel, L., Ilten, C., Kroener, I., Neyland, D., Postigo H. (eds.) Managing Privacy through Accountability. Springer (2012)

Bovens, M.: Two Concepts of Accountability: Accountability as a Virtue and as a Mechanism, West European Politics, pp. 946–967 (2010)

Council of the EU, Delegations Comments on Risk Based Approach (12267/2/14), 2 September 2014. http://register.consilium.europa.eu/doc/srv?l=EN&f=ST%2012267%202014%20REV%202

Council of Europe, Modernisation proposals adopted by the 29th Plenary meeting (2012)

Council of Europe, Ad Hoc Committee on Data Protection (CAHDATA), Working Document on Convention 108 with Additional Protocol and Modernisation proposals, Strasbourg, 25 March 2014

Council of the EU, Risk Based Approach (11481/14 July 3, 2014). http://register.consilium.europa.eu/doc/srv?l=EN&f=ST%2011481%202014%20INIT

Council of the EU, Proposal for a Regulation of the European Parliament and of the Council on the protection of individuals with regard to the processing of personal data and on the free movement of such data (General Data Protection Regulation) - Chapter IV (12312/14 August 1, 2014). http://register.consilium.europa.eu/doc/srv?l=EN&f=ST%2012312%202014%20INIT

Council of the EU, Proposal for a Regulation of the European Parliament and of the Council on the protection of individuals with regard to the processing of personal data and on the free movement of such data (General Data Protection Regulation) - Preparation of a general approach (9565/15 June 11, 2015). http://data.consilium.europa.eu/doc/document/ST-9565-2015-INIT/en/pdf

De Hert, P.: From the principle of accountability to system responsibility key concepts in data protection law and human rights discussions. In: Guagnin, D., Hempel, L., Ilten, C., Kroener, I., Neyland, D., Postigo, H. (eds.) Managing Privacy through Accountability. Springer (2012)

Directive 95/46/EC of the European Parliament and of the Council of October 24, 1995 on the Protection of Individuals with Regard to the Processing of Personal Data and on the Free Movement of Such Data (O.J. L 281 31) (Directive 95/46/EC)

EC, Proposal for a Regulation of the European Parliament and of the Council on the protection of individuals with regard to the processing of personal data and on the free movement of such data (General Data Protection Regulation), January 2012a

EC, Explanatory Memorandum to the proposal for a General Data Protection Regulation, 20 January 2012b, 10. http://eur-lex.europa.eu/legal-content/EN/TXT/PDF/?uri=CELEX: 52012PC0011&from=en

European Conference of Data Protection Authorities, Resolution on the revision of the Convention for the Protection of Individuals with regard to Automatic Processing of Personal Data (Convention 108), Strasbourg, 5 June 2014

European Data Protection Supervisor (EDPS), Opinion 4/2015 Towards a new digital ethics

European Digital Rights (EDRi), Everything you need to know about the Data Protection Regulation (2012). http://protectmydata.eu/topics/tasks-and-obligations/

European Parliament, Legislative resolution of 12 March 2014 on the proposal for a regulation of the European Parliament and of the Council on the protection of individuals with regard to the processing of personal data and on the free movement of such data (General Data Protection Regulation) (COM(2012)0011 – C7-0025/2012 – 2012/0011(COD))

OECD: The Recommendation of the Council concerning Guidelines Governing the Protection of Privacy and Transborder Flows. amended on 11 July 2013. http://www.oecd.org/sti/ieconomy/oecd_privacy_framework.pdf

Raab, C.: The Meaning of 'Accountability' in the information privacy context. In: Guagnin, D., Hempel, L., Ilten, C., Kroener, I., Neyland, D., Postigo, H. (eds.) Managing Privacy through Accountability, vol. 1–27. Palgrave Macmillan (2012)

Wright, D., Gellert, R., Gutwirth, S., Friedewald, M.: Precaution and privacy impact assessment as modes towards risk governance. In: Von Schomberg, R. (ed.) Towards Responsible Research and Innovation in the Information and Communication Technologies and Security Technologies Fields. Publications Office of the European Union, Luxembourg (2011)

Towards Authenticity and Privacy Preserving Accountable Workflows

David Derler[1]($\boxtimes$), Christian Hanser[1], Henrich C. Pöhls[2], and Daniel Slamanig[1]

[1] IAIK, Graz University of Technology, Graz, Austria
{david.derler,christian.hanser,daniel.slamanig}@tugraz.at
[2] Institute of IT-Security and Security Law and Chair of IT-Security,
University of Passau, Passau, Germany
hp@sec.uni-passau.de

Abstract. Efficient and well structured business processes (and their corresponding workflows) are drivers for the success of modern enterprises. Today, we experience the growing trends to have IT supported workflows and to outsource enterprise IT to the cloud. Especially when executing (interorganizational) business processes on third party infrastructure such as the cloud, the correct execution and documentation become very important issues. To efficiently manage those processes, to immediately detect deviations from the intended workflows and to hold tenants (such as the cloud) accountable in such (decentralized) processes, a mechanism for efficient and accountable monitoring and documentation is highly desirable. Ideally, these features are provided by means of cryptography in contrast to organizational measures.

It turns out that variants of *malleable* signature schemes, i.e., signature schemes where *allowed modifications* of signed documents do not invalidate the signature, as well as *proxy (functional)* signature schemes, i.e., signature schemes which allow the *delegation of signing rights* to other parties, seem to be a useful tool in this context. In this paper, we review the state of the art in this field, abstractly model such workflow scenarios, investigate desirable properties, analyze existing instantiations of aforementioned signature schemes with respect to these properties, and identify interesting directions for future research.

1 Introduction

To efficiently handle frequently recurring processes within enterprises, it is advantageous to define standardized business processes. An ICT supported technical realization of a business process is usually denoted as a workflow [30]. Such a workflow can be seen as an abstract process, which defines a certain sequence of tasks as well as conditions on how participating entities have to complete these tasks. In such a context, workflows may span various departments within an enterprise or even various enterprises (interorganizational workflows).

The authors have been supported by EU H2020 project PRISMACLOUD, grant agreement no. 644962.

To always have an overview of the current state of concrete workflow instances and to be able to react to deviations from the defined workflows, it is important to document each step and to report it to some entity. Thereby, an inherent requirement is that these reports allow to verify whether delegatees acted within their boundaries and that each task can be attributed to a certain delegatee. This shall hold true especially if the process is interorganizational. In addition, it is desireable to automatically derive information, e.g., to issue warnings if certain constraints in a workflow are not met. Furthermore, it is often required that documentations of certain workflows are retained in an unforgeable recording for auditing or legal purposes. For example, the European data protection law requires an organization to document the usage of data [6]. However, the boundaries within each participating entity can act in a workflow might already be a sensitive business internal. Hence, it should not be disclosed to other parties (e.g., other enterprises in interorganizational workflows). Thus, an additional requirement is that the defined boundaries are not revealed to entities verifying a report, i.e., to ensure privacy, while still being able to check whether delegatees acted within their boundaries. We stress that this goal is in contrast to confidentiality of task reports. In particular, privacy requires that—even when the task reports are available in plain—the defined boundaries are not recoverable.

A suitable application is outsourcing inter- or intra-enterprise workflows to some environment that is not under full control, e.g., to the cloud. An automated process outsourced to the cloud may then run on behalf of the participants to carry out a task within such a workflow. A participating enterprise will be interested in the correctness of the workflow, the compliance with associated privacy requirements and to hold the cloud accountable. We note that especially in context of accountability there are significant efforts to provide and standardize frameworks for cloud accountability, e.g., as demonstrated within the A4CLOUD project [44]. We note that we are interested in a more abstract view on workflows and cryptographic tools that allow to realize the aforementioned requirements.

1.1 Related Work

Besides [34,39,40], not much attention has been paid to cryptographically enforcing certain properties of workflows. Subsequently, we review the existing approaches and other related concepts.

In [39,40], the authors investigate traceability and integrity aspects of decentralized interorganizational workflow executions. This work focuses on preserving authenticity and integrity with respect to logical relations (AND, OR, XOR) among certain tasks in a priori defined workflows, while the concrete agents executing the workflow tasks do not need to be pre-specified (these could be dynamically chosen with the help of some discovery service). To do so, they use policy-based cryptography [4], where every agent gets issued credentials from some central authorities (specifying attributes that the agent satisfies). Then, for each workflow step a policy defines what needs to be satisfied for the execution of the respective task (basically the required decryption keys can only be obtained if the policy is satisfied). In addition they use group signatures to guarantee anonymity of honest agents, but support traceability of malicious ones.

In contrast, [34] allows to dynamically define those workflows during the workflow execution. That is, they map the workflow to a (dynamically extendable) tree, where each node in the tree is interpreted as one particular workflow task. Then, building upon the hierarchical identity based signature scheme in [35], one can build a hierarchy of signing keys (i.e., each node in possession of a signing key can issue signing keys for its child nodes). These signing keys are then used to sign some task-dependent information and, due to the hierarchical nature of the underlying primitive, this delivers an authentic documentation of the workflow execution regarding the logical relations among subsequent tasks.

Orthogonal to our goals of authenticity, accountability and privacy, variants of attribute-based encryption were used for cryptographically ensured access control with respect to some policy in [2,22,43]. Recent work [21], thereby, also considers the possibility to hide the access policy.

Somehow close to our goal is [28], but it does not target the enforcement of properties of workflows. However, the authors use malleable signatures to allow to remove (potentially confidential) information from signed data, while not influencing source authentication in service oriented architectures (SOAs). In their approach, workflow participants exchange signed data based on predecessor-successor relationships. This is not what we are looking for in this case.

Finally, the work done in this paper relates to data provenance, which deals with identifying the origins of data and also giving a record of the derivation [41]. More precisely, this work relates to the aspect of process documentation found in data provenance, i.e., the proposed solutions will allow to verify whether a certain workflow was carried out as intended. This and other aspects of data provenance have been surveyed and studied in the literature, for example in [23,42,47]. Our work may be considered as realizing some aspects of provenance with cryptographic guarantees, i.e., to ensure that any deviation from a planned workflow will be detectable and that each workflow participant can be held accountable for it's actions.

1.2   Motivation and Contribution

The few existing approaches to authenticity, accountability and privacy in workflows [34,39,40] rely on rather non-standard and often complex schemes. Given the importance of outsourcing computations and processes to cloud providers, it is thus an interesting challenge to look for simpler and more efficient solutions that rely on standard cryptographic primitives.

We propose two generic patterns to document the workflow executions, which can be instantiated using various different signature primitives. These patterns follow the well-known *delegation-by-certificate* approach from proxy signatures [37], and—in contrast to existing solutions—allow to obtain particularly efficient schemes which only make use of standard cryptographic primitives with multiple efficient instantiations. In addition to existing work, which only considers tasks from an abstract point of view, we also consider the outputs of tasks and their corresponding documentation (reports).[1] In this context, we discuss means to predefine the structure of reports to ease an automated processing and also cover related privacy issues. We develop a set of requirements for workflow documentation systems and analyze possible instantiations of our generic patterns from different types of signature schemes with respect to these requirements. Finally, we discuss open problems and future directions.

2   Preliminaries

Throughout the paper we require the notion of digital signature schemes, which we recall subsequently. A digital signature scheme (DSS) is a triple KeyGen, Sign, Verify) of efficient algorithms. Thereby, KeyGen is a probabilistic key generation algorithm that takes a security parameter $\kappa \in \mathbb{N}$ as input and outputs a secret (signing) key sk and a public (verification) key pk. Further, Sign is a (probabilistic) algorithm, which takes a message $M \in \{0,1\}^*$ and a secret key sk as input, and outputs a signature σ. Finally, Verify is a deterministic algorithm, which takes a signature σ, a message $M \in \{0,1\}^*$ and a public key pk as input, and outputs a single bit $b \in \{0,1\}$ indicating whether σ is a valid signature for M under pk.

A digital signature scheme is required to be *correct*, i.e., for all security parameters κ, all (sk, pk) generated by KeyGen and all $M \in \{0,1\}^*$ one requires Verify(Sign(M, sk), M, pk) = 1. Additionally, for security one requires existential unforgeability under adaptively chosen-message attacks (EUF-CMA) [24].

3   Workflow Model

In the following we align our notation largely with the one used in [34]. A *workflow* W comprises some central entity called the *workflow manager* (WM) who wants to outsource a workflow to some set A of entities denoted as *agents*. Thereby, every workflow can be decomposed into single atomic *tasks* $t_i \in T$, where every task is executed by some agent. For instance, task $t_i \in T$ may be executed by agent $A_j \in A$, which we denote by $A_j(t_i)$.

As it is common when modeling workflows (e.g., [29]), we define a workflow as a directed acyclic graph $W = (T, E)$, where each vertex $t_i \in T$ represents one particular task and edges $e_j \in E \subseteq T \times T$ represent task dependencies, i.e., a vertex $(t_u, t_v) \in E$ means that task t_v follows after the completion of task t_u. Now, we augment such a simple workflow by the following semantics and in the remainder of the paper we always mean such an augmented workflow when we speak of a workflow. Each vertex $t_i \in T$ with at least two outgoing edges (i.e., where outdegree $\deg^+(t_i) \geq 2$) is called a *split* and each vertex t_i with at least two incoming edges (i.e., where indegree $\deg^-(t_i) \geq 2$)) is called a *join*. Each split and join is associated with a logical type {AND,OR,XOR}. In case of an

---

[1] This could also be interesting in the context of data provenance.

AND split all edges are executed in parallel; in case of an XOR split exactly one edge must be executed; and in an OR split at least one edge needs to be executed. To illustrate this idea, we present an example of a simple workflow in Fig. 1. For ease of presentation we label each outgoing edge with the respective type.

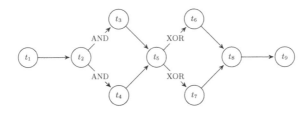

Fig. 1. A simple workflow example.

To distinguish between successful and unsuccessful workflow executions, we need the notion of a *trace*. A trace τ of a workflow is a sequence of tasks in the order of their execution and a trace is called *valid* if it is compatible with the workflow. Let us look at the example in Fig. 1. For instance, the trace $\tau = (t_1, t_2, t_3, t_5, t_7, t_8, t_9)$ is invalid, but $\tau' = (t_1, t_2, t_3, t_4, t_5, t_7, t_8, t_9)$ is a valid trace.

Another issue that needs to be addressed is that not every agent may be allowed to execute every task. Consequently, we use *assignment* $\alpha(\tau)$ to denote the sequence indicating which agents have executed the respective task. For instance, we may have $\alpha(\tau') = (A_1, A_2, A_3, A_4, A_5, A_6, A_7, A_8)$. Furthermore, either the WM may specify which potential set of agents is allowed to execute each task (*static assignment*) or each agent may dynamically decide which agents may execute the subsequent task(s) (*dynamic assignment*). In case of a static assignment, we call an assignment $\alpha(\tau')$ valid if it is compatible with the restrictions set by the WM. We note that our above notation deviates from the one in [34] who only consider dynamic assignments. Also, in contrast to [34] who solely look at the tasks in a workflow from a very abstract level, we are also interested in properties of the outputs of the tasks and thus get a bit more concrete. Therefore, we introduce the notion of the documentation of one particular task in a workflow and denote it as the report of a task, or *report* in short.

Subsequently, we introduce desirable properties for the documentation of workflow executions. Firstly, the most crucial requirement in our setting is that reports are protected against unauthorized modifications. Recall, that we do not consider the orthogonal feature of providing confidentiality for workflow data.

Requirement 1. *The integrity of the reports needs to be ensured.*

Furthermore, it is required that only the workflow manager and the execution agent, which is actually performing a certain task, can produce a valid report.

Requirement 2. *For a particular task t_i, no one except the workflow manager and the agent(s) assigned to t_i is/are capable of creating task reports that are accepted by an auditor.*

In this context, it is also important that each report can be used to identify the respective execution agent (workflow manager), i.e., to ensure accountability.

Requirement 3. *The execution agent (workflow manager) that performs a certain task can be held accountable for its actions.*

However, as long as the work is done correctly, a delegator might want to account for the work of a delegatee, while still being able to accuse the delegatee in case of a dispute.[2]

Requirement 4. *One can not publicly verify whether a delegator or a delegatee created a certain report, while it is still possible to provide a proof assigning the task execution to one of the aforementioned parties.*

In addition, it is desirable to *automatically derive information*, e.g., to issue warnings if certain constraints in a workflow are not met.

Requirement 5. *Task reports allow to derive the order of the tasks in a certain workflow instance.*

3.1   Bringing Signatures to Workflows

We can model workflows using the well-known *delegation-by-certificate* approach from proxy signatures [37]. Subsequently, we describe two useful patterns.

Static Assignment. Figure 2 illustrates the pattern for a statically assigned workflow. Here, the workflow manager computes a signature σ_0 on a sequence of (sets of) public keys PK together with the respective split/join operations.

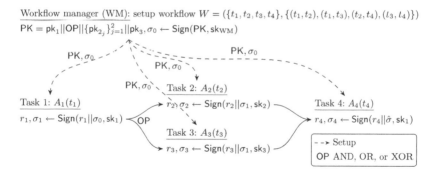

Fig. 2. Pattern for statically assigned workflows. The tuples (r_i, σ_i) denote the task reports corresponding to $A_i(t_i)$. If OP = AND then $\hat{\sigma} \leftarrow \sigma_2 || \sigma_3$, if OP = OR then $\hat{\sigma} \leftarrow \sigma_2$, $\hat{\sigma} \leftarrow \sigma_3$, or $\hat{\sigma} \leftarrow \sigma_2 || \sigma_3$, if OP = XOR then $\hat{\sigma} \leftarrow \sigma_2$ or $\hat{\sigma} \leftarrow \sigma_3$.

---

[2] When following the paradigm in Fig. 2, the workflow manager is the delegator, whereas the agents are the delegatees. In contrast, following the paradigm in Fig. 3, agents act as both, delegatees and delegators, while only the first delegation is performed by the workflow manager.

Then, for each task, (one of) the authorized agent(s) can sign the respective report using its secret key sk_i corresponding to the public key pk_i in PK. To be able to reconstruct the order of the task executions, agent A_j also includes the signature(s) of the agent(s) executing the preceding tasks in its signature σ_i.

Dynamic Assignment. Figure 3 describes the pattern for dynamically assigned workflows. In this approach, the workflow manager only delegates to the first agent within the workflow and the agents can further delegate the execution rights for subsequent tasks to subsequent agents.

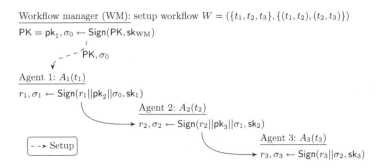

Workflow manager (WM): setup workflow $W = (\{t_1, t_2, t_3\}, \{(t_1, t_2), (t_2, t_3)\})$
$PK = pk_1, \sigma_0 \leftarrow Sign(PK, sk_{WM})$

PK, σ_0

Agent 1: $A_1(t_1)$
$r_1, \sigma_1 \leftarrow Sign(r_1\|pk_2\|\sigma_0, sk_1)$

Agent 2: $A_2(t_2)$
$r_2, \sigma_2 \leftarrow Sign(r_2\|pk_3\|\sigma_1, sk_2)$

Agent 3: $A_3(t_3)$
$r_3, \sigma_3 \leftarrow Sign(r_3\|\sigma_2, sk_3)$

$--\rightarrow$ Setup

Fig. 3. Pattern for dynamically assigned workflows. The tuples (r_i, σ_i) denote the task reports corresponding to $A_i(t_i)$. For simplicity, we omit split/join (cf. Fig. 2).

3.2   Structuring Task Reports

Orthogonal to the requirement to ensure logical relations among tasks, it might also be interesting to automatically verify certain constraints regarding particular decisions upon execution of a task t_i. For instance, it would be convenient to predefine certain sets of possible actions of an agent per task. As a simple realization one can think of a form containing several multiple-choice fields, where each multiple-choice field corresponds to a subtask of a specific task in a workflow. Then, an application monitoring reports can easily define constraints in the fashion of: **if** *Option A was chosen in Subtask 1.1* **and** *Option B was chosen in Subtask 1.2* **then** *issue a warning*. If required, this can easily be extended to arbitrarily complex forms per task (Fig. 4).

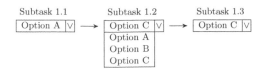

Subtask 1.1	Subtask 1.2	Subtask 1.3
Option A ∨	Option C ∨	Option C ∨
	Option A	
	Option B	
	Option C	

Fig. 4. A simple task report for a task $t_1 = (t_{1.1}, t_{1.2}, t_{1.3})$, composed of three multiple choice elements.

Adding a structure to the task reports, suggests to introduce the following additional requirements.

Requirement 6. *It is possible to predefine the structure of task reports.*

Besides addressing the structure of the report, allowing the delegatee to predefine sets of admissible choices for certain parts of task reports would help to improve the quality and help to automate the processing.

Requirement 7. *It is possible to predefine sets of admissible choices for certain fields in the task report.*

However, such detailed workflow reports also impose privacy requirements, since it is crucial that business internals remain confidential, e.g., when reports are revealed for auditing purposes.

Requirement 8. *Task reports do not reveal additional information that is available to the delegator and/or the execution agent (e.g., the unused choices of the predefined sets of admissible replacements).*

4 Instantiations

Using standard digital signatures, one can straightforwardly instantiate the patterns in Figs. 2 and 3. Subsequently, we revisit the instantiation of these patterns with other variants of digital signatures. We stress that we provide algorithmic descriptions for the schemes as we believe that this makes the presentation unambiguous and clearer than any informal textual description.

Append-Only Signatures. Append only signatures [32] allow to publicly extend signed messages and to update the signature correspondingly. An append only signature scheme (AOS) is a tuple of efficient algorithms (Setup, Append, Verify), which are defined as follows:

Setup : On input of a security parameter κ, this algorithm outputs a keypair (sk, pk), where sk constitutes the signature on the empty message.

Append : On input of a public key pk, a signature σ_{n-1} on a message $(m_1, \ldots, m_{n-1})$, and a message m_n, this algorithm outputs a signature σ_n on the message $(m_1, \ldots, m_n)$.

Verify : On input of a public key pk, a signature σ and a message $M = (m_1, \ldots, m_n)$, this algorithm outputs a bit $b \in \{0, 1\}$, indicating whether σ is valid.

For security, AOS are required to provide AOS-unforgeability under chosen message attacks. Informally this means that the only way of creating a valid signature of length n on a message $M = (m_1, \ldots, m_n)$ is to extend a valid signature on message $M' = (m_1, \ldots, m_{n-1})$.

Application to Workflows: Using append-only signatures, the workflow manager creates a signature on the empty message and each agent can append its documentation. Due to their public-append capabilities, AOS are suited for unauthorized delegations, which only ensure the integrity of the signed reports.

Redactable Signatures. Informally, redactable signatures [31,38,48] allow to sign documents, where certain predefined parts can later be blacked out (or cloaked) without signer interaction and without invalidating the signature. A redactable signature scheme (RSS) is a tuple of efficient algorithms (KeyGen, Sign, Verify, Redact), which are defined as follows (using the notation of [19]):

KeyGen : On input of a security parameter κ, this algorithm outputs a key-pair (sk, pk).

Sign : On input of a secret key sk, a message M and admissible redactions ADM, this algorithm returns a message-signature pair (M, σ) (where ADM can be derived from σ).

Verify : On input of a public key pk, a message M and a signature σ, this algorithm outputs a bit $b \in \{0, 1\}$, indicating the validity of σ.

Redact : This algorithm takes a public key pk, a signature σ, a message M and modification instructions MOD, computes an updated signature σ' and outputs an updated message signature pair $(\mathsf{MOD}(M), \sigma')$.

Essentially the redaction can be done by everyone, meaning that (1) the entity that performs the redaction is not accountable for the changes and (2) one is only able to *black out* certain document parts. For security, redactable signatures are required to be *unforgeable* and *private*.

Unforgeability captures the infeasibility to output a valid message signature pair (M, σ) without knowing sk, unless (M, σ) was obtained by redaction.

Privacy requires it to be infeasible for every efficient adversary to reconstruct the redacted message parts, given the redacted message and its signature.

See [19] for a formal security model. Besides these properties, the security model for RSS has been refined and extended several times. Firstly, [45] introduced the notion of *accountability*, which requires that signers and redactors can be held accountable for their signatures/redactions. Secondly, [14,45] independently introduced *unlinkability* for RSS as an even stronger privacy notion. *Unlinkability* essentially requires multiple redactions of the same document to be unlinkable. We, however, note that we do not further consider unlinkability here, since privacy already provides the required security guarantees in our context. We also mention that redactable signatures are related to the more general framework of P-homomorphic signatures [1].

Application to Workflows: In context of workflows, RSS can be used in two different ways:

(1) One uses RSS in the same way as conventional DSS. Then, when it is required to publish reports (e.g., for auditing purposes) it can be useful to redact certain confidential parts of the reports.

(2) Provided that all potential reports are known prior to designating a task to an agent, one could enumerate all variants of the reports and sign this list using an RSS. The agent then simply redacts—thus removes—all reports that are not required. While conventional RSS do not provide accountability in this setting, accountable RSS (ARSS) [45] can be used to additionally provide accountability.

Sanitizable Signatures. Sanitizable signatures [3,9–13,46] split messages in fixed and variable message parts and allow to issue signatures on them. A designated party (the sanitizer) is then able to modify the variable parts of the message without invalidating the signature. A sanitizable signature scheme (SSS) is a tuple of efficient algorithms ($\mathsf{KeyGen_{sig}}$, $\mathsf{KeyGen_{san}}$, Sign, Sanit, Verify, Proof, Judge). Subsequently, we recall the definitions from [9]:

$\mathsf{KeyGen_{sig}}$: On input of a security parameter κ, this algorithm outputs a signer key-pair ($\mathsf{sk_{sig}}$, $\mathsf{pk_{sig}}$).

$\mathsf{KeyGen_{san}}$: On input of a security parameter κ, this algorithm outputs a sanitizer key-pair ($\mathsf{sk_{san}}$, $\mathsf{pk_{san}}$).

Sign : On input of a message M, corresponding admissible modifications ADM, the keypair of the signer ($\mathsf{sk_{sig}}$, $\mathsf{pk_{sig}}$), as well as the verification key of the sanitizer $\mathsf{pk_{san}}$, this algorithm outputs a message-signature pair (M, σ), where it is assumed that ADM can be reconstructed from σ.

Sanit : On input of a valid message-signature pair (M, σ), modification instructions MOD, some auxiliary information aux, the verification key of the signer $\mathsf{pk_{sig}}$ and the secret key of the sanitizer $\mathsf{sk_{san}}$, this algorithm outputs an updated message signature pair ($\mathsf{MOD}(m), \sigma'$) and $\perp$ if the modification instructions are incompatible with ADM.

Verify : On input of a message-signature pair (M, σ) and the verification keys of the signer $\mathsf{pk_{sig}}$ and the sanitizer $\mathsf{pk_{san}}$, this algorithm outputs a bit $b \in \{0, 1\}$ indicating whether σ is a valid signature on M.

Proof : On input of a message-signature pair (M, σ), q message-signature pairs (M_j, σ_j)$_{j=1}^q$ created by the signer, the keypair ($\mathsf{sk_{sig}}$, $\mathsf{pk_{sig}}$) of the signer and the verification key of the sanitizer $\mathsf{pk_{san}}$, this algorithm outputs a proof π.

Judge : On input of a message-signature pair (M, σ), the verification keys of the signer $\mathsf{pk_{sig}}$ and the sanitizer $\mathsf{pk_{san}}$, and a valid a proof π, this algorithm outputs a bit $b \in \{\mathtt{sig}, \mathtt{san}\}$, indicating whether the respective signature was created by the signer or the sanitizer.

Subsequently, we informally discuss the security properties of sanitizable signatures (introduced in [3] and formalized in [9]):

Unforgeability requires that only honest signers and sanitizers are able to produce valid signatures.

Immutability requires that malicious sanitizers are not able to modify fixed message parts.

Transparency requires that no one (except the signer and the sanitizer) can distinguish signatures of the signer from signatures of the sanitizer.

Privacy requires that no one (except the signer and the sanitizer) can recover sanitized information.

Signer-/Sanitizer-accountability Requires that no signer can falsely accuse a sanitizer of having created a certain signature and vice versa.

The above properties have seen some refinement and gradual extension since their formalization in [9], e.g., by [12,13,16,20,25,33,45].

In [33], among others, an extension that additionally allows to define sets of admissible replacements per message block (LimitSet) was introduced and later formalized in [15] (henceforth called extended sanitizable signatures or ESSS). Their formalization, however, does not require the sets of admissible modifications to remain concealed upon verification, and, thus, does not define privacy in the original sense. Thus, [20] introduced the notion of *strong privacy*, that additionally covers this requirement. In [20], it is also shown that ESSS providing strong privacy can be black-box constructed from every secure SSS in the model of [9] and indistinguishable accumulators [18].

Orthogonal to that, [13] discusses that accountability can be modeled in two ways: non-interactive or interactive. The model presented above is tailored to interactive (non-public) accountability. In contrast, non-interactive (public) accountability requires that Judge works correctly on an empty proof π.[3] We emphasize that non-interactive accountability might be helpful in workflows, where the original signer can not be involved for certain reasons, e.g., efficiency.

Application to Workflows: By definition, SSS include a delegation mechanism, i.e., a signer grants a sanitizer permission to modify certain parts of a signed message without invalidating the signature. Thus, using this primitive, one can not only pre-specify the execution agent, but also the structure of the report.[4] In other words, SSS allow to split the report into several fields; then, according to the pre-defined workflow, one specifies which agent (i.e., by specifying the sanitizer) is allowed to put arbitrary content into certain fields of the report. In addition, SSS provide *transparency*, which is useful if it is required to hide whether a certain task was outsourced or not. In case of a dispute, the {Proof, Judge} algorithms still guarantee accountability. In case the additional level of privacy given by transparency is not needed, one can use non-interactively (publicly) accountable SSS, e.g., [12,13].

ESSS [15]: Extended sanitizable signatures, as defined in [15], extend SSS by the possibility to limit the admissible modifications per message block to sets of allowed messages. This allows for an even more fine grained definition of the report structure. However, the model of [15] does not require the unused choices in the sets of admissible modifications to remain hidden upon verification. While this extension eases the automatic processing of reports, the limited privacy features limit the practical applicability of this instantiation.

---

[3] Note that this obviously contradicts transparency, meaning that no scheme can be transparent and non-interactively accountable at the same time.

[4] Using SSS supporting multiple sanitizers [16], one can even pre-specify multiple possible agents for a single task.

ESSS [20]: Extended sanitizable signatures, as defined in [20], fix the aforementioned privacy problems, which, in turn, extends their applicability to workflow documentation systems.

Proxy Signatures. Proxy signature (PS) schemes, introduced in [37] and formalized in [7] allow a delegator to delegate the signing rights for a certain message
space $\mathcal{M}$ to a proxy. A proxy can then produce signatures for messages $m \in \mathcal{M}$
on behalf of the delegator. Subsequently, we recall the definitions from [7]:

(D, P) : The originator and the proxy jointly compute a delegation for the message space $\mathcal{M}$ as well as a proxy signing key skp. The originator runs D and
outputs the delegation σ computed using its signing key sk_i, whereas the
proxy verifies the delegation and obtains the proxy signing key skp, which
consists of its private signing key sk_j and the originators delegation.

Sign : This algorithm computes and outputs a proxy signature σ_P for message
$m \in \mathcal{M}$ using the proxy signing key skp.

Verify : This algorithm verifies whether proxy signature σ_P is a valid proxy signature for message m under pk_j, delegated by pk_i. On success, this algorithm
outputs 1, and 0 otherwise.

ID : This algorithm outputs the identity j of the proxy, when given a proxy
signature σ_P.

For security, proxy signatures are required to be *unforgeable*, which informally
means that no one can produce valid signatures for messages $m \notin \mathcal{M}$ and only
the designated proxy can produce valid signatures for $m \in \mathcal{M}$. In [27], the
model was extended by introducing *privacy*, which essentially requires that—
upon verification of a signature σ_P on a message $m \in \mathcal{M}$—the verifier learns
nothing about $\mathcal{M}$ (except that $m \in \mathcal{M}$). Signatures secure in this model are
called warrant-hiding proxy signatures (WHPS). We note that proxy signatures
are one instantiation of the more general concept of functional signatures [5,8].

Application to Workflows: Here, a delegator grants a proxy the signing rights for
messages out of a certain message space $\mathcal{M}$. This delegation mechanism can be
used to predefine all possible reports and the executing agent only chooses the
suitable report. In addition, WHPS additionally provide privacy with respect to
the unused reports in the designated message space.

Blank Digital Signatures. Blank digital signatures, introduced in [26], allow
an originator O to define and sign forms (so-called templates $\mathcal{T}$) consisting of
fixed and exchangeable (multiple-choice) elements. These forms can then be filled
in (instantiated) by a designated party (the proxy P). Upon verification, the verifier only learns the values chosen by the designated party. A blank digital signature scheme (BDSS) is a tuple of efficient algorithms (KeyGen, Sign, Verify$_T$, Inst,
Verify$_I$), which are introduced subsequently. Thereby, we assume that DSS signing keys for the originator (sk_O, pk_O) and the proxy (sk_P, pk_P) already exist.

KeyGen : On input of a security parameter κ and an upper bound for the template
size t, this algorithm outputs public parameters pp. We assume pp to be an
implicit input to all subsequent algorithms.

Sign : On input of a template $\mathcal{T}$, the signing key of the originator $\mathsf{sk_O}$ and the verification key of the proxy $\mathsf{pk_P}$, this algorithm outputs a template signature $\sigma_{\mathcal{T}}$ and a secret instantiation key $\mathsf{sk_P^{\mathcal{T}}}$ for the proxy.

Verify$_\mathsf{T}$: On input of a template $\mathcal{T}$, a template signature $\sigma_{\mathcal{T}}$, the instantiation key of the proxy $\mathsf{sk_P^{\mathcal{T}}}$ and the public verification keys of the originator $\mathsf{pk_O}$ and the proxy $\mathsf{pk_P}$, this algorithm outputs a bit $b \in \{0, 1\}$, indicating whether $\sigma_{\mathcal{T}}$ is valid.

Inst : On input of a template $\mathcal{T}$, a template signature $\sigma_{\mathcal{T}}$, an instance $\mathcal{M}$, the signing key $\mathsf{sk_P}$ and the instantiation key $\mathsf{sk_P^{\mathcal{T}}}$ of the proxy, this algorithm outputs an instance signature $\sigma_{\mathcal{M}}$ on $\mathcal{M}$ if $\mathcal{M}$ is a valid instance of $\mathcal{T}$ and $\perp$ otherwise.

Verify$_\mathsf{I}$: On input of an instance $\mathcal{M}$, an instance signature $\sigma_{\mathcal{M}}$ and the verification keys of the originator $\mathsf{pk_O}$ and the proxy $\mathsf{pk_P}$, this algorithm outputs a bit $b \in \{0, 1\}$, indicating whether $\sigma_{\mathcal{M}}$ is valid.

The security requirements for BDSS are (informally) defined as follows:

Unforgeability requires that only the honest originator and proxy can create valid signatures.

Immutability requires that even malicious proxies cannot create instance signatures for invalid instances $\mathcal{M}$ of $\mathcal{T}$.

Privacy requires that no one (except the proxy and the originator) can recover the unused choices for the exchangeable elements.

Application to Workflows: BDSS are—up to the missing transparency and accountability properties—similar to ESSS in [20] and can, thus, be used for similar purposes. We note that all known instantiations of BDSS [17,26] provide public accountability, since they require an explicit signature of the delegatee (proxy).

4.1   Comparison and Discussion

In Table 1, we bring the various possible instantiations discussed above into the context of the previously defined requirements, where we exclude naive instantiations. Depending on the used scheme, we can cover different subsets of previously posed requirements. While choosing a concrete instantiation always depends on the requirements, we note that ESSS and BDSS seem to be particularly well suited for the considered applications. Note that—mainly due to the imposed overhead—we do not consider naive solutions such as achieving Requirements 6 and 7 by enumerating all possible task reports. We again stress that the instantiations discussed in this paper are very simple and only make use of standard cryptographic primitives with multiple efficient instantiations. Thereby, we only require to assume the existence of some public key authority.

Outlook. In this paper we have discussed potential solutions for authentic and accountable, yet privacy maintaining documentation of outsourced workflows. While we, thereby, followed a rather high-level and informal approach, it would

Table 1. Requirements covered by the respective instantiations. Legend: ✓... supported, A... supported by ARSS [45], †... if scheme is transparent

Inst.	R1	R2	R3	R4	R5	R6	R7	R8
DSS	✓	✓	✓		✓			
AOS	✓				✓			
RSS (1)	✓	✓	✓		✓			✓
RSS (2)	✓	✓	A	A†	✓			✓
SSS	✓	✓	✓	✓†	✓	✓		
ESSS [15]	✓	✓	✓	✓†	✓	✓	✓	
ESSS [20]	✓	✓	✓	✓†	✓	✓	✓	✓
PS	✓	✓	✓		✓			
WHPS	✓	✓	✓		✓			✓
BDSS	✓	✓	✓		✓	✓	✓	✓

be interesting to model the desired security properties more formally (as for instance done in [36] for cloud provenance). Furthermore, it would be interesting to evaluate the practical value of our proposed solutions in a real world setting. Finally, we note that it seems to be straight forward to extend our approach by cryptographic access control solutions (e.g., [21,22]) to restrict the access to task reports. We leave these points as future work.

References

1. Ahn, J.H., Boneh, D., Camenisch, J., Hohenberger, S., Shelat, A., Waters, B.: Computing on authenticated data. In: Cramer, R. (ed.) TCC 2012. LNCS, vol. 7194, pp. 1–20. Springer, Heidelberg (2012)
2. Al-Riyami, S.S., Malone-Lee, J., Smart, N.P.: Escrow-free encryption supporting cryptographic workflow. Int. J. Inf. Sec. **5**(4), 217–229 (2006)
3. Ateniese, G., Chou, D.H., de Medeiros, B., Tsudik, G.: Sanitizable signatures. In: di Vimercati, S.C., Syverson, P.F., Gollmann, D. (eds.) ESORICS 2005. LNCS, vol. 3679, pp. 159–177. Springer, Heidelberg (2005)
4. Bagga, W., Molva, R.: Policy-based cryptography and applications. In: FC Patrick, A.S., Yung, M. (eds.) FC 2005. LNCS, vol. 3570, pp. 72–87. Springer, Heidelberg (2005)
5. Bellare, M., Fuchsbauer, G.: Policy-based signatures. In: Krawczyk, H. (ed.) PKC 2014. LNCS, vol. 8383, pp. 520–537. Springer, Heidelberg (2014)
6. Bier, C.: How usage control and provenance tracking get together - a data protection perspective. In: IEEE Security and Privacy Workshops (SPW). IEEE (2013)
7. Boldyreva, A., Palacio, A., Warinschi, B.: Secure proxy signature schemes for delegation of signing rights. J. Cryptol. **25**(1), 57–115 (2012)
8. Boyle, E., Goldwasser, S., Ivan, I.: Functional signatures and pseudorandom functions. In: Krawczyk, H. (ed.) PKC 2014. LNCS, vol. 8383, pp. 501–519. Springer, Heidelberg (2014)

9. Brzuska, C., Fischlin, M., Freudenreich, T., Lehmann, A., Page, M., Schelbert, J., Schröder, D., Volk, F.: Security of sanitizable signatures revisited. In: Jarecki, S., Tsudik, G. (eds.) PKC 2009. LNCS, vol. 5443, pp. 317–336. Springer, Heidelberg (2009)

10. Brzuska, C., Fischlin, M., Lehmann, A., Schröder, D.: Sanitizable signatures: how to partially delegate control for authenticated data. In: BIOSIG. LNI, vol. 155 (2009)

11. Brzuska, C., Fischlin, M., Lehmann, A., Schröder, D.: Unlinkability of sanitizable signatures. In: Nguyen, P.Q., Pointcheval, D. (eds.) PKC 2010. LNCS, vol. 6056, pp. 444–461. Springer, Heidelberg (2010)

12. Brzuska, C., Pöhls, H.C., Samelin, K.: Efficient and perfectly unlinkable sanitizable signatures without group signatures. In: Katsikas, S., Agudo, I. (eds.) EuroMPI 2013. LNCS, vol. 8341, pp. 12–30. Springer, Heidelberg (2014)

13. Brzuska, C., Pöhls, H.C., Samelin, K.: Non-interactive public accountability for sanitizable signatures. In: De Capitani di Vimercati, S., Mitchell, C. (eds.) EuroPKI 2012. LNCS, vol. 7868, pp. 178–193. Springer, Heidelberg (2013)

14. Camenisch, J., Dubovitskaya, M., Haralambiev, K., Kohlweiss, M.: Composable and modular anonymous credentials: definitions and practical constructions. In: Iwata, T., Cheon, J.H. (eds.) ASIACRYPT 2015. LNCS, vol. 9453, pp. 262–288. Springer, Heidelberg (2015)

15. Canard, S., Jambert, A.: On extended sanitizable signature schemes. In: Pieprzyk, J. (ed.) CT-RSA 2010. LNCS, vol. 5985, pp. 179–194. Springer, Heidelberg (2010)

16. Canard, S., Jambert, A., Lescuyer, R.: Sanitizable signatures with several signers and sanitizers. In: Mitrokotsa, A., Vaudenay, S. (eds.) AFRICACRYPT 2012. LNCS, vol. 7374, pp. 35–52. Springer, Heidelberg (2012)

17. Derler, D., Hanser, C., Slamanig, D.: Privacy-enhancing proxy signatures from non-interactive anonymous credentials. In: Atluri, V., Pernul, G. (eds.) DBSec 2014. LNCS, vol. 8566, pp. 49–65. Springer, Heidelberg (2014)

18. Derler, D., Hanser, C., Slamanig, D.: Revisiting cryptographic accumulators, additional properties and relations to other primitives. In: Nyberg, K. (ed.) CT-RSA 2015. LNCS, vol. 9048, pp. 127–144. Springer, Heidelberg (2015)

19. Derler, D., Pöhls, H.C., Samelin, K., Slamanig, D.: A general framework for redactable signatures and new constructions. In: Kwon, S., Yun, A. (eds.) ICISC 2015. LNCS, vol. 9558, pp. 3–19. Springer, Heidelberg (2016). doi:10.1007/978-3-319-30840-1_1

20. Derler, D., Slamanig, D.: Rethinking privacy for extended sanitizable signatures and a black-box construction of strongly private schemes. In: Au, M.-H., et al. (eds.) ProvSec 2015. LNCS, vol. 9451, pp. 455–474. Springer, Heidelberg (2015). doi:10.1007/978-3-319-26059-4_25

21. Ferrara, A.L., Fuchsbauer, G., Liu, B., Warinschi, B.: Policy privacy in cryptographic access control. In: CSF. IEEE (2015)

22. Ferrara, A.L., Fuchsbauer, G., Warinschi, B.: Cryptographically enforced RBAC. In: CSF. IEEE (2013)

23. Freire, J., Koop, D., Santos, E., Silva, C.T.: Provenance for computational tasks: a survey. Comput. Sci. Eng. 10(3), 11–21 (2008)

24. Goldwasser, S., Micali, S., Rivest, R.L.: A digital signature scheme secure against adaptive chosen-message attacks. SIAM J. Comput. 17(2), 281–308 (1988)

25. Gong, J., Qian, H., Zhou, Y.: Fully-secure and practical sanitizable signatures. In: Lai, X., Yung, M., Lin, D. (eds.) Inscrypt 2010. LNCS, vol. 6584, pp. 300–317. Springer, Heidelberg (2011)

26. Hanser, C., Slamanig, D.: Blank digital signatures. In: ASIACCS. ACM (2013)
27. Hanser, C., Slamanig, D.: Warrant-hiding delegation-by-certificate proxy signature schemes. In: Paul, G., Vaudenay, S. (eds.) INDOCRYPT 2013. LNCS, vol. 8250, pp. 60–77. Springer, Heidelberg (2013)
28. Herkenhöner, R., Jensen, M., Pöhls, H.C., de Meer, H.: Towards automated processing of the right of access in inter-organizational web service compositions. In: WSBPS. IEEE (2010)
29. ISO, IEC 19510: Information Technology - Object Management Group Business Process Model and Notation (2013)
30. Jablonski, S.: On the complementarity of workflow management and business process modeling. SIGOIS Bull. **16**(1), 33–38 (1995)
31. Johnson, R., Molnar, D., Song, D., Wagner, D.: Homomorphic signature schemes. In: Preneel, B. (ed.) CT-RSA 2002. LNCS, vol. 2271, p. 244. Springer, Heidelberg (2002)
32. Kiltz, E., Mityagin, A., Panjwani, S., Raghavan, B.: Append-only signatures. In: Caires, L., Italiano, G.F., Monteiro, L., Palamidessi, C., Yung, M. (eds.) ICALP 2005. LNCS, vol. 3580, pp. 434–445. Springer, Heidelberg (2005)
33. Klonowski, M., Lauks, A.: Extended sanitizable signatures. In: Rhee, M.S., Lee, B. (eds.) ICISC 2006. LNCS, vol. 4296, pp. 343–355. Springer, Heidelberg (2006)
34. Lim, H.W., Kerschbaum, F., Wang, H.: Workflow signatures for business process compliance. IEEE Trans. Dependable Sec. Comput. **9**(5), 756–769 (2012)
35. Lim, H.W., Paterson, K.G.: Multi-key hierarchical identity-based signatures. In: Galbraith, S.D. (ed.) Cryptography and Coding 2007. LNCS, vol. 4887, pp. 384–402. Springer, Heidelberg (2007)
36. Lu, R., Lin, X., Liang, X., Shen, X.S.: Secure provenance: the essential of bread and butter of data forensics in cloud computing. In: ASIACCS. ACM (2010)
37. Mambo, M., Usuda, K., Okamoto, E.: Proxy signatures for delegating signing operation. In: CCS. ACM (1996)
38. Miyazaki, K., Iwamura, M., Matsumoto, T., Sasaki, R., Yoshiura, H., Tezuka, S., Imai, H.: Digitally signed document sanitizing scheme with disclosure condition control. IEICE Trans. Fundam. Electron. Commun. Comput. Sci. **88–A**(1), 239–246 (2005)
39. Montagut, F., Molva, R.: Enforcing integrity of execution in distributed workflow management systems. In: SCC. IEEE (2007)
40. Montagut, F., Molva, R.: Traceability and integrity of execution in distributed workflow management systems. In: Biskup, J., López, J. (eds.) ESORICS 2007. LNCS, vol. 4734, pp. 251–266. Springer, Heidelberg (2007)
41. Moreau, L., Groth, P., Miles, S., Vazquez-Salceda, J., Ibbotson, J., Jiang, S., Munroe, S., Rana, O., Schreiber, A., Tan, V., et al.: The provenance of electronic data. Commun. ACM **51**(4), 52–58 (2008)
42. Moreau, L., Ludäscher, B., Altintas, I., Barga, R.S., Bowers, S., Callahan, S., Chin, G., Clifford, B., Cohen, S., Cohen-Boulakia, S., et al.: Special issue: the first provenance challenge. Concurr. Comput. Pract. Exp. **20**(5), 409–418 (2008)
43. Paterson, K.: Cryptography from pairings: a snapshot of current research. Inf. Secur. Tech. Rep. **7**(3), 41–54 (2002)
44. Pearson, S., Tountopoulos, V., Catteddu, D., Südholt, M., Molva, R., Reich, C., Fischer-Hübner, S., Millard, C., Lotz, V., Jaatun, M.G., Leenes, R., Rong, C., Lopez, J.: Accountability for cloud and other future internet services. In: CloudCom. IEEE (2012)
45. Pöhls, H.C., Samelin, K.: Accountable redactable signatures. In: ARES. IEEE (2015)

46. Pöhls, H.C., Samelin, K., Posegga, J.: Sanitizable signatures in XML signature — performance, mixing properties, and revisiting the property of transparency. In: Lopez, J., Tsudik, G. (eds.) ACNS 2011. LNCS, vol. 6715, pp. 166–182. Springer, Heidelberg (2011)
47. Simmhan, Y.L., Plale, B., Gannon, D.: A survey of data provenance in e-science. ACM Sigmod Rec. **34**(3), 31–36 (2005)
48. Steinfeld, R., Bull, L., Zheng, Y.: Content extraction signatures. In: Kim, K. (ed.) ICISC 2001. LNCS, vol. 2288, p. 285. Springer, Heidelberg (2002)

A Technique for Enhanced Provision of Appropriate Access to Evidence Across Service Provision Chains

Isaac Agudo[1], Ali El Kaafarani[2], David Nuñez[1(✉)], and Siani Pearson[3]

[1] NICS Lab, University of Malaga, Malaga, Spain
{isaac,dnunez}@lcc.uma.es
[2] Mathematical Institute, University of Oxford, Oxford, UK
ali.elkaafarani@maths.ox.ac.uk
[3] Security and Manageability Lab, Hewlett Packard Labs, Bristol, UK
siani.pearson@hp.com

Abstract. Transparency and verifiability are necessary aspects of accountability, but care needs to be taken that auditing is done in a privacy friendly way. There are situations where it would be useful for certain actors to be able to make restricted views within service provision chains on accountability evidence, including logs, available to other actors with specific governance roles. For example, a data subject or a Data Protection Authority (DPA) might want to authorize an accountability agent to act on their behalf, and be given access to certain logs in a way that does not compromise the privacy of other actors or the security of involved data processors. In this paper two cryptographic-based techniques that may address this issue are proposed and assessed.

Keywords: Accountability · Attribute based encryption · Auditing · Cloud computing · Proxy Re-Encryption

1 Introduction

There are a variety of data protection concerns related to cloud computing that include ongoing questions of jurisdiction and exacerbation of privacy risk through sub-processing and de-localisation, as well as legal uncertainty[1].

Auditing and verification of accounts by third parties are a necessary part of provision of accountability in complex service provision ecosystems, and the related building of trust [1]. However, the implementation of certain accountability measures themselves could introduce data protection risks, such as breach risks. For example, personal data would be included both in accounts and also in

---

A. El Kaafarani—Work done while at Hewlett Packard Labs.

[1] European DG of Justice (Article 29 Working Party): Opinion 05/12 on Cloud Computing (2012).

© IFIP International Federation for Information Processing 2016
Published by Springer International Publishing Switzerland 2016. All Rights Reserved
D. Aspinall et al. (Eds.): Privacy and Identity 2015, IFIP AICT 476, pp. 187–204, 2016.
DOI: 10.1007/978-3-319-41763-9_13

logs that are gathered for evidence. Hence, for both privacy and security reasons it is not the case that all actors should be able to see all logs, nor even that actors that may need to have a view on parts of certain logs in order to provide appropriate audit or verification should even be able to see all parts of those logs. This is the main problem that we address. In this paper we present and compare two novel approaches for controlling access to logs (or other forms of evidence that may be used when assessing accountability) and provide examples of their usage within cloud data transfer scenarios.

Specifically, we describe two cryptographic schemes which provide a fine-grained access control mechanism to the logged data. The different actors may be authorised to have different views on relevant log files, in various ways. For example, data subjects may disclose their data to data processors based on a privacy policy which states how their data will be processed by data processors, and who can access its related log files that are possibly distributed across multiple log servers. A data subject should be always able to access data logged about his data, but (s)he might want to delegate this right to some auditing agents of his or her choice.

2   Related Work

In general, technical security measures (such as open strong cryptography) can help prevent falsification of logs, and privacy-enhancing techniques and adequate access control should be used to protect personal information in logs. More specifically, relevant techniques for addressing accountability in the context described above include non repudiable logs, backups, distributed logging, forward integrity via use of hash chains and automated tools for log audits; for example, a log analyser and framework that link obligations right through to lower level distributed evidence in cloud supply chains that show whether or not the obligations are met [2]. Core techniques from the field of secure logging are described in [3–5]; the first paper about using chains of values of cryptographic hash functions for proofs of integrity dates from a paper about time-stamping by Haber and Stornetta [6]. Closely related research related to secure logging for accountability has been carried out within Daniel Le Metayer's group in INRIA (for example [7,8]). While secure logging techniques mainly focus on integrity (for example via the use of hash chains), our research is concerned with access control in logging systems. Of course, there has been a great deal of work on various techniques for access control, including Role-Based Access Control (RBAC) techniques, protection of data during database query [9], etc.

Our research provides contextual access to logs to governance actors (such as regulators) and other third parties. There is some analogous research carried out that instead takes a data subject centric approach, providing a transparency-enhancing tool for informing users about the actual data processing that takes place on their personal data [10]. But the range of applications is therefore smaller. Some of the assumptions and techniques vary, although there are a number of strong similarities to that approach. *Transparency Log* (TL) [11] is a transparency enhancing tool that plays an essential role in the A4Cloud EU project[2], namely, to facilitate the communication of data from data controllers to data subjects. In order to provide *secrecy*, TL uses an encryption scheme that is indistinguishable against chosen plaintext attacks (IND-CPA) (see [12]); however, using this type of encryption scheme, an entity has to encrypt multiple copies of the same data if it wants to send them to different recipients even if they are allowed to see the same subset of log information.

Our research relies on technical means to protect evidence, whereas there is other (potentially complementary) research that aims to improve transparency (for example, by exposing additional evidence to actors that can then be assessed). An example is the Cloud Security Alliance (CSA) Cloud Trust Protocol (CTP)[3], which works at the transport interface layer and which allows cloud service consumers to ask for and receive information about "elements of transparency" from cloud service providers. Indeed, transparency is an important aspect of accountability [1]. At present, end users have an unequal relationship with service providers, exacerbated by current cloud providers offering "take it or leave it" terms of service: users have no bargaining power *vis-a-vis* cloud service providers and no means of verifying that cloud providers behave as they claim they do. Furthermore, this transparency should be provided in a way that does not impinge on privacy, especially since there can be tension between privacy and transparency [10]. The Privacy by Design approach strives to reach a positive sum, which allows both privacy and accountability/transparency to be implemented [13]. Such a positive sum can be achieved by pseudonymity schemes with the help of cryptography which allow revocation of anonymity for misbehaving users, making them accountable for their actions while guaranteeing strong anonymity for honest users (see for instance [14,15]). Previous work has been done on pseudonymisation of log files [16] for enhancing privacy of accountability tools, such as intrusion detection systems (see e.g. Revocable Privacy[4]). Further related research on privacy aspects of transparency has been conducted by the Revocable Privacy project[5], the FIDIS [17], PrimeLife [18,19] and A4Cloud EU projects.

There is a need for provenance logs for accountability, and yet there is a potential tension with privacy. This issue is not confined to cloud service provision chains, but is a broader issue that also relates to scenarios relating to internet of things, smart cities and so on, where there can be many logs reflecting what has been happening in the system. Quite often, to solve this problem, some degree of approximation could be introduced into the logs [16], but data linkage could reduce any pseudonymisation used and make it obsolete. It is not clear what the noise added in should be, and how that should match the context (and especially the purpose of usage). Deciding how to structure the information

---

[2] http://www.a4cloud.eu/.

[3] https://cloudsecurityalliance.org/research/initiatives/cloud-trust-protocol.

[4] http://www.cs.ru.nl/jhh/revocableprivacy/.

[5] http://www.fidis.net/fileadmin/fidis/deliverables/fidiswp7-del7.
12_behaviouralbiometric_profiling_and_transparency_enhancing_tools.pdf.

and how to obfuscate it and which parts to obfuscate is non trivial and requires further research. Prior research in the area of data provenance[6] needs to be combined with new privacy preserving methodologies. The approach described in this paper could potentially be combined with such an approach: our work addresses certain tensions between log access, accountability and privacy, given existing logs within a system, rather than addressing the generation of logs in an appropriate format or the provenance of such logs.

The logs that are protected may relate to data creation, access, flow, type, deletion or handling [20]. The proposed research is not dependent on particular means used to produce logs, and could build on top of logs produced by existing Security Information and Event Management (SIEM or SIM/SEM) solutions [21]. These include, for example, RSA envision[7] and HP ArcSight[8], which provide a standardized approach to collect information and events, store and query and provide degrees of correlations, usually driven by rules. SIEM solutions do not cover business audit and strategic (security) risk assessment but instead provide inputs that need to be properly analysed and translated into a suitable format to be used by senior risk assessors and strategic policy makers. Risk assessment standards such as ISO 2700x[9], NIST[10], etc. operate at a macro level and usually do not fully leverage information coming from logging and auditing activities carried out by IT operations. Similarly, there exist a number of frameworks for auditing a company's IT controls, most notably COSO[11] and COBIT[12].

3   Scenario

We consider the aspect of controlling access to the logs (and related accountability evidence) involved within cloud ecosystems. Accountability evidence can be defined as a collection of data, metadata, routine information, and formal operations performed on data and metadata, which provide attributable and verifiable account of the fulfilment (or not) of relevant obligations; it can be used to support an argument on the validity of claims about appropriate functioning of an observable system [22]. Logging can be performed at different levels and evidence can have different sources as well [20]. In particular, at the data level we might be interested in: data creation, data access, data flow, data type, data deletion, data handling and data notification.

Since data that is collected for accountability might itself be data that can be abused, it might need to be protected as much as the processed data. The potential conflict of accountability with privacy is somewhat reduced as the focus

---

[6] See for example http://workshops.inf.ed.ac.uk/tapp2015/.

[7] http://www.rsa.com/experience/envision/3n1/.

[8] http://www.arcsight.com/.

[9] http://www.27000.org/.

[10] http://csrc.nist.gov/publications/nistpubs/800-30/sp800-30.pdf.

[11] http://www.coso.org.

[12] http://www.isaca.org.

in data protection is not on the accountability of data subjects but rather of data controllers, who need to be accountable towards data subjects and trusted intermediaries, and the identities of the service providers do not need to be hidden.

As discussed in Sect. 1, we consider the subproblem of how appropriate views may be provided to selected cloud stakeholders on logs and evidence-related information. The overall scenario is shown in Fig. 1, where governance actors, or indeed the cloud subjects or the cloud customers, may need to have a view on logs or other accountability evidence produced within the cloud ecosystem. In this figure we use the extension of the NIST cloud actor roles defined in the A4Cloud project, by which in a data protection context data subjects whose information is being processed in the cloud are relevant parties called cloud subjects. In addition, there may be an organisational cloud customer with the role of a data controller, there can be more than one cloud service provider, and accountability agents may be acting on behalf of the cloud customer or of data protection authorities (a form of cloud supervisory authority). The organisational cloud customer, and indeed the cloud service providers, will have their own internal business governance. For further details, see [1].

Rules need to be enforced about who may access what aspects of the logs. We require authorized entities that may be for example a cloud customer, their clients, data subjects, auditors, cloud service providers and regulators to be given different views on the logs and evidence derived from logs, in a way that satisfies data minimization. That is to say, such that they should be able to see only the source or derived data from logs that is necessary to provide the level of assurance that they need. Furthermore, this must be without revealing personal or other types of confidential information (either in the processed data, source data logs or evidence derived from these logs) that they do not need to see.

In some scenarios it might also be needed that governance actors that oversee the way that data is handled in the Cloud (for example as shown on the left hand side of Fig. 1) delegate access to some parts of the logs in an accountable way. For example, an authorised cloud auditor might require the assistance of some other auditor. Instead of sharing the logs directly it would be preferable that access by the secondary auditor to the logs is also performed in an accountable way, subject to the same (or more constrained) rules as the primary auditor.

The specific requirements that are addressed by this scheme are as follows:

- **R1** (Secrecy). Confidentiality of the logs regarding data processing, as parts of the logs may reveal personal or confidential data.
- **R2** (Fine-grained Access Control). Data should be structured in a way that makes it possible to give different views of the logs to different entities, without necessitating an all-or-nothing approach.
- **R3** (Audit). It should be possible to track access to the different views of the logs, namely recording in a trustworthy way who accessed what and when that happened.

Confidentiality of the personal and/or confidential data processed within the cloud service provision chain is of course a very important aspect too, but is

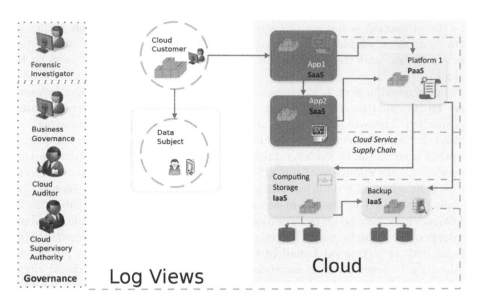

Fig. 1. High level overview of the scenario

not included in the requirements above as this problem is not the focus of our attention. Furthermore, the confidentiality of the logs regarding access to the data processing logs, i.e. auditing logs is in general much less of an issue than integrity requirements concerning those logs, so we do not here include it in **R1**.

Note that in our approach we are relaxing some of the security requirements defined in [11] as we leave some secure logging aspects (such as log integrity) to other well known techniques to address and we are not making the presumption that the logs are readable only by the associated data subject. For example, we are not covering Forward Integrity [3], i.e. the adversary should not be able to make undetectable modifications to logged data (committed prior to compromise). Another assumption we make in this paper is that cloud providers follow the honest-but-curious adversary model [23], which means they follow the established protocols, but will try to access the protected information.

We will now discuss some particular solutions that address the above requirements.

4   Solutions

We propose an alternative solution to existing transparency logs [11] that overcome some of their previously identified issues, mainly the lack of flexibility when different auditing agents with different privileges or views are involved. Also, we allow the CSP to delegate to a logging module or some other component the task of granting access to different auditing entities.

We propose a transparency-enhancing tool in the form of a cryptographic scheme that enables data processors to control access to auditors, regulators, data subjects and other authorized parties to information about the data processing that is carried out within a service provision chain.

In this new approach, we deal with cases where data subjects might have a say in deciding *who* can play the role of an auditor, or simply when data controllers want to encrypt different levels of sensitive information presented in the logs once and yet allow more than one party to access different parts of them, based on their roles in the whole scenario. Figure 2 presents a generic diagram of our approach that shows the key components, namely, logging of the processing of personal and/or confidential data, access to those logs by authorised parties, and auditing about that data access, grouped in the following domains:

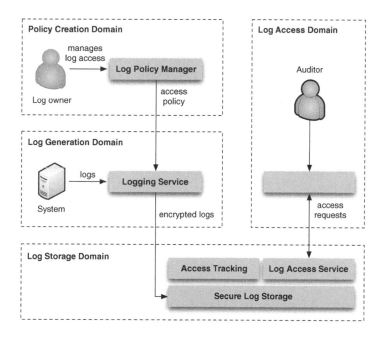

Fig. 2. Domains and processes in our solution

- **Policy Creation Domain**. This domain involves the definition of access policies to protect the logs, using a Log Policy Manager.
- **Log Generation Domain**. This domain encompasses the logged system (i.e., CSP) and an associated Logging Service, which generates the logs regarding the processing of data and protects them according to an access policy, encrypting all entries of the log or some parts of them. Depending on the kind of approach we take we might need to also categorise logs based on their contents and decide what roles would have access to them.
- **Log Storage Domain**. This domain is in charge of storing encrypted logs, and more importantly, of providing and tracking access to these logs by authorised governance actors. We are generally agnostic as to the particular cloud

storage service provided. The enforcement of access control policies is done in the Log Access Service component. In addition, for every access, there should be an audit log produced by the Access Tracking component, indicating who accessed what and when.

– **Log Access Domain**. This domain involves the access to the logs by the governance actors (e.g., auditors), using a Log Access Client.

This architecture supports different implementations. We differentiate between two main strategies for instantiating our proposal:

– **A *priori* or Agent centric**. In the a priori approach we put the focus on the agents that can audit the log. We aim at providing a solution that can *protect* log entries based on who should be entitled to access them. This way, data is protected with some embedded access control policies before reaching the data storage. When using this approach, agents can directly access the protected data and consume it according to the embedded policies.

– **A *posteriori* or Data centric**. In the a posteriori or data centric approach we put the focus on the log (or other evidence). We aim to provide a solution that can *protect* logs based on its content. This way, no policy is taken into account when protecting the log but dependent on the content, the level of protection will be different. When using this approach we need to provide an *a posteriori* mechanism for access control that will be enforced when requesting access to the log.

In the following section we introduce two implementation strategies for each of the approaches, but it would not be hard instead to implement hybrid approaches using any of the strategies. We also discuss pros and cons of both of them.

5   *A Priori* Approach: Attribute Based Encryption

A cryptographic technique which we can employ in order to provide both confidentiality and access control mechanisms is a suitable attribute-based encryption (ABE) scheme. For instance, one can use either of [24,25], knowing that in [26], they show how to construct a Verifiable Computation scheme with *public delegation* and *public verifiability* from any ABE scheme. On the other hand, Sahai and Seyalioglu provide in [27] an ABE scheme that enjoys both delegation of access rights and revocation of private keys. Similar to [11], data subjects in our approach can always have *full* access to data logged about their data. But now, they (or the data controllers) can delegate this right to some accountability agents.

All they need to do is to include them in the encryption policy part of the privacy policy. As an example of an encryption policy, one can think of the following boolean combination:

$$\Psi := (\mathsf{DataSubject}) \vee ((\mathsf{AuditorLocation} = \mathsf{EU}) \wedge (\mathsf{BSI\ accredited}))$$

Encrypting logs with respect to this policy means that the corresponding data subject can access the *full* data presented in the logs, but so can any auditor who is located in EU with a British Standards Institution (BSI) accreditation. Other encryption policies will be defined for potential accountability agents, to share the access of the same subset of metadata. Some scenarios would allow data subjects and data processors to agree on the full privacy policy when they start their negotiation (if there is any). The encryption policy could be then a part of the privacy policy.

5.1   Building Blocks: ABE

Attribute-based Encryption was first presented to surpass one of the drawbacks of *sharing* encrypting data on the cloud; namely, we were able to share data *only* at a coarse-grained level; i.e. by giving away a private key to whoever we want to share our data with. Attribute based encryption offers a way for fine-grained sharing of encrypted data. Informally speaking, someone can encrypt his data with respect to a certain predicate (aka policy), and only people who have enough credentials to satisfy the predicate are granted access to the data.

In our approach we propose to use the Ciphertext-Policy variant of ABE (or CP-ABE). In this paradigm, encryption is done using a function Enc which takes a message m, the policy Ψ and any other public parameters PK established at the beginning of the protocol. The decryption key (which is issued by an attribute authority to entities satisfying policy Ψ or a suitable subset of that policy) is computed from the attributes $\mathcal{A}$ of the entity and the master key established at the beginning of the protocol. Once an entity has been issued a decryption key corresponding to its attribute set $\mathcal{A}$, it can decrypt ciphertexts associated to policy Ψ. For illustrative purposes, the following is the generic syntax of a CP-ABE scheme:

- Setup($1^\lambda, U$): For a given security parameter, it generates a set of global parameters, represented by PK, and the set of attributes U. The global parameters include the master key MSK.
- Enc(PK, Ψ, m): The encryption function takes as input the message m, the public key PK and an encryption policy Ψ, and produces a ciphertext CT.
- KeyGen(MSK, $\mathcal{A}$): Taking as input the master secret key MSK and a set of attributes $\mathcal{A}$, it creates the private key $\mathsf{SK}_{\mathcal{A}}$ associated to $\mathcal{A}$.
- Dec(CT, SK): The decryption function takes as input a ciphertext CT and a private key SK for a set $\mathcal{A}$. If $\mathcal{A}$ satisfies the encryption policy associated to CT, then this function returns the original message m.

The important thing to note is that decryption can only succeed in such a scheme if the entity trying to decrypt satisfies the policy that has been specified for the ciphertext, namely, if the entity holds the attributes which are required. A given key can decrypt a particular ciphertext only if there is a match between the attributes of the ciphertext and that key.

5.2   Mapping/Integration

Using ABE as building blocks, the following are the main architectural components of our approach:

- Attribute Authority (AA). There are one or more of these entities, which deal with attribute management, i.e. issuing, revoking and updating users' attributes. They create and distribute secret keys that are associated with attributes. The AAs run KeyGen, which gives a user a set of secret keys corresponding to the attributes that s/he holds, and these are distributed to the appropriate entities. This process is likely to be integrated to some extent to existing business processes, some of which may be offline. It is important that the mechanisms by which the attributes are allocated, distributed and kept up to date can be trusted by other entities in the system, but some of this process is necessarily out of scope for the proposed architecture as it will vary across different scenarios and related infrastructures.
- Trusted Authority (TA) (optional). Optionally, a central authority can be used, whereby all the users and attribute authorities in the system register with a central certification authority to obtain certificates, i.e. this entity underpins a PKI, distributing global secret and public keys. In an initial phase, the TA sets up the system by running Setup. Alternatively, a different approach can be taken by which this entity is not needed, and instead of the legal users in the system having public keys distributed by this entity, they have credentials corresponding to their attributes, issued by multiple attribute authorities.
- Log Policy Manager (LPM). This deals with policy creation and modification aspects, as well as building of lists of standardized attributes for relevant domains, which may correspond to more than one attribute authority.
- Logging Service (LS). This allows generation of a fresh symmetric key (e.g. for AES) using a random number generator, encryption of log entries using said key and encryption of the symmetric key using ABE. This hybrid encryption is used to make the process more efficient, relative to encrypting potentially large data objects directly using ABE. More formally, for a given log entry ℓ_i, LS generates a fresh symmetric key k_i and encrypts it using ABE with respect to a policy Ψ, which results in the ciphertext $c_{i,1} = \mathsf{Enc}(\mathsf{PK}, \Psi, k_i)$. The log entry is encrypted with k_i using symmetric encryption, which produces $c_{i,2} = \mathsf{SymEnc}(k_i, \ell_i)$. Therefore, the hybrid encryption produces a pair $(c_{i,1}, c_{i,2})$. Overall, LPM interacts with log owners to allow them to form/modify policies (using a standardised set of attributes for a given domain), and LS encrypts a symmetric key with this policy using ABE, that is used to encrypt the log entries and store them in the cloud storage. This component would run as a separate service, probably using the cloud storage service (CSS) to store encrypted policies and other customer related data needed for the functioning of the service (using keys generated by LS).
- Log Access Client (LAC). This process involves decryption of the symmetric key using ABE as well as decryption of log entries using the symmetric key. In response to an auditor request for access to the logs, LAC fetches the corresponding encrypted logs from CSS, and decrypts them using auditors'

secret keys, if the auditor has enough attributes to satisfy the policy Ψ. The LAC is likely to be run as a separate service, optionally integrated with LS for business reasons.

- Revocation Manager (RM). This component handles revocation and delegation. This may be handled in a number of different ways (e.g. time windows, revocation lists or more advanced techniques) and is the subject of further research which mechanisms would be most appropriate in the context of the project. Depending upon the decision about which one is chosen, aspects related to revocation may be integrated within the TA or AC, or run as a separate service.
- Cloud Storage Service (CSS). This entity stores encrypted logs, and provides them to governance actors (e.g., auditors) by means of a Log Access Services (LAS).

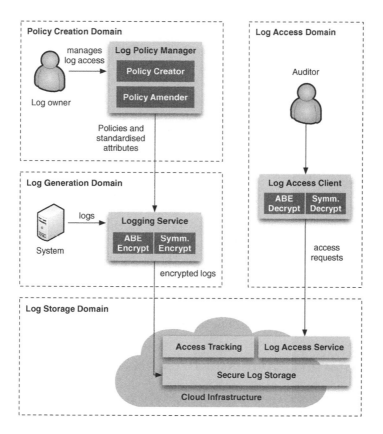

Fig. 3. ABE-based architecture

Figure 3 depicts the main components of this architecture. In addition, there can be optional integration with existing services (e.g. key storage service, authentication service).

The protocol has a setup phase and an operational phase; the purpose of the former is to establish all security parameters and to codify in machine-readable form the policy of the log owner with regards to access to its logs and encrypt a symmetric key that encrypts the log using that policy as an encryption key. The operational phase comprises the steps that are carried out in order to grant auditors access to certain logs in the cloud system in accordance with the policy that has been established in the setup phase, or subsequently modified (with associated re-encryption).

Finally, we note that we could replicate this pattern for the Tracking and Audit Access processes in case we also want to protect the audit logs.

5.3   Analysis/Assessment of Level of Fulfillment of Requirements

The requirement **R1** (Secrecy) is satisfied as long as we use an ABE scheme that achieves a proper security notion, such as IND-CPA or IND-CCA. The requirement **R2** (Fine-grained access control) is met by encrypting different parts of the log with different policies. The requirement **R3** (Audit) is fulfilled through the Access Tracking component in the Log Storage Domain, which records all access requests received by the Log Access Service.

The main advantage of this approach is that the log information does not need to be encrypted multiple times, each with the public key of the entity that is to be given access to this information, but instead just needs to be encrypted once. Also, the identity of the accessors does not need to be known in advance, so this suits scenarios where the role of an auditor that can access information (together potentially with other properties) is known, but the specific person holding this role (and satisfying any additional constraints) is not necessarily known in advance.

The main drawback of this approach relates to the necessity of a pre-phase in which attributes are distributed, and in which the actors distributing these attributes need to be trusted, as well as the attributes themselves needing to be standardised and understandable (across the actors that use them) as well as revocation mechanisms needing to be in place (although there are various options for this). In addition, if the policy relating to access changes, then the log information would need to be re-encrypted based upon that.

6   *A Posteriori* Approach: Proxy Re-Encryption

In this section we discuss an alternative approach based on Proxy Re-Encryption (PRE) [28,29], which is a type of asymmetric encryption that allows a proxy to transform ciphertexts under Alice's public key into ciphertexts decryptable by Bob; this transformation is called *re-encryption*. The main idea behind the use of PRE in our scenario is that the re-encryption process can be seen as a way of enforcing the access delegation decision, and therefore, it is an ideal place to implement the auditing capability (i.e., recording all access requests), such that it cannot be bypassed, since the re-encryption is necessary to access the information. First we propose a preliminary version using a regular PRE scheme, and next we extend this proposal to support the requirement of fine-grained access control using a variant of PRE called Conditional PRE.

6.1   Building Blocks: PRE, Conditional PRE

As described before, PRE allows a proxy to re-encrypt ciphertexts intended for Alice into ciphertexts for Bob. In order to do this, the proxy is given a re-encryption key $rk_{A \rightarrow B}$, which makes this process possible. It can be seen that Proxy Re-Encryption materialises the functionality of delegation of decryption rights. In this case, a delegator Alice can delegate decryption rights into a delegatee Bob, and a proxy can enforce such rights by means of re-encryption. The re-encryption key act as a token of delegation. Therefore, PRE is an ideal candidate for constructing an access control system where information is outsourced (e.g., the cloud).

In our scenario, the parties that are interested on accessing the encrypted information are the consumers of the accountability evidence, in the form of logs. These consumers include auditors, data protection authorities, and data subjects, among others. Logs are encrypted under the public key of the data owner (i.e., the CSP). The CSP will grant access to specific consumers by means of re-encryption keys, which will be handed to log servers. In turn, log servers will act as proxies, enforcing the access control through the re-encryption procedure. When an auditor requests access to some log, the log server will verify if s/he is authorised (i.e., the corresponding re-encryption key exist) and will re-encrypt the data to the consumers's public key. The log servers are then capable of recording all access requests.

This solution can be extended to support a finer-grained access control using Conditional Proxy Re-Encryption (CPRE) [30,31]. CPRE is a specialization of PRE, where ciphertexts are tagged during decryption with a keyword (the "condition"); similarly, re-encryption keys are also tagged with a condition when they are generated, so only ciphertext tagged with the same condition is re-encryptable by that key. Therefore, for a given ciphertext CT_A with condition w, originally encrypted under A's public key, the proxy can only re-encrypt the ciphertext to user B if he has the re-encryption key $rk_{A \xrightarrow{w} B}$.

Using CPRE, the data owner can provide finer-grained access by means of a set of re-encryption keys with different conditions. The extension is essentially identical to the basic proposal, but ciphertexts (i.e., logs) are tagged during encryption with a specific condition (e.g., "contains personal information"). The proxies will be able to re-encrypt encrypted logs (or not) depending on whether they have the corresponding re-encryption keys. For the sake of completeness, we show here the generic syntax of a CPRE scheme:

- Setup(1^λ): For a given security parameter, it computes a set of global parameters $params$.
- KeyGen($params$): It computes a pair of public and private keys (pk_i, sk_i).

- Enc(pk, w, m): For a given public key pk and a message m, it computes a ciphertext CT tagged with keyword w.
- Dec(CT, sk): It decrypts a ciphertext CT for a given private key sk.
- ReKeyGen(sk_i, w, pk_j): For a given private key sk_i, a keyword w, and a public key pk_j, it computes a conditional re-encryption key $rk_{i \overset{w}{\to} j}$.
- ReEnc($CT_i, rk_{i \overset{w}{\to} j}$): Using conditional re-encryption key $rk_{i \overset{w}{\to} j}$, it re-encrypts a ciphertext CT_i, encrypted under pk_i and keyword w, into a ciphertext CT_j decryptable by sk_j.

6.2   Mapping/Integration

In order to deploy a CPRE-based access control system for logged data, it is necessary to agree first on a set of public parameters, generated by the Setup algorithm. Next, interested parties should possess a keypair, generated by the KeyGen algorithm; these parties not only include data consumers (e.g., auditors), but also the data owner. Based on off-line authorisation decisions, the data owner can grant access to data consumers using the ReKeyGen algorithm, producing re-encryption keys that act as authorization tokens; additionally, in the Conditional PRE setting, a condition tag will be associated during this process. These re-encryption keys are handed to the log servers, which will act then as re-encryption proxies, enforcing access control. Finally, data consumers can read the encrypted data using the Dec algorithm.

Figure 4 depicts our approach based on the use of Conditional Proxy Re-Encryption. The architecture is similar to the ABE-based one, but using CPRE for the encryption and decryption of logs; consequently, the components are adapted here to this cryptosystem. A fundamental difference, however, is that the CSS now provides a Log Access Service (LAS), which implements the re-encryption functionality. It can be seen that this approach can be easily mapped to the elements shown in Fig. 2, which depicts CSP internals. In this case, the functionality of log servers, which act as re-encryption proxies, is twofold: on the one hand, they enable log access through the re-encryption procedure; on the other hand, since they control re-encryption they can record access control requests in order to support tracking and audit access. In order to make the re-encryption possible, it is necessary that the system logs generated on the CSP side are encrypted under its own key, so it can be re-encrypted to the consumer's public key.

6.3   Analysis/Assessment of Level of Fulfillment of Requirements

Requirement **R1** (Secrecy) is clearly fulfilled by using this approach. As with any public key encryption scheme, the idea is to use a hybrid encryption approach, where data is encrypted with a symmetric scheme under fresh random keys, and then these keys are encrypted with the PRE scheme. This way logged data is stored encrypted and the corresponding keys are only provided to authorised entities using public key cryptography.

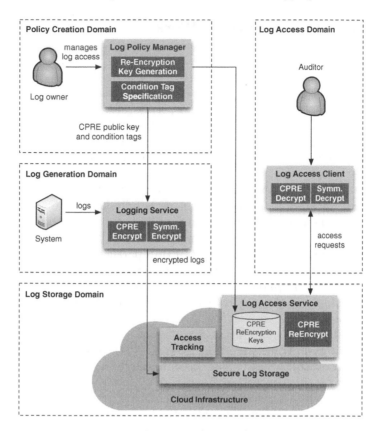

Fig. 4. CPRE-based architecture

It can be seen that this approach for access control partially supports requirement **R2** (Finc-grained access control). Using a conditional PRE scheme we can discriminate which data to grant access to (i.e., produce different logs views) and with the issuance of the corresponding re-encryption keys we can also decide who will have access to the different views of the logs.

We require that log servers perform a cryptographic operation on logs in order to ultimately grant access to other parties based on the existence of the corresponding re-encryption key. This forces us to place some extra burden on the log servers compared to the approach using ABE but on the other hand, when implemented properly, e.g., using some trusted module, it makes it easier to audit or track the actual of access to the logs because the log server is in the position of tracking access to the stored logs, by recording the re-encryption requests from auditors, supporting in this way requirement **R3** (Audit). The idea is that the same module in charge of re-encrypting will do the audit as an atomic operation. This process can even be implemented in a trusted platform module (TPM) in order to increase reliability.

7 Conclusions and Further Work

In this paper, we presented two different transparency-enhancing mechanisms that support provision of appropriate views on audit logs, based on the use of Attribute-Based Encryption (ABE) and Conditional Proxy Re-Encryption (CPRE). These approaches provide confidentiality of logs with respect to unauthorized users, and fine-grained access control over the information about the data processing that is carried out within a service provision chain (although CPRE is more limited than ABE with respect to the satisfaction of this requirement). In both approaches, different cloud actors (e.g., auditors, regulators, data subjects and other authorised parties) may be given different views of the logs.

As further work, we plan to document more fully how these schemes would work, and assess in more detail related security aspects. In addition, we are considering the potential use of yet another advanced cryptographic technique, i.e. multi-party computation, in the context of transparency logging. Briefly, secure multi-party computation can be defined as follows [32]: *n players want to compute a function of their **private** inputs in a secure way, i.e. it should guarantee both the correctness of the output and the privacy of the players' inputs, even when some players cheat.* In this case, we consider a scenario in which different accountability agents have access to different levels of sensitive information presented in a certain transparency log. Bar the data subjects, we assume that none of the accountability agents has access to the *full* log. In this case, we want these agents to be able to work *together* in order to tell whether or not there is any breach, i.e. a given service provider is compliant with the privacy policy on which he agreed with a certain data subject. This can assure that no single auditor knows *all* the sensitive information about some data subjects. This clearly is not a trivial task, and therefore it can be considered as an intriguing idea for some future work that needs more investigation on many levels; first, to fully understand the way the current logs are formed and how flexible they are in the sense that if a certain log is divided into different chunks, how would the absence of *at least* one of them help in providing further protection of the privacy of the data subjects? Second, to study the practicality of current multi-party computation (MPC) systems because MPC is a complicated cryptographic tool and extra care must be taken to give an estimate of its impact on the practicality of the whole system.

Acknowledgements. The research leading to these results has received funding from the European Union Seventh Framework Programme (FP7/2007-2013) under grant agreement no. 317550 (A4Cloud) and by the Junta de Andalucía through the project FISICCO (P11-TIC-07223). The third author has been funded by a FPI fellowship from the Junta de Andalucía through the project PISCIS (P10-TIC-06334).

References

1. Pearson, S.: Accountability in cloud service provision ecosystems. In: Bernsmed, K., Fischer-Hübner, S. (eds.) NordSec 2014. LNCS, vol. 8788, pp. 3–24. Springer, Heidelberg (2014)
2. Chaum, D., Fiat, A., Naor, M.: Untraceable electronic cash. In: Goldwasser, S. (ed.) CRYPTO 1988. LNCS, vol. 403, pp. 319–327. Springer, Heidelberg (1990)
3. Bellare, M., Yee, B.S.: Forward integrity for secure audit logs. Technical report (1997)
4. Bellare, M., Yee, B.S.: Forward-security in private-key cryptography. In: Joye, M. (ed.) CT-RSA 2003. LNCS, vol. 2612, pp. 1–18. Springer, Heidelberg (2003)
5. Schneier, B., Kelsey, J.: Cryptographic support for secure logs on untrusted machines. In: Proceedings of the 7th Conference on USENIX Security Symposium, SSYM 1998, Berkeley, CA, USA, vol. 7, p. 4. USENIX Association (1998)
6. Haber, S., Stornetta, W.: How to time-stamp a digital document. J. Cryptol. 3(2), 99–111 (1991)
7. Métayer, D.L., Mazza, E., Potet, M.L.: Designing log architectures for legal evidence. In: 8th IEEE International Conference on Software Engineering and Formal Methods (SEFM), pp. 156–165, September 2010
8. Butin, D., Chicote, M., Metayer, D.L.: Log design for accountability. In: 2013 IEEE Security and Privacy Workshops (SPW), pp. 1–7, May 2013
9. Agrawal, R., Kiernan, J., Srikant, R., Xu, Y.: Hippocratic databases. In: Proceedings of the 28th International Conference on Very Large Data Bases, VLDB Endowment, pp. 143–154 (2002)
10. O'Hara, K.: Transparent government, not transparent citizens: a report on privacy and transparency for the cabinet office (2011)
11. Pulls, T., Peeters, R., Wouters, K.: Distributed privacy-preserving transparency logging. In: Proceedings of the 12th ACM Workshop on Workshop on Privacy in the Electronic Society, WPES 2013, pp. 83–94. ACM, New York (2013)
12. Pulls, T., Martucci, L.: D: D-5.2 User-centric transparency tools. In: A4Cloud (2014)
13. Camenisch, J., Groß, T., Heydt-Benjamin, T.: Accountable privacy supporting services. Identity Inf. Soc. 2(3), 241–267 (2009)
14. Flegel, U.: Privacy-Respecting Intrusion Detection, vol. 35. Springer Science & Business Media, New York (2007)
15. Øverlier, L., Brekne, T., Årnes, A.: Non-expanding transaction specific pseudonymization for IP traffic monitoring. In: Desmedt, Y.G., Wang, H., Mu, Y., Li, Y. (eds.) CANS 2005. LNCS, vol. 3810, pp. 261–273. Springer, Heidelberg (2005)
16. Flegel, U.: Evaluating the design of an audit data pseudonymizer using basic building blocks for anonymity. In: Proceedings of SSZ, no. P-62 in Lecture Notes in Informatics, pp. 221–232. GI SIGs SIDAR and PET (2005)
17. WP7: D 7.12: Behavioural biometric profiling and transparency enhancing tools. In: FIDIS (2009)
18. WP4.2: D 4.2.2 - end user transparency tools: UI prototypes. PrimeLife (2010)
19. Hedbom, H., Pulls, T., Hjärtquist, P., Lavén, A.: Adding secure transparency logging to the PRIME core. In: Bezzi, M., Duquenoy, P., Fischer-Hübner, S., Hansen, M., Zhang, G. (eds.) IFIP AICT 320. IFIP AICT, vol. 320, pp. 299–314. Springer, Heidelberg (2010)

20. Rübsamen, T., Reich, C., Taherimonfared, A., Wlodarczyk, T., Rong, C.: Evidence for accountable cloud computing services. In: Pre-Proceedings of International Workshop on Trustworthiness, Accountability and Forensics in the Cloud (TAFC), p. 1. Citeseer (2013)
21. Nicolett, M., Kavanagh, K.M.: Critical capabilities for security information and event management technology. Gartner report (2011)
22. Agrawal, B., Molland, H., Gulzar, H., Rübsamen, T., Reich, C., Azraoui, M., Onen, M., Pulls, T., Royer, J.C.: D: C-8.1 framework of evidence. In: A4Cloud (2014)
23. Smart, N.P.: Cryptography: An Introduction, vol. 5. McGraw-Hill, New York (2003)
24. Bethencourt, J., Sahai, A., Waters, B.: Ciphertext-policy attribute-based encryption. In: 2007 IEEE Symposium on Security and Privacy, SP 2007, pp. 321–334. IEEE (2007)
25. Waters, B.: Ciphertext-policy attribute-based encryption: an expressive, efficient, and provably secure realization. In: Catalano, D., Fazio, N., Gennaro, R., Nicolosi, A. (eds.) PKC 2011. LNCS, vol. 6571, pp. 53–70. Springer, Heidelberg (2011)
26. Parno, B., Raykova, M., Vaikuntanathan, V.: How to delegate and verify in public: verifiable computation from attribute-based encryption. In: Cramer, R. (ed.) TCC 2012. LNCS, vol. 7194, pp. 422–439. Springer, Heidelberg (2012)
27. Sahai, A., Seyalioglu, H., Waters, B.: Dynamic credentials and ciphertext delegation for attribute-based encryption. Cryptology ePrint Archive, Report 2012/437 (2012). http://eprint.iacr.org/
28. Ateniese, G., Fu, K., Green, M., Hohenberger, S.: Improved proxy re-encryption schemes with applications to secure distributed storage. ACM Trans. Inf. Syst. Secur. (TISSEC) 9(1), 1–30 (2006)
29. Canetti, R., Hohenberger, S.: Chosen-ciphertext secure proxy re-encryption. In: Proceedings of the 14th ACM Conference on Computer and Communications Security, pp. 185–194. ACM (2007)
30. Weng, J., Deng, R.H., Ding, X., Chu, C.K., Lai, J.: Conditional proxy re-encryption secure against chosen-ciphertext attack. In: Proceedings of the 4th International Symposium on Information, Computer, and Communications Security, pp. 322–332. ACM (2009)
31. Weng, J., Yang, Y., Tang, Q., Deng, R.H., Bao, F.: Efficient conditional proxy re-encryption with chosen-ciphertext security. In: Samarati, P., Yung, M., Martinelli, F., Ardagna, C.A. (eds.) ISC 2009. LNCS, vol. 5735, pp. 151–166. Springer, Heidelberg (2009)
32. Cramer, R., Damgård, I.B., Maurer, U.M.: General secure multi-party computation from any linear secret-sharing scheme. In: Preneel, B. (ed.) EUROCRYPT 2000. LNCS, vol. 1807, pp. 316–334. Springer, Heidelberg (2000)

Evidence-Based Security and Privacy Assurance in Cloud Ecosystems

Saul Formoso and Massimo Felici[✉]

Security and Manageability Lab, Hewlett Packard Labs,
Bristol BS34 8QZ, UK
{saul.formoso,massimo.felici}@hpe.com

Abstract. This paper is concerned with the problem of security and privacy assurance in cloud ecosystems. Different controls are deployed in order to guarantee security and privacy across cloud ecosystems. It is yet challenging to assess their effectiveness in operation. Therefore, it is necessary to devise methodologies and technologies for providing assurance of whether security and privacy controls are effective and appropriate for specific cloud ecosystems. This paper discusses the rationale and requirements for evidence-based security and privacy assurance. It also discusses the underlining mechanisms shaping a software defined storage system for gathering evidence drawn from a cloud ecosystem. It explains such requirements and mechanisms in the context of a sample use case. In conclusion, it provides insights for evidence-based security and privacy assurance of cloud ecosystems.

1 Introduction

Cloud computing provides an alternative way of providing and using Information Technology (IT) that differs from traditional systems [1, 2]. It can be characterized in terms of its main features [3], i.e. on-demand self-service, broad network access, resource pooling, rapid elasticity, and measured service. Alternative cloud computing deployments (e.g. public cloud, private cloud, and hybrid cloud) can accommodate different customer needs [1]. Alongside the new opportunities offered by cloud computing, there are new challenges related to security and privacy of data stored in the cloud [4]. Cloud customers as well as cloud providers are concerned with such challenges. Security and privacy are therefore shared responsibilities among the parties involved in cloud supply chains – that is, all actors that participate in the provision and consumption of cloud services.

In order to mitigate emerging security and privacy threats, consequently reducing risks in the cloud, different security and privacy controls are deployed across cloud supply chains [2]. Such security and privacy controls diffuse organisational boundaries as emphasised by the security conservation principle: *"for a particular service migrated to the cloud, the full set of necessary Security Components and controls that must be implemented to secure the cloud Ecosystem is always the same; however, the division of responsibility for those Components and controls changes based upon the characteristics of the cloud, particularly the service deployment."* [2].

D. Aspinall et al. (Eds.): Privacy and Identity 2015, IFIP AICT 476, pp. 205–219, 2016.
DOI: 10.1007/978-3-319-41763-9_14

This paper is related to the Cloud Accountability Project, which has defined an approach and related mechanisms for accountability in the cloud [5]. In particular, this paper looks into how different technologies are deployed in order to support security and privacy in a cloud ecosystem – *"A cloud computing business ecosystem (cloud ecosystem) is a business ecosystem of interacting organisations and individuals – the actors of the cloud ecosystem – providing and consuming cloud services"* [6]. Although the security and privacy controls are easy to identify, it is yet challenging to assess their effectiveness operationally. There is yet a lack of support for assessing how such technologies work as a whole and how they are appropriate for the specific cloud ecosystems they are deployed in. It is necessary to understand how security and privacy controls enable organisations to comply with high level policies (drawn from relevant regulatory regimes).

This paper is structured as follows. Section 2 highlights relevant security and privacy research and industry practices, which provide a background to the research and development work presented here. The problem is then to provide evidence-based assurance that security and privacy controls are appropriate and operationally effective for the cloud ecosystems they are deployed in. Section 3 characterises the problem of security and privacy assurance in cloud supply chains. Section 4 discusses mechanisms that are necessary in order to implement evidence-based assurance in practice. These mechanisms have been used for tailoring a software defined storage system for the cloud in order to gather evidence related to the security and privacy controls deployed in the ecosystem. The evidence collected supports assurance and eases auditing the cloud supply chain. This aims to map the security and privacy controls deployed in the cloud supply chain for monitoring and auditing purposes. Section 5 explains the resulting implementation for evidence-based assurance in the context of a use case demonstrator drawn from the Cloud Accountability Project. This shows how the implemented system is useful in order to support assurance. An example explains how two sample SLAs between different cloud actors can be monitored. To sum up, this paper provides practical insights for implementing and supporting evidence-based assurance for security and privacy controls in cloud ecosystems.

2   Security and Privacy Practices

Cloud environments, due to their different nature, have an additional set of security and privacy requirements compared to traditional systems [1, 2]. While traditional systems require a large emphasis on the infrastructure, cloud computing focuses mainly on the provision of the services, relegating the former to a secondary level. Cloud environments' inherent ubiquity brings along security and privacy risks that need to be addressed (e.g. broad, network access, decreased visibility and control by customers, multi-tenancy, data residency, etc. [2]). These have originated practices, certification schemes (including guidelines), and technologies.

As this is a topic of increasing interest, there are research projects putting effort into complying with the aforementioned requirements. The main point is that in order to support security and privacy, it is necessary to adopt diverse mechanisms, from technical tools to process-oriented approaches, including certification and auditing. A brief overview of security and privacy practices, in particular, frameworks, certification schemes, technologies, and research projects, is provided hereunder:

- **Frameworks:** different frameworks capture industry best practices that guide stakeholders in order to enhance security and privacy in operations. For example, at the architectural level, it is possible to identify different security controls that organisations need to implement [2]. From a management viewpoint, it is possible to identify critical processes (e.g. security risk assessment and privacy management) that address the mitigation of security and privacy threats [7].
- **Certification Schemes:** ENISA released the Cloud Certification Schemes Metaframework (CCSM) that classifies the different types of security certifications for cloud providers [8]. This metaframework is used to compare and compile a list (CCSL, Cloud Certification Schemes List) of different cloud certification schemes and map detailed security requirements to security objectives existing in them. The overall objective is to make the cloud transparent for cloud customers, in particular, in the way cloud providers meet specific security objectives. Relevant examples are the CSA STAR Certification and the ISO/IEC 27017 (cloud security) and ISO/IEC 27018 (cloud privacy) standards.
- **Technologies:** among the various security and privacy technologies, Security Information and Event Management (SIEM) technologies have a critical role in monitoring operational security and supporting organisations in decision-making. These can be deployed to monitor computational resources in a cloud ecosystem, generating evidence that can be used to prove that security and privacy controls are complied with. Gartner reviews the most widely adopted SIEM technologies (e.g. Hewlett Packard Enterprise's ArcSight, IBM Security's QRadar, McAfee's Enterprise Security Manager, etc.) in industry [9].
- **Research:** recent and ongoing research projects (with a particular attention to European projects) have been concerned with providing the conceptual and technological foundations underpinning the European Cloud Computing Strategy [10]. For example, research has focused on accountability (A4Cloud[1]), data sharing agreement (CocoCloud[2]), security assurance (MUSA[3]), certification, and many other aspects of security and privacy. This highlights an increasing interest in providing assurance in the cloud.

3   Assurance in Cloud Ecosystems

This section points out the role of evidence in supporting assurance. In particular, it recalls the concept of accountability which highlights the responsibilities of an organisation in order to be accountable [5]. This is central to the concept of accountability [6]: *"Accountability for an organisation consists of accepting responsibility for*

---

[1] http://www.a4cloud.eu/.

[2] http://www.coco-cloud.eu/.

[3] http://www.tut.fi/musa-project/.

data with which it is entrusted in a cloud environment, for its use of the data from the time it is collected until when the data is destroyed (including onward transfer to and from third parties). It involves the commitment to norms, explaining and demonstrating compliance to stakeholders and remedying any failure to act properly". Underpinning the concept of accountability is the provision of an account, which involves the gathering of evidence supporting organisational practices. This section then discusses the problem of assurance in a sample cloud supply chain. This discussion helps clarifying the requirements for supporting security and privacy assurance in cloud ecosystems.

3.1   Evidence-Based Accountability

The Cloud Accountability Project points out the need for evidence-based accountability in order to support the assessment of whether adopted security and privacy solutions (e.g. technologies, processes, etc.) are suitable for the specific cloud ecosystems, and hence provide assurance [5]. Cloud ecosystems involve various actors with different responsibilities. Emergent relationships among cloud actors give rise to the need for chains of evidence – *"A process and record that shows who obtained the evidence; where and when the evidence was obtained; who secured the evidence; and who had control and possession of the evidence"* [6] – and evidence in terms of organisational practices. On the one hand, it is necessary to validate gathered evidence and trace its source. On the other hand, evidence (is transformed and) propagates across system and organisational boundaries. From a technical viewpoint, evidence is considered among the three fundamental capabilities of an accountable system [11]:

- **Validation:** "It allows users, operators and third parties to verify a posteriori if the system has performed a data processing task as expected"
- **Attribution:** "In case of a deviation from the expected behaviour (fault), it reveals which component is responsible"
- **Evidence:** "It produces evidence that can be used to convince a third party that a fault has or has not occurred".

Therefore, gathering evidence has a critical role in supporting assurance – *"Assurance is about providing confidence to stakeholders that the qualities of service and stewardship with which they are concerned are being managed and maintained appropriately"* [12]. This is also particularly important while dealing with emergent threats [13] due to a certain extent to the shift required while deploying new technological paradigms like cloud computing.

3.2   Example of Cloud Supply Chain

Figure 1 shows a sample supply chain involving different actors: a cloud customer and two cloud service providers. The emergent relationships among actors form cloud supply chains defined in terms of cloud roles [5]. From a data protection perspective [14], cloud actors also have different roles and responsibilities (i.e. data subject, data controller, and data processor).

It is challenging to support operational compliance to policies and regulations. Security and privacy depend on the operational effectiveness and appropriateness of deployed controls and their dependencies. It is desirable to build and maintain dynamic assurance cases of security and privacy controls (providing security and privacy assurance of the cloud supply chain through continuous monitoring). The following points characterise some aspects of assurance in cloud supply chains (Fig. 1):

1. Different security and privacy controls are deployed across a cloud supply chain.
2. It is challenging to provide transparency and assurance to cloud customers.
3. It is necessary to provide technological solutions to support continuous assurance.
4. Operational evidence of security and privacy controls is required to provide assurance. This evidence can then be used for certification.

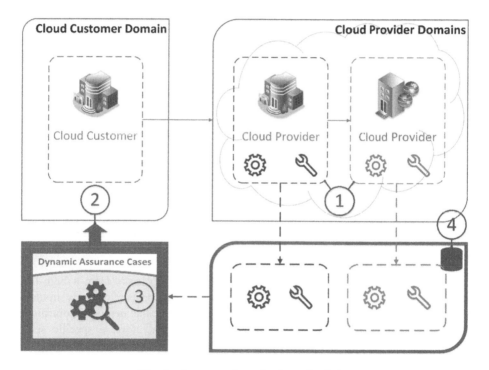

Fig. 1. Assurance in a cloud supply chain

Throughout the cloud supply chain, cloud actors share the overall responsibility of security and privacy. These objectives are achieved and supported by adopting and deploying different security and privacy technologies (as depicted in Fig. 1). Such technologies provide different support within and across cloud actors' domains. The problem then is how to provide assurance that the adopted technologies as a whole support security and privacy objectives across the supply chain, that is, how to provide supporting evidence that the adopted security and privacy technologies are appropriate and effective for the specific cloud supply chain.

4 Implementing Assurance

Keeping in mind what has been introduced so far, this section discusses various aspects of implementing assurance in cloud supply chains, that is, emerging technical considerations to be addressed while implementing a system supporting assurance. System functionalities that support assurance for the whole cloud supply chain are discussed. Notice that specific technical points are not implementation steps to follow, but rather insights which aim to inform on how assurance can be implemented in a concrete scenario.

4.1 Evidence of Cloud Controls

Cloud service providers often work together (e.g. sub-contract services or relies on third-party resources constrained by specific service level agreements) in order to provide specific services to cloud customers. This may result in complex cloud supply chains involving several cloud service providers working jointly (as depicted in Fig. 1). In a cloud supply chain, security is therefore a shared responsibility among the actors involved. Cloud providers deploy different security and privacy controls in order to guarantee critical service features.

In order to support accountability, cloud providers need to gather evidence as proof that security and privacy controls are effective and suitable in addressing emerging threats. Cloud providers can then be entrusted with sensitive data. Table 1, for example, lists some controls drawn from the CSA Cloud Control Matrix v3.0.1 [15], in particular, controls from two different domains: *Data Security & Information Lifecycle Management*, and *Supply Chain Management, Transparency, and Accountability*. Similarly, the NIST Cloud Computing Security Reference Architecture identifies a list of controls (requirements) to mitigate security risks [2].

However, both NIST and CSA aim mitigating security risks from a high-level perspective, providing no guidelines on which operational aspects of controls should be supervised and which data should be stored in order to prove that deployed controls are effective and suitable in addressing emerging threats. Therefore, a specific set of controls and associated (type of) evidence should be defined for each specific cloud environment. However, independently of any cloud environment, it is possible to build a general framework that will ease the task of managing these controls and evidence.

It is necessary that each security and privacy control clearly defines which (type of) evidence it requires to be gathered in a cloud supply chain. Evidence should focus on operational aspects of deployed controls that need to be monitored. If such evidence is not produced, controls cannot be regarded as supporting security and privacy objectives (e.g. in terms of compliance with security and privacy policies). The proposed CloudTrust Protocol (CTP), for example, provides a basic mechanism for sharing evidence across cloud supply chains [16], hence supporting transparency in the cloud.

Table 1. Examples of controls from the CSA Cloud Control Matrix v3.0.1

Control Domain	CCM V3.0 Control ID	Updated Control Specification
Data Security & Information Lifecycle Management: Classification	DSI-01	Data and objects containing data shall be assigned a classification by the data owner based on data type, value, sensitivity, and criticality to the organization
Data Security & Information Lifecycle Management: Handling/ Labeling/Security Policy	DSI-04	Policies and procedures shall be established for the labeling, handling, and security of data and objects which contain data. Mechanisms for label inheritance shall be implemented for objects that act as aggregate containers for data
Data Security & Information Lifecycle Management: Ownership/Stewardship	DSI-06	All data shall be designated with stewardship, with assigned responsibilities defined, documented, and communicated
Supply Chain Management, Transparency and Accountability: Supply Chain Metrics	STA-07	Policies and procedures shall be implemented to ensure the consistent review of service agreements (e.g., SLAs) between providers and customers (tenants) across the relevant supply chain (upstream/downstream). Reviews shall performed at least annually and identity non-conformance to established agreements. The reviews should result in actions to address service-level conflicts or inconsistencies resulting from disparate supplier relationships

4.2 Control-Evidence Data Model

As discussed in the previous section, it is necessary to associate controls to evidence about them. Such evidence can be gathered in a dedicated permanent storage platform (e.g. a software defined storage). There should be an entity in charge of creating, reading, updating, and deleting these controls and relating them to specific evidence. The same entity would also be in charge of the transactions to and from the storage platform. We will call this entity *Control Manager*. Our proposed implementation framework will hence include three main classes: (1) *Control Manager*, (2) *Control*, and (3) *Evidence Item*. Figure 2 provides a diagrammatic representation of the proposed data model.

Each *Control Manager* may handle several Controls, and each of these may have different types of Evidence Items associated with it. Note that the same type of Control may be configured differently in operation, hence, it may be necessary to store different types of evidence. The only way to associate Controls and Evidence Items should be through a Control Manager. While instantiating specific controls, changes will be immediately applied to the storage platform. A Control Manager may also include some metadata defined by the cloud actor using the Control Manager. This metadata, for example, may include information about specific instances of controls which it handles and their associated types of evidence. The Control Manager should be able to communicate directly with the storage platform via a dedicated Application Program Interface (API).

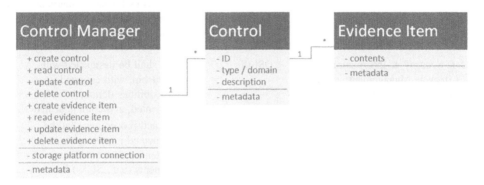

Fig. 2. Proposed Control-Evidence data model

A *Control* will be described by (at least) three fields, as listed by the CSA Cloud Control Matrix [15]: ID, control domain and description. Each Control should be supported by at least one Evidence Item. This evidence will support auditing of the Control (e.g. in terms of policy compliance). Each Control should keep track of its associated Evidence Items. It can also include user-defined metadata (e.g. what type of evidence it is associated with, timestamps like when was the last time this control was audited, etc.).

Finally, an *Evidence Item* is a collection of information that needs to be kept for a Control to support auditing. It can be regarded as a wrapper for the required information. Its contents are, a priori, not of interest for the Control Manager. On the contrary, they will be necessary for an auditor to grant that the deployed set of controls is suitable and effective in order to mitigate security and privacy threats. As with Controls, an Evidence Item may include user-defined metadata (e.g. type of evidence stored such as log file, configuration file, performance metrics, who generated it, etc.).

4.3   Roles in Providing Assurance

A cloud supply chain will need to meet certain controls to prove its accountability. These controls require evidence as proof of their fulfilment. As it was mentioned previously, it is necessary that there exists some permanent storage platform in the cloud supply chain where this evidence will be stored. This responsibility will be assigned to one cloud provider. This storage platform should be accessible by the other providers in the cloud supply chain, as this is where they will store their Evidence Items. It should count with the required security measures to guarantee confidentiality, integrity, and availability (e.g. access control, encryption, backups, etc.). Figure 3 shows a sample cloud supply chain in terms of actors and their associated responsibilities in sharing and contributing to an evidence storage for controls.

In this example, different controls (numbered 1 to 5) are deployed to guarantee security and privacy of data. The evidence associated with them is stored in specific locations which are managed according to the responsibilities in the cloud supply chain. In this example, Cloud Provider A is in charge of managing a software defined storage platform, as well as it is responsible for providing the evidence for controls 1, 2, and 3. On the other hand, Cloud Provider B (subprovider) is only responsible for providing the evidence for controls 4 and 5, which are the ones that affect it. Once that all the evidence is produced, Cloud Provider A is able to reason over it and, if everything is correct, eventually demonstrate to the Cloud Costumer that all the controls are implemented adequately, hence providing assurance.

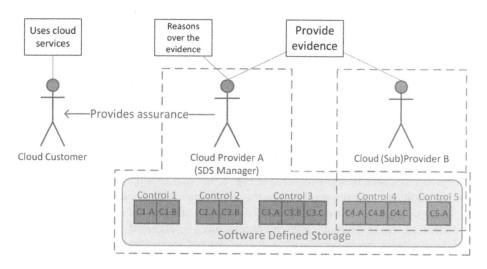

Fig. 3. Sample cloud supply chain

4.4 Evidence Access

As depicted in the previous section, specific Evidence Items are to be provided by specific cloud providers. The access to this evidence should be limited only to the providers who are responsible for them (and, when appropriate, to the auditors).

A Control may require several Evidence Items in order to be considered complied with. These Evidence Items could be supplied by different cloud providers. In this case, it would be desirable that each provider is only allowed access to its related Evidence

Items and no others, hence preventing them from being tampered with by unrelated providers. This scenario is shown in Fig. 4, where Control B requires evidence coming from two different sources. Evidence Items 4 and 5 should only be accessed by Cloud Provider A and Evidence Item 6 only by Cloud Provider B. In this case, an object-level access control is required.

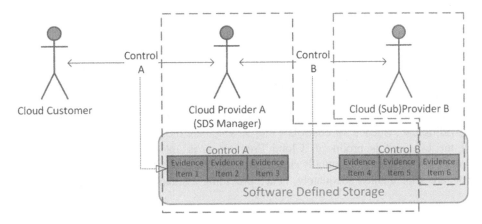

Fig. 4. Desirable requirements for access control

Three of the major software defined storage platforms – OpenStack Swift, Google Cloud Storage, and Amazon S3 – have a two-level hierarchy where the upper level serves as a container[4] for the objects which contain the relevant information to be stored. One can think of a container as a folder where only files (objects) can be stored, not allowing nested folders. The finest granularity that some software defined storage platforms allow (for example, OpenStack Swift [17]) is per container. This means that a user who is granted access rights to a specific container (Control) may then access all its objects (Evidence Items) – depicted in Fig. 5. In order to support object-level access control, additional security mechanisms that allow finer access granularity are required.

Alongside access control, there are other security and privacy concerns that need to be addressed. As an example, integrity checks must be enforced in order to guarantee that the Evidence Items kept in the software defined storage platform have not been tampered with. Enabling monitoring of events at the object level could be useful in small scenarios. However, this may involve dealing with a remarkable amount of data in large scenarios, making it a hardly scalable solution.

In scenarios where two different cloud providers need to share the same Evidence Items, there is a risk of data aggregation. If this situation is likely to arise, additional mechanisms which filter the shared information to specific actors should be implemented – for example, transparency logs [18].

---

[4] "Containers" in OpenStack Swift and Google Cloud Storage and "buckets" in Amazon S3.

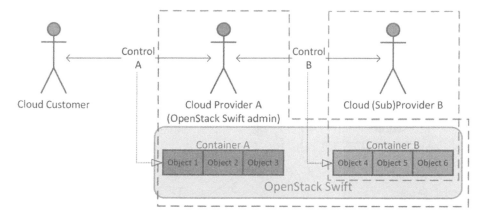

Fig. 5. Access control using OpenStack Swift

5 An Assurance Use Case

The main goal for the Cloud Accountability Project (A4Cloud) is to increase trust in cloud computing by devising methods and tools, through which cloud stakeholders can be made accountable for the privacy and confidentiality of information held in the cloud. Among other milestones, it has specified an accountability model for cloud supply chains ([5]) and several tools to support accountability have been implemented.

In order to prove the application of the accountability model and related tools, a demonstrator scenario has been developed [19]. In this section, we recall this scenario in order to explain a realistic situation where the system depicted in the previous sections can prove useful.

5.1 Wearable Service Use Case Explained

Wearable Co. is a manufacturer of wearable devices that collect well-being data from its wearers. It uses the SaaS[5] provider Kardio-Mon to provide additional services to its customers. Kardio-Mon integrates Map-on-Web's services into their own. Kardio-Mon and Map-on-Web use the IaaS[6] provider DataSpacer to run their services. This scenario is depicted in Fig. 6, where the interactions among the different actors have been numbered. For the sake of simplicity, only interactions between two actors have been considered.

These interactions are subject to be monitored (implementing controls), either continuously or occasionally. The evidence collected to support this process, supplied by the different cloud providers, will be stored in an OpenStack Swift server whose administrator will be Kardio-Mon. The reasons to use this platform are that the demonstrator scenario for the Cloud Accountability Project uses an OpenStack

---

[5] SaaS: Software as a Service.
[6] IaaS: Infrastructure as a Service.

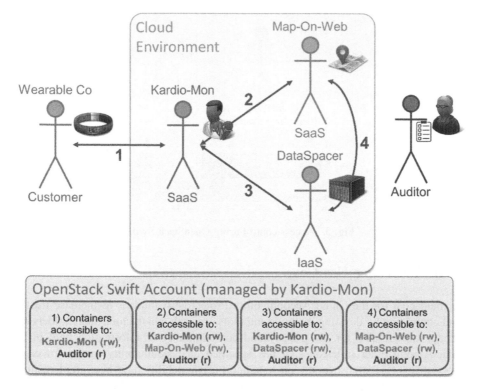

Fig. 6. Wearable service use case: environment and storage platform with access permissions

deployment and also because it is open-source. In the event of having an external auditor to audit these controls, she will require access to read this evidence. Figure 6 shows also the access permissions[7] for all actors involved in the demonstrator use case.

5.2   An Assurance Example: Implementing SLAs

Given the scenario presented in the previous section, let's consider an example where service level agreements (SLA) among the different cloud providers are to be implemented and reviewed, as defined in control STA-07 from the CSA Cloud Control Matrix v3.0.1 (see Table 1). Each SLA will be considered as a separate Control.

For the sake of simplicity we will ignore one of the cloud providers (Map-On-Web) and we will focus on the SLAs between (1) Wearable Co and Kardio-Mon and (2) Kardio-Mon and DataSpacer. The case of having an external auditor in the system will also be considered.

As specified previously, Kardio-Mon will be the OpenStack Swift server administrator. Each Control – one per SLA – needs to be associated with a container in

---

[7] Note that each control will be associated with a container in OpenStack Swift.

OpenStack Swift. These will be named STA-07-SLA1 and STA-07-SLA2. Kardio-Mon is responsible for creating them and for granting the expected access rights. Let's consider that each Control requires only three Evidence Items to support its proper operation: (1) the SLA definition, (2) some performance metrics, and (3) some operation logs.

Let's consider that Kardio-Mon is the cloud provider in charge of supplying the SLA definitions and the updated performance metrics. The logs are to be supplied by the cloud provider running the service. This means that Kardio-Mon is responsible for all the Evidence Items from Control STA-07-SLA1 and for the SLA definition and performance metrics for STA-07-SLA2. With respect to DataSpacer, it should only provide the logs for STA-07-SLA2. This scenario is depicted in Fig. 7.

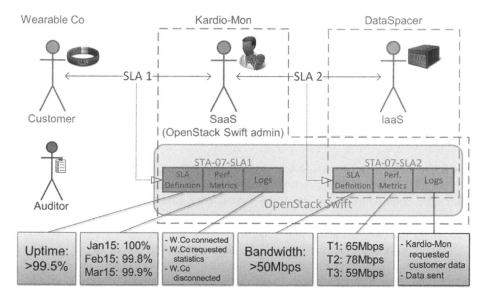

Fig. 7. Example of a cloud environment with SLAs in place

As pointed out in Sect. 4.4, OpenStack Swift does not support object-level access controls. This means that both Kardio-Mon and DataSpacer are able to access the Evidence Items from Control STA-07-SLA2. Consequently, it needs to be ensured that none of the cloud providers have modified – either intentionally or accidentally – the Evidence Items whose responsibility falls on the other provider.

As an auditor is to be expected to join the scenario, her access rights should be set in OpenStack Swift. She should be granted reading permissions to all the Controls. On a different note, the role of Wearable Co is limited to cloud customer, hence not being part of the cloud. Therefore, it should have no access rights whatsoever to the storage platform. All the access rights are collected in Fig. 8.

Actor	Wearable Co		Kardio-Mon		DataSpacer		Auditor	
Operation	Read	Write	Read	Write	Read	Write	Read	Write
SDS*	x	x	✓	✓	x	x	x	x
SLA1	x	x	✓	✓	x	x	✓	x
SLA2	x	x	✓	✓	✓	✓	✓	x

*SDS: Create/Delete containers and modify privileges

Fig. 8. Access rights for the different actors

Wearable Co is the one who, ultimately, is interested in receiving assurance that the data that it puts in the cloud will be adequately protected using privacy and security measures. This assurance may be provided by an external auditor or by an auditor within the cloud environment. In the latter case, one of the cloud providers should act as an auditor, providing comprehensive assurance about the cloud supply chain to the customer. Note that this system can be used as well for such internal auditing.

6 Concluding Remarks

This paper has briefly discussed security and privacy assurance in cloud ecosystems and provided some guidelines on how it can be implemented throughout a cloud supply chain. The controls to be set should be associated with evidence that supports compliance with security and privacy policies. This evidence should be saved in a permanent storage platform accessible to the different could providers.

The discussion provides a rationale for the assurance problem in the cloud and highlights some preliminary requirements. In order to provide support for security and privacy assurance throughout the cloud supply chain, it is necessary:

1. to regard security and privacy solutions as deployed across the cloud supply chain rather than from a single organisation viewpoint,
2. to design and implement means for supporting assurance,
3. to understand emergent dependencies among security and privacy solutions deployed in cloud ecosystems,
4. to assess how security and privacy solutions comply with (or enable to comply with) organisational as well as regulatory policies,
5. to gather operational evidence that supports security and privacy assurance across the cloud supply chain.

A system that can help gather and classify assurance evidence and control which users can access it is also introduced. This system can ease auditing the cloud supply chain, eventually contributing to providing security and privacy assurance.

Future research and development activities will focus on continuous monitoring of the cloud supply chain in order to address the security and privacy risks as soon as they arise, hence avoiding jeopardizing its assurance.

Acknowledgements. This work has been partly funded by the European Commission's Seventh Framework Programme (FP7/2007-2013), grant agreement 317550, Cloud Accountability Project – http://www.a4cloud.eu/ – (A4Cloud).

References

1. NIST Cloud Computing Reference Architecture, Special Publication 500-292
2. NIST Cloud Computing Security Reference Architecture, Special Publication 500-299
3. The NIST Definition of Cloud Computing, Special Publication 800-145
4. ENISA: Cloud Computing Benefits, risks and recommendations for information security
5. Felici, M., Pearson, S.: Accountability for data governance in the cloud. In: Felici, M., Fernández-Gago, C. (eds.) A4Cloud 2014. LNCS, vol. 8937, pp. 3–42. Springer, Heidelberg (2015)
6. Felici, M.: Cloud accountability: glossary of terms and definitions. In: Felici, M., Fernández-Gago, C. (eds.) A4Cloud 2014. LNCS, vol. 8937, pp. 291–306. Springer, Heidelberg (2015)
7. NYMITY Inc.: Privacy Management Accountability Framework (2014)
8. ENISA: Cloud Certification Schemes Metaframework, Version 1.0, November 2014
9. Gartner: Magic Quadrant for Security Information and Event Management, June 2014
10. European Commission: Unleashing the Potential of Cloud Computing in Europe (2012)
11. ENISA: Privacy, Accountability and Trust – Challenges and Opportunities. European Network and Information Security Agency (ENISA) (2011)
12. Baldwin, A., Pym, D., Shiu, S.: Enterprise Information Risk Management: Dealing with Cloud Computing. In: Pearson, S., Yee, G. (eds.) Privacy and Security for Cloud Computing. Computer Communications and Networks, pp. 257–291. Springer, London (2013)
13. CSA: The Notorious Nine Cloud Computing Top Threats in 2013. Top Threats Working Group, Cloud Security Alliance (2013)
14. Pearson, S.: Accountability in Cloud Service Provision Ecosystems. In: Bernsmed, K., Fischer-Hübner, S. (eds.) Secure IT Systems. LNCS, vol. 8788, pp. 3–24. Springer, Heidelberg (2014)
15. CSA: Cloud Control Matrix v3.0.1, October 2014
16. CSC: A Precis for the CloudTrust Protocol (V2.0). Computer Sciences Corporation (CSC) (2010)
17. Arnold, J.: OpenStack Swift, O'Really (2015)
18. Pulls. T.: Preserving Privacy in Transparency Logging. (Doctoral dissertation). Karlstads Universitet (2015)
19. Wiktor Wlodarczyk, T., Pais, R. (eds.): Deliverable D38.2 Framework of evidence (final), A4Cloud (2015)

Enhanced Assurance About Cloud Service Provision Promises

Michela D'Errico$^{(\boxtimes)}$ and Siani Pearson

Hewlett Packard Enterprise, Security and Manageability Lab, Bristol, UK
{michela.derrico, siani.pearson}@hpe.com

Abstract. It is envisaged that in future cloud service providers will increasingly be using a Privacy Level Agreement (PLA) to disclose their data protection practices. This is essentially a self-assessment relating to data protection compliance. Many cloud customers may wish for greater ease in comparing PLAs from different providers, as well as increased assurance about what is being claimed. We tackle this issue by proposing: a standardised representation for PLAs that can be used in a number of ways, including automated comparison by software tools; an ontological approach that can be used as a basis for such automated analysis; a way of expressing evidence that supports statements made in the PLA. Evidence plays a core role when obtaining assurance and building trust, so we also present an ontology for evidence and show how the linkage between evidence elements and data protection aspects in PLAs can be realised through an ontology-aware tool prototype we have developed.

Keywords: Assurance · Evidence · Policy enforcement · Privacy Level Agreement · Privacy policy

1   Introduction

Cloud Service Providers (CSPs) can disclose the level of data privacy and protection offered in a Privacy Level Agreement (PLA) [1], which is a Cloud Security Alliance (CSA) standard intended to be used by potential customers to assess data protection related offerings. In this work we envisage the modelling and representation of key information required to be provided in a PLA for different data protection related aspects.

An important source of requirements for CSPs is data protection legislation, which imposes obligations that have to be considered and complied with when offering cloud services. A PLA specifies how the CSP will be compliant with the applicable data protection law; therefore, PLAs are produced by privacy officers of a CSP in the form of natural language documents. Information about how CSPs address different aspects relating to data protection and privacy are reflected in the various sections in which the document is structured. The standardised structure of the agreement is of great help as it provides a way to group the statements found in a privacy policy by the aspect addressed (such as Data Transfer or Breach Notification). PLAv2 [1] has specifically been developed with the aim of creating an agreement template suitable for containing statements about how a CSP is going to meet obligations set out by the European

D. Aspinall et al. (Eds.): Privacy and Identity 2015, IFIP AICT 476, pp. 220–238, 2016.
DOI: 10.1007/978-3-319-41763-9_15

Union (EU) Data Protection Directive 95/46/EC [2] (DPD in short, hereafter) and other current European data protection requirements[1]. The guidelines provided for each section in the PLA inform CSPs about which information is to be provided. This information will enable a customer to analyse and evaluate how a particular CSP has planned to comply with the European legal data protection framework.

Although the PLA is an important achievement, the evaluation of the information contained within it involves humans analysing the agreement's statements. If we consider an organisational customer wanting to compare services based on the provided PLAs, this task may take a long time as it requires humans to read and compare, section by section, the data protection-related statements. With respect to this issue we see the utility of having a machine readable representation of the policy statements. In fact, the information modelling behind the representation of the PLA policy statements constitutes the basis on which tools supporting the comparison among PLAs can be built. The idea here is to automate as many human-performed tasks as possible, primarily for efficiency reasons (as would be needed for example if hundreds of agreements were available). What we seek to model is the set of core information that can be extracted from the agreements and that are likely to be looked for by consumers when searching for a suitable service. The representation of key PLA privacy policy statements will thus highlight the main offerings from the data protection perspective.

We have been researching the topic of privacy policies and machine readable versions within the A4Cloud project [3], which has been developing a set of tools enabling an accountability based-approach that includes managing policies for fulfillment of obligations. As shown in Fig. 1, the implementation of privacy policies can be seen as a two-phase process. During the first phase (*design time*) CSPs define the set of policies setting out the different aspects of the service provision. This policy definition step can result in the production of formal agreements such as Service Level Agreements (SLA) [4] or PLAs. In the following step the CSP selects the controls that are more suitable to fulfil the defined policies. At the end of this step enforcement systems should be appropriately configured to make the overall service components work as they should.

At runtime the components should behave as they have been instructed during the design time phase, and appropriate monitoring components should run to keep track of actions performed and the results of those actions. This is necessary to verify whether operationally the systems are behaving effectively as planned. From an accountability perspective, as we will expand on in Sect. 2, CSPs need to be prompt to prove deployed controls and performed actions; therefore, each step of the implementation process needs to produce evidence of the specific tasks that have been carried out. This is represented in Fig. 1 with the arrows linking each single step with an exemplary evidence repository. If not appropriately described, evidence and its handling can be complex. This is why we propose an ontology for the semantic annotations of evidence elements that can specify the nature of the evidence element and what this latter is evidence of.

---

[1] On December 15th 2015 the European Commission, the European Parliament and the Council agreed on the draft text of the General Data Protection Regulation that, once approved, will update and replace the DPD. It is likely to come into force in spring 2016 with a two-year transition period for organisations to comply. The PLA WG will continue to work on the PLA to keep it aligned with current privacy laws in Europe.

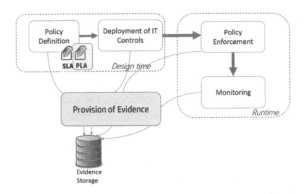

Fig. 1. Provision of evidence for accountable implementation of privacy policies

We have analysed the capability of software components in a specific instance of a cloud environment to enforce privacy statements. For statements enforceable by the means of software, we extend the PLA ontology that we have developed by adding properties that allow us to enrich the agreement representation. Specifically, we want to augment the representation with the technical policies created for policy enforcement. We see a technical policy, in itself, as an element that may need to be provided as evidence for demonstration purposes. The technical policy is one of the elements of evidence needed to prove that a policy statement has not just been claimed in an agreement but has also been turned into a software artifact. Evidence produced at runtime contributes to further back up the fulfilment of the policy statements. To establish a link between evidence elements and the policy statements whose demonstration they contribute to support, we propose an ontologically based-approach. Specifically, we create a machine understandable representation of the PLA and then we propose a model to semantically describe evidence elements and link them to the privacy statements.

The remainder of the paper is structured as follows. In Sect. 2 we present the concept of evidence, along with some definitions, highlighting its importance for the sake of accountability. In Sect. 3 we present the approach we have taken to turn PLA into a software-exploitable tool. We illustrate an example of ontology modelling applied to the data transfer section of PLA. Then we propose an ontology modelling the concept of evidence (about data processing in the cloud), proposing in particular an approach to link evidence elements to the data protection aspect they underpin. In Sect. 4 we present the tool that we developed within the context of the A4Cloud project to facilitate the translation of policy statements into instances of the PLA-related ontology models. The tool also enables the creation of system level policies for the setup and configuration of enforcement components that are added to the ontology-based representation of the PLA as evidence elements. In Sect. 5 related work is presented. Section 6 concludes the paper by providing some considerations about the work done and outlining directions for future work.

2   Evidence and Assurance in Relation to CSPs' Promises

As considered above, the information provided in the PLA represents data protection related promises that a CSP commits to keep with regard to the provision of a service. A customer selects a service based on an evaluation of the PLAs of the available services. Once a specific service is selected, the related CSP needs to set up and configure the systems so that the PLA terms are met when the customer starts to use the service.

Moving towards the adoption of an accountability-based approach in the provision of a service [5], the CSP must be able to provide the customer with further assurance that the policies are being enforced as stated in the agreement. This assurance can be built upon the evidence elements that the provider can produce and make available to authorised and interested parties in different phases of the cloud service provision.

From the customer point of view, the result of the evaluation of evidence is meant to be used as an indicator of what they can expect from the service in terms of adherence to the promised policies. From the provider standpoint, being able to produce evidence can be an advantage in service markets. Enterprise businesses are more likely to select services provided by CSPs that can guarantee a certain level of assurance with regard to the fulfillment of obligations, especially when the latter are required legally. Provision of evidence is not just a business-driven choice, though. In fact, for providers that want to disclose their practices by using the last release of CSA PLA [1], provision of evidence has been turned into a requirement to be addressed to demonstrate the CSPs' accountability in fulfilling obligations.

2.1   The Role of Evidence

Evidence is strictly bound to the concept of accountability, as it is one of the elements that must be produced and provided to appropriate parties by an organisation that wants to adopt an accountable approach for the provision of a cloud service. A strong accountability approach requires moving from accountability of policies and procedures to accountability of practices [5]. This move requires an organisation to be prompt in providing evidence about how obligations have been fulfilled and not just producing reports based on elements that have been analysed and elaborated by the provider itself. Elements that can be provided as proof of the correct (or incorrect) behaviour of a provider are likely to play an important role. In the PLA the way the provision of evidence has to be disclosed is explained in the guidelines accompanying the accountability section[2] within it, as the provision of evidence is central to the concept of accountability. Evidence is viewed as encompassing different levels. Specifically, *"Evidence elements need to be provided at the (i) Organizational policies level to demonstrate that policies are correct and appropriate; at (ii) IT Controls level, to demonstrate that appropriate controls have been deployed; at (iii) Operations level,*

---

[2] The A4Cloud project, through the authors, has contributed to the text of the accountability section in the PLA.

to demonstrate that systems are behaving (or not) as planned" [1]. Therefore the availability of evidence elements can support the demonstration of the fulfilment of an obligation at different levels, from a declaration level through a documented policy to an operational level through the production of logs or any other system level tangible representation of the processing carried out by the systems. The willingness to produce evidence also reflects the transparency of an organisation and can contribute to building the trust of the customer in the provider.

The need to provide evidence is explicitly stated in the definition of accountability from the EDPS glossary [6] (see text we have underlined), which reads: *"Accountability requires that controllers put in place internal mechanisms and control systems that ensure compliance and provide evidence – such as audit reports – to demonstrate compliance to external stakeholders, including supervisory authorities."*

The Article 29 WP (Opinion 05/12, 2012) [7] also introduces the notion of (documentary) evidence to be provided to back up the asserted compliance to the data protection principles, *"[…] cloud providers should provide documentary evidence of appropriate and effective measures that deliver the outcomes of the data protection principles".*

CSPs need therefore to support assertions about practices adopted with related and relevant evidence artifacts. Example of these types of elements are certifications, logs and technical policies. These elements can be evaluated by customers who will make their choice by taking into account, in addition to the more common privacy policy statements, the information that a provider discloses about the evidence that it is able to produce. Some obligations may matter more than others for a specific customer. For those obligations, a customer is likely to view more favourably a provider that is able to produce a larger set, or more compelling, evidence elements.

2.2 Evaluation of Evidence Upfront and During Service Provision

As considered above, CSPs may want to provide a tangible demonstration to customers and/or auditors that they adopt an accountable approach. Such accountable CSPs would need to design their systems in such a way that they would be prompted to produce the evidence elements that will be required and analysed for demonstration purposes. The evidence can take different forms and can be used to demonstrate accountability at different levels, namely the organizational, controls and operations levels [8].

Evidence has to be produced by CSPs before entering into an agreement with a customer and also just after the contract is signed. In the first phase, CSPs need to provide evidence so that customers can make a more informed service selection. During this phase, customers can evaluate tangible evidence elements, such as documented policies, certifications and privacy seals. These elements represent a type of evidence that has been already produced. A different type of evidence is *promised evidence*, which refers to the elements that CSPs commit to produce. Logs are an example of promised evidence, as they can be produced when the service is in operation. Access to logs and other forms of evidence produced at runtime may be required to assess whether the provider and the systems set up have behaved as agreed or not. *Promised evidence* is thus key for holding a provider accountable. The two different set of evidence elements that result from this distinction can be used for the evaluation of the accountability attributes *appropriateness* and *effectiveness*. According to the definition of these attributes[3] [9], appropriateness evaluates the *capability* of contributing, therefore evidence provided upfront shall be used for this purpose; effectiveness evaluates the *actual* contribution to accountability, therefore for the purpose of this attribute *promised evidence* elements shall be evaluated when produced at runtime.

Information about the evidence elements available and to be produced can be difficult to analyse and evaluate. We would like to model some aspects of the evidence related disclosure that can be of use for its evaluation. We want to create a model that allows the building of tools that, with reference to a service, can answer questions like "Which types of elements can be produced to demonstrate the fulfilment of this data transfer policy?" To achieve this goal we create an evidence ontology and then link it to the ontology models we created for the PLA sections. In this way it will be possible for a provider to specify whether a specific evidence element has to be used for evaluating the fulfilment of a specific data privacy aspect. Establishing this link will be of help for customers, as there may be some data protection aspects that matter more than others for a customer, and knowing that a CSP can provide a larger set of evidence elements than another CSP, with respect to that aspect, may determine the choice that the customer will make.

The ontology model we build would be used by a provider to create instances of classes and properties that reflect information disclosed about the service. As mentioned above, the duty to produce evidence does not end with the signing of an agreement. The ontology-based representation of the PLA can be enriched with new elements as they are created within the enforcement environment. Ontology classes can be used for tagging the evidence produced at runtime by the enforcement components. Let us consider the case of data transfer policy statements, and let us assume there is a component in charge of monitoring the fulfilment of the restriction about the data processing location. The component can be configured so that the logs for the monitoring of those statements are tagged with the instance of the Data Transfer section being monitored. This would facilitate gathering logs about the monitoring of a specific policy. Our work on PLA formal representation seeks then to structure the concept of evidence into an ontology model and link it to the policy statements that the specific evidence elements aim to prove. This modelling constitutes the base element that can enable the development of a tool that help cloud customers to query, for a specific service, the type of evidence that can be produced to demonstrate the fulfilment of a specific policy.

In the following section we will present the approach taken for the modelling of the PLA ontology. We will give details about the modelling of the Data Transfer section, as we will be referring to it as an example in Sect. 4 when we will present the ontology-enabled tool to create the PLA representation.

---

[3] **Appropriateness**: the extent to which the technical and organisational measures used have the capability of contributing to accountability.
Effectiveness: the extent to which the technical and organisational measures used actually contribute to accountability.

3 PLA and Evidence Ontology Models

We present in the following subsections a set of classes and properties forming part of our PLA ontology. We present the Data Transfer section as an example of section ontology modelling that shows the approach taken. Then we move to the modelling of evidence.

3.1 PLA Model Overview

We would like the PLA ontology model to reflect the structure of the agreement; thus we model the top level class PLA and link it to the Service class and to the DataProtectionAspect class. A PLA is associated with one and only one service; a service can have just one PLA, therefore we model this two-way relation through the property isProvidedFor and its inverse provides. The DataProtectionAspect class has a list of subclasses which correspond to the sections in the PLA. To give an example, DataTransfer and PersonalData-Breach are two subclasses.

Data Transfer. In the Data Transfer section of the PLA, CSPs are required to set out the following set of information:

- Whether data will be transferred
- The reason of the transfer (regular operations or emergency)
- The country where data are transferred to (EEA or outside)
- The legal grounds for the transfer
- The Data Protection role of the recipient of the data being transferred

The Data Transfer ontology is then modelled by turning the above information into the set of properties described below. We give just two examples of the properties we have modelled to represent the information above, as we will be using them in Sect. 4.

Object Property toCountry: this specifies the country where data will be transferred. This property ranges over instances of the class Country, which can be described by exhaustively listing all the possible instances of the class. The individuals of Country class are grouped into relevant areas so that we are able to retrieve additional information from the specific recipient country specified. As we know, for the implementation of DPD the knowledge about the area the country belongs to plays an important role. Knowing whether the country is within or outside the European Economic Area (EEA) is important as it establishes whether additional safeguards have to be guaranteed by the recipient organisation. For this reason we create an EEACountry subclass so that we can also directly obtain the information about the area. For completeness we also model a EUCountry class, a subclass of EEACountry, as it can be useful in other contexts.

Modelling the data transfer policy by specifying not just the area (within or outside EEA) but also the specific country (or set of countries) is of importance for organisations that have stricter requirements in this regard. In fact, there are countries where organisations have to maintain stronger data protection policies because it is required by tougher local laws. Having this piece of information represented in the machine readable version of the Data Transfer section allows customers to search for services able to address their specific need about the location.

Object Property `hasAdequacyBase`: this property specifies the means by which data transfer adequacy criteria are met. An instance of `DataTransfer` class is linked to an instance of the class `AdequacyBase`. We describe the class by enumerating some individuals belonging to this class, among which there are well known legal grounds enabling the transfer of data, namely `ECApprovedModelContractClauses`, `BindingCorporateRules`, `EEAInternalTranfer`, `OtherContractual-Agreement`, `Consent`, `Exception`. The instantiation of this property is of high importance when the transfer is to be done towards a country outside the EEA.

3.2 An Ontology for Evidence

Cloud customers evaluate capabilities of CSPs in demonstrating accountability by taking into consideration the set of evidence artifacts that have been produced in advance. The set of evidence elements is enriched as new evidence artifacts are produced while the service is in operation. This type of evidence may be requested at any time for the purpose of monitoring the behaviour of the provider and therefore assessing whether actions (and their effects) are compliant with what is expected.

Before building our evidence ontology, let us review a few definitions drawn for Evidence and Accountability Evidence. This initial analysis will allow us to extract the main properties that characterise an evidence element and possible connections between an evidence element and other concepts. The result of this analysis will be a set of elements which will drive the modelling of the evidence ontology, which will make the knowledge about evidence explicit.

A4Cloud has defined Accountability Evidence [10] as "*collection of data, metadata, routine information and formal operations performed on data and metadata which provide attributable and verifiable account of the fulfilment of relevant obligations with respect to the service and that can be used to support an argument shown to a third party about the validity of claims about the appropriate and effective functioning (or not) of an observable system*". This definition is broad enough to account for evidence provided in different forms, whether raw or derived. What we highlight from this definition is the established linkage between the evidence and the *claims*. In our context, where claims are made in the PLA's sections and the capabilities of producing evidence are stated in the PLA Accountability section, we model the link between a specific evidence artifact and the specific data protection aspect that the evidence backs up.

From the guidelines accompanying the accountability section in PLA [1] we gather a view on the different forms of evidence, namely evidence "*can take different forms, such as attestations, certifications, seals, third-party audits, logs, audit trails, system maintenance records, or more general system reports and documentary evidence of all processing operations*". This characterisation of the nature of evidence can be translated into an ontology that can be used for classification purposes. Referring to the same section in PLA, evidence can be provided to demonstrate the level of depth that the implementation of the policies has reached. The information about the level is additional information than can be used to augment the description of an evidence artifact. Organisations wanting to adopt an accountable approach need to be prepared to provide evidence at all the levels mentioned above, to prove that policies have not only been declared but are actually being followed in practice. The property of being able to provide evidence at different levels is another feature we aim to model in our ontology so that the populated evidence ontology (i.e. the evidence knowledgebase) can be queried to return the data protection aspects for which all levels have been implemented. It is not the case though that evidence can be provided at all the levels mentioned for all policy statements. For example, operationally, there may not be software-based mechanisms for policy enforcement. This consideration should be taken into account by the actors tasked with evaluation of the evidence-related guarantees.

Evidence Ontology Concepts. In the ontology we aim to model the evidence elements and their use for assessments. At the core of our ontology there is the broad *Evidence* concept that we want to better characterise by specifying specific evidence elements along with their definitions. Our context is cloud service provision and evidence is used for demonstration of effective implementation of organisational policies, IT controls and operations; therefore, in our ontology we model the evidence elements that can be used for these purposes.

A first characterisation can be done by introducing the concept of *Derived Evidence*, which is a form of evidence that has been created by examining a set of evidence elements. We introduce the *Assessment* concept as the general term to express the evaluation of evidence elements that generate *Assessment Reports*, which are therefore classified as *Derived Evidence*. We distinguish two main types of assessment, namely *Audit-Based Assessment* and *Continuous Monitoring Assessment*. The knowledge about the assessment type affects the level of confidence that stakeholders have about the result of the assessment, therefore it is important to be transparent about this type of information. Audit, according to the ISO/IEC 27000 definition [11], is a *"systematic, independent and documented process for obtaining audit evidence and evaluating it objectively to determine the extent to which the audit criteria are fulfilled"*. Audit can be performed in different ways, based on what the audit results are to be used for. We distinguish the type of audit based on the actor playing the role of the auditor. *Internal Audit* (also called first party audit) is conducted by the organisation itself for internal purposes, such as process management review. The results of internal audits, in the form of *Audit Reports*, may be requested by customers, and therefore CSPs may wish to include this among the type of (derived) evidence generated. Internal audits can be used to self-assess conformance of organisations to standards/best practices. *Third-Party Audit* is another type of audit-based assessment which is performed by parties external to the organisation. The results of this type of audit may result in certification, or be used for legal and/or regulatory purposes. They are typically conducted by accredited auditors following specific standard audit procedures. Being produced by actors that have no interest in the organisations being audited, third party audit reports assume importance as they provide a higher level of assurance and consequently customers would show greater trust in them. This is also due to the different factors that may affect the trust relationships between CSPs and customers [12].

Certification is defined in our ontology as a type of derived evidence, whose issuance is based on the result of an assessment. As specific type of certifications we include *Attestation* and *Privacy Seal*. Following the classification by ENISA [13], the *Cloud Certifications* class includes the certification schemes relevant for cloud customers. Each certification has a set of underlying standards or best practices. We model this connection through the relationship *underlyingPractices* between *Certification* and *Practices*, which includes *Standards* and *Best Practices*.

There are many artifacts produced during a cloud service lifecycle, which encompasses phases such as service design, development, deployment, advertisement, operation. Each produced artifact can be seen as evidence associated with a specific activity carried out during a specific phase. It can be very complex to classify every possible evidence element. The objective within this paper is to include most known and used types of evidence, based on their possible exploitation during the service procurement phase. We model the *Policies* evidence type and its two main subclasses *Privacy Policy* and *Security Policy*. Evidence elements can be classified as belonging to this category if they document respectively the privacy policy and the security policy adopted in an organisation. As an example of privacy policy evidence we have added the *Notice* class, which can also be associated to an URL pointing to the resource location where the notice has been published.

Agreements represent evidence of what has been promised to customers. We distinguish *Legal Agreements*, which are legally binding, and *Service Specification Agreements*, which are documents describing the features of the service. As agreements addressing specific aspects of a service description we include *Privacy Level Agreements* (PLAs) and *Service Level Agreements* (SLAs), which focus on, respectively, data protection aspects and quality of service aspects. A SLA may refer to a PLA, therefore this link should be represented (although it is not explicitly modelled in this ontology).

Enforcement systems, which are in charge of the technical enforcement of what has been described in policies and agreements, need to be configured and set up appropriately before being deployed. The main artifacts produced at this stage can be classified as *Technical Policies* and *Configuration Files*. Technical policies are the representation of documented policies and procedures in low level policy languages. An example is the policy language denoted as A-PPL [14]; policies in A4Cloud are represented by using A-PPL and then enforced by an A-PPL Engine (A-PPLE) [15] able to process A-PPL policies. A component provided with a set of technical policies should act in a way consistent with that established by those policies. The accountability-driven view of the provision of a cloud service requires provision of proof also about the correct behaviour of the system corresponding to a set of correctly specified policies. Proof of the appropriateness of the policies specified does not imply their effectiveness once they are enforced. Logs will be produced to give evidence of that. *Logs* are the main source of evidence to prove effectiveness of measures. As a specific type of logs we mention *Audit Trails*, which represent records of the sequence of operations leading to a relevant event.

Communications also constitute evidence. The main distinction is between *Informal Communications*, which includes messages exchanged in the form of emails, and

Formal Communications. This latter, in turn, includes *Notifications,* which represent formal reporting of relevant events, and *Account,* which is defined as a report or description of an event or a process and may be used to communicate audit results and system state. The account provides answers to the "six reporters' questions" by using evidence elements [16].

We want to code the implicit linkage between policy statements in a PLA and the evidence that can be evaluated upfront by a customer to assess to which extent the CSP can be considered accountable for specific data protection aspects. This linkage makes explicit the relation between an evidence artifact and a specific data protection aspect. This linkage can be useful to advise customers on the correct use of the evidence elements available. Evidence elements can apply to different data protection aspects but may also target the demonstration of a specific part of the privacy policy. This is modelled in the ontology through the relationship *isEvidenceOf* which maps evidence elements to the data protection aspect which is the target of the evidence-based demonstration.

This linkage created can also be exploited at runtime. Components creating evidence as a result of the enforcement of a privacy policy statement should be enabled to exploit this link to enrich the knowledge base with a reference, such as a Uniform Resource Identifier (URI), to the evidence being created. The reference can also be an accessible Uniform Resource Locator (URL) that points to a web service endpoint to gather evidence elements of that type being continuously collected. We used the Protégé tool [17] to draw the evidence ontology, which is shown in Fig. 2. This ontology shows the classes to be used for describing the evidence artifacts, along with some relationships that hold among some concepts.

The ontology produced should be seen as a living document to be updated as the knowledge about evidence to be used for accountability purposes is enriched.

3.3   Discussion About Use of the Ontologies

The use of the ontology can help to gather and classify the evidence artifacts produced. Metadata describing a specific evidence element can help answer the following questions: "What is the data protection aspect whose demonstration this evidence is meant to contribute to?" About this question, we remark that in the guidelines of the Accountability section of the PLA there is no linkage suggested to be established between the evidence elements provided and a specific data protection aspect. The evidence ontology model we are going to design will also be of use in this respect. The reasoning capabilities of the ontology will be exploited as the semantic description of instances of classes such as Logs will automatically be classified as instances of *Evidence* holding the properties of having been produced by *Software Tools.* Information about the type of evidence element can be used to handle this in the right way, based for example on the format of the element provided.

About the use of ontologies there are two main issues that arise which we try to address in the following paragraphs by proposing approaches we may take, in a later stage of our work.

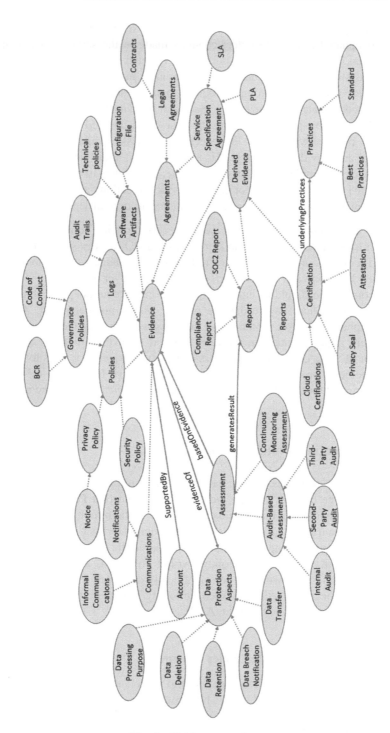

Fig. 2. Evidence ontology

Change Management. Privacy Policies can change over time to adapt the service offerings to updated laws or to reflect changes made in the service implementation. Providers need to track changes and inform the affected customers to let them check that the terms still meet their requirements. Providers need then to have processes in place that track changes and promptly require them to take actions on different tasks that are affected by detected changes. Changes can be handled as events, which can be automatically or manually created (as in the case of an updated law), and the change management process will trigger the execution of tasks which involve the active interaction of the provider. Signatu [18] is an example of a tool that creates the natural language policy and implements a process that alerts providers in case of changes to the law. Iubenda [19], another tool for privacy policy creation, also promises to keep tracking the privacy policy for necessary adaptation to current legislation.

Regulatory Compliance. Use of the Data Protection Policies Tool (DPPT) facilitates the creation of a privacy policy compliant with the DPD. It does so by presenting the provider with options in UI elements that reflect the knowledge we have about possible practices used by providers. However, an additional layer specifically designed to verify the compliance should be introduced to take into account dependencies between different statements that may render the privacy policy not compliant. Application specific compliance checker modules can be designed to verify the compliance with more stringent requirements than the ones derived from the DPD. We see that the development of these compliance checkers can be built by adding rules to be verified over the statements produced. For the time being we have focused on the use of the ontologies for creation of statements to show what the result would be like and how we envisage to use it.

4   Data Protection Policies Tool

We illustrate how instances of the data transfer ontology concepts introduced in Subsect. 3.1 can be created with the aid of a Data Protection Policies Tool (DPPT), which is a user-friendly tool that we have developed. Data introduced by the user (who typically would be a policy manager or policy administrator) can be used to create the technical representation of the policy that is then sent to the component tasked with the policy enforcement. This technical policy (written in A-PPL as this is the A4Cloud reference policy language) will then be semantically described as evidence of the data transfer policy. The result will be a Web Ontology Language (OWL) [20] file containing the data transfer policy and the A-PPL policy.

4.1   Creation of Data Transfer Policy Statements

The GUI of the tool presents different panels and reflects the structure of the PLA. The Data Transfer panel is shown in Fig. 3. The elements available in the GUI are bound to the Data Transfer ontology concepts. Actions performed through the GUI, such as typing values in text fields and selecting an option from a combo box, result in the instantiation of corresponding ontology concepts. The GUI layer hides the ontology layer and helps the user in handling ontology-related operations. To clarify this point, let us consider the text field with the label "Country where personal data will be transferred". The name of the country entered by the user, "US" in this example, is an individual of `Country` class and is linked through the object property `toCountry` to the instance of the `DataTransfer` class.

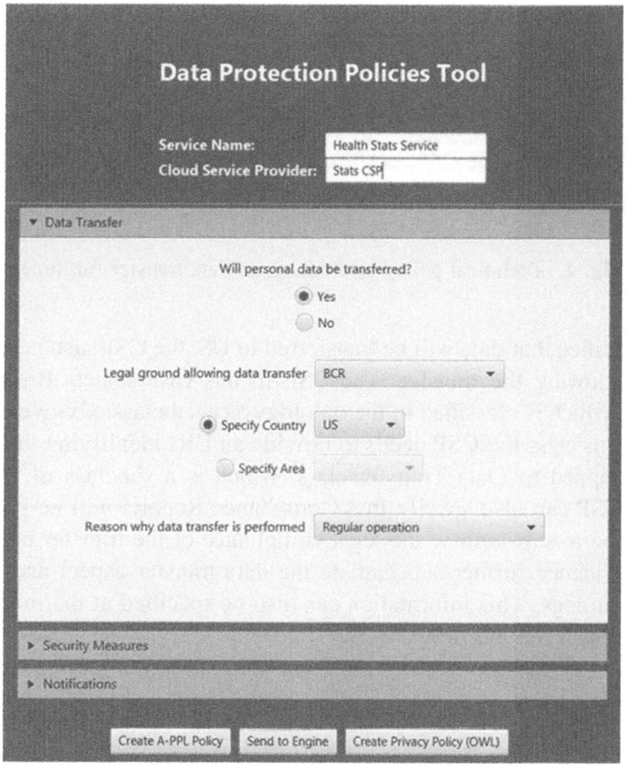

Fig. 3. GUI of data transfer section

Once the user has provided all the data, an A-PPL policy can be created. We have created A-PPL templates for expressing various policy statements. When we click the "Translate into A-PPL" button, the template for data transfer is used and filled in with the needed data. Depending on the language used and the capability of the enforcement components, all or only a subset of the data may be used. Once the A-PPL policy is created, the tool generates an assertion that declares the policy as an instance of the class `TechnicalPolicy` that is evidence of the Data Transfer instance, as shown in Fig. 4. The A-PPL policy can also be sent to the A-PPLE engine by clicking the related button on the GUI. The policy is sent by using the web service APIs provided by A-PPLE, therefore an URL identifying the endpoint of the web service is used. This information can be integrated into the ontology-based representation of Data Transfer if we add classes describing the enforcement components. In this case we can model an

EnforcementComponent class and create an instance identifying the A-PPLE engine. We can provide more specific information about A-PPLE by adding the object property hasEnpoint which links the A-PPLE instance with an instance of the class WebServiceEndpoint, which is a URL.

```
- <xacml:Actions>
  - <xacml:Action>
    - <xacml:ActionMatch MatchId="urn:oasis:names:tc:xacml:1.0:function:string-equal">
        <xacml:AttributeValue DataType="http://www.w3.org/2001/XMLSchema#string">data transfer</xacml:AttributeValue>
        <xacml:ActionAttributeDesignator DataType="http://www.w3.org/2001/XMLSchema#string" AttributeId="action:action-id"/>
      </xacml:ActionMatch>
    </xacml:Action>
  </xacml:Actions>
    <!-- Data must be transferred only the following locations -->
  - <xacml:Environments>
    - <xacml:Environment>
      - <xacml:EnvironmentMatch MatchId="urn:oasis:names:tc:xacml:1.0:function:string-equal">
          <xacml:AttributeValue DataType="http://www.w3.org/2001/XMLSchema#string">Germany</xacml:AttributeValue>
          <xacml:EnvironmentAttributeDesignator DataType="http://www.w3.org/2001/XMLSchema#string" AttributeId="environment:environment-
              id"/>
        </xacml:EnvironmentMatch>
      </xacml:Environment>
    </xacml:Environments>
```

Fig. 4. Technical policy as evidence of data transfer fulfillment

Having specified that data will be transferred to US, the CSP also needs to select the legal ground allowing the transfer. The CSP in this case selects Binding Corporate Rules (BCRs), which is classified in the ontology as a subclass of Governance Policies. To instantiate this class the CSP needs to provide an URI identifying the BCR text that can then be mapped to Data Transfer class, which is a subclass of Data Protection Aspects. The CSP can also specify that Compliance Reports will be produced during service operation to substantiate the legal compliance of the transfer being performed. This type of evidence further substantiate the data transfer aspect and its production may be based on logs. This information can also be specified at the moment manually (that is, not through the aid of a GUI).

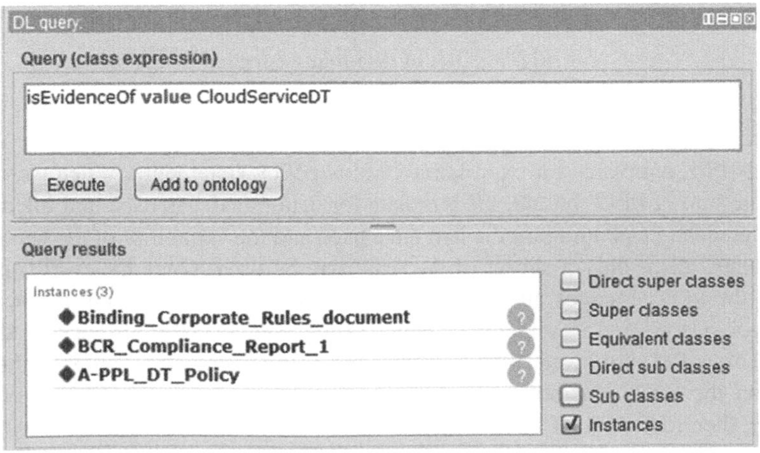

Fig. 5. Evidence elements query

The instances created will be exploited to answer queries about the evidence available for the data transfer data protection aspect.

If we want to know which evidence elements are available for the Data Transfer policy, we need to query the populated ontology by using the DL Query Tab in the Protégé tool, and we obtain references to BCR, compliance report and technical policy (this latter is added to the knowledge base by the DPPT tool). The query and the result are shown in Fig. 5.

5 Related Work

PLA as a research initiative was launched only in 2012 and PLA v2 was released in June 2015. We are not aware of available examples of real instances of PLA, nor of published work about software-based exploitable PLA, which we introduce with our work. However, there has been significant research in the area of SLAs [4], of which PLA is positioned to be supplementary and privacy-focused, and there are a few projects that have addressed the modelling of a machine readable SLA to be exploited by software tools. In particular, the SLA@SOI project [21] has created a SLA model for service lifecycle management [22, 23]. The SPECS project [24] addresses the topic of automating the management of security-oriented SLA. To this aim, the problem of the definition of a machine readable format for the SLA is tackled. SPECS introduces a SLA security conceptual model and proposes an XML schema for this model [25]. As an example of an ontology-based approach to enable SLA management we cite [26]. Significant research has been carried out on the representation of privacy policies in a machine readable format. Among relevant background in this area we cite W3C P3P [27], which developed a platform enabling web sites to express their data collection privacy practices in an XML standard format known as a *P3P policy*, and extensions of this approach in the PRIME project [28] and PRIMELife project [29], although many other approaches have been taken.

There has also been prior work in ontology supported policy generation [30] based on the mapping between single eXtensible Access Control Markup Language (XACML) syntax elements and legal requirements modelled in an ontology. The advantage of the approach we propose is that we can utilize a task that needs to be completed by organisations in any case (namely the provision of SLAs and PLAs), and then automatically generate information that has a clear business benefit (namely, provision of assurance that can be used to generate trust).

Evidence-related topics have been tackled in different work for different purposes that relate to evidence generation, the gathering/collection of evidence, secure storage of produced evidence, protocols for evidence retrieval and evidence analysis. For example, Ruebsamen et al. in [31], as part of work carried out within the A4Cloud project, have tackled the design of a system for secure collection and storage of digital evidence to address the requirements imposed for the purpose of accountability audits. Various evidence sources are considered for evidence collection, with software agents specifically developed for collection of evidence from a specific source. The knowledge about the features of the source and the evidence produced has been used to design the software agents but has not been made explicit once the evidence is generated. This is one of the purposes of our work, to add metadata to evidence elements by means of ontologies so that they are given meaning by different systems being made to be ontology-enabled.

The role of logs and the importance they assume as accountability evidence is discussed by Ruebsamen et al. in [32], where the need for mappings between evidence data and high level requirements is also raised.

Semantic description of evidence has been tackled in the field of digital investigations for automating the process of integration of evidence [33], which often relies on expertise of expert practitioners who manually perform this task. Dosis et al. [33] in their work describe their ontology-based method to integrate digital evidence. They have specified a number of ontologies for describing sources of evidence commonly used in digital investigations, such as storage media and network traffic. With respect to this work, our ontology can be considered as an upper ontology of evidence, whose concepts can be expanded into additional ontologies in which the knowledge of a specific component can be modeled. Brady et al. [34] also propose an ontology – the Digital Evidence Semantic Ontology (DESO) – to describe devices that are sources of digital evidence. DESO has been developed to support digital evidence examiners in their job of entailing the classification and comparison of digital evidence artifacts.

The Cloud Trust Protocol [35] is a research initiative launched by CSA that aims to provide cloud customers with mechanisms to make queries about *elements of transparency* that can help build evidence-based trust towards the CSP. The link with accountability is not explicitly mentioned but, according to the view developed in the A4Cloud project [2], this type of mechanism contributes to displaying accountability.

Evidence for demonstrating accountability is addressed by the Privacy Office Guide produced by the Nymity Research Initiative [36]. Evidence is seen as one of the three fundamental elements of accountability (together with ownership and responsibility). Nymity has developed a Privacy Management Accountability Framework which identifies 13 processes for which accountability has to be supported through assessments based on collected evidence.

6   Conclusions

In this paper we have presented an ontology-based approach to create a machine readable representation of the PLA. To ease the creation of PLA ontology instances we have developed a prototype of a GUI-based tool which presents the user with policy statements that have to be disclosed for a specific section of the PLA, and automatically generates a corresponding machine readable representation that can be used in a number of ways.

Provision of evidence is key for an organisation that wants to adopt an accountable approach for service provision. We propose an ontology modelling the concept of evidence and its linkage with privacy policy statements. This modelling allows a semantic description of the evidence elements produced according to their nature. Information about evidence is added to the ontology-based representation of the PLA and can be processed and exploited by customer side tools to extract information about the evidence produced to demonstrate the fulfilment of a data protection aspect. We have shown a specific example related to a Data Transfer policy where the evidence is provided in the form of a technical policy and BCRs, but additional elements could be added in the same way.

Future directions of this research include that we seek to keep working on the tool and the ontologies to keep these aligned with current legal obligations and formal evidence documents being produced and used. We also plan to integrate the tool into a specific real enforcement environment to test the usefulness of the ontology-based tagging.

Acknowledgment. This work has been partly funded from the European Commission's Seventh Framework Programme (FP7/2007-2013) under grant agreement no. 317550 (A4CLOUD) Cloud Accountability Project.

References

1. CSA Privacy Level Agreement. https://downloads.cloudsecurityalliance.org/assets/research/pla/downloads/2015_05_28_PrivacyLevelAgreementV2_FINAL_JRS5.pdf
2. European Commission (EC): Directive 95/46/EC of the European Parliament and of the Council of 24 October 1995 on the protection of individuals with regard to the processing of personal data and on the free movement of such data (1995)
3. Cloud Accountability Project (A4Cloud). http://www.a4cloud.eu/
4. Patel, P., Ranabahu, A.H., Sheth, A.P.: Service Level Agreement in Cloud Computing (2009)
5. Pearson, S.: Privacy management and accountability in global organisations. In: Hansen, M., Hoepman, J.-H., Leenes, R., Whitehouse, D. (eds.) Privacy and Identity 2013. IFIP AICT, vol. 421, pp. 33–52. Springer, Heidelberg (2014)
6. European Data Protection Supervisor (EDPS): Glossary of terms (2012). http://www.edps.europa.eu/EDPSWEB/edps/site/mySite/pid/71#accountability
7. European DG of Justice (Article 29 Working Party): Opinion 05/12 on Cloud Computing (2012). http://ec.europa.eu/justice/data-protection/article-29/documentation/opinion-recommendation/files/2012/wp196_en.pdf
8. Felici, M., Pearson, S. (eds.): D:C-2.1 Report detailing conceptual framework. Deliverable D32.1, A4CLOUD (2014)
9. Jaatun, M., Pearson, S., Gittler, F., Leenes R.: Towards strong accountability for cloud service providers. In: IEEE 6th International Conference on Cloud Computing Technology and Science (CloudCom), pp. 1001–1006. IEEE (2014)
10. Felici, M.: Cloud accountability: glossary of terms and definitions. In: Felici, M., Fernández-Gago, C. (eds.) A4Cloud 2014. LNCS, vol. 8937, pp. 291–306. Springer, Heidelberg (2015)
11. ISO/IEC 27000, Information technology — Security techniques — Information security management systems — Overview and vocabulary. European DG of Justice (Article 29 Working Party), Binding Corporate Rules. http://ec.europa.eu/justice/data-protection/document/international-transfers/binding-corporate-rules/index_en.htm
12. Pearson, S.: Privacy, security and trust in cloud computing. In: Pearson, S., Yee, G. (eds.) Privacy and Security for Cloud Computing. Computer Communications and Networks, pp. 3–42. Springer, London (2013)
13. Cloud Computing Certification - CCSL and CCSM. https://resilience.enisa.europa.eu/cloud-computing-certification

14. Azraoui, M., et al.: A-PPL: An Accountability Policy Language. Technical report, Eurecom, (2014)
15. Azraoui, M., Elkhiyaoui, K., Önen, M., Bernsmed, K., De Oliveira, A.S., Sendor, J.: A-PPL: an accountability policy language. In: Garcia-Alfaro, J., Herrera-Joancomartí, J., Lupu, E., Posegga, J., Aldini, A., Martinelli, F., Suri, N. (eds.) DPM/SETOP/QASA 2014. LNCS, vol. 8872, pp. 319–326. Springer, Heidelberg (2015)
16. A4Cloud Consortium: Cloud Accountability Reference Architecture. http://www.a4cloud.eu/content/cloud-accountability-reference-architecture
17. Protege Ontology Editor. http://protege.stanford.edu
18. Signatu (Beta version as of 18 November 2015). https://signatu.com/home
19. Iubenda. http://www.iubenda.com/en
20. Owl 2 web ontology language document overview, 2nd edn. http://www.w3.org/TR/owl2-overview/
21. SLA@SOI Project. http://sla-at-soi.eu/
22. Kearney, K.T., Torelli, F., Kotsokalis, C.: SLA*: an abstract syntax for Service Level Agreements. In: 2010 11th IEEE/ACM International Conference on Grid Computing (GRID), pp. 217–224. IEEE (2010)
23. Kotsokalis, C., Yahyapour, R., Gonzalez, M.A.R.: SAMI: the SLA management instance. In: 2010 Fifth International Conference on Internet and Web Applications and Services (ICIW), pp. 303–308. IEEE (2010)
24. SPECS Project. http://www.specs-project.eu/
25. SPECS Consortium: Report on conceptual framework for cloud SLA negotiation – Initial. Technical Report D2.2.1 (2014)
26. Labidi, T., Mtibaa, A., Gargouri, F.: Ontology-based context-aware SLA management for cloud computing. In: Ait Ameur, Y., Bellatreche, L., Papadopoulos, G.A. (eds.) MEDI 2014. LNCS, vol. 8748, pp. 193–208. Springer, Heidelberg (2014)
27. Cranor, L.: Web Privacy with P3P. O'Reilly & Associates, Sebastopol (2002)
28. Camenisch, J., Leenes, R., Sommer, D. (eds.): Digital Privacy: PRIME – Privacy and Identity Management for Europe. LNCS, vol. 6545. Springer, Heidelberg (2011)
29. Ardagna, C.A., Bussard, L., Di, S.D.C., Neven, G., Paraboschi, S., Pedrini, E., Preiss, S., Raggett, D., Samarati, P., Trabelsi, S.: Primelife policy language (20009)
30. Rahmouni, H.B., Solomonides, T., Mont, M.C., Shiu, S.: Privacy compliance in European healthgrid domains: an ontology-based approach. In: 22nd IEEE International Symposium on Computer-Based Medical Systems, CBMS 2009, pp. 1–8. IEEE (2009)
31. Ruebsamen, T., Pulls, T., Reich, C.: Secure evidence collection and storage for cloud accountability audits. In: Proceedings of the 5th International Conference on Cloud Computing and Services Science, pp. 321–330. ISBN 978-989-758-104-5 (2015)
32. Rübsamen, T., Reich, C., Taherimonfared, A., Wlodarczyk, T., Rong, C.: Evidence for accountable cloud computing services. In: Pre-Proceedings of International Workshop on Trustworthiness, Accountability and Forensics in the Cloud (TAFC) (2013)
33. Dosis, S., Homem, I., Popov, O.: Semantic representation and integration of digital evidence. Procedia Comput. Sci. 22, 1266–1275 (2013)
34. Brady, O., Overill, R., Keppens, J.: Addressing the increasing volume and variety of digital evidence using an ontology. In: 2014 IEEE Joint Intelligence and Security Informatics Conference (JISIC), pp. 176–183. IEEE (2014)
35. CSA Cloud Trust Protocol Initiative. https://cloudsecurityalliance.org/research/ctp/
36. Nymity Research Initiative: A Privacy Office Guide to Demonstrating Accountability (2014). https://www.nymity.com/data-privacy-resources/data-privacy-research/privacy-accountability-book.aspx

ALOC: Attribute Level of Confidence for a User-Centric Attribute Assurance

Salameh Abu Rmeileh[✉], Esther Palomar, and Hanifa Shah

Birmingham City University, Birmingham, UK
{salameh.aburmeileh,esther.palomar,hanifa.shah}@bcu.ac.uk

Abstract. The proliferation of online services leads to an increasing number of different digital identities that each user has. In order to enforce access control policies, service providers need assurance that the information associated with users' identities, either received by the user or a federation partner, are correct and trustworthy. Current identity assurance frameworks assess the trustworthiness of identity providers but do not define trust on the user attribute level of granularity. In this paper, we consider the user attribute as a dynamic structure that extends the foundation of attribute authenticity and trustworthiness by introducing the attribute level of confidence (ALOC). Basically, the ALOC encompasses additional information on attributes' lifecycle and issuing mechanisms. We present the architecture design and demonstrate its components. This paper concludes discussing future research directions.

Keywords: Attribute assurance · Attribute-based identity · Trust · Level of confidence

1 Introduction

A significant amount of our daily activities have been replaced by their digital counterparts (online services) such as banking, social networking, and shopping, to name a few. As their real life former selves, some online service providers (SPs) must be able to identify and authenticate their consumers in order to make informed access control decisions while others can be more flexible depending on the nature of the service. However, as [19] state, "modern businesses see data as a gold mine." This reliance on data incite inappropriate practices. For online service providers the certainty of proving a subjects digital identity is limited by the strength and/or some level of trust on one or more authentication attributes. On the other hand, consumers need to trust SPs to handle their personal information properly [16].

However, todays online activities have evolved beyond what the username/password format can effectively protect. Users then create multiple digital identities, one for each service provider that requires an acceptable level of security when granting access to the service [13]. These identities may partly

D. Aspinall et al. (Eds.): Privacy and Identity 2015, IFIP AICT 476, pp. 239–252, 2016.
DOI: 10.1007/978-3-319-41763-9_16

overlap, but can also be mutually inconsistent, e.g. shaving few years off their age or few pounds off their weight on online social networks, or a minor pretending to be a certain age in order to gain eligibility for certain entitlements. From users' perspective, this generates a huge burden for users to manage their identities, remember associated credentials, and keep their information up-to-date [4] while from a business perspective, SPs will suffer from critical deficiencies in their access control decisions in case of false or inconsistent information been provided by the users.

A digital identity is the information about individual characteristics, distributed in the digital world, by which an entity, a thing or person, in the real world can be recognised or known [22]. Technically, a digital identity comprises a limited set of attributes that holds the information about the entity's characteristics. These attributes are attested by some party (either the entity itself or a third party). Some attributes are for identification purposes and some others are not. While an attribute may not uniquely identify an entity, the aggregation of them could potentially cause entities to be uniquely identified within a scope. Identity is also *dynamic*. Assertions of someone's age, passport, email, phone number, friendships, convictions and beliefs change over time.

This leads to identity management (IDM) becoming one of the most pervasive parts of IT systems [20]. IDM comprises the whole processes and all underlying technologies for the creation (provision), usage, update and revocation (de-provision) of a digital identity once it is not needed anymore [3]. Thus, IDM systems are about controlling and using digital identities, enabling businesses to select and share user information [10]. Trying to overcome the limitations of traditional IDM models, Federated identity management emerged as a way of sharing identity information across several trust domains [1]. However, inherent issue in these open models is heavy reliance on online identity providers.

Identity assurance frameworks then appeared to assess the trustworthiness of identity providers [2]. As a result, identity providers obtain a level of assurance (LoA) that reflects the degree of confidence in the assertions they make. On the other hand, current identity assurance approaches do not consider the definition of trust at the level of attribute and mostly consider identity as a whole lacking distinction amongst different qualities of trust, and the ability to cope with changes of trust level over time, e.g. attributes are gathered during the registration phase and often fixed.

In this paper, we propose a privacy-enhanced user-centric attribute assurance model to ensure that identity attributes are authentic and accurately associated with the user while enabling the user to have control over his attributes. We assign trust levels to individual attributes not only registration and authentication process and we extend the attribute structure to hold the aggregation of its assertions by introducing attribute level of confidence (ALOC). Basically, ALOC is a data structure, within the attribute itself, which comprises a set of elements reflecting the correctness, authenticity, timeliness and integrity of the attribute value. Being a fundamental component of the attribute structure, ALOC defines trust on the same granular level as the attribute information.

In particular, ALOC utilises the attribute's usage history, combined with its life cycle[1] [12], to build its reputation and quantify its trust level. The user identity is then a unique dynamic structure compiling the attributes that can be selectively disclosed to the SP and according to a certain policy.

The rest of the paper is organised as follows. Section 2 overviews the related work. In Sect. 3 we present the new user attribute data structure. The architecture and our proposal integration into potential real scenarios and platform are described in Sect. 4. Finally, Sect. 5 concludes with the immediate future work.

2 Related Work

This work builds on and contributes to the fields of identity management, attribute assurance, attribute aggregation, trust, and privacy. Thus, related work has been investigated in these main different areas: trust and reputation systems, level of assurance and credibility of claims.

Several approaches have been proposed regarding trust levels for users' attributes. In [6–8], Chadwick et al. build on NIST's concept of assurance levels and propose to have separate metrics for the Registration LoA and the Authentication LoA instead of NIST's compound metric which is dependent upon both. The Registration LoA reflects the strength of the registration method the identity provider (IdP) used e.g. registering online is much weaker than registering in person while the Authentication LoA reflects the strength of the authentication method the IdP used e.g. username/password is weaker than public key certificates and private keys. Prior to any authentication taking place, a user needs to register with a service, and provide various credentials to prove his identity. After successful registration the SP creates a profile for the user and may offer different authentication mechanisms for the user to access, such as username/password with Kerberos, username/password with SSL, etc. Thus, Chadwick et al. argue that no Authentication LoA can be higher than the Registration LoA, since it is the latter that originally authenticated who the user is. In [17], Mohan et al. propose the AttributeTrust framework for evaluating trust in aggregated attributes which are provided by trusted attribute authorities. Similar to our approach, in AttributeTrust, service providers are asked to provide attribute authorities with feedback after each successfully completed transactions. However, Mohan et al. do not outline differences between trust in attribute authority and the attribute itself. Compared to this, in our work, we assign trust levels to individual attributes not only registration and authentication process and we extend the attribute structure to hold the aggregation of its assertions. Additionally, the proposed approaches by Chadwick et al. and Mohan et al. assess the trustworthiness of IdPs not the individual attributes.

Several approaches to enhance the quality of attributes, user-centricity and privacy within national eIDs exist. In [14,15], Laube and Hauser propose a service, as an extension to the SuisseID [9] infrastructure, to handle and provide,

---

[1] Attribute lifecycle consists of four phases: creation, usage, update, and revocation. These phases are inspired by the IDM life cycle.

to some extent, assurance of personal attributes with no official authority certifying or owning. Similar to our approach, the MyIdP service reuses data the user has already used as part of a transaction with a web application in order to assess the quality and trustworthiness of the data. In particular, the assessment is based on the freshness of information, quality of the attribute issuer and the recurrence of information. In [21], Slamanig et al., propose an identification and authentication model to be applied for eIDs which allows for selective disclosure to better protect citizen's privacy. Both approaches rely on the existence of IdPs.

In [23], Thomas and Meinel propose a model to consider trust on a claim basis. Their approach is to extend the notion of claim in claim-based identity management by a *credibility* value enabling service providers to specify the expected trust quality for attributes and the required user attributes. However, the *credibility* value is based on two factors: (i) whether the issuer is trusted or not and (ii) whether the claim is verified or not limiting the attributes' trustworthiness to only three possibilities, namely trusted, untrusted, and a third vague possibility where claim is verified by an untrusted issuer. In our approach we go beyond the *credibility* value by considering other attribute properties resulting in a more compliant and scalable level of confidence for user attributes and provide more choices for a SP to express its policy demands and for users to protect their privacy. In another study [24], Thomas and Meinel present an attribute assurance framework for federated identity management based on a verification context class. However, their attribute assurance framework only offers the possibility to express which attribute has been verified by a federated IdP using a particular verification method in addition to which attributes are required. By contrast, our approach offers users and SPs a wider spectrum to express their policy demands.

The aforementioned models do not address the attribute dynamic nature nor its lifecycle which in reality affects attribute's correctness and timeliness. Drawbacks of these existing solutions motivated us to design an improved, more fine granulated yet more applicable user-centric attribute assurance model.

3   Our Model

In this section, we propose a new user-centric attribute assurance model which is applicable for the public cloud in terms of data assurance and privacy. Our model enables the users to have full control over their information while providing SPs with assured and well qualified attributes.

3.1   Roles

The following entities are involved in the architecture:

User. A set of attributes will allow system users to be authenticated and authorised. For authentication reasons, the user can reveal a subset of these attributes that are endorsed by different types of endorsers and mechanisms. the user can ask for endorsements as well as endorsing other users' attributes.

Endorser. This represents a trusted certification authority, a TTP, a SP, a user, or combination of all. The endorser issues an endorsement to the user for a particular set of attributes using a specific endorsing mechanism.

Service Provider. The SP offers different resources or services which require user identity information. Also, a SP can act as an endorser.

3.2   Requirements

The model fulfills the following requirements:

Assurance. The model must provide qualified but not necessarily certified attributes utilising various mechanisms to quantify attributes' trust levels, i.e. timeliness, correctness, and reputation as well as certification and verification by either TTPs and also fully distributed mechanisms such as crowdsourcing.

User-Centricity. The user always remains in full control over his attributes and benefits from the selective disclosure property when the SP supports it. However, the user cannot alter the $ALOC$ part of the attributes structure. Nonetheless, the user can view all information about his attributes such as which attributes have been endorsed by whom.

Selective Disclosure. In addition to disclose only required attributes' values to SP, the user must have the option to provide the SP with information about the attributes quality and authenticity.

Privacy. The privacy of user attributes must be preserved in the presence of an honest but curious cloud storage, i.e., the cloud storage must not learn anything about the user's attributes, policies or transactions.

Dynamic and Self-contained. User attributes must be dynamic and self-contained by holding all necessary information required to assess their trustworthiness without the involvement of any third party during a given transaction. The model must not involve IdPs. The user acts as its own attribute provider and only interact with third parties that endorse their attributes.

3.3   Extending Identity Attributes

Digital identities are *dynamic*, so are the online services they interact with. Similarly, attribute must be *dynamic* too. Traditionally, an attribute is defined as an ordered pair of label and value, i.e. attribute $x = \langle l, v \rangle$, e.g. $\langle Name, John \rangle$, $\langle Address, London \rangle$. The current static structure of attribute does not provide any information about the authenticity, integrity, or correctness of the value the attribute holds. Our approach is not only to provide attribute assurance and trust but to also make attribute self-contained and more dynamic. We extend the current structure with third element, called *Attribute Level of Confidence (ALOC)*. This element holds all required information to express attribute trustworthiness as we believe this information must be part of the attribute itself and nowhere else. Therefore, we define a dynamic attribute as follows:

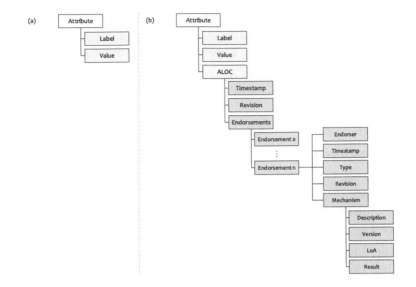

Fig. 1. Current (a) vs Proposed (b) Attribute structure

Dynamic Attribute is a data structure that holds some property or piece of data about an entity as well as the required information to verify the trustworthiness of this property or data. Technically, it is tuple of label, value and $ALOC$, i.e. attribute $x = \langle l, v, aloc \rangle$ where $ALOC$ is a data structure that comprises a set of elements, illustrated in Fig. 1.

The following section explains $ALOC$ in detail.

3.4   Attribute Level of Confidence

Basically, $ALOC$ is a data structure which comprises a set of elements that are required to assess an attribute's trust level. These elements reflect the attribute completeness, timeliness, reputation, and authenticity. The following is a detailed explanation of $ALOC$ elements.

Timestamp. This element represents the attribute's timeliness. It is important to measures the extent to which the age of an attribute is appropriate for the value it holds. We quantify timeliness as the time elapsed from the last update/revision of the attribute's value. In other words, It holds the date and time of the last revision.

Revision. Represents the number of times the attribute's value has been changed, e.g. an attribute with a revision value of 7 shows that the attribute's value has been updated 7 times.

Endorsements. This element holds a list of assertions by different entities, e.g. users, authorities, SPs. Each **endorsement** is a data structure comprising a number of elements as follows:

- **Endorser.** Represents the entity that issued the endorsement.
- **Timestamp.** The issuance date and time of the endorsement.
- **Type.** This element represents the type of the endorsement. We have identified 4 types of endorsements, namely: *Creation, Registration, Authentication* and *Authorisation* endorsement, see Sect. 3.5.
- **Revision.** Shows the attribute's revision the endorsement has been issued for.
- **Mechanism.** Contains information about the certification mechanism used by the endorser.
  - **Description.** Defines the type of certification mechanism, e.g. X.509 certificate, username/password token, SAML assertions, digital signature, etc.
  - **Version.** The version number of the mechanism.
  - **LoA.** Level of assurance of the mechanism indicates the strength of the mechanism, e.g. a X.509 certificate will have a higher LoA than a username/password token.
  - **Result.** This element holds the result of the endorsing mechanism, e.g. if the mechanism is a digital signature then result is the signature itself.

Issuance and acceptance of endorsements depend on the *ALOC* policies of both the endorser and the attribute owner.

3.5   Endorsements Types and Mechanisms

We define four types of endorsements based on the phases of the attribute life cycle. Firstly, *Creation* endorsement is attached to the creation phase of the attribute. Secondly, we break down attribute's usage phase into 3 endorsements: *Registration, Authentication*, and *Authorisation*. We will further elaborate on these phases' processes in Sect. 4.2. For example, attribute 'Academic Qualification' gets a *Creation* endorsement issued by the corresponding academic institution upon the user request; when the user registers with a SP he gets a *Registration* endorsement. A single authority may not be able to certify every attribute and not all attributes have certifying authorities. Thus, the user is able to get endorsements not only from trusted third parties and SPs but also from referral-based trust models such as crowdsourcing.

A wide range of mechanisms are used for adding endorsements namely digital signature, reputation systems, voting schemes, or referral-based mechanisms. The result of the mechanism, i.e. signature, score, value, is stored in the *Result* element of the endorsement.

SPs also define own classifications and trust of endorsers, endorsement mechanisms and mechanisms' results expressed using *ALOC* policies.

4   Architecture

System architecture comprises 4 components: User-centric *ALOC* Agent, Service Provider, Secure Storage, and the User. Figure 2 depicts the proposed architecture. The designed architecture adopts Kim Cameron's Laws of Identity [5] that are widely accepted as a guideline for the design of identity systems.

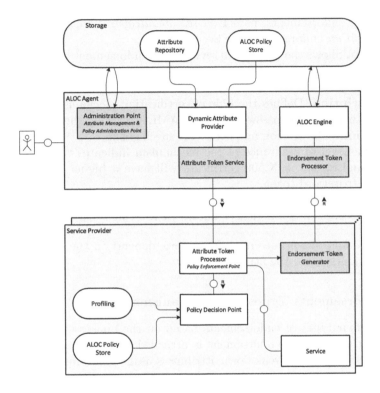

Fig. 2. Proposed architecture for ALOC-based user-centric attribute assurance

4.1   Components

Components of the architecture are explained in detail.

Attribute Token. Is an encrypted token containing a set of attributes' elements to be sent to a SP by the user. The attributes' elements contained in the token are based on the user *ALOC* policies.

ALOC Policy. Represents the storage for the user to express rules and semantics of the attribute information to reveal, to whom, and under what conditions. The SP can also establish its own policies to express the conditions under which a service can be accessed. See Sect. 4.3.

Endorsement Token. For every endorsing process, an endorsement token is created by the issuer containing the elements depicted in Fig. 1.

ALOC Agent. ALOC Agent is a software application that implements the Attribute Level of Confidence model presented in Sect. 3.4 and comprises several components:

- **Administration Point.** This component enables the user to manage his attributes (view, add, update, revoke), define own *ALOC* policies, and request endorsements from other entities.
- **Dynamic Attribute Provider.** This component builds a set of dynamic attributes based on the requested attributes and on dependence of the user's *ALOC* policies.
- **Attribute Token Service.** This component is responsible to provide the Dynamic Attribute Provider with the requested attributes by the SP and to provide the SP with an encrypted token which contains what the Dynamic Attribute Provider returned.
- **Endorsement Token Processor.** This component parses and validates endorsement tokens received from a SP and pass it on to the *ALOC* Engine.
- **ALOC Engine.** This component is responsible for updating the user's attributes *ALOC* element after receiving information from the Endorsement Token Processor according to the user's *ALOC* policies.
- **Storage.** In order to preserve the users' privacy without violating the 8th Law of Location Independence [11] (which states that IDMs should not rely on any persistent data stored locally at the user's machine), the users' dynamic attributes and ALOC policies are stored encrypted on the public cloud. The cloud storage comprises two persistent storage components. The information stored in both components can only be accessed through an ALOC Agent. The data is encrypted by the ALOC Agent before being sent for storage; none of the data is revealed to the storage provider.

Service Provider. The SP consists of several components:

- **Attribute Token Processor/PEP.** This component is responsible for validating attribute tokens. In order to decide whether the information in the token is accepted or not, a request is sent to the Policy Decision Point component. If the information is accepted the Attribute Token processor provides the Endorsement Token Generator component with required information to issue an endorsement token and send it back to the user's *ALOC* Agent.
- **Policy Decision Point.** The Policy Decision Point compares the token information it receives to the *ALOC* policies of the service provider.
- **Endorsement Token Generator.** This component issues encrypted endorsement tokens back to the user's *ALOC* Agent based on requests from the Attribute Token Processor.

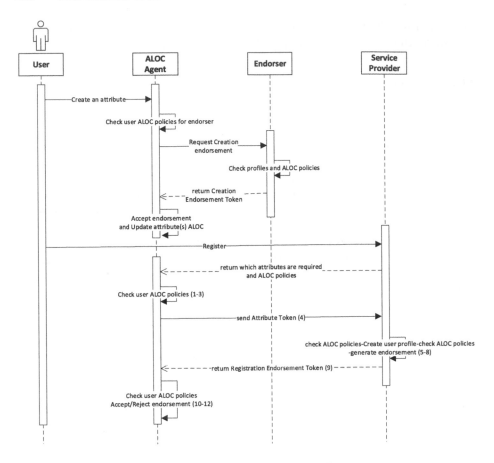

Fig. 3. Attribute creation and registration endorsing processes

4.2   Processes

Creation and Management of Attributes. A user access the ALOC Agent (Mobile app, web app, browser extension) using a passphrase, a smartcard, or a biometric credential. The user creates and manages (view, update, delete) his attributes, i.e. attributes values and ALOC policies through the Administration Point within the *ALOC* Agent.

The user is able to set label and value for an attribute. Also, the user can send a request to a TTP, SP, another user, or collection of them asking for a *Creation* endorsement depending on the attribute type and the user's ALOC policies. Figure 3 shows the attribute creation and registration endorsing processes.

Endorsing Process. The following steps describe the endorsing process for the *Registration* endorsement. See also Fig. 3.

When the user register with a SP:

1. The Attribute Token Service asks the Dynamic Attribute Provider for a set of the requested attributes by the SP.
2. The Dynamic Attribute Provider checks the user *ALOC* policies and accordingly builds the set of requested attributes from the Attribute Repository.
3. The Dynamic Attribute Provider returns the set of dynamic attributes to the Attribute Token Service to issue a token.
4. The Attribute Token Service creates a token, in the requested format, which contains the set of dynamic attributes and sends it to the SP.
5. Upon receipt, the Attribute Token Processor parses the token, checks its validity then passes the information within the Token to the Policy Decision Point.
6. The Policy Decision Point checks the SP *ALOC* policies against the received information.
7. The SP applies the required verification mechanism.
8. Upon success of steps 6 and 7, the Attribute Token Processor requests the Endorsement Token Generator to issue a *Registration* endorsement token for the accepted attributes after providing it with the required information, i.e. the accepted attributes and the endorsing mechanism used.
9. The Endorsement Token Generator issues a token, which contains this information, signs it and then sends it back to the user's *ALOC* Agent.
10. The Endorsement Token Processor receives it, parses it, verifies and checks its validity, and then passes it on to the *ALOC* Engine.
11. The *ALOC* Engine checks the user's *ALOC* policies and accordingly decides whether to accept the endorsement or not.
12. If the endorsement is accepted, the *ALOC* Engine computes the attributes *ALOC* elements, i.e. weight and endorsements, and applies it the Attribute Repository.

The aforementioned steps also apply for the authentication and authorisation processes. However, the endorsement type changes to *Authentication* or *Authorisation*. Additionally, in the authentication process step (8) the Attribute Token Processor checks if the received dynamic attributes have a *Registration* endorsement by the SP, otherwise it applies a required verification mechanism. Lastly, to securely and reliably support these processes, we assume that whenever we speak of public parameters or public keys, they are available in an authentic fashion, e.g., via a PKI. Furthermore, the channels between all parties provide confidentiality, as well as authenticity, e.g., via the use of TLS.

4.3   ALOC Policies

ALOC policies are a crucial part of the ALOC trust model as they enhance the decision making process at SPs, and the selective and/or minimal disclosure of users' attributes. There are two types of *ALOC* policies namely SP *ALOC* policies and user *ALOC* policies. Whereas the latter allows the users to control what to reveal to SPs the former allow SPs to define the trust requirements for user attributes.

User ALOC Policies. Users can create their own policies to control information disclosure and endorsement acceptance. For instance, a user may create a policy that constraints what can be revealed out of the attribute data structure, e.g. a policy for particular when interacting with particular SPs to only disclose the attribute's label, timestamp, revision, and endorsements. Though the value of the attribute is not revealed, the SP will have some degree of assurance based on the *ALOC* elements. Additionally, the user can create policies for endorsement acceptance, e.g. a user policy for attribute *DateOfBirth* forces to be endorsed for *Creation* by *An Interior Ministry* or attribute *Fullname* can be endorsed for all endorsement types by any endorser.

SP ALOC Policies. SPs can create policies for particular attribute information to be verified. In other words, a SP may create a policy that expresses what attribute elements required to compute the level of trust (confidence) of an attribute. For example, the SP expresses its requirements for 2 attributes (Fullname and DateOfBirth) to access a particular resource. For the Fullname attribute the SP enforces exactly one policy, in this case (A) which expresses that the attribute value is required, and it is willing to endorse the attribute if requirements are met. For DateOfBirth attribute the SP enforces 2 policies, A and B, and requires both policies to be met. In policy A the SP expresses that providing the value of the attribute is optional leaving the decision to the user. However, in policy B the SP requires the attribute weight, revision, and an endorsement from a particular endorser by a certain endorsing mechanism whether the user provides the attribute value or not.

In case of a conflict between a user policy and a SP policy then it is up to the user to make a decision to change his policy or not.

5   Conclusion and Future Work

In this paper, we dealt with attribute assurance by extending the structure of digital attributes and defining trust within the attribute itself without the involvement of a third party during a given transaction. We consider the user attribute as a dynamic data structure that extends the foundation of user attribute authenticity and trustworthiness by introducing the attribute level of confidence (ALOC). ALOC enables a multi-level selective disclosure where the user can reveal particular attributes' elements that can be to the SP and according to a certain policy. We also proposed a user-centric attribute assurance architecture based on ALOC. An ALOC agent can be locally-installed software running on a user's device, or its functionality can be distributed between a local and cloud-based entities to reach a higher level of security and accomplish the 8th law of identity, although the problem of protecting stored data on cloud is out of our work's scope. We also showed that our architecture does not require major changes to SPs, however, requires the addition of certain components.

Our implementation consists of developing a user side and a SP side applications. For the SP side, we are developing a simple online store web service that requires user registration and authentication. For the user side, we are developing a browser add-on where the user manages his attributes, attribute endorsements and policies. In our design the user's registration, authentication and policy negotiation will be managed by the add-on. Thus, the user does not need to create a username, a password or provide attributes or ALOC elements manually, e.g. when the user clicks the registration button in the service the service and the add-on will establish communication, exchange policies, and then make a decision either the user will be registered or not based on both policies and provided ALOC elements. *ALOC* policies will adopt XACML policy language standard [18]. Currently, both parts of the implementation are under development and will be evaluated against the requirements mentioned in Sect. 3.2.

Although our architecture satisfies the major properties of a user-centric IDM system, there are still some properties to be improved. It is our immediate future work to finish the implementation of both, the SP and user sides, to evaluate the architecture usability, security, and test the ALOC policy negotiation between users and SPs as well as to making the endorsement mechanism strong against collusion and Sybil attacks.

References

1. Alpár, G., Hoepman, J., Siljee, J.: The identity crisis. security, privacy and usability issues in identity management, pp. 1–15 (2011). arXiv preprint. arXiv:1101.0427
2. Baldwin, A., Mont, M., Shiu, S.: On identity assurance in the presence of federated identity management systems. In: Proceedings of the 2007 ACM Workshop on Digital Identity Management, No. 1, pp. 1–19. ACM, New York (2007)
3. Bertino, E., Takahashi, K.: Identity Management: Concepts, Technologies, and Systems (2011)
4. Bertino, E., Martino, L., Paci, F., Squicciarini, A.: Security for Web Services and Service-Oriented Architectures, 1st edn. Springer, Berlin (2010)
5. Cameron, K.: The laws of identity. Microsoft Corp, May 2005. http://myinstantid.com/laws.pdf
6. Chadwick, D.W., Inman, G.: Attribute aggregation in federated identity management. Computer **42**, 33–40 (2009)
7. Chadwick, D.W., Inman, G.: The Trusted Attribute Aggregation Service (TAAS) - Providing an attribute aggregation layer for federated identity management. In: Proceedings - 2013 International Conference on Availability, Reliability and Security, ARES, pp. 285–290 (2013)
8. Chadwick, D.W., Inman, G., Klingenstein, N.: A conceptual model for attribute aggregation. Future Generation Comput. Syst. **26**(7), 1043–1052 (2010)
9. ECH: eCH-0113: Spezifikation SuisseID. Technical report, eCH (2012)
10. Hansen, M., Berlich, P., Camenisch, J., Clauß, S., Pfitzmann, A., Waidner, M.: Privacy-enhancing identity management. Inf. Secur. Tech. Rep. **9**(1), 35–44 (2004). http://www.sciencedirect.com/science/article/pii/S1363412704000147
11. Hoepman, J.h., Joosten, R., Siljee, J.: Comparing Identity Management Frameworks in a Business Context (2008)
12. Jensen, J.: Identity management lifecycle - exemplifying the need for holistic identity assurance frameworks. In: Mustofa, K., Neuhold, E.J., Tjoa, A.M., Weippl, E., You, I. (eds.) ICT-EurAsia 2013. LNCS, vol. 7804, pp. 343–352. Springer, Heidelberg (2013)

13. Jøsang, A., Fabre, J., Hay, B.: Trust requirements in identity management. In: Proceedings of the 2005, pp. 99–108 (2005). http://dl.acm.org/citation.cfm?id=1082305

14. Laube, A., Hauser, S.: myIdP-The personal attribute hub. In: The Fifth International Conferences on Advanced Service Computing, pp. 1–5 (2013)

15. Laube, A., Hauser, S.: myIdP-The personal attribute hub: prototype and quality of claims. Int. J. Adv. Intell. Syst. **7**(1), 1–10 (2014)

16. Lopez, J., Oppliger, R., Pernul, G.: Authentication and authorization infrastructures (AAIs): a comparative survey. Comput. Secur. **23**(7), 578–590 (2004). http://linkinghub.elsevier.com/retrieve/pii/S0167404804001828

17. Mohan, A., Blough, D.M.: AttributeTrust - A framework for evaluating trust in aggregated attributes via a reputation system. In: Proceedings - 6th Annual Conference on Privacy, Security and Trust, PST 2008, pp. 201–212 (2008)

18. OASIS: eXtensible Access Control Markup Language (XACML) Version 3.0 (2013). http://docs.oasis-open.org/xacml/3.0/xacml-3.0-core-spec-os-en.html

19. Ethan McCallum, Q., Gleason, K.: Business Models for the Data Economy. O'Reilly (2013)

20. Sharman, R.: Digital Identity and Access Management: Technologies and Frameworks. IGI Global (2011)

21. Slamanig, D., Stranacher, K., Zwattendorfer, B.: User-centric identity as a service-architecture for eIDs with selective attribute disclosure. In: ACM Symposium on Access Control Models and Technologies (SACMAT) (2014)

22. Suriadi, S.: Strengthening and formally verifying privacy in identity management systems. Ph.D. thesis, Queensland University of Technology (2010)

23. Thomas, I., Meinel, C.: Enhancing claim-based identity management by adding a credibility level to the notion of claims. In: 2009 IEEE International Conference on Services Computing, pp. 243–250 (2009)

24. Thomas, I., Meinel, C.: An attribute assurance framework to define and match trust in identity attributes. In: 2011 IEEE International Conference on Web Services, pp. 580–587, July 2011

Identity-Theft Through e-Government Services – Government to Pay the Bill?

Jessica Schroers[✉] and Pagona Tsormpatzoudi

K.U. Leuven - Centre for IT & IP Law - iMinds,
Leuven, Belgium
{jessica.schroers,
pagona.tsormpatzoudi}@kuleuven.be

Abstract. The expansion of e-Government and online authentication possibilities in recent years increases the risk of not properly implemented authentication systems. This may often give rise to subsequent risks, such as identity theft. Whereas the legal framework has primarily focused on identity theft as a criminal act, less attention has been given to the way the Government handles information in its identity management systems. This paper considers traditional theories of European extra-contractual liability/tort law to assess whether the Government can be liable for failures in the authentication procedure.

1 Introduction

In the digital age, strong online authentication is an important step in fostering online services with a higher risk but also higher value (OECD 2011). With that in mind, different states have developed their own national eID systems through which citizens can access e-Government services on the basis of secure citizen authentication. This has opened the stage for a new era in citizens' interaction with governments. Transactions on a government's portal are often inherently related to the official identity of a person and involve personal data. In that sense, simple online activities, such as access to portals and modifications of personal details may entail significant risks to citizens' identity information. One of such risks which is rapidly growing and affects all types of stakeholders, including governments and citizens, is the phenomenon of identity theft (European Commission 2004a). Identity theft is described as any unlawful activity where the identity of another person is used as a target or principal tool without that person's consent (Koops and Leenes 2006). The harmful consequences of identity theft do not end with the compromise of one's identity but rather often lead to financial loss. For instance, in case a thief replaces the bank details of an account holder with his own on a web-tax portal, the person entitled to the tax return will not receive it.

The risk of identity theft can appear as a result of faulty online authentication and may lead to potential liability risks for all participants in the Identity Management ("IdM") system, including the government as a relying party[1]. Furthermore, a denial for

---

[1] Typically participants in an IdM system are: i. User ii. Identity Provider (party providing identity assertion on the user) iii. Relying Party (the party relying on the identity assertion provided by the Identity Provider).

© IFIP International Federation for Information Processing 2016
Published by Springer International Publishing Switzerland 2016. All Rights Reserved
D. Aspinall et al. (Eds.): Privacy and Identity 2015, IFIP AICT 476, pp. 253–264, 2016.
DOI: 10.1007/978-3-319-41763-9_17

access to e-Government services or unauthorised access to personal files may be some of the harmful consequences. In order to prevent such consequences, there is a need to enhance the privacy and security of citizens' identity information and ensure that all participants perform their obligations properly (Smedinghoff 2012).

This paper examines the potential civil liability of the government for failures in e-Government authentication systems resulting in identity theft. Departing from the general notions of e-Government (Sect. 2), Sect. 3 describes the way the European extra-contractual liability/tort law could create liability of public services providing e-Government services. Namely the paper first studies the three most common elements that need to be fulfilled in order to establish liability: fault, damage, causation (Sub-sects. 3.2, 3.3 and 3.4). In addition, it illustrates whether each of these elements can be applied to establish liability in case of identity theft caused by failures in e-Government authentication systems.

2 The Rise of e-Government

The use of ICT in administration is not new and has been present for quite some time. Nevertheless, it significantly expanded in the last couple of years and the notion of 'e-Government' has become "one of the topics most frequently debated in administration". (Schedler and Summermatter 2003) As per van der Meer et al., e-Government could be generally understood as

> "the major initiatives of management and delivery of information and public services taken by all levels of government [...] on behalf of citizens, business, involving using multi-ways of internet, website, system integration, and interoperability, to enhance the services (information, communication, policy making), quality and security, and as a new key (main, important) strategy or approach."[2]

Even though e-Government covers an extensive range of services and technologies, the scope of this paper covers the provision of public services using electronic authentication (i.e., e-Government services) which is growing at a fast pace. One factor fostering the use of e-Government services are legal and policy developments at both the European and national level. An example at the European level is Article 6 of the Directive 2006/123/EC which requires Member States to establish 'Points of Single Contact' (PSCs) in order to simplify procedures and formalities relating to access to a service activity. The Directive provides that all procedures and formalities "may be easily completed, at a distance and by electronic means" (Article 8). This entails the provision of the service online, and often necessitates electronic authentication. At the national level, an example can be found in § 2 of the German e-Government law[3],

---

[2] T. van der Meer, D. Gelders, S. Rothier, "E-Democracy: Exploring the current stage of e-Government", Journal of Information Policy 4 (2014), p. 489; referring to: Guanwei Hu, Wenwen Pan, Mingzin Lu and Jie Wang, "The Widely Shared Definition of E-Government. An Exploratory Study.", The Electronic Library 27 (2009): 979.

[3] Entered into force on the 1st of January 2015; § 2 (3) Gesetz zur Förderung der elektronischen Verwaltung (E-Government Gesetz – EGovG) from 25.7.2013 (BGBl. I S. 2749) ('EGovG').

which requires every federal authority in Germany to provide the possibility to use the eID in administrative procedures when identification of a citizen is required by law or necessary for other reasons.

2.1 The Government as Relying Party

The increase of e-Government services necessitates ways to authenticate the citizen in order to ensure that the person authenticating online, accessing the service and eventually receiving the benefit, is indeed the eligible person. Traditionally, citizens had to go to the public authority in order to authenticate and use a public service, or at least send a personally signed document in paper (e.g., the application for a new ID card or filing a tax return form). In e-Government this can be done electronically and at a distance. However, such an electronic action requires reliable electronic authentications. As a result, different states have developed their own national eID systems through which citizens can authenticate themselves to use e-Government services.

These systems are often linked to the national ID card of the country, such as in Germany (i.e. the nPA) or in Belgium (i.e. the eID). Other national eID systems may differ, such as the Austrian 'Citizen Card' (Bürgerkarte), which is a logical unit that can be integrated on different tokens (e.g. a smart card or cell phone)[4]. The national eID systems can vary extensively, but often the current systems use certificates and require the relying party to integrate specific software or hardware for the authentication system. Implementation of authentication systems in e-Government services not only takes place in large scale systems (for example for purposes of tax administration), but also by small scale regional e-Government public services.

In the future, local government services which generally operate on a smaller scale and might not have the necessary IT know-how will need to be able to accept different types of eIDs and keep the information secure. This obligation results from the new eIDAS Regulation (No 910/2014) of the European Parliament and of the Council of 23 July 2014 on electronic identification and trust services for electronic transactions in the internal market and repealing Directive 1999/93/EC. The Regulation introduces obligations for mutual recognition of electronic identity means in order to facilitate cross border authentication and improvement of the availability of interoperable e-Government services in the EU (Recital 6). The Regulation ensures that Member States also have to accept eID means of notified eID schemes of other countries for access to their own public services, if they require their national eID means for access (Article 6).

Considering that public services often have neither extensive IT resources/ knowledge nor much funding to implement systems able to accept foreign eIDs, the obligation to accept notified foreign eIDs might result in poorly implemented authentication systems and a reduced security level. Although the eIDAS Regulation includes provisions on liability, it only entails liability for (1) the Member State, (2) the issuing party and (3) the operating party of the eID systems, yet not for the relying party (i.e. the

---

[4] E. Schweighofer, W. Hötzendorfer, "Electronic identities – public or private", International Review of Law, Computers & Technology, 27:1–2, 230–239, 2013, p. 233. In case of a 'handy signature', the authentication with a cell phone the secure signing module is on a special server.

government in this case). Therefore traditional approaches to extra-contractual liability/tort law and laws entailing certain obligations for the relying party may form the basis of liability for failures attributed to the relying party.

3 Liability of Government as Relying Party

In most cases e-Government services are provided by public services, which may in principle be held liable under specific provisions on the liability of public services as well as general extra-contractual liability or tort law. This section analyses how the latter may be applied in case of poorly implemented authentication systems which resulted in identity theft.

3.1 Extra-Contractual or Tort Law Liability in Europe

Civil or tort law liability has developed in different ways across Europe. European legal traditions have adopted various approaches vis-à-vis the concept of extra-contractual liability or tort law. Terminology has varied accordingly. In civil law traditions, extra-contractual liability is derived from an unlawful conduct which causes damage, whereas in common law this notions is referred to as "tort". According to Van Dam, '*European extra-contractual liability law excluding agency without authority and unjust enrichment*' might be a more accurate description, however, it has become common to use the word tort in English academic writing (Van Dam 2013). For the purposes of this paper, we will use the term "tort" as a general term.

Tort liability has different functions. The main one is generally the restitutory function, i.e. the duty to indemnify the damage caused, which can be assigned to the person who commits a tort (i.e. the tortfeasor) (Dimitrov 2007). In certain legal systems civil liability also has other functions, such as a punitive function. In this case the objective is to punish the tortfeasor for the negligent non-performance of his/her duties, in order to discourage future negligent behaviour (Dimitrov 2007). In this regard, it is important to assess whether a relying party can be liable under tort law for faulty online authentication and whether potential liability might provide incentives to increase security.

In order to derive liability from tort in Europe, there are certain elements that have been generally accepted as relevant despite the fact that there is no generally applicable European law:

1. Most countries base tort liability on the principle of **fault**. Fault liability refers to liability for intentional as well as negligent conduct (Van Dam 2013). However, nearly all systems also have some categories of tort liability that are not based on fault, usually a form of strict liability (Widmer 2005). Strict liability implies that someone is liable regardless of whether he acted intentionally or negligently (Van Dam 2013).
2. Another requirement for liability is **damage**. Damage refers to the harm one suffers.
3. A final requirement is that there should be a **causal connection** between the damage and the harmful behaviour (causation).

3.2   Fault

Requirements to prove fault may differ in various countries. For example in France, liability is established when the requirement of fault (faute) stemming from negligent conduct is fulfilled. In England, however, this would not be sufficient, as two requirements need to be fulfilled to establish fault: duty of care and breach of duty. In Germany, there are even three requirements: the violation of a codified normative rule (Tatbestand), unlawfulness (Rechtswidrigkeit) and intention or negligence (Verschulden) (Van Dam 2013). Aside from the differences, the common denominator amongst these cases is the basic requirement for fault liability, namely intentional or negligent conduct (Van Dam 2013). English and German law do contain additional requirements which mean that not every type of misconduct is sufficient for liability (Van Dam 2013).

It is difficult to define fault in a universal way, since its building blocks vary in different countries. Additionally, the way it is interpreted has changed overtime from a more subjective approach to a more objective one. The subjective fault approach considers the individual qualities of the tortfeasor, while the objective fault approach considers the behavior itself (Widmer 2005). Since it is difficult for the judge to evaluate the personal qualities of the tortfeasor, the definition changed towards a more objective standard. Therefore, at the moment, the majority of European countries use the objective standard, frequently presented as the famous 'bonus pater familias'. The 'bonus pater familias' is a model of an average person, "not exceptionally gifted, careful or developed, neither underdeveloped nor someone who recklessly takes chances or who has no prudence" (Widmer 2005). For some countries the concept can be adapted to the personal circumstances or time and place ('reasonable surgeon', 'careful barkeeper') (Widmer 2005) and for specialists generally a higher 'due care' is evaluated according to their above average capacities. The behaviour of the tortfeasor is then measured against this standard. If the behaviour does not comply with this standard and the tortfeasor did not act with due care, the fault criterion is fulfilled.

Other factors that form part of the fault assessment can be, for example, foreseeability (Widmer 2005). In Germany, the foreseeability of the damage-producing situation and preventability of the damage are considered a factor of fault, since "if a certain situation or damage never occurred before, it might have been impossible for the tortfeasor to anticipate its emergence" (Widmer 2005). Another factor can be conformity or lack of conformity with prescriptions, technical or deontological norms (Widmer 2005). This conformity or lack of conformity can serve as a yardstick for the assessment of fault.

Fault of the Government as Relying Party.   This section examines on what conditions a conduct of an e-Government service can constitute a fault if the authentication service has not been properly implemented. An example of a faulty implementation could be a system that does not perform a necessary check of a (certificate) revocation list. In this case the risk arises that an unauthorised person gets access to the service with a stolen eID, even if the owner of the eID has reported the eID theft and blocked the eID.

Another example could be when a system for the provision of a public service does not adequately check whether the user requesting the service is actually entitled to do this. This happened in the Netherlands, where identity theft and fraud cases took place when the tax authority allowed to make requests in the name of someone else. Since no adequate checks were put in place, unauthorised users could make requests through the Dutch eID system in the name of other persons, to receive benefits on their own bank account.[5] As possible under the Dutch social system, the tax administration requested the money back from the beneficiaries.[6] In a relevant court case, the court decided that since the official beneficiaries never received the benefit, the tax administration could not request benefit return from them.[7] It also underlined that since unlawful activity with the DigiD system was possible and had happened before, the tax administration should have checked the bank accounts to which the money was transferred. Additionally, the court stated that the tax administration was not able to discover whether the beneficiary possessed a DigiD (the Dutch eID) or with the use of whose DigiD the request had been placed.[8] In this case the court decided that the request could not be attributed with sufficient certainty to the official beneficiary, however, in similar other cases it was attributed and the beneficiaries had to pay the benefit back.

This shows that a general problem to establish liability remains the challenge to notice failures and to identify and prove one's fault. In this regard logging or specific accountability mechanisms might be helpful. However, if the relying party logs the actions, it would still be necessary that these logs are tamper proof and possibly time stamped, in order to be usable as evidence. An additional difficulty might be the fact that the user might not be able to obtain the information of the logs, as they are in the hands of the relying party. Furthermore, the recognition of failures could often appear on the relying party's side, which is in a better position to recognise if the system does not work/has not been implemented adequately. However; considering that a part of the system might be the responsibility of the IdP, in case failures appear on the IdP's side, it might be more difficult for the relying party to prove the failure.

Independent from the problem of recognising failures, for establishing fault one should examine what can be expected from a public service providing an e-Government service, and whether this was fulfilled or not. In this regard laws and generally accepted standards can be useful. Laws and standards describe the 'duty' of the public services and their employees. Breaching such duties may hold them liable under tort law.

An example of such a law is the main provision with regard to tort liability § 823 of the German Civil Code 'Bürgerliches Gesetzbuch' ('BGB'). For liability based on this provision, it is either necessary that an absolute right has been infringed, which in case of identity theft could be a misuse of the identity or rather the name of the identity

---

[5] See e.g. RvS 201202458/1/A2 en 201202462/1/A2, with noot of Prof. G. Overkleeft-Verburg, Jurisprudentie Bestuursrecht 2013 – 125; RvS 201400357/1/A2; Rechtbank Midden-Nederland, 16-994253-13.

[6] In the Netherlands, a specific system of benefits exists, in which case the benefits will first be disbursed, and later be checked if the person was entitled to receive it, and in case not, the benefits need to be returned.

[7] See RvS 201202458/1/A2 noot 5.3.

[8] RvS, 201202458/1/A2 en 201202462/1/A2, 2.4.2013, Rn. 5.3.

owner, which is considered an absolute right according to § 12 BGB (Borges, 2010, p. 182). Or a "protective law" needs to have been infringed. "Protective law" in the German legal system is a law which protects a person; according to the legislator's incentives, such a law in its substance serves protection of an individual against a defined type of damage (BGH Urteil 1982). For instance when government tortious behaviour leads to an unauthorised access to data which may be related to identity theft, such a protective law could be § 9 of the German federal data protection law, 'Bundesdatenschutzgesetz' (BDSG). This clause requires the relying party to take the necessary technical and organisational measures to ensure the implementation of the provisions of the data protection act, ensuring especially the security of the data (Borges 2010, p. 199).

Data protection liability.   The above example shows that laws can provide the basis of tort liability. However, laws often provide liability clauses themselves. An example of a law providing a basis for potential liability for the government as a relying party in case of unauthorised transmission of data is the Data Protection Directive of the European Parliament and of the Council of 24 October 1995 on the protection of individuals with regard to the processing of personal data and on the free movement of such data (1995/46/EC). Article 23 para 1 and Recital 55 of the Data Protection Directive provide that any person who has suffered damage as a result of an unlawful processing operation is entitled to receive compensation from the controller for the damage suffered. Such damage may occur to the actual identity owner in the case of unauthorised access to his/her data in a governmental portal without his/her consent. In such a case the relying party acting as a data controller had the responsibility to implement appropriate technical and organisational measures to protect the actual identity owner from identity theft (Article 17).

The data controller is in principle liable for the damage caused to citizens when data processing is not compatible with data protection law. In that sense, the lack of technical and organisational measures and in general the way data has been treated has led to wrong online authentication and possibly to identity theft. Article 23 paragraph 2 states that the controller may be exempted from this liability, in whole or in part, if he proves that he is not responsible for the event giving rise to the damage. As Huysmans explains, the mentioned article is an "objective" liability provision, because there is no need to prove the fault of the data controller to hold him/her accountable for a certain action: the mere fact that he/she infringed the data protection law leads to liability, of course only if there is a causal link between the damages and this infringement of the law (Huysmans 2008).

All Member States have implemented this provision in their national legislation, often using identical or similar terms (Korff 2002). For instance, in Germany § 7 and § 8 BDSG provide for liability of breaches of the German federal data protection law, whereby § 8 BDSG provides a liability for public services in case of automated data processing. Yet, the General Data Protection Regulation to be adopted by the European Parliament in 2016 and to enter into force in 2018 (Council of the European Union, 15 December 2015), having a direct application in all Member States may lead to further harmonization of the handling of liability issues with respect to data protection. The regulation provides a detailed regime for liability issues stemming from data protection law infringements in Chapter VIII and in particular underlines that both material or immaterial damage suffered by the data subject grant her the right to receive compensation from the controller or processor (Article 77).

3.3 Damage

Most Member States do not include a definition of damage in their legislation. An exception is Austria, which has a statutory definition (§ 1293 Austrian Code: "Damage is called every detriment which was inflicted on someone's property, rights or person. This is distinguished from the loss of profit which someone has to expect in the usual course of events") (Magnus 2001). Even though it may start from a 'natural' meaning of damage, damage is a legal concept and only that damage which can be recovered is damage in the eyes of the law (Magnus 2001). Courts and scholarly writing provide definitions in other countries, for instance in Germany 'any loss that somebody suffered with respect to his legally protected rights, goods and interests', in Italy 'a detriment capable to be evaluated from an economic standpoint' and in the Netherlands 'factual detriment arising from a certain occurrence' (Magnus 2001). All attempts agree that they presuppose a negative change (attributable to the wrongdoer) which must have taken place in the legally protected sphere of the injured party (Widmer 2005). In order to judge whether a change is negative, the judge will draw a comparison between two states of affairs (the "Differenzhypothese") (Magnus 2001). However, the outcome depends on the positions which are included in the comparison and which worth is attributed to them. Therefore the comparison is a method of assessing damages, but it does not in itself decide what constitutes recoverable damage (Magnus 2001).

Damage in the Case of e-Government. Smedinghoff (Smedinghoff 2012) has observed several consequences resulting from failed authentication. First, the government as relying party and/or citizens may suffer damages when the former either acts in reliance on a false credential or assertion which they considered as valid (e.g., by granting unauthorized access or allowing transaction), or fails to act in reliance on a valid credential that it mistakenly believes to be false. Second, citizens may suffer damages when either their personal information is misused or compromised or, when they are improperly denied access or are unable to conduct a transaction they are otherwise entitled to.

In sum, damages mainly occur at the side of the relying party/government and/or the citizens. As illustrated in the previous section, the scope of these damages depends upon the specific situation and is subject to the discretion of the judge.

It is unlikely that the government providing the e-Government service would request compensation in case it suffers damage from its own negligent behaviour. On its turn this may result in two possible consequences. On one hand, the damage itself would be high enough to provide an incentive to increase security, which ensures no repetition of the resulted damage. On the other hand, the service would accept the damage since the costs related for example to increased security or better organisation might be higher than the damage. A court proceeding will in this case not be initiated.

With regards to the citizen, tort law provides a possibility to indemnify the citizen for the damage suffered. In case of denial of access, the damage would be difficult to prove, as the purpose of e-Government services is to provide an alternative to contacting the public services through traditional channels. As long as these traditional alternatives are available, the only harm caused is reduced convenience, which may not qualify as a damage in the sense of recoverable negative change as presented above.

Consequently, the most prevalent case of damage which might occur to a citizen would result from granting access (and allowing transactions) to unauthorised persons. This will be further explained in the next section.

Damage in the Case of Identity Theft? A lack of secure online authentication systems may have detrimental consequences, since unauthorised access and information misuse may cause a domino of further risks. As described above, identity theft is a risk that has gained momentum in recent years and entails severe consequences for governments and citizens. (European Commission 2004a). But its consequences do not end when it has been completed as in the aftermath of identity theft additional risks may occur. Identity theft may be part of a conspiracy to commit other crimes, an aggravating circumstance in other crimes or it may be included in other forms of crime such as fraud, forgery, computer crimes, counterfeiting (European Commission 2004b). For instance, if someone (with or without stolen credentials) accesses personal data in an e-Government portal because of poorly implemented authentication in an e-Government portal, this may subsequently lead to tax fraud. Tax fraud involves circumstances where an identity thief receives money from the government to which he is not entitled (McKee and McKee 2011), as in the case of DigiD in the Netherlands as described above.

Overall, it is difficult to assess and prove recoverable damage in case of stolen personal data. There is often a gap between the real damage and what can be claimed as damages. For example, the largest costs of identity theft arguably is the time lost due to administrative procedures amongst others, and not the money stolen per se. A recent study showed that victims in the US spend on average $1400 to clear up an identity theft crime, but also spend on average 600 h. Further, it takes up to 10 years to clear up the crime with creditors (Demby 2005). Victims are often faced with increased insurance, credit card fees and similar costs.

In general only direct pecuniary losses, i.e. measurable financial losses are typically considered damage. In this regard a recent UK case provides a change of the current understanding of damage in the UK Data Protection Act (Vidal-Hall & Ors v Google 2015). This is interesting, since, as previously explained, data protection legislation includes provisions regarding security, whose breach could give rise to liability. In the UK Data Protection Act damage was considered pecuniary loss, and only distress was not acceptable for compensation except for certain specific cases. However, in Vidal-Hall & Ors v Google the court ruled that misuse of private information, which cannot be considered as pecuniary loss as such, is a tort. The judges concluded that article 23 Directive 95/46/EC has a wide meaning, including both material and non-material damage. As the definition of damage in the UK act only referred to material damage, the judges ruled that the definition of damage in the UK act is not in line with the European Data Protection Directive 95/46/EC.

3.4 Causation

In order to establish liability for a certain damage there needs to exist a causal link between the liable person/entity and the damage. To establish such causality the different legal systems have developed similar tests. Most legal systems consider conditio sine qua non as a first test. Only in Belgium conditio sine qua non is the sole requirement to be established and officially rejects the two step-approach which other jurisdictions take as a theoretical framework (Spier and Haazen 2000). Conditio sine qua non means that in order to determine whether an act or omission was a cause of the loss, consider whether the loss would still appear if the act or omission was eliminated. If the loss does not occur, the act or omission was not causal for the loss, if it does, the loss has been caused by the act or omission (Spier and Haazen 2000).

The second step can vary in the different legal systems. Common law considers the 'proximate cause', which includes proximity in time and space, foreseeability of the harm and other factors (Spier and Haazen 2000). Other countries such as France, Germany, Greece and Austria use the test of adequate causation (Spier and Haazen 2000). In this regard the degree of probability is decisive. For example in Austria, adequacy is established if the damaging event was to a considerable extent generally suitable for increasing the possibility of such a damage as in fact occurred (Spier and Haazen 2000).

Causation Between e-Government Fault and Identity Theft. It should be noted that vulnerabilities in the governments' authentication systems are not created by the identity thief; but rather, as Solove points out, exploited by him (Solove 2003). Unauthorised access to personal files is then a result of an inadequately protected architecture with flawed security safeguards and limited degree of participation on the citizen in the collection, dissemination, and use of personal data. This is something that the traditional approaches to identity theft focusing on it from a criminal law perspective fail to capture; identity theft which occurred as a result of vulnerabilities in an information system forms part of a larger problem regarding the way our personal information is handled (Solove 2003). Even the term of "identity theft" views it as an instance of crime - a "theft" rather than as the product of inadequate security (Solove 2003). This is why to counter the risks of identity theft, amongst other, particular attention should be paid to the development and deployment of secure identity management systems (Meulen 2006).

Useful for the claimant with regard to her awareness of security breaches could be the notification obligation in the proposed Regulation of the European Parliament and of the Council on the protection of individuals with regard to the processing of personal data and on the free movement of such data. The choice to introduce a general obligation for data controllers to notify personal data breaches (Article 31) (Council of the European Union) is in line with the proposal for a NIS Directive and may be an element to help the claimant establishing the causal link.

In order to establish causation, it has to be assessed whether the identity theft still could have taken place without the failure of the e-Government service. If it can be established that the identity theft could not have taken place without the failure, the e-Government service might be held liable for its failure.

4 Conclusion

The paper has demonstrated that bringing claims to court in cases of identity theft due to a failure of authentication in e-Government services could be complex. Difficulties relate to all the three elements that need to be fulfilled in order to establish liability from tort law. Firstly, with regard to the fault criterion, victims might not be aware that the relying party was at fault or find it difficult to prove that the relying party was at fault. Secondly, with regards to causation, it might be hard to prove that the identity theft resulted from a failure of the relying party. Finally, proving damages would often be a problem, especially in case of misuse of data without obvious pecuniary loss. The difficulties explain why the amount of court cases so far has remained limited.

However, this might change in the future. As described, the amount of e-Government services is increasing, and with them the opportunities for identity thieves to use them for fraudulent acts. Additionally, the implementation of various software might, if not conducted properly, in the frame of adhering to the provisions of the eIDAS Regulation, provide security lacunas, which can be used by identity thieves. This might result in rising numbers of identity theft in the future.

Also the reluctance of citizens to sue the government might reduce in time. Considering that the UK court recently ruled that pecuniary damage is not necessary for a tort claim for breach of the data protection act, privacy advocates already foresee a rising amount of claims based on breaches of the data protection act.[9] Data protection law may also provide a legal basis for liability in case of failures of security of authentication for e-Government services.

Since it will be in future easier for data subjects to become aware of security breaches (because of breach notification obligations), they might be encouraged to bring claims based on a breach of data protection law. In turn, this may lead to an increased risk of liability for the relying party.

In any case, relying parties will need to be able to document and proof that they adhered to the state of the art security standards. This might not completely avert security breaches, but at least will make them more difficult. The increased liability risk stemming from tort law could therefore exert pressure to public services to improve the security of their e-Government systems.

Acknowledgments. This paper was made possible by the funding of the project FutureID (Shaping the future of electronic identity), EU FP7, under the Grant Agreement No. 318424 and the project EKSISTENZ (Harmonized framework allowing a sustainable and robust identity for European Citizens), EU FP7, under the Grant Agreement No. 607049.

---

[9] See e.g. Jon Baines, http://informationrightsandwrongs.com/2015/03/27/vidal-hall-v-google-and-the-rise-of-data-protection-ambulance-chasing/.

References

BGH Urteil, VI ZR 33/81, BGH, 29 June 1982

Borges, G.: Rechtsfragen der Haftung im Zusammenhang mit dem elektronischen Identitätsnachweis - Ein Gutachten für das Bundesministerium des Innern (2010). http://www.bmi.bund.de/SharedDocs/Downloads/DE/Themen/Sicherheit/PaesseAusweise/rechtsfragen_npa.html

Council of the European Union. Proposal for a Regulation of the European Parliament and the Council on the protection of individuals with regard to the processing of personal data and on the free movement of such data - Analysis of the final compromise text with a view to agreement. Presidency to Permanent Representatives Committee, 15 December 2015. http://www.statewatch.org/news/2015/dec/eu-council-dp-reg-draft-final-compromise-15039-15.pdf

Demby, E.: Identity theft insurance - is it worthwile? Collections & Credit Risk 10–11 (2005)

Dimitrov, G.: Liability of Certification Service Providers, Ph.D. KU Leuven, Leuven (2007)

European Commission. A New EU Action Plan 2004–2007 to Prevent Fraud on Non-cash Means of Payment. COM (2004) 679 final, Brussels, 20 October (2004a)

European Commission. Minutes of the Forum on Identity Theft (2004b)

Huysmans, X.: Privacy-friendly identity management in eGovernment. In: Hubner, S.F., Duquenoy, P., Zuccato, A., Martucci, L. (eds.) The Future of Identity in the Information Society: Proceedings of the Third IFIP WP9.2, 9.6/11.6, 11.7 FIDIS Summer School on the Future of Identity in the Information Society, pp. 245–258. Springer, New York (2008)

Koops, B.-J., Leenes, R.: Identity theft, identity fraud and/or identity related crime. Datenschutz und Datensicherheit 30, 553–556 (2006)

Korff, D.: EC Study on Implementation of Data Protection Directive - Comparative Summary of National Laws, Cambridge (2002)

Magnus, U.: Unification of Tort Law: Damages. Kluwer, The Hague (2001)

McKee, T., McKee, L.: Helping taxpayers who are victims of identity theft. CPA J. 81(7), 46 (2011)

van der Meulen, N.: The Challenge of Countering Identity Theft: Recent Developments in the United States, the United Kingdom, and the European Union Report Commissioned by the National Infrastructure Cyber Crime program (NICC). NICC (2006)

OECD. OECD report on "Digital Identity Management of Natural Persons: Enabling Innovation and Trust in the Internet Economy" (2011)

Schedler, K., Summermatter, L.: e-Government: what countries do and why: a European perspective. In: Curtin, G., Sommer, M., Vis-Sommer, V. (eds.) The World of e-Government. The Haworth Press, Inc. (2003)

Smedinghoff, T.: Solving the legal challenges of trustworthy online identity. Comput. Law Secur. Rev. 28, 532–541 (2012)

Solove, D.: Identity, privacy and the architecture of vulnerability. Hastings Law J. 54, 1228–1277 (2003)

Spier, J., Haazen, O.: Comparative conclusions on causation. In: Spier, J. (ed.) Unification of Tort Law: Causation. Kluwer (2000)

Van Dam, C.: European Tort Law. Oxford University Press, Oxford (2013)

Vidal-Hall & Ors v Google, EWCA Civ 311 (Court of Appeal 2015)

Widmer, P.: Unification of Tort Law: Fault. Kluwer, The Hague (2005)

«All Your Data Are Belong to us». European Perspectives on Privacy Issues in 'Free' Online Machine Translation Services

Paweł Kamocki[1,2,3]($\boxtimes$), Jim O'Regan[4], and Marc Stauch[5]

[1] Université Paris Descartes, 75006 Paris, France
[2] Westfälische Wilhelms-Universität Münster, 48149 Münster, Germany
[3] Institut für Deutsche Sprache, 68161 Mannheim, Germany
kamocki@ids-mannheim.de
[4] Centre for Language and Communication Studies, Trinity College, Dublin, Ireland
[5] Leibniz Universität Hannover, 30167 Hannover, Germany

Abstract. The English language has taken advantage of the Digital Revolution to establish itself as the global language; however, only 28.6 % of Internet users speak English as their native language. Machine Translation (MT) is a powerful technology that can bridge this gap. In development since the mid-20th century, MT has become available to every Internet user in the last decade, due to free online MT services. This paper aims to discuss the implications that these tools may have for the privacy of their users and how they are addressed by EU data protection law. It examines the data-flows in respect of the initial processing (both from the perspective of the user and the MT service provider) and potential further processing that may be undertaken by the MT service provider.

Keywords: Personal data · Machine Translation · Privacy · Directive 95/46/EC · Google Translate

1 Introduction

The digital revolution, which started with the proliferation of personal computers in the late 1970s and continues to the present day, has (just as any revolution worthy of its name) changed our everyday life in more ways than one may want to admit. Most importantly, new modes of communication developed in this Digital Age allow people to exchange information across the globe within seconds. A live chat with a contractor from another continent or an online search for the most

---

This is a paraphrase of '*All your base are belong to us*', a phrase from the 1991 video game *Zero Wing*, poorly translated from the original Japanese. The phrase has become an Internet phenomenon which had its peak in 2004 (see: Know Your Meme, http://knowyourmeme.com/memes/all-your-base-are-belong-to-us).

D. Aspinall et al. (Eds.): Privacy and Identity 2015, IFIP AICT 476, pp. 265–280, 2016.
DOI: 10.1007/978-3-319-41763-9_18

obscure items sold in the four quarters of the Earth is now as easy as pie. Or is it...?

Not yet, and for a reason as old as the hills: the language barrier. Even though English has undoubtedly taken advantage of the Digital Revolution to establish itself as the global language[1]; it has recently been estimated that it is used only by 54.3 % of all websites (as of November 24, 2015). Moreover only 26 % of Internet users speak English as a native language (as of June 30, 2015) (Internet World Stats 2013). While it is true that a certain percentage of the remaining Internet users speak (some) English as their second or third language, it remains a fact that a substantial part of the global Internet community does not speak it at all and, thus, can only take advantage of a fraction of the content available on the World Wide Web. In response the Digital Revolution has provided a number of tools for linguistic support. Foremost among these is the technology of Machine Translation (MT).

In this paper, while accepting the importance of MT as a prima facie beneficial technology for enhancing global communication, we aim nonetheless to consider a problematic aspect to it that has so far received little attention: this is the potential incompatibility of the technology – or at least the typical way it is made available to users – with key tenets of data protection law (our focus is EU data protection rules). We shall next describe further the development of the technology, and the way it operates, so as to provide some context for the subsequent legal analysis.

2   MT in Context

MT (or automatic translation) can be defined as a process in which software is used to translate text (or speech) from one natural language to another. This section will briefly present the history of MT and various technologies used in the process.

2.1   History

The idea to mechanize the translation process can be traced back to the seventeenth century (Hutchins 1986, chap. 1); however, the field of machine translation is usually considered to have begun shortly after the invention of the digital computer (Koehn 2010, chap. 1). Warren Weaver, a researcher at the Rockefeller Foundation, published a memorandum named "Translation" in which he put forward the idea to use computers for translation (Hutchins 1999), proposing the use of Claude Shannon's work on Information Theory to treat translation as a code-breaking problem[2].

---

[1] Which was pointed out as early as 1997: (Crystal 2012, p. 22).

[2] Weaver also cited work by McCullough and Pitts on neural networks, which, due to recent advances in "deep" neural networks, have been applied to Statistical Machine Translation.

During the Cold War, researchers concentrated their efforts on Russian-to-English (in the US) and English-to-Russian MT (in the USSR). In January 1954 the first public demonstration of an MT system (used to translate more than sixty sentences from Russian to English) took place in the headquarters of IBM (the so-called Georgetown-IBM experiment) (Hutchins 2004). In the following years, imperfect MT systems were developed by American universities under the auspices of such players as the U.S. Air Force, Euratom or the U.S. Atomic Energy Commission (Hutchins 1986, chap. 4).

In 1964 the U.S. government, concerned about the lack of progress in the field of MT despite significant expenditure, commissioned a report from the Automatic Language Processing Advisory Committee (ALPAC). The report (the so-called ALPAC report), published in 1966, concluded that MT had no prospects of achieving the quality of human translation in the foreseeable future (Hutchins 1986, chap. 8.9). As a result, MT research was nearly abandoned for over a decade in the U.S.; despite these difficulties, the SYSTRAN company was established successfully in 1968: their MT system was adopted by the U.S. Air Force in 1970 and by the Commission of the European Communities in 1976 (Hutchins 1986, chap. 12.1).

Research and commercial development in Machine Translation continued in the "rule-based" paradigm, in which a dictionary, a set of grammatical rules, and varying degrees of linguistic annotation are used to produce a translation, until the early 1990s, when a group of IBM researchers developed the first "Statistical Machine Translation" system, Candide (Berger et al. 1994). Building on earlier successes in Automatic Speech Recognition, which applied Shannon's Information Theory, the group applied similar techniques to the task of French-English translation. In place of dictionaries and rules, statistical MT uses word alignments learned from a corpus (Brown et al. 1993): given a set of sentences that are translations of each other, translations of words are learned based on their co-occurrence (the *translation model*); of the possible translations, the most likely is chosen, based on context (the *language model*).

"Phrase-based MT" (Koehn 2003) is an extension of statistical MT that extends word-based translation to "phrases"[3], which better capture differences between languages. Although attempts have been made to include linguistic information (e.g. Koehn and Hoang 2007), phrase-based MT is still the dominant paradigm in Machine Translation. Google started providing an online translation service in 2006[4], initially using SYSTRAN's rule-based system, but switched to a proprietary phrase-based system in 2007 (Tyson 2012).

2.2   Technology and Challenges

Machine Translation is used for two primary purposes: *assimilation* (to get the gist of text in a foreign language), and *dissemination* (as an input to publication, typically post-edited by translators). Free online services, such as Google

---

[3] Contiguous chunks of collocated words, rather than a "phrase" in the linguistic sense.
[4] According to the company's history posted on Google's website.

Translate, are usually intended for assimilation; the translation services in use at the EU, for dissemination. Consequently, systems for assimilation may trade accuracy for broader coverage, and vice versa.

Rule-based systems can be classified into three main categories: *direct translation*, where no transformation of the source text is performed; *transfer-based*, where the input is transformed into a language-dependent intermediate representation[5]; and *interlingua*, where the input is transformed into a language independent representation. Rule-based systems tend to be costly and time-consuming to build, as they require lexicographers and linguists to create dictionaries and rules. Transfer-based and interlingua, as they operate on abstract representations, generalize well: if a word is in the dictionary, it can be handled in all forms; but they tend to handle exceptions, such as idioms, poorly: specific rules must be written, and multiple rules may conflict with each other.

The prerequisite for building statistical MT systems is the existence of human-translated bilingual (or multilingual) corpora – and the bigger the better. An obvious source of professionally translated multilingual corpora are international organizations such as the United Nations or the European Union, generating a substantial amount of freely available, high-quality multilingual documents (in 24 languages for the EU[6] and in 6 languages for the UN[7]).

Compared to rule-based MT systems, statistical MT systems are cheaper (at least for widely-spoken languages) and more flexible (a statistical system is not designed specifically for one language pair, but can accommodate to any language pair for which a corpus is available). Also, because statistical MT systems are based on human-translated texts, the output of statistical MT is (or at least can be) more natural, and it naturally adapts well to exceptions (if the corpus contains the phrase, it is effectively not an exception).

Zipf's law[8] states that in a given corpus, the frequency of a word is inversely proportional to its frequency rank: the most frequent word will occur (approximately) twice as often as the second, three times as often as the third, and so on. Conversely, the majority of words (40–60%) are *hapax legomena* (words which only occur once). As statistical MT is corpus-based, it therefore suffers from the problem of *data sparsity* due to the high proportion of hapax legomena: longer phrase matches are absent from the translation model; contextual information is absent from the language model, affecting the quality ("fluency") of the output.

Data sparsity is the biggest problem in statistical MT. Although there have been attempts to solve it by using linguistic information, dating back to Candide,

---

[5] Typically, *lemma* (the citation form of the word), *morphological analysis* (details such as case, number, person, etc.), and possibly *semantic analysis* (subject of a verb, etc.).

[6] Art. 1 of the Regulation No. 1 of 15 April 1958 determining the languages to be used by the European Economic Community.

[7] Rule 51 of the Rules of Procedure of the General Assembly of the United Nations; rule 41 of the Provisional Rules of Procedure of the United Nations Security Council.

[8] See, e.g., https://en.wikipedia.org/wiki/Zipf%27s_law.

the most common approach is to simply add more data[9]. A large amount of websites are available in multiple languages, so crawling the web for parallel text is a common method of collecting corpora (Smith et al. 2013), particularly for the providers of free online MT, such as Google and Microsoft, who also operate search engines and therefore already have access to such data. The use of such data, however, has its own problems, as such documents are often not just translated, but *localized*: different units of measurement, currency, and even country names (Quince 2008), because of their collocation, become "translations".

Crowdsourcing, where online communities are solicited for content, is also in increasing use. Amazon's Mechanical Turk, an online market place for work, provides an easy way to pay people small amounts of money for small units of work, which has been used in MT (Zaidan and Callison-Burch 2011). Google has made use of crowdsourcing since the earliest days of Google Translate, by providing users with a means of improving translation suggestions (Chin 2007), by providing a translation memory system (Galvez and Bhansali 2009), and more directly, with Translate Community (Kelman 2014).

Finally, the quality of MT output depends on the quality of the input. Even the most banal imperfections such as misspellings or grammar mistakes – not uncommon in electronic communications – even if they are barely noticeable to a human translator, can compromise the most elaborate MT systems (Porsiel 2012).

2.3 'Free' Online MT Tools

A number of 'free' online MT services are available today. This section will present the most popular of them and try to very briefly evaluate their quality.

2.3.1 Examples

The most popular 'free' online MT service is Google Translate, which is reported to be used by 200 million people every day (in 2013) (Shankland 2013) and to translate enough text to fill 1 million books every day (in 2012) (Och 2012). Launched in 2006, it can now support an impressive number of 80 languages, from Afrikaans to Zulu, including artificial (Esperanto) and extinct (Latin) languages. Google's proprietary MT system is based on the statistical approach. Google Translate is also available as an application for Android and iOS; it is integrated in Google Chrome and can be added as a plug-in to Mozilla Firefox.

Bing Translator (http://www.bing.com/translator/) has been provided by Microsoft since 2009. It currently supports 44 languages and is integrated in Internet Explorer, Microsoft Office and Facebook.

---

[9] On the other hand, it has been claimed that translation quality can be increased by simply discarding infrequent phrases: (Johnson and Martin 2007).

2.3.2   Are They 'good Enough'?

Erik Ketzan argued in 2007 that the fact that MT had not attracted much attention from legal scholars was a consequence of the low quality of the output (Ketzan 2007). He predicted that *'if MT ever evolv[ed] to "good enough," it [would] create massive copyright infringement on an unprecedented global scale'*. While this article is not about copyright issues in MT, the question *'is MT good enough?'* remains relevant.

The user's expectations related to such services have to be reasonable, but we believe that they can be satisfied to a large extent. 'Free' online MT tools can definitely help users understand e-mails or websites in foreign languages. Moreover, it is apparent that the quality of MT tools is improving. For example, in his article Ketzan quoted *'My house is its house'* as machine translation of the Spanish proverb *'Mi casa es su casa'*[10].

If we take into account Moore's law (according to which computers' speed and capacity double every 18 months (Moore 1965)), as well as the exponentially growing number of digital language data that may be used to increase the accuracy of statistical MT systems, the future of MT technology looks promising. The number of users of 'free' online MT services will probably keep growing – it is therefore important to discuss the impact that such tools may have on user privacy.

3   Data Protection Issues in Respect of Data Processed in 'free' Online MT Services

3.1   Background

'Free' online MT services allow users to translate texts of different length: from single words and phrases to multiple paragraphs (while Bing Translator is limited to 5000 characters, Google Translate can handle several times more). These texts can be of various types, including private and professional correspondence, blog entries, social media content, newspaper articles, etc. It is therefore not surprising that these texts may contain information that is sensitive from the point of view of privacy, and more specifically, constitute personal data. If we take into account the fact that MT is an integral part of such privacy-sensitive services as Gmail or Facebook, this becomes even more obvious.

The concept of personal data is defined in art. 2(a) of the Directive 95/46/EC on the protection of individuals with regard to the processing of personal data and on the free movement of such data (hereinafter: the Directive). According to this, personal data shall mean *'any information relating to an identified or identifiable natural person'*. This definition has been further analysed by the Article 29 Data Protection Working Party (hereinafter: WP29) in its Opinion 4/2007,

---

[10] This result was obtained on August 6, 2006 using Google Translate (then based on SYSTRAN); using the current version of Google Translate (October 23, 2014) the proverb is translated correctly as *'My house is your house'*.

which advocates a broad understanding of the concept[11]. In particular, according to WP29's analysis it covers not only 'objective' information (i.e. facts), but also 'subjective' information (i.e. opinions and assessments)[12]. The information 'relates to a person' not only if it is 'about' a person (the 'content' element), but also if it is used to evaluate or influence the status or behaviour of the person (the 'purpose' element), or if it has an impact on the person's interests or rights (the 'result' element)[13].

As regards the processing of personal data, the effect of the EU data protection regime is that processing this requires a legal basis, either in the form of the consent of the person in question (the 'data subject'), or another legitimate ground specified under the Directive.[14] In addition, the processing must respect certain principles of fairness, set out in art. 6 of the Directive. For its part, 'processing' is another broad concept defined in the Directive: in fact, every operation performed on data (be it manual or automatic) is 'processing' in the sense of art. 2(b).

As we have seen in the previous sections, MT services perform a series of automatic operations on input data which certainly qualifies as 'processing' of data. Though, as noted, in principle MT software installed on the user's computer could perform the translation locally (with data never leaving the computer), in practice most MT services – including the main 'free' applications offered by providers such as Google – operate by transferring the data to a remote location for processing. As described in Part 1, this is partly to take advantage of the far higher processing capacity available (allowing a superior and faster service), but is also an innate part of the 'data-capturing' business model of those providers. From the perspective of data protection law, it is the latter model, involving as it does a transfer or disclosure of the data by the MT service user to the service provider, that undoubtedly presents the key challenges.

For the purposes of this paper, we shall accordingly focus on remote MT services. The processing involved in such services can in fact be divided into two discrete stages. The first concerns the activity of the user of the MT service when he enters data into the MT tool in order to have it translated. The second stage relates to the processing that is then performed by the MT service provider, who then performs a series of operation on the input data and sends the translated output back to the user. The processing operations at this stage may reflect different purposes; most obviously, there will be a need to perform the translation as requested by the user. However, in addition there will generally be further processing (referred to below as secondary processing), where the MT service provider processes the input data for purposes, other than the return of the translation. This may be part of the evaluation and development of the service,

[11] Article 29 Data Protection Working Party, *Opinion 4/2007 on the concept of personal data adopted on 20th June 2007*, 01248/07/EN, WP 136.

[12] *Idem*, 6.

[13] *Idem*, 10–11.

[14] Art. 7 of the Directive; as discussed below, there are also 'special categories' of personal data, which are subject to more stringent conditions for processing under art. 8 of the Directive.

including through the use of statistical techniques (see Part 1); another possibility is of user profiling with a view to direct marketing. The following sections will analyse the data protection implications of these various processing operations separately, as they present substantially different legal considerations.

3.2   Processing by the MT Service User

For each stage of processing, it is essential to identify the data controller, i.e. 'the person who determines (alone or jointly with others) the purposes and means of the processing of personal data'[15]. It may seem that as far as initial input of text data into the MT tool is concerned, the user should be regarded as the controller, whereas the MT service provider is merely a processor (i.e. a person who processes data on behalf of the controller[16]). However, given that the MT provider plays a crucial role in determining the functioning of an MT service (including the required format of input data, etc.), he can also be regarded as a controller[17]. Indeed, the Directive, in art. 2(d), expressly allows for there to be more than one controller in respect of a single processing operation. Moreover, it seems possible that – to the extent that the MT provider makes use of third party software in the process – even more data controllers could be identified (albeit this hypothesis will not be considered in detail in this study).[18]

From the MT service user's perspective, two main categories of personal data can be processed at this stage: data concerning the user himself and data relating to a third person. For example, a Polish person wishing to book a hotel room in Italy, may feed the sentence, "Please could I have a single room for the second half of August?" into the MT service, and communicate the result to the hotel (first-person processing). Quite often, though, there may also be an element of third-person processing, insofar as the user introduces another person within the communication, as in, "Please could I have a double room for myself and my wife for the second half of August?" A further instance of third-person processing would be when the guest writes to the Italian hotel in Polish, and the hotel (as MT service user) utilises the translation service to understand the message.

As regards the case of pure first-person processing this does not seem to raise any particular concerns as far as the lawfulness of the user's own activity is concerned. In fact, it seems that a person can always process his own data; in this situation the rights and duties of the data controller, the data processor and the data subject are all merged in one person and the idea of informational self-determination can be realised to its fullest extent. Equally, from the privacy perspective, and recalling that an aim of the Directive is to concretise the right

---

[15] Art. 2(d) of the Directive.

[16] Art. 2(e) of the Directive.

[17] See the CJEU judgement in Case C-131/12 Google Spain SL, Google Inc. v Agencia Española de Protección de Datos, Mario Costeja González, par. 23: 'The operator of a search engine is the 'controller' in respect of the data processing carried out by it since it is the operator that determines the purposes and means of that processing'.

[18] See the Article 29 Data Protection Working Party, *Opinion 02/2013 on apps on smart devices adopted on 27 February 2013*, 00461/13/EN, WP 202, 9-13.

to private and family life under art. 8 of the European Convention on Human Rights,[19] it can be argued that the legal rules are not directed at the use made by individuals of data about themselves.

Turning to cases where the MT service user processes data of another person, matters are more complex. As noted, such a scenario is presented where our hotel seeker refers to his wife as well as himself in his booking request. Here a preliminary question is whether the user might invoke the so-called 'household exemption'. According to this, processing of third person data may be exempted from the Directive if this is done in the course of a purely personal or household activity[20]. It is not clear how to interpret this category. Textbook examples of such activities include private correspondence and keeping of address books; in its 2009 Opinion on online social networking, the Article 29 Working party also implied that sharing of information among a limited circle of 'friends' could be covered.[21] This would suggest that the use of MT tools in order to translate information about one's private activities into another language may be exempted from the Directive, as long as neither the input nor the output data are made public. The scope of the 'household exemption', however, has been recently interpreted narrowly by the CJEU in the *Rynes case*[22] concerning a camera system installed by an individual on his family home, which also monitored a public space. In its ruling the Court emphasised that the exclusion concerns not all the personal and household activities, but only those that are of purely personal and household nature. The camera system in question was *'directed outwards from the private setting'*[23] and as such it was not covered by the exemption. It is possible to draw an analogy between such a camera system and the use of an MT system, which is also 'directed outwards', as its functioning involves (which may however not be obvious to an ordinary user) transmitting data over a network. It is possible, therefore, that the private user of an MT service will have to comply with the Directive. In other cases, where a person uses the service in the course of a business (as in the example of the Italian hotel translating a message received in Polish), there will be no basis to argue the exemption in the first place.

Assuming the Directive applies, the user will need to comply with the requirements relating both to the lawfulness and the fairness of data processing. As far as the grounds for lawfulness of processing are concerned, the default legal basis for processing should be the data subject's consent. Consent is defined in art. 2(h) of the Directive as *'any freely given specific and informed indication of [the data subject's] wishes by which [he] signifies his agreement to personal data relating to him being processed'*. This definition does not require that consent be given e.g. in writing. Rather, as the WP29 suggested in its 2011 Opinion

---

[19] Recitals 10 and 11 of the Directive.
[20] art. 3(2) of the Directive.
[21] WP29 Opinion 5/2009 (WP 163), at p. 6.
[22] C-212/13, 11 December 2014.
[23] Idem, par. 33.

on consent, it allows for consent implied from the data subject's behaviour[24]. Therefore, it might be argued for example that if the user receives an e-mail in a language that he does not understand, he can imply the sender's consent to enter it into an MT system, especially if the sender knew that the addressee was unlikely to understand the language in which the message was written. After all, the purpose of sending an e-mail is to communicate, i.e. to be understood.

In our view, however, there are several difficulties with implying consent in this way. First of all, it will likely miss the 'informed' element, as it may be doubted that the sender of the email (assuming he has the knowledge of an average computer user) fully understands the implications of having his data entered into an online MT service[25]. As such he arguably cannot validly consent to the processing unless this information is given to him up front. Secondly, the Directive sets forth other conditions for consent, namely that it is *unambiguous* (i.e. leaving no doubt as to the data subject's intention[26]; art. 7(a)). Moreover, when it comes to processing of special categories of 'sensitive' data (relating to the subject's health, sex life, political or religious beliefs, etc.), the Directive requires consent to be *explicit* (art. 8.2(a)), which excludes implied consent. Indeed this points up an underlying problem in the context of MT, namely that the recipient of a message in an unfamiliar language is not in a position to assess the contents of the data he will process. This problem would arguably persist even in a case where the sender of the message expressly invites the recipient to have it translated, for this consent can only concern processing of data relating to the data subject, and not a third person. And yet how is the recipient to tell the difference? For example, if a hotel owner uses a 'free' online MT system to translate a message "Ground floor please, my wife has an artificial hip", he may suddenly find he is unlawfully processing data concerning the sender's wife's health.

It is true that the Directive also allows alternative legal bases for processing (other than the data subject's consent), in particular when processing is necessary for the the performance of a contract to which the data subject is party or in order to take steps at the request of the data subject prior to entering into a contract (art. 7(b)); or for purposes of the legitimate interests of the data subject, the data controller or a third party (art. 7(f)). In our view, though, the same fundamental difficulty remains of ruling out (in the event sensitive data are present) that the more stringent processing conditions under art. 8 will apply.

3.3   Processing by the MT Service Provider

We now turn to the processing of the data by the service provider. What are the potential rights and obligations of the latter under the Directive? Here some of

---

[24] Article 29 Data Protection Working Party, *Opinion 15/2011 on the definition of consent adopted on 13 July 2011.* 01197/11/EN, WP187, 11.

[25] For a description of the discrepancy between the user expectations and reality regarding online privacy on the example of Facebook see, e.g., (Liu et al. 2011).

[26] Idem, 21.

the major players on the 'free' online MT market (such as Google and Microsoft) could attempt to argue that the Directive does not apply to them because they are not established on the territory of an EU Member State, and nor do they use equipment situated on the territory of such a state (art. 4 of the Directive). This argument (which has already been rejected by European courts[27] and data protection authorities[28]), however, will soon be precluded as the proposed text of the new General Data Protection Regulation extends its applicability to the processing activities related to the offering of services (such as MT services) to data subject in the EU (see Tene and Wolf 2013, p. 2).

A second possibility, if MT providers were seeking to avoid the effect of the Directive, might be to invoke the liability limitation of art. 14 of the Directive 2000/31/EC on e-commerce (hereafter the E-commerce Directive)[29], claiming that all they do is to provide a service that consists of processing data provided by the users, and lack control over the content that is being processed in these services. However, this argument also has little chance of success in court – the CJEU held recently that a search engine provider is responsible for the processing of personal data which appear on web pages, even if they were published by third parties[30].

Therefore, MT providers are bound by the provisions of the Directive (which cannot be altered or waived by a contractual provision, e.g. in Terms of Service[31]), such as those according to which processing may only be carried out on the basis of one of the possible grounds listed in its art. 7. In our view, the only two grounds that can be taken into consideration here are: the data subject's consent (art. 7(a)) and performance of a contract to which the data subject is party (art. 7(b)). It is, however, not clear if such a consent in case of MT services would be regarded as sufficiently informed, given the fact that in practice no information about the functioning of the service is given to the user[32]. Thus, in the case of Google Translate, neither the Terms of Service nor the Privacy Policy can be regarded as sufficiently informative, especially given that, since 2012, they attempt to cover all the services provided by Google (Gmail, Google Docs, Google Maps...) in a composite way.

Another legal ground that can be thought of in the context of 'free' online MT services is performance of a contract to which the data subject is party. In fact, the MT provider offers an MT service to the user who, by entering

---

[27] Cf.: CJEU judgement in Case C-131/12 Google Spain SL, Google Inc. v Agencia Española de Protección de Datos, Mario Costeja González.

[28] See e.g. Délibération de la Commission Nationale Informatique et Libertés no. 2013-420 prononçant une sanction pécuniaire à l'encontre de la société Google Inc.

[29] This provision has received rather extensive interpretation from the CJEU, especially in case Google France SARL and Google Inc. v Louis Vuitton Malletier SA (C-236/08) concerning the AdWords service.

[30] Case C-131/12.

[31] Article 29 Data Protection Working Party, *Opinion 02/2013 on apps on smart devices adopted on 27 February 2013*, 00461/13/EN, WP 202.

[32] Article 29 Data Protection Working Party, *Opinion 02/2013 on apps on smart devices adopted on 27 February 2013*, 00461/13/EN, WP 202, 15.

data in the service accepts the offer[33]. Without entering into details of contract law theory, we believe that these circumstances (offer and acceptance) may be sufficient for a contract to be formed, at least in jurisdictions that do not require consideration (i.e. something of value promised to another party) as a necessary element of a contract (however, the data itself may be regarded as consideration for the translation service).

The processing of data is therefore necessary for the performance of such a contract – which in itself may constitute a valid legal basis for processing.

In reality, however, these legal bases are only valid for the processing of data relating to the user. Once again, by processing data relating to a third party, the MT service provider is potentially in breach of the Directive. Just as in the case of processing by the user, processing by the MT provider fits with difficulty within the framework of the Directive.

3.3.1   Data Processing Obligations of the MT Service Provider

What then are the processing obligations of the MT service provider in respect of the data fed into the translator by the user? In the first place, the provider will undertake processing of the text to provide the specific translation for the user. Such primary processing is exactly what the user expects, and consents to when he uses the service and is not further problematic. Some users may imagine that the data entered in a 'free' online MT service 'disappear' once the MT process is accomplished. In fact, MT service providers are interested in keeping the data and re-using them in the future. For example, Google's Terms of Use expressly state that by entering content in one of Google services, the user grants Google *'a worldwide [IP rights] license to use, host, store, reproduce, modify, create derivative works (. . .), communicate, publish, publicly perform, publicly display and distribute such content'*. The text further specifies that *'the rights [the user] grant[s] in this license are for the limited purpose of operating, promoting, and improving our Services, and to develop new ones'*.

In this regard, the business model behind 'free' online MT services is likely not very different from the one on which SNS (Social Networking Services) are based[34]: they allow the service provider to harvest data from users which can then be re-used (either directly by the MT provider or by a third party) for direct or indirect marketing or advertising purposes (in Google's case: advertising is actually one of the services that the quoted passage refers to). Naturally, the data can also be used to improve the tool (by enriching the corpus on which the translation model can be based). In this model, the data (together with additional input from the user provided e.g. by accomplishing crowdsourced tasks, such as resolving Captcha challenges or proposing an alternative translation, or choosing the most appropriate one) are in fact a form of payment for the service (hence, the services are not really 'free'). Such services can be called

---

[33] Cf. idem, 16.

[34] Article 29 Data Protection Working Party, *Opinion 5/2009 on Online Social Networking adopted on 12 June 2009*, 01189/09/EN, WP 163, 4-5.

'Siren Services', by analogy with Lanier's 'Siren Servers' (Lanier 2014). These services (or servers) lure users (just like sirens lured sailors in The Odyssey) into giving away valuable information in exchange for services. In this scheme the users receive no payment (or any other form of acknowledgment) for the value they add to the service.

Apart from raising ethical concerns, such behaviour of MT service providers is also of doubtful conformity with the Directive. Firstly, art. 6.1 (e) prohibits data storage for periods *'longer than necessary for the purposes for which the data were collected'*, which in itself may be a barrier to any form of secondary processing of MT data. Secondly, given that an average user may well be unaware of this processing taking place, the requirement of informed consent is arguably missing. Equally, the user will be denied the practical possibility to exercise rights that are granted to him by the Directive, such as the right of access (art. 12) or the right to object (art. 14).

From the point of view of the Directive, two scenarios for such re-use of data by the MT-providers should be distinguished: firstly, secondary processing for such purposes as research, evaluation and development of the MT service (translation model); secondly, secondary processing for marketing and advertising purposes. For the sake of simplicity, these two scenarios will be referred to as 'service-oriented' and 'commercial' secondary processing.

3.3.2 Service-Oriented Secondary Processing

In our view, in some cases service-directed secondary processing may be allowed by the Directive even without the additional consent of the data subject. First of all, art. 6.1 (b) interpreted *a contrario* allows for further processing of data for purposes which are compatible with the purposes for which they were initially collected. The same article specifies that processing for historical, statistical and research purposes shall not be considered incompatible with the initial purpose. Therefore, it may seem that the processing for the purposes of statistics and research (including, arguably, the improvement of the translation model) may be allowed by the Directive. However, according WP29's opinion one of the key factors in assessing purpose compatibility should be *'the context in which the data have been collected and the reasonable expectations of the data subjects as to their further use'*[35]. As explained above, any form of secondary processing of MT data does not seem to meet 'reasonable expectations' of MT users, as most of them may simply expect the data to be deleted after the MT is accomplished. Independently of this point, to the extent it is no longer necessary – for the purpose of the secondary processing – any reference to real data subjects, the service provider should anonymise the data, as set out in art. 6(e) of the Directive.

Additionally, MT service provider may also seek to rely on another 'safety valve', provided by art. 7(f) of the Directive, which allows for processing of

---

[35] Article 29 Data Protection Working Party, *Opinion 03/2013 on purpose limitation adopted on 2 April 2013*, 00569/13/EN, WP 203, 24.

personal data *'necessary for the purposes of the legitimate interests pursued by the controller or by the third party or parties to whom the data are disclosed'*. The problem here, however, is that this provision of the Directive further specifies that fundamental rights and freedoms of the data subject may override other legitimate interests; therefore, the fact that in case of secondary processing users cannot exercise their rights, and in particular their right to be forgotten, may lead a court to reject art. 7(f) as a valid legal ground for such processing[36]. Finally, it might be argued that service-oriented data use falls within the scope of processing for research purposes, even though the Directive does not provide a specific research exemption (apart from the one in the art. 6.1 (b) quoted above), some Member States, relying on more general principles of the Directive (such as e.g. the art. 7(f)), introduced it in their national laws. This is the case of UK law as well as the laws of German federal states[37]. In each case, though, additional measures, including anonymisation of the data would again appear mandatory to adequately safeguard the user's interests.

3.3.3   Market-Oriented Secondary Processing

The providers of 'free' online MT data may want to further process the input data for commercial purposes, such as direct and indirect marketing or advertising. It is clear, however, that the Directive does not allow for such form of secondary processing, which falls neither within the scope of art. 6.1 (b), nor art. 7 (f). Such processing would therefore necessitate the data subject's consent, distinct from that given for primary processing, which this time certainly cannot be implied. In particular, in order to validly consent for such secondary processing, the user would need to be thoroughly informed. Even if such detailed information is provided to the user, some forms of commercial secondary processing may, in our view, fail to meet the requirement of fairness, distinct from the one of lawfulness (art. 6.1 (a) of the Directive), and therefore violate the principles of the Directive.

4   Conclusions

MT is a very useful and constantly improving technology which may contribute in a very efficient way to crossing the language barrier in digital communications. Nonetheless, the use of this technology also raises some important privacy risks, of which many users may be insufficiently aware. The current EU data protection framework, if applied and respected by all actors involved should serve to shield

---

[36] Cf. CJEU case C-131/12 (Google Spain), para 91.

[37] A research exception was also contained in art. 83 of the General Data Protection Regulation as initially proposed by the Commission; after numerous amendments introduced by the Parliament, its future, however, remains uncertain. If adopted, such an exception would under certain conditions allow for some forms of secondary processing of MT input data.

the users from many of those privacy risks. However, it some cases it may also place bona fide users or providers of these services in danger of breach of law.

More generally, solving the ethical dilemmas raised by 'siren services' such as 'free' online MT remains a difficult challenge. It is true that these services are - at least in part - built on users' data and other input. Realistically speaking, more information about the functioning of 'free' online MT services should be provided to the community. Private users should consider translating only those bits of texts that do not contain any information relating to third parties (which in practice may limit them to translating text into, and not from, a different language to their own). Businesses in particular may find such a limitation rather constricting and to protect their own data and the data of their clients, may prefer to opt for a payable offline MT tool instead of a 'free' online service.

References

Berger, A.L., Brown, P.F., Della Pietra, S.A., Della Pietra, V.J., Gillett, J.R., Lafferty, J.D., Mercer, R.L., Printz, H., Ureš, L.: The candide system for machine translation. In: Proceedings of the Workshop on Human Language Technology, pp. 157–162. Association for Computational Linguistics (1994)

Brown, P.F., Della Pietra, V.J., Della Pietra, S.A., Mercer, R.L.: The mathematics of statistical machine translation: parameter estimation. Comput. Linguist. **19**(2), 263–311 (1993). ISSN 0891-2017

Chin, J.: Suggest a better translation, March 2007. http://googleblog.blogspot.com/2007/03/suggest-better-translation.html. Accessed 2 Nov 2014

Crystal, D.: English as a Global Language. Canto Classics. Cambridge University Press, Cambridge (2012)

Galvez, M., Bhansali, S.: Translating the world's information with Google Translator Toolkit, June 2009. http://googleblog.blogspot.com/2009/06/translating-worlds-information-with.html. Accessed 2 Nov 2014

Hutchins, W.J.: Machine Translation: Past, Present, Future. Ellis Horwood Series in Computers and Their Applications. Prentice Hall, Englewood Cliffs (1986)

Hutchins, W.J.: Warren weaver memorandum: 50th anniversary of machine translation. In: MT News International, issue 22, pp. 5–6. MT News International (1999)

Hutchins, W.J.: The Georgetown-IBM experiment demonstrated in January 1954. In: Frederking, R.E., Taylor, K.B. (eds.) AMTA 2004. LNCS (LNAI), vol. 3265, pp. 102–114. Springer, Heidelberg (2004)

Internet World Stats: Internet World Users by Language (2013). http://www.internetworldstats.com/stats7.htm. Accessed 23 Oct 2014

Johnson, J.H., Martin, J.: Improving translation quality by discarding most of the phrasetable. In: Proceedings of EMNLP-CoNLL 2007, pp. 967–975 (2007)

Kelman, S.: Translating the world's information with Google Translator Toolkit, July 2014. http://googletranslate.blogspot.com/2014/07/translate-community-help-us-improve.html. Accessed 2 Nov 2014

Ketzan, E.: Rebuilding babel: copyright and the future of online machine translation. Tulane J. Technol. Intellect. Property **9**, 205 (2007)

Koehn, P.: Statistical Machine Translation. Cambridge University Press, Cambridge (2010). ISBN 9780521874151

Koehn, P., Hoang, H.: Factored translation models. In: Proceedings of the 2007 Joint Conference on Empirical Methods in Natural Language Processing and Computational Natural Language Learning, EMNLT, pp. 868–876, Prague. Association for Computational Linguistics, June 2007

Koehn, P., Och, F.J., Marcu, D.: Statistical phrase-based translation. In: Proceedings of the Conference of the North American Chapter of the Association for Computational Linguistics on Human Language Technology, vol. 1 of NAACL 2003, pp. 48–54, Stroudsburg, PA, USA. Association for Computational Linguistics (2003)

Lanier, J.: Who Owns the Future? Simon & Schuster, New York (2014). ISBN 9781451654974

Liu, Y., Gummadi, K.P., Krishnamurthy, B., Mislove, A.: Analyzing Facebook privacy settings: user expectations vs. reality. In: Proceedings of the ACM SIGCOMM Conference on Internet Measurement Conference, pp. 61–70. ACM (2011)

Moore, G.E.: Cramming more components onto integrated circuits. Electronics **38**(8), 114 (1965)

Och, F.: Breaking down the language barrier-six years in, April 2012. http://googleblog.blogspot.co.uk/2012/04/breaking-down-language-barriersix-years.html. Accessed 23 Oct 2014

Porsiel, J.: Machine Translation and Data Security, February 2012. http://www.tcworld.info/e-magazine/content-strategies/article/machine-translation-and-data-security/. Accessed 23 Oct 2014

Quince, M.: Why Austria is Ireland, March 2008. http://itre.cis.upenn.edu/~myl/languagelog/archives/005492.html. Accessed 1 Nov 2014

Shankland, S.: Google Translate now serves 200 million people daily, May 2013. http://www.cnet.com/news/google-translate-now-serves-200-million-people-daily/. Accessed 23 Oct 2014

Smith, J.R., Saint-Amand, H., Plamada, M., Koehn, P., Callison-Burch, C., Lopez, A.: Dirt cheap web-scale parallel text from the Common Crawl. In: Proceedings of the 51st Annual Meeting of the Association for Computational Linguistics (Volume 1: Long Papers), pp. 1374–1383, Sofia, Bulgaria. Association for Computational Linguistics, August 2013

Tene, O., Wolf, C.: Overextended: jurisdiction and applicable law under the EU general data protection regulation. Technical report, The Future of Privacy Forum, Washington, DC (January 2013)

Tyson, M.: Google Translate tops 200 million active users, April 2012. http://hexus.net/tech/news/software/38553-google-translate-tops-200-million-active-users/. Accessed 23 Oct 2014

Zaidan, O.F., Callison-Burch, C.: Crowdsourcing translation: professional quality from non-professionals. In: Proceedings of the 49th Annual Meeting of the Association for Computational Linguistics: Human Language Technologies - vol. 1, HLT 2011, pp. 1220–1229, Stroudsburg, PA, USA. Association for Computational Linguistics (2011). ISBN 978-1-932432-87-9

Identification of Online Gamblers in the EU: A Two-Edged Sword

Dusan Pavlovic[1,2(✉)]

[1] LAST-JD, CIRSFID University of Bologna, Bologna, Italy
serpavlovic@gmail.com
[2] TILT, Tilburg University, Tilburg, The Netherlands

Abstract. Online gambling in Europe is a challenge for all stakeholders – service providers, gamblers, regulators and academic researchers. Despite a lack of harmonization of national gambling-specific legislations and consequent legal uncertainty, online gambling is the most progressive online service in the European Union (EU). Service providers are supposed to promote and implement strategies and measures that ensure an acceptable level of gamblers' protection and prevention of problem gambling. At the same time, the online environment offers numerous novel opportunities for business development. Data is the central online business focus and, for that reason, it can be used for multifold purposes. This paper discusses how data collected for identifying online gamblers could include additional functions, both negative and positive, from the gamblers' protection perspective. Thus, the paper answers the research question: What are the tensions in gamblers' protection that derive from the identification of online gamblers in the EU?

Keywords: European Union · Identification · Online gambling · Problem gambling

1 Introduction

Online gambling is a rapidly growing service in the EU. This relatively new form of entertainment has been taken up on a massive scale by European gamblers. However, the current EU regulatory landscape in the gambling domain does not appear to favor business development, nor to facilitate optimal gamblers' protection.

1.1 The Growing Popularity of Online Gambling Experiences

Online gambling in Europe is a lucrative reality with a peculiar nature [29]. Statistical data show that this branch of industry is the fastest growing service activity in Europe. Around 6.8 million online players in Europe generate significant economic outcomes.[1] Many reasons account for online gambling's progress and general popularity, including the greater acceptance of this new form of gambling among both traditional and new

---

[1] Annual revenues in 2015 were expected to be about 13 billion EUR. http://ec.europa.eu/growth/sectors/gambling/index_en.htm, accessed 24 February 2016.

© IFIP International Federation for Information Processing 2016
Published by Springer International Publishing Switzerland 2016. All Rights Reserved
D. Aspinall et al. (Eds.): Privacy and Identity 2015, IFIP AICT 476, pp. 281–295, 2016.
DOI: 10.1007/978-3-319-41763-9_19

gamblers. The growing popularity of online gambling among European consumers is a consequence of easier and more convenient access to gambling than is the case with traditional, offline gambling [20, p. 1396]. Gamblers have the opportunity to gamble 24/7 without leaving their house or wherever they are. Among the desirable features of this shift are the possibilities to gamble for those who cannot access brick-and-mortar gambling premises, and the accessibility of gambling instructions, manuals and other useful information. In addition, a variety of gambling options, better payout rates, higher odds and a better reward system as consequences of a cheaper online business model all favor online gambling [20, p. 1389]. A combination of these factors creates positive attitudes among consumers regarding online gambling, and subsequently influences industrial progress and potential [20, p. 1397].

1.2   The EU and Online Gambling

The history of online gambling starts in 1994, when the small Caribbean country of Antigua and Barbuda adopted the Free Trade and Processing Zone Act. The main point of the act was liberal licensing, including the licensing necessary for gambling operations on the Internet. This new situation attracted business opportunity seekers from all over the world. The first online casino, *Interactive Casino Inc.*, was established in August 1995 [26]. In the first decade of operation, the online gambling industry was primarily focused on the American (US) market. However, the US authorities were concerned about the regulation of the industry abroad as well as the risk of money laundering. Therefore, in 2006 the US authorities announced the *Unlawful Internet Gambling Enforcement Act* (UIGEA), as a measure that prevents the use of illegally-gained proceeds for terrorism financing, and banned the realization of financial transactions derived from gambling via the Internet. Taking into consideration that gambling in Europe has been very popular and well developed for a long time (for more information see [31, Ch. 1]), the online gambling industry shifted its focus to Europe.

Today, Europe is the most developed online gambling market worldwide [18]. The EU regulatory institutions are supposed to play an important role in regulating gambling activities; however, EU Member States draw upon different cultural, social, religious and political elements regarding gambling in order to justify regulation on the national level [17]. As a consequence, online gambling is controlled, organized and regulated exclusively by the Member States as a service with distinctive attributes separate from harmonized services. This approach is officially justified by the protection of national policies (e.g. on public health and youth). Several rulings by the Court of Justice of the European Union (CJEU) represent the cornerstones for regulating gambling at the national level. The CJEU case law can be viewed as providing a carte blanche for the Member States to regulate gambling in accordance with national policies, going so far as to justify a state monopoly or gambling bans as measures to regulate (online) gambling [25, p. 2]. Consequently the current state of the art in the domain of gambling in the EU can be described as legislatively fragmented (28 Member States with 28 different gambling legislations), diverging from the principle of the freedom to provide services in the EU. Thus, all 28 Member States require online gambling providers to ensure that their operations comply with national, regional or local legislations, as otherwise service providers are considered to be illegal.

Nevertheless, the Internet is a global network where national borders and national legislations are not crucial limiting factors for data transmission. Therefore, insisting on the enforcement of current online gambling legislation is almost meaningless. Despite national governments' activities toward the suppression of illegal gambling activities in their jurisdictions, in the case of online gambling, so-called "gray" [14, Ref. 3] and illegal online markets are well-developed due to the co-existence of different Member States regulatory models and various problems related to their enforcement [14]. Illegal online gambling service providers in the EU can be classified as follows:

- Service providers that are not licensed and formally established in any jurisdiction.[2]
- Service providers that are licensed outside the EU, but whose services are accessible in the EU's Member States.
- Service providers licensed in one or more EU Member States, but whose services are also provided in Member States in which they are not licensed.

The European Commission (EC) and the European Parliament have undertaken an initiative to harmonize gambling and online gambling regulations. The European Parliament adopted two resolutions related to online gambling matters [15, 16]. In addition, the European Commission strengthened public discussion on online gambling in the EU with a Green Paper on on-Line Gambling in the Internal Market [14]. Despite extensive political and public discussions, overall efforts toward harmonizing gambling regulations have so far only resulted in legally non-binding documents. The latest outcome is the EU Commission's "Recommendation on the Principles for the Protection of Consumers and Players of Online Gambling Services and for the Prevention of Minors from Gambling Online" (EC Recommendation) [13]. The EC Recommendation promotes principles that serve to protect online gamblers and encourages Member States to adopt these principles.

2   Contribution of This Paper

Gambling-specific legislation is mainly concerned with protecting gamblers from various kinds of risks in order to prevent problem gambling. There are several groups of measures in gambling-specific legislations, including the identification of gamblers. The identification of gamblers is a legal requirement imposed by all EU Member States' gambling legislations. Despite non-harmonized regulations in the field of gambling at the EU level, the purposes of players' identification are not dissimilar in different national legislations. The EC Recommendation proposes the registration process of players with the aim to verify players' identity and track players' behavior [13, Recital 18]. However, there is a lack of empirical knowledge regarding the additional purposes for which providers process gamblers' personal data that are initially collected for players' identification and tracking.

---

[2] In 2011 more than 85 % of the gambling sites in Europe were operating without any license [13].

This paper focuses on online gamblers' identification in the EU, and discusses its function as a two-edged sword. The paper addresses the following research question: What are the tensions in gamblers' protection that derive from the identification of online gamblers in the EU? In order to answer this question, three tasks have been undertaken. Firstly, the paper briefly explains the main concerns regarding online gambling and presents the EC Recommendation, particularly the part that recommends rules for the identification of players. Secondly, the paper sheds light on service providers' self-regulation regarding the identification of online gamblers, through a comparative analysis of 11 privacy policies announced by selected online gambling service providers. Thirdly and finally, the paper explains the advantages and disadvantages of gamblers' personal data processing in the context of identification of online gambling and reveals that it is a "two-edged sword". This two-edged sword refers to how personal data processing used for identification purposes can have two completely opposite effects – prevention of problem gambling on the one hand, and causing problem gambling on the other. For the purpose of the analysis, the paper pays special attention to behavioral tracking tools as the instruments for the prevention of problem gambling and to commercial communication as an important provocation of problem gambling.

3   Gambling-Related Concerns and the EC Recommendation

3.1   The Importance and Functions of Gamblers' Protection

In general, the greatest concerns regarding gambling are the prevention of problem gambling. Notwithstanding the lack of a widely accepted concept of "problem gambling" [11, pp. 20–21], this term refers to a broad spectrum of negative consequences of gambling. Problem gambling may refer to a health disorder, economic problems, various individual harms, to classification of certain groups of gamblers, or to broad social problems [27, p. 5]. Clear boundaries between these categories do not exist, but they are identifiable. It could be said that problem gambling as a health disorder is a foundation for all other forms of problem gambling. The prevention of problem gambling as a health disorder is the main focal point in the protection of gamblers from other gambling-associated risks. Thus, maintaining public order is tightly knit with the prevention of problem gambling. In favor of this claim is the fact that gamblers with a health disorder are more prone to commit crimes than people without this kind of problem [30, pp. 47–52].

A general approach toward the regulation of gambling in Europe follows principles of restrictivism [10, p. 597]. In other words, gambling is not prohibited, but is rather considered to be a service that deserves a special regulatory approach necessary to mitigate gambling-related harms. In line with this approach, the EC Recommendation encourages EU Member States "to achieve a high level of protection for consumers, players and minors through the adoption of principles for online gambling services and for responsible commercial communication of those services in order to safeguard health and also to minimize a possible economic harm that may result from compulsive or excessive gambling" [13, Art. 1]. Despite Member States' strong opposition to the harmonization of national gambling-related legislations, the EC Recommendation could be considered as an outline of the very principles for online gambling that already exist in Member States' national gambling legislations.[3] As can be seen, the goal of the national gambling-related legislations is not only to protect human health, but also to minimize the negative effects that problem gambling has on the economy. The legislator sets up a hypothesis that the effective protection of online gamblers, besides preventing individual harm, has a broad societal importance that is reflected in economic impacts.

The EC Recommendation is formally designed "to improve the protection of consumers, players and to prevent minors from gambling online" [13, Recital 2]. This document intends to ensure that gambling remains a source of entertainment and to provide a safe gambling environment. The purpose of the proposed measures is to "counter the risk of financial or social harm as well as to set out action needed to prevent minors from gambling online" [13, Recital 2]. Key measures toward improved gamblers' protection proposed by the EC Recommendation can be grouped into the following eight categories:

- Information requirements.
- Protection of minors.
- Player account and registration.
- Player funds and activity.
- Time-out and self-exclusion.
- Advertising.
- Sponsorship.
- Education and supervision.

3.2   The EC Recommendation and Identification of Gamblers

A substantial part of the EC Recommendation that is supposed to enhance online gamblers' protection relates to gamblers' personal data processing. Section 5 of the EC Recommendation sets up norms related to the registration of gamblers and the creation of their gambling accounts. Any person who intends to gamble online has to register and open an account. Therefore, online gambling service providers request several types of personal data for registration purposes. The EC Recommendation, which is in line with Member States' national legislations, suggests that the following information has to be revealed for the purpose of player registration and gambling account creation: the player's name, address, date of birth, electronic mail address or mobile telephone number. In addition, a unique username and password have to be created [13, Ch. 5]. The email address and telephone number should be validated by the player or verified by the operator [13, Art. 17]. In cases where direct electronic verification is not possible, "Member States are encouraged to facilitate access to national registers, databases

---

[3] Harrie Temmink, Deputy Head of the Online and Postal unit at DG Internal Market and Services, European Commission, in his speech given at 10th European Conference on Gambling Studies and Policy Issues (Helsinki, Finland; September 2014) stressed the fact that EU Recommendations are a non-legally binding source that outline common principles for online gambling from all Member States' gambling legislations.

or other official documents against which operators should verify identity details" [13, Art. 18]. For that reason, Member States are encouraged to adopt an electronic identification system for the registration purposes [13, Art. 20].

The full registration of a gambler's account is composed of two sets of actions. Gamblers have to provide the requested data and their identity has to be verified afterwards. Considering that the verification of the identity details provided takes some time, service providers should ensure that players have access through temporary accounts [13, Art. 22(a)]. Verification should be done in a reasonable period of time and for that purpose "the registration system allows alternative means to verify iden-tification" [13, Art. 21(b)]. In the case when the identity or age of the person cannot be verified, the registration process should be cancelled. Cancelation includes the sus-pension of temporary accounts [13, Art. 19]. In practice, this solution allows gambling subsequent to the creation of an account, but before the completion of a registration process. Thus, gamblers may gamble even if their personal data are not verified. However, if they cannot verify their personal data their accounts will be suspended and the situation provokes certain consequences (e.g. the retention of funds without the possibility of withdrawal). The consequences depend on the particular gambling ser-vice provider and its related policy.

According to the EC Recommendation, players' activities have to be monitored. Operators have to be able to inform players and alert them about their winnings and losses and about the duration of play. This sort of information has to be sent on a regular basis [13, Art. 26]. Moreover, operators' policies and procedures should facilitate players' interaction whenever a player's gambling behavior indicates a risk of devel-oping a gambling disorder [13, Art. 30]. Players whose behavior indicates problem gambling should be supported and offered professional assistance [13, Art. 25].

Players themselves can initiate the limitation of their own gambling activities using self-exclusion mechanisms. The self-exclusion mechanism is a voluntary tool that should be at the gamblers' disposal so as to restrict their access to gambling services for a certain period of time. According to the EC Recommendation, any player who excludes himself or herself should not be allowed to gamble for at least for six months from the moment of self-exclusion. In addition, commercial communication should not target players who have excluded themselves from gambling or who have been excluded from receiving online gambling services due to problem gambling [13, Art. 43]. The EC Recommendation encourages Member States to establish a national registry of self-excluded players [13, Art. 37]. Member States should facilitate the access of operators to the national registries of self-excluded players and ensure that operators regularly consult registries in order to prevent self-excluded players from continuing to gamble [13, Art. 38].

4 Identification and Personal Data Processing: Business Practice

This part of the paper highlights service providers' self-regulation regarding the identification of online gamblers. For the purpose of the analysis, 11 online gambling service providers' privacy policies have been examined. The selection of online gambling service providers operating in Europe was based on their presence in the most developed market – the United Kingdom (UK) – and on their size (large and small providers). Relevant data were taken from the Data Report created by Gambling Compliance [21], a global provider of independent business intelligence to the gambling industry. The five largest online sports betting providers' policies were examined (*Betfair, Bet 365, William Hill, Paddy Power*, and *Ladbrokes*), who together have a UK market share of about 75 %. The privacy policies of an additional six operators (*Betfred, Stan James, Coral, BetClick, Betwin* and *Bet at Home*) were also assessed, who have from 2.5 % to less than a 1 % presence on the UK online sports betting market. In total, the market presence of the listed companies was around 84 % in UK online sports betting. The privacy policies of these providers have been examined to identify which data they process for gambler identification and for which (other) purposes they allow these data to be used (Table 1).

Table 1. Service providers' presence on the UK online sport betting market in 2012

Service provider	Market share
Betfair	22.0 %
Bet 365	19.0 %
William Hill	15.0 %
Paddy Power	12.0 %
Ladbrokes	7.5 %
Betfred	2.5 %
Stan James	2.0 %
Coral	2.5 %
BetClick	<1 %
Betwin	<1 %
Bet at Home	<1 %
Overall	Approx. 84 %

The first step in gambling online is a registration process that a gambler must complete on a chosen service provider's web page. In order to conduct this procedure, a new gambler has to open an account, accept several policies (terms and conditions), verify his/her identity and provide the personal data requested by a service provider. By registering with any of the service providers analyzed here, a gambler accepts its privacy policy and provides consent for further personal data processing. According to *Betfair*'s regulations, registering as well as logging onto its website is considered to indicate an explicit consent to processing and disclosing personal information [5]. Other policies consider the first registration to be a sufficient condition for any further personal data processing. A common feature of all policies is that personal data processing is a necessary condition for the registration process.

Considering the scope of the collected data and the purpose of data processing, the policies mainly regulate these issues in a similar manner. *Paddy Power* collects information about players during the account registration process and during service provision. This information may include, but is not limited to, name, postal address, e-mail address, phone number, credit/debit card details and "any other details" [28, Art. 4.1]. Similarly, *Bet 365* enumerates how and which data could be collected by describing the purposes of the collected data. It emphasizes that data could be used for different purposes, including but not limited to bet processing, account management, complying of legal duties, research and analyses, promotional or monitoring purposes [3]. In the case of *Bet at Home*, "collection or processing of customer data is a necessary condition for the conclusion of contract and is solely for this purpose" [4, Art. 2]. *Ladbrokes* explicitly lists reasons why personal data are collected [24]. *Bwin* collects gamblers' personal data to deliver the service, to provide customer support, undertake security and identify verification checks, process online transactions, assist participation in third-party promotions, meet certain business requirements, and for any other purpose related to the operation of the service [8]. *Betfair* processes personal data to allow access and use of the website and participation in the services offered, to administer accounts, to maintain accounts and records, to monitor website usage levels and the quality of the service provided, and to share information about products and services it considers interesting for gamblers [5].

Taking into consideration the important role of gambling advertisement in provoking gambling problems (see next section), particular attention was paid in this research to the parts of policies that regulate the use of personal data for commercial communication purposes. All privacy policies allow service providers to send gambling advertisements to players. Players provide consent for various purposes including service providers' right to send gambling-related advertisements. However, in the case of *Betfair*, if a player does not wish to receive future marketing, promotional or sales material, he/she may notify the company to stop sending further material [5]. In that sense, players can "qualify, vary, modify or limit consent in relation to marketing communications or in circumstances where any processing of personal data is likely to cause damage or distress or such other circumstances as the law allows (...)" [5]. *Bet 365*'s privacy policy prescribes that the information collected about players can be used for "providing information about promotional offers, products and services, where players have consented" [3]. *Ladbrokes'* policy allows this service provider to provide information about promotional offers to its customers [24]. However, if players do not wish to receive this kind of information they have to opt out of this option in the account registration form. *William Hill*'s privacy policy prescribes that this company is allowed to use players' personal data for "preparing and displaying appropriate individualized marketing material and content" [32, Art. 3.2.6]. As in the case of *Ladbrokes*, *William Hill*'s customers can opt out from being informed about gambling events, promotions and offers [32, Art. 2.6]. Also, *Paddy Power* uses players' data to send appropriate marketing material and content via "SMS, email, phone, post or otherwise" [28, Art. 6.2]. *Coral* uses personal information, such as the email address and telephone number, to send promotional material to players if they agree on that [9, Art. 4.6]. Thus, all privacy policies regulate commercial communication between service providers and their customers in a largely similar manner. Service providers are allowed to use collected data for marketing activities in order to share information regarding offers, promotions and events. However, the majority of policies also include a possibility for players to change their consent given in the part of the website related to advertisements or to later adjust their own preferences related to commercial communication.

All privacy policies contain rules regarding the flow of gamblers' data. Despite slight differences among policies related to this issue, a common feature in all the policies examined is that gamblers' data can be transferred to third parties. Very large parts of the policies are devoted to the use of cookies. By registering online and consenting to all the rules in the privacy policies, gamblers accept the use of cookies for different purposes. From the observed privacy policies, it can be concluded that the purpose of cookies is not only to improve the performance of webpage functioning and the facilitation of users' identification, but also for advertising and analytical purposes.

5 Prevention and Provocation of Problem Gambling – The Context of Behavioral Tracking Tools and Commercial Communication

Gambling-related regulations in the EU Member States govern the monitoring of gamblers' activities for the sake of finding indications of problematic gambling. Gambling service providers should warn gamblers about their gambling behavior where this is supposed to be risky. Apart from gamblers' protection measures imposed by gambling-specific legislation, it is up to online gambling service providers to decide whether to use additional protective measures as well as on the kind of measures for gamblers' protection from gambling-associated risks.

In recent years, the online gambling industry introduced behavioral tracking tools that alert gamblers to their problematic gambling behavior while they are playing (these are called "in-play" notifications) or after gambling. New intelligent real-time systems combine gamblers' personal data and their gambling behavior in order to recognize patterns of problematic gambling. Sophisticated technological tools can calculate gambling trends from the processed data and thus generate personalized feedback.[4] Despite the fact that the use of the above-described technology is still non-mandatory, initial scientific findings have demonstrated that the use of this kind of technology is beneficial for the prevention of problem gambling [1, 2, 19].

The concept of problem gambling as a health disorder is a challenge not only for practical prevention, but also in the scientific domain. Despite various opinions and findings, scientific studies support claims that problem gambling as a health disorder (i.e., addiction) can be observed in many contexts [22]. Earlier, Blaszczynski and Nower tried to outline common features of gambling addiction in their "pathway models of problem and pathological gambling" [6]. They agreed on ecological factors as important stimulants of a gambling addiction. The notion of "ecological factors" refers to activities and components that increase the availability and accessibility of a rewarding activity. Advertising, for example, is considered to be an important ecological factors.

---

[4] Some of the examples used by the online gambling industry are software *Playscan* (http://playscan. com/, accessed on 24 February 2016), and *Mentor* (developed by Neccton ltd, see http://www. neccton.com/en/about-mentor-en.html, accessed on 24 February 2016).

Advertising is an inseparable part of today's business development. However, measuring the impact of advertising is very complex. Different types of advertising strategies, target groups of consumers, market features, as well as different advertising effects lead to a variety of methodological problems for assessing advertising effects. Although there is a relative paucity of scientific research about the influence of advertising on problem gambling, so far studies have shown causal relations between the advertising of gambling-related content and problem gambling. Gambling advertising does not have the same impact on everyone within the overall gambling population. However, certain groups of gamblers who are affected by gambling advertising are triggered to gamble above a constant level [7]. Derevensky et al. found that gambling advertising has a particularly strong influence on adolescents. Among this group of consumers, advertising is suitable to attract new gamblers as well as to maintain already created gambling behavior [12]. Hing et al. conducted a study about the contribution of advertising to the increased consumption of online gambling [23]. The authors' findings confirm that "the role of advertising and promotions of online gambling in attracting new users" is limited [23, p. 404]. However, advertising and promotions of online gambling increase gambling among the current population of gamblers, especially among online gamblers and particularly among gamblers who have been treated for addiction. Gambling-related advertisements tempt gamblers who try to leave or to limit the scope of gambling [23, p. 405]. In addition, the largest population of the researched sample agreed that promotion and advertising cause longer time spent on gambling [23, p. 404].

6 Discussion

The preceding findings reveal a number of problems regarding gambling-related regulation in the EU. In addition, certain relations between the encouragement of problem gambling and gamblers' data processing have been indicated. This section of the paper analyses these issues and discusses the presented findings. Firstly, observations on the protection of online gamblers in the EU are made. Secondly, some controversies regarding online gamblers' data processing are discussed. Finally, attempting a balance between business needs and problem gambling is addressed.

6.1 Protection of Online Gamblers in the EU

The development of online gambling imposed a need for higher consumer protection and better prevention of problematic gambling, especially in Europe. Gambling legislation in Europe is fragmented and is limited by national borders. Mandatory gambling legislations in the EU Member States tally with broad societal interests of gamblers' protection. However, the enforcement of the law with conventional standards that should be applied in the online context is not ideal. Considering non-harmonized regulations at the EU level as well as the lack of enforceable regulations in the domain of online gambling, service providers' activities can be easily operate beyond the legal zone into the "gray" or illegal zone.

It is a widely held view that risk is a part and parcel of gambling. Personal health, personal wealth, personal relations, health policy, youth policy, public policy, economy and public finances could be disrupted by undesirable harms deriving from gambling. Taking into consideration the progressive growth of the online gambling industry, it can be assumed that gambling-related problems will continue to occur more frequently. Thus, the EC Recommendation for the stronger protection of online gamblers is quite a desirable document. The proposed regulation regarding the identification of gamblers would tend to decrease the possibilities for vulnerable groups of people (e.g. under-aged and problem gamblers) to gamble. However, the enforcement of the EC Recommendation regarding the identification of players occurs at the expense of personal data protection. The EC Recommendation involves the processing of a large volume of gamblers data both by service providers and states. However, pro-privacy oriented policy makers and researchers argue that such extensive personal data processing jeopardizes the privacy of data subjects. Despite these claims, which are not incorrect in themselves, processing online gamblers' data is an essential means that can also be used for their own protection. Thus, it can be reasonably concluded that one of the main challenges regarding gamblers' protection will be to reach a proper balance between the protection of gamblers' privacy on the one hand and the prevention of gambling-related problems on the other.

6.2   Treatment of Online Gamblers' Personal Data

From the previous findings, it can be concluded that the online gambling industry processes a broad range of gamblers' data. Privacy policies usually do not limit service providers' opportunities to request different personal data. They enumerate different purposes (including the identification of players), but they always leave room for collecting data that may serve additional purposes. In addition, policies assert a long period of data retention (in case of *Labrokes*, a data retention period lasts seven years) or do not even mention how long they retain data (e.g. *Paddy Power*).

All privacy policies impose commercial communications. The gambling registration system relies on a "take it or leave it" approach. In other words, gamblers have to accept policies, including an obligation to receive promotional material about further games. Practically speaking, advertising is an "option" that is included in the same gambling package. This default option could be turned off through self-exclusion from certain lists by consumers not wishing to receive certain promotional materials. Nevertheless, it is questionable how effective the opportunities are to stop receiving gambling-related advertisements. On the one hand, privacy policies contain rules that allow gamblers to change their consent related to receiving promotional material, offers and information about events. On the other hand, these rules are explained in one or two sentences that are usually integrated in very exhaustive lists of rules that compose the privacy policies. Moreover, responsible gambling policies that explain the use of responsible gambling tools are usually presented separately from privacy policies and they do not contain manuals on how to stop or limit gambling advertisements.

Intertwined aspects of the gambling business thus create possibilities that identification data can be used for other purposes. Different activities overlap throughout the process of online gambling (e.g. transfer of funds cannot be initiated without player identification; commercial communication cannot be realized without player registration). Therefore, it is difficult to clearly delineate the purpose of processing particular data. In any case, it is without doubt that online gambling service providers can process huge amounts of gamblers' data. Online gambling service providers have to process a large volume of gamblers' personal data in order to comply with mandatory legal requirements, but they can use that data processing also for commercial reasons.

Finally, collecting and processing personal data for various reasons without the explicit delineation of the scope of the collected data and the purpose of data processing are not unusual in the online environment. Service providers, including those in the e-commerce sector, often do not limit themselves in terms of their possibilities for data collection and data processing. However, it has to be recalled that gambling is not an ordinary service. It is a service that deserves special regulatory treatment aimed toward, inter alia, the prevention of problem gambling.

6.3   Balance Between Business and Problem Gambling Concerns

With the wide variety of purposes for which gamblers' personal data processing occurs, data could be used for advertising as well as for the indication of risky ways of gambling and the prevention of problem gambling. Advertising gambling content and related commercial communication are not prohibited. The EC Recommendation proposes the organization of commercial communication so as to be socially responsible [13, recital 12]. Although it is beyond this paper's scope to discuss relevant academic studies on social responsibility in the marketing and advertising industries, it could be argued that personal data is the most valuable source of online commercial communication. The online environment is a quite desirable playground for sophisticated advertising strategies and personalized commercial communications. The consensus view from the domain of gambling studies seems to be that advertising influences the consumption of gambling [7, 12, 23]. In addition, the increased consumption of gambling leads toward risky gambling and health disorders. In contrast, behavioral tracking techniques could detect problem gambling and prevent further harm. Gamblers' personal data serves to support both online gambling commercial communication and behavioral tracking tools. In this context, personal data processing turns out to be a means for decreased as well as increased levels of gamblers' protection.

Therefore, it is in the scope and modes of gamblers' personal data processing that business, public interests and private interests will have to be balanced. However, the use of behavioral tracking tools for gamblers' protection purposes is not mandatory. It seems that the business sector has the discretion to decide whether and to what extent these different interests should be balanced. Thus, it appears that this industrial sector holds a two-edged sword in its hands: an expression that refers to a very sharp tool that can be used precisely to separate wrong from right. But can we leave it up to the industry to decide for themselves how to wield this sword? The online gambling business industry has its own interests that are legitimate from a business perspective. Its interests do not, however, fully coincide with more general public interests. From the above-mentioned examples of concerns, it can be concluded that the business sector may use gambling advertisements as tools that could injure gamblers by opening them up to the serious consequences provoked by a health disorder. Therefore, advertising as a powerful encouragement of problem gambling deserves further attention both from both regulators and researchers.

7 Conclusion

Gamblers' personal data processing for identification purposes can be used for various goals. Data processing can be practiced for both gambling purposes that are beneficial for the protection of gamblers and as a business model that is not necessarily in favor of gamblers' protection. Data processing is used for commercial communication purposes which is just one, but a very important, factor that may increase the impetus for additional gambling and may provoke problematic gambling. In contrast, gamblers' personal data could also be analyzed for signs of risky gambling, such as an increased amount of time or money spent, and any loss chasing or increased tolerance of losses. However, it appears that the gambling industry favors a particular approach in regard of its own interests, which is not surprising given the lack of harmonized mandatory legislation stipulating measures to prevent problem gambling. As a consequence, gambler protection can be easily put in danger.

From the gamblers' protection perspective, it would be beneficial to have an obligation imposed by Member States' gambling legislations that includes limitations to or the exclusion of gambling advertisement in relevant gambling policies. Easier exclusion (i.e., an opt-out) from receiving gambling related advertisements would probably decrease the risks of new problem gambling. If Member States develop national registers of self-excluded gamblers in accordance with the EC Recommendation, it can be conceivably believed that gamblers' protection will be strengthened. The EC Recommendation prescribes that self-exclusion from gambling should include an opt-out from gambling-related commercial communication (which is not currently a regular business practice). Furthermore, the development of national registers of self-excluded players and the use of electronic identification systems could also be pro-consumer-oriented. Despite potential polemics that could be provoked by developing centralized systems for collecting large amounts of gamblers' personal data (especially from the part of pro-privacy-oriented researchers and policy makers responsible for high levels of personal data protection), it is likely that the use of such an electronic identification system could shorten the period between gamblers' identification and verification. In such a case, the possibilities for manipulating temporary accounts and gambling by minors would be decreased.

Service providers have at their disposal tools that can influence gamblers' protection. Working on the prevention of problem gambling does not necessarily decrease business opportunities. Gamblers' personal data processing can contribute to the prevention or mitigation of gambling-related harms: these are beneficial not only for gamblers, but also for society at large. In doing so, online gambling service providers can improve their own reputation. As a result of this, they can present themselves as being corporate socially responsible companies, a feature which could be particularly appreciated by the public sector and certain groups of consumers, and which can make the industry more sustainable in the long run.

Finally, scientific research should be used to avoid assumption-based solutions and regulations. To date, there has been little evidence provided about the status or use of online gamblers' personal data processing. There is a lack of knowledge how data are processed by service providers, regulatory bodies or third parties. As in many other online services, data processing provides the foundation for the functioning of the online gambling market. Notwithstanding the variety of opinions and findings, there is now a consensus view that a causal relation exists between the provision of gambling opportunities and problem gambling. In addition, it is likely that the ways in which gamblers' personal data are processed for different purposes influence how online gambling is provided and consumed, and thus also affects – for better or for worse – problem gamblers. Therefore, for the sake of preventing and mitigating problem gambling, further in-depth research is needed to better understand the practices of online gamblers' personal data processing and how these influence gamblers' behavior. Such empirical knowledge can help to assess the ethical and legal dimensions of online gambling business practices, and thus help regulators to take measures that ensure that providers wield the two-edged sword of gamblers' data processing in a balanced way.

References

1. Auer, M.M., Griffiths, M.D.: The use of personalized behavioral feedback for online gamblers: an empirical study. Front. Psychol. **6**, Article 1406 (2015). http://journal.frontiersin.org/article/10.3389/fpsyg.2015.01406/full, Accessed 25 February 2016
2. Auer, M.M., Griffiths, M.D.: Behavioral tracking tools, regulation, and corporate social responsibility in online gambling. Gaming Law Rev. Econ. **17**, 579–583 (2013)
3. Bet365 Privacy Policy. https://help.bet365.com/en/privacy-policy. Accessed February 2016
4. Bet at Home Privacy Policy. https://www.bet-at-home.com/en/privacypolicy. Accessed 25 February 2016
5. Betfair, Privacy and Data Protection policy. http://www.betfair.com/aboutUs/Privacy.Policy/. Accessed 25 February 2016
6. Blaszczynski, A., Nower, L.: A pathways model of problem and pathological gambling. Addiction **97**, 487–499 (2002)
7. Binde, P.: Exploring the impact of gambling advertising: an interview study of problem gamblers. Int. J. Mental Health Addict. **7**, 541–555 (2009)
8. Bwin Privacy Policy. https://help.bwin.com/ca/general-information/security/privacy-policy. Accessed 25 February 2016
9. Coral Privacy Policy. http://coral-eng.custhelp.com/app/answers/detail/a_id/2132/ ∼ /privacy-policy. Accessed 25 February 2016
10. Collins, P., Blaszczynski, A., Ladouceur, R., Shaffer, H.J., Fong, D., Venisse, J.: Responsible gambling: conceptual considerations. Gaming Law Rev. Econ. **19**, 594–599 (2015)
11. Committee on the Social and Economic Impact of Pathological Gambling, Committee on Law and Justice, Commission on Behavioral and Social Sciences and Education, National Research Council: Pathological gambling: a critical review. National Academy of Sciences, USA (1999)
12. Derevensky, J., Sklar, A., Gupta, R., Messerlian, C.: An empirical study examining the impact of gambling advertisements on adolescent gambling attitudes and behaviors. Int. J. Mental Health Addict. **8**, 21–34 (2010)

13. EU Commission: Recommendation of 14 July 2014 on Principles for the Protection of Consumers and Players of Online Gambling Services and for the Prevention of Minors from Gambling Online. O.J. L214, 38–47, 19 July 2014

14. European Commission: Green Paper on on-Line Gambling in the Internal Market. COM (2011) 128 final, Brussels (2011)

15. European Parliament: European Parliament resolution of 10 March 2009 on the integrity of online gambling (2008/2215(INI)). O.J. C 87 E, 30-35, 1 April 2010

16. European Parliament: European Parliament resolution of 10 September 2013 on online gambling in the internal market (2012/2322(INI)). P7_TA(2013)0348, Strasbourg, 10 September 2013

17. European Parliament Portal: The Principle of Subsidiarity. http://www.europarl.europa.eu/ftu/pdf/en/FTU_1.2.2.pdf. Accessed 25 February 2016

18. EGBA Facts and Figures. http://www.egba.eu/facts-andfigures/market-reality/. Accessed 25 February 2016

19. Forsström, D., Hesser, H., Carlbring, P.: Usage of a responsible gambling tool: a descriptive analysis and latent class analysis of user behavior. J. Gambl. Stud., January 2016. doi:10.1007/s10899-015-9590-6

20. Gainsbury, S.M., Wood, R., Russell, A., Hing, N., Blaszczynski, A.: A digital revolution: comparison of demographic profiles, attitudes and gambling behavior of Internet and non-Internet gamblers. Comput. Hum. Behav. **28**, 1388–1398 (2012)

21. Gambling Compliance: European Regulated Online Markets. Data Report. Gambling Data, Summer 2012. http://gamblingcompliance.com/files/attachments/RegMarketsfactsheet2.pdf

22. Griffiths, M., Larkin, M.: Conceptualizing addiction: the case for the complex system account. Addict. Res. Theor. **12**, 99–102 (2004)

23. Hing, N., Cherney, L., Blaszczynski, A., Gainsbury, S.M., Lubman, D.I.: Do advertising and promotions for online gambling increase gambling consumption? An Exploratory Study. Int. Gambl. Stud. **14**, 394–409 (2014)

24. Ladrokes Privacy policy. http://helpcentre.ladbrokes.com/app/answers/detail/a_id/272/∼/privacy-policy. Accessed 25 February 2016

25. Littler, A.: Member states versus the European Union: The Regulation of Gambling. Martinus Nijhoff Publishers, Leiden (2011)

26. Manzin, M., Biloslavo, R.: Online Gambling: Today's Possibilities and Tomorrow's Opportunities. Managing Global Transitions Int. Res. J. **6**, 96–110 (2008)

27. Neal, P., Delfabbro, P., O'Neil, M.: Problem Gambling and Harm: Towards a National Definition. Published on behalf of Gambling Research Australia by the Office of Gaming and Racing Victorian Government Department of Justice: Melbourne, Victoria, Australia, November 2005

28. Paddy Power Privacy and Cookie Policy. https://support.paddypower.com/app/answers/detail/a_id/9/∼/privacy-%26-cookie-policy. Accessed 25 February 2016

29. Planzer, S.: Empirical Views on European Gambling Law and Addiction. Springer, Heidelberg (2013)

30. Spapens, T.: Crime problems related to gambling: an overview. In: Spapens, A., Fijnaut C., Littler, A. (eds.) Crime, Addiction and the Regulation of Gambling, pp. 10–54. Martinus Nijhoff Publishers, Leiden (2008)

31. Schwartz, D.G.: Roll the Bones: The History of Gambling. Gotham Books, New York (2006)

32. William Hill Privacy Policy. https://williamhill-lang.custhelp.com/app/answers/detail/a_id/6721. Accessed 25 February 2016

Can Courts Provide Effective Remedies Against Violations of Fundamental Rights by Mass Surveillance? The Case of the United Kingdom

Felix Bieker[✉]

Walther Schücking Institute for International Law at the University of Kiel
and ULD (Independent Centre for Privacy and Data Protection),
Kiel, Schleswig-Holstein, Germany
fbieker@datenschutzzentrum.de

Abstract. This case comment examines the Investigatory Powers Tribunal's jurisdiction and critically analyses its recent finding of compatibility of the GCHQ's mass surveillance of telecommunications in the case of Liberty v. GCHQ with human rights. The analysis shows that the Tribunal's human rights assessment fails to meet ECtHR standards. It provides a brief outlook on the cases concerning UK mass surveillance pending before the ECtHR and the reform of the RIPA regime, which expands the GCHQ's competences even further. It concludes that neither the Tribunal's jurisprudence nor the current reform process alleviate concerns regarding the mass surveillance's compatibility with human rights.

Keywords: Investigatory Powers Tribunal · GCHQ · NSA · RIPA · Draft Investigatory Powers Bill · Mass surveillance · Privacy · Snowden Documents · European Convention on Human Rights · Tempora · Prism

> *Indeed, it would defy the purpose of government efforts to keep terrorism at bay, thus restoring citizens' trust in their abilities to maintain public security, if the terrorist threat were paradoxically substituted for by a perceived threat of unfettered executive power intruding into citizens' private spheres by virtue of uncontrolled yet far-reaching surveillance techniques and prerogatives – ECtHR, Szabo and Vissy v. Hungary, App. no. 37138/14, Judgment of 12 January 2016, para. 68.*

1 Introduction

The documents leaked by Edward Snowden in 2013 informed the general public about the practices of the US National Security Agency (NSA) and its UK counterpart, the Government Communications Headquarters (GCHQ) to tap into electronic communications on a massive scale. This case comment, as the judgments analysed, will focus on the major programs: With its Upstream program the NSA accesses information from fibre-optic cables, while under its Prism program it obtained access to the networks of technology companies such as Google, Microsoft, Facebook and Apple for in-depth

D. Aspinall et al. (Eds.): Privacy and Identity 2015, IFIP AICT 476, pp. 296–311, 2016.
DOI: 10.1007/978-3-319-41763-9_20

surveillance of online communication [1]. This information is shared with GCHQ [2], which in turn shares information it gathers in its own mass surveillance program: Tempora enables GCHQ to access the fibre-optic cables transporting internet traffic and phone calls, which cross the British isles [3].

In the meantime, further details about surveillance programmes of both the NSA and GCHQ, as well as similar programmes of inter alia the French intelligence services, have become public [4]. Additionally, cooperation between NSA and other European intelligence services, such as the German BND, has been in the focus [5, 6].

However, as only Tempora and Prism/Upstream have been subject to judicial scrutiny, the present article will address these programmes. The UK Investigatory Powers Tribunal (IPT or the Tribunal) as well as the European Court of Human Rights (ECtHR) were asked to rule on the compatibility of these programmes with the European Convention on Human Rights (ECHR), namely the right to privacy as guaranteed by Article 8 ECHR [7–12].

In line with this Summer School's topical question concerning the need for a revolution, this case comment analyses the judicial response to the Snowden revelations. As a substantial amount of time has passed since the first revelations on the activities of GCHQ, the question is whether the existing legal framework is apt to provide sufficient remedies for these actions or whether they require a revolutionary reform. In the following, this article will set out the UK legal framework for the exchange of information with other intelligence services and the operation of interception of communications by GCHQ (2), detail the requirements of the ECHR with regard to measures of secret surveillance (3) and focus on the proceedings before the IPT (4). It will then critically evaluate the Tribunal's findings (5) and in an outlook turn to the proceedings instigated before the ECtHR, to provide guidance on possible outcomes and outline efforts to reform the regime of surveillance as well as judicial oversight (6), before drawing final conclusions (7) on this matter.

2 The UK Legal Framework

2.1 The Mission of the Intelligence Services

According to Section 3 of the Intelligence Services Act (ISA), GCHQ is competent to monitor electronic signals and gather information relating to national security, the economic well-being of the United Kingdom and to support the prevention and detection of serious crime. Under Section 4(2) ISA it is for the Director of GCHQ to ensure that information is obtained only in as far as it is necessary for the proper achievement of its functions. Similar clauses are contained in the relevant provisions for the Security Service, also known as MI5, and the Secret Intelligence Service, better known as MI6. All information obtained by an intelligence service may be used in relation to any of its functions, as emphasized by Section 19(2) Counter-Terrorism Act.

2.2   Measures of Secret Surveillance

Measures of secret surveillance and their review are laid down in the Regulation of Investigatory Powers Act (RIPA). Section 1 RIPA contains a general prohibition of any interception of communications, unless there is an interception warrant as prescribed by Section 5 RIPA. In order to obtain such a warrant GCHQ must apply to the Secretary of State under Section 6 RIPA, who may order the interception and disclosure of communications during their transmission in the interests of national security, the economic well-being of the United Kingdom or the prevention and detection of serious crime. According to Section 5(2) RIPA the Secretary of State has to believe that the warrant is necessary and proportionate to achieve one of these goals.

Interception warrants based on national security or the economic well-being are valid for six months, those relating to the detection and prevention of serious crime for three. Both kinds may be repeatedly extended for another six or three months, respectively, according to Section 9(1) and (6) RIPA, if the Secretary of State believes that this continues to be necessary for the reasons set out under Section 5(3) RIPA.

Section 8 RIPA then distinguishes between targeted and strategic warrants: targeted warrants under Section 8(1) RIPA are directed against specific individuals or premises. Strategic warrants according to Section 8(4) and (5) RIPA concern the interception of external communications, which is of interest here. This term is defined in Section 20 RIPA as any communication, which is either sent or received outside the United Kingdom. As, on a technical level, such a differentiation is not possible, the interception entails a two-step process: firstly, all communications are intercepted. In a second step, intercepted material may only be processed where it has been verified that its examination is necessary for the reasons of Section 5(3)(a–c) RIPA and it is believed that the person concerned is not within the United Kingdom, as prescribed by Section 16 RIPA.

As a safeguard, Section 15 RIPA demands that any information obtained under Section 8 RIPA must be made accessible or distributed only as much as necessary and be destroyed once this is no longer the case. Under Section 15(4)(a) RIPA necessity means that it is likely that the information is needed for the any of the purposes of Section 5(3) RIPA, i.e. national security, the economic well-being or the detection and prevention of serious crime.

3   Requirements of the ECHR

As any national legislation, the RIPA regime has to adhere to the human rights requirements of the ECHR, as implemented by the Human Rights Act. It is not the task of the ECtHR to review national legislation in abstracto, but rather to assess whether the application of a law gives rise to a violation of the Convention. This is due to the fact, that the ECtHR is competent to interpret the ECHR under Art. 32(1) ECHR, while it is the task of national courts to interpret national legislation. Thus, in order to lodge an individual complaint under Art. 34 ECR, the applicant has to submit that he or she is directly affected by the measure concerned. However, when it comes to measures of secret surveillance, this requirement has to be adjusted, as – due to the very nature of the measure – the individual concerned is unaware whether he or she is affected. Consequently, an applicant can possibly be affected by a measure either because he or she belongs to a group of persons targeted by the legislation or because the provisions directly affect all users of a communication service as the communications are intercepted in bulk [13, para. 171]. In a second step, the standard of review by the ECtHR depends on the availability of remedies to persons suspecting to be subjects of secret surveillance: if such remedies are not available, the sole menace of surveillance is a direct interference with the rights of the ECHR. In contrast, if there are effective remedies available, the applicant must demonstrate that due to his or her personal situation he or she is potentially at risk.

Article 8 ECHR is the relevant provision for the questions at hand in this case, as it protects the private life of a person. The provision itself contains various individual rights, which are all related to the notion of private life.

Most relevant here is the right to privacy, as enshrined in Article 8(1) ECHR: the right to privacy awards protection from measures of surveillance even beyond a person's home [14, para. 27]. This includes individual communications, whereby e.g. communications by telephone are protected as correspondence as well as under aspects of privacy [14, para. 28]. An interference with the right to privacy occurs, where measures to obtain information are used by the State, inter alia measures of secret surveillance [15, para. 41]. With regard to the protection of personal correspondence it is not necessary that contents are accessed – even where only metadata, i.e. data concerning the subscriber, the receiver, the time and duration of a communication, are made accessible to public authorities there is an interference [16, paras. 83 et seq.].

Article 8(1) ECHR further includes the right to the protection of personal data as a subcategory of the right to privacy [17, § 22 para. 10]. Each collection, storage or processing of such data constitutes a separate interference with this right [18, para. 48].

Like most rights of the ECHR, Article 8 it is not an absolute right, but may be restricted in accordance with the justifications clause of Article 8(2) ECHR. It may inter alia be restricted with regard to national security, the economic well-being of the State and for the prevention of serious crime, if the restriction is accordance with the law and necessary in a democratic society. The ECtHR has introduced specific requirements concerning the quality of a law in order to justify interferences under Article 8(2) ECHR: while the provisions do not necessarily have to be statutory law, they have to be sufficiently accessible and foreseeable [18, para. 67; 19, para. 76]. Particularly with regard to measures of secret surveillance there can be no unfettered discretion of public authorities; there must be limitations in order to allow for the review of such acts [19, para. 78]. Further, there have to be sufficient signposts to enable individuals to foresee on an abstract level, when they may become subjects of surveillance measures in order to prevent arbitrariness in the exercise of these powers [15, paras. 42 and 49]. While this must not be read as an obligation to inform an individual of specific surveillance measures – which, of course, would be detrimental to their very purpose – there have to be sufficient and effective safeguards against abuse [16, para. 67]. Measures striving to protect national security must not undermine or even destroy democracy [15, paras. 49 et seq.].

Accordingly, there can be no indiscriminate collection of data without provisions limiting the powers of a secret police [20, paras. 57 et seq.]. In its seminal *Weber* decision, the ECtHR set out specific requirements for telephone-tapping: the law has to define the offences which may trigger surveillance measures as well as the persons potentially affected by such measures [21, para. 95]. Further, limitations as to the duration of the measures and the procedure of processing the data have to be laid out. Lastly, there have to be safeguards with regard to the sharing of the data and their proper destruction.

Regarding a measure's necessity in a democratic society, the ECtHR generally awards the Contracting Parties a wide margin of appreciation when it comes to measures concerning national security [18, para. 59]. As the ECHR is an international treaty between 47 European States, it is intended to provide a minimum standard for the protection of fundamental rights. In order to accommodate the different political systems and to respect the national sovereignty of the Contracting Parties, the ECtHR allows them a certain amount of discretion in justifying national measures which interfere with fundamental rights. This discretion varies, depending on the measure and the area of concern. However, the ECtHR has embraced the approach of the European Court of Justice to apply a test of strict necessity in the assessment of secret surveillance measures, due to their great potential for abuse [22, para. 73].

As a last step, the assessment of proportionality calls for the striking of a balance between the interest of national security and the effect of secret surveillance measures on an individual [21, para. 106]. Thus, the result also depends on the gravity of the interference with the individual's rights [14, para. 98].

4 Oversight by the Investigatory Powers Tribunal

4.1 The Functions of the Investigatory Powers Tribunal

The judicial supervision of surveillance measures rests with the Investigatory Powers Tribunal as a specialized court for the intelligence services established under Section 65 RIPA. According to Section 65(2)(a) RIPA this includes applications for judicial review concerning individual rights of the ECHR under Section 7(1)(a) HRA, when they concern actions of the intelligence services. At the end of the proceedings, the IPT makes a Determination as to whether it upholds the claims brought before it according to Section 68(4) RIPA.

4.2 The Judgments Against GCHQ

Soon after the Snowden revelations, British advocacy groups Liberty, Privacy International and Amnesty International applied for judicial review before the IPT. They claimed violations of their right to privacy under Article 8 ECHR and their right to freedom of speech according to Article 10 ECHR [7, paras. 5, 14 and 79]. The claimants saw no appropriate provisions for the exchange of information with the NSA and found the legal requirements for the interception of information transmitted by fibre-optic cables insufficient. The Tribunal, however, decided that Article 10 ECHR did not entail any questions beyond those posed by Article 8 ECHR and thus restricted its review to the right to privacy [7, para. 12].

4.3   The Judgment of 5 December 2014

In its judgment of 5 December 2014, the Tribunal addressed two substantive points raised by the claimants.

4.3.1   The Exchange of Information (Prism/Upstream)

Concerning the first part of the action, the Tribunal assumed that the NSA collected communications from US service providers and that among those were such of the claimants, which was then forwarded to the British intelligence services [7, para. 14]. This raised the question, whether the legal regime was in accordance with the law as prescribed by Article 8(2) ECHR.

The intelligence services and the government as respondents argued that the competence to exchange information with other intelligence services followed from the general functions of the intelligence services as detailed above (2.1), which included appropriate limitations [7, paras. 19 et seq.]. They had access only with regard to their functions, which corresponded to those of interception warrants under Section 8 RIPA. The respondents strove to show that while there was an interference with the right of privacy of individuals concerned by this practice, it was a much lighter interference as it would be in cases where the GCHQ itself intercepted communications [7, paras. 34–36].

The Tribunal first examined whether the legal regime was in accordance with the law. It therefore referred to the ECtHR's judgments in *Malone* and *Bykov* when stating that for an interference to be in accordance with the law, public authorities were not to be given unfettered discretion and there needed to be appropriate safeguards against abuse [7, para. 37]. Further, the provisions needed to be sufficiently clear and foreseeable. The IPT held that the rules did not have to be implemented as statutory law, when there was sufficient signposting and effective supervisory mechanisms [7, paras. 38 et seq.]. While the arrangements further specifying the general provisions where confidential, they were monitored by the parliamentary Intelligence and Security Committee and the Interception of Communications Commissioner, who ensured that the intelligence services acted in compliance with these rules [7, paras. 42–44 and 22–24]. Further, judicial oversight was provided by the IPT itself with its extensive powers of investigation under Section 68(6) RIPA [7, para. 47]. In the course of a confidential hearing, the intelligence services disclosed that requests for information were made to foreign intelligence services only under an international mutual legal assistance agreement or in analogy to the rules on interception warrants under Section 8(1) or (4) RIPA. In cases where there was no interception warrant, communications could only be requested exceptionally, if RIPA was not thereby circumvented and it was necessary and proportionate for the intelligence services to receive the information. These latter requests could be issued only by the Secretary of State and had so far never occurred in practice [7, paras. 47 and 51]. In any case, all information thus obtained was treated in accordance with the safeguard clauses of Sections 15 and 16 RIPA.

Thus, the IPT concluded that there were appropriate provisions to ensure that the exchange of information was in accordance with national law as well as Articles 8 and 10 ECHR and that after the disclosures made by the respondents, these rules were sufficiently accessible [7, para. 55]. It was also satisfied with the level of supervision and found that the limitations on the discretion of the security services were adequate to prevent arbitrary interferences.

4.3.2   The Interception of External Communications (Tempora)

For examining the compatibility of the interception of external communications with Article 8 ECHR, the Tribunal assumed that the claimants' communications could have been intercepted and parts thereof might have been processed [7, para. 59]. The claimants argued that GCHQ with its Tempora programme intercepted all communication contents and their metadata which were transmitted by fibre-optic cables [7, para. 78]. These were then stored for an undefined period of time and searched automatically with selectors provided inter alia by the NSA and eventually forwarded to other public authorities.

It thus had to be assessed whether the difficulty in differentiating between internal and external communications led to an incompatibility of Section 8(4) RIPA with the requirements of Article 8(2) ECHR. As even communications only sent within the UK could entirely or partly be transmitted via cables outside the UK, this did not make them external communications [7, paras. 93 et seq. and 68 et seq.]. However, this was the reason why Section 8(5)(b) in conjunction with Section 5(6) RIPA allowed the interception of internal communications as a collateral. Yet, the Tribunal found that these collaterally intercepted communications were concerned only at a preliminary stage and subsequently treated differently for the purposes of Section 16 RIPA [7, paras. 101 et seq.]. As under this provision, material intercepted under Section 8(4) RIPA may only be accessed where it is assumed that the person concerned is not within the UK, it was ensured that internal communications were not used. However, Section 16 RIPA only concerns intercepted material, which under the definition of Section 20 RIPA includes only contents of communications, whereas related communications data, which are also defined by Section 20 RIPA, are not covered [7, paras. 107–109]. Related communications data can also be described as metadata. The respondents argued that the collection of metadata was a much lighter interference with the right to privacy than the collection of contents of communications. In order to underline this argument, the respondents referred to the judgment of the Court of Justice of the European Union (CJEU) in the *Digital Rights Ireland* case.[1] In this case, the CJEU invalidated the EU Data Retention Directive 2006/24/EC on the grounds that the bulk collection of online and telephone communications metadata was incompatible with the rights to privacy and data protection under the EU's fundamental rights. The respondents in the case at hand argued that the CJEU did so only due to the directive's missing nexus to a threat to the public order and missing limitations on the access of national authorities [23, paras. 59 et seq.]. Unlike the EU directive the national legislation of the UK, more precisely Section 8(4) RIPA on strategic warrants, was explicitly linked with a threat to national security or serious crime according to Section 5(3) RIPA. Furthermore, the metadata were required to make the determination under Section 16 RIPA whether the person

---

[1] For an in-depth assessment of the judgment cf. Bieker, F.: The Court of Justice of the European Union, Data Retention and the Rights to Data Protection and Privacy – Where are we now? In: Camenisch, J., et al. (eds.) Privacy and Identity 2014. IFIP AICT 457, pp. 73–86. Springer, Heidelberg (2015).

concerned was within the UK [7, para. 112]. The IPT concurred, stating the limiting of the access to metadata for this purposes appeared as a "impossibly complicated or convoluted course" [7, para. 113]. The collection of metadata could also be justified under Section 15(3) and (4) RIPA for later use by the intelligence services for the reasons set out in Section 5(3) RIPA. As these data were not to be stored longer than necessary, the IPT held that the ECtHR's requirements concerning the minimum safeguards for surveillance measures were also satisfied [7, paras. 112 and 114].

When assessing the rules of RIPA as a whole, the Tribunal recapitulated the ECtHR's requirements as set out in the *Weber* case. Firstly, it thus examined whether the nature of the offences which could trigger an interception warrant and the persons potentially affected, were sufficiently clear to prevent abuse. Concerning the aim of national security, it cited the case of *Kennedy*, where the ECtHR determined that the notion of national security was sufficiently clear and explicitly mentioned in Article 8 (2) ECHR [7, para. 116 (i)]. While it was not possible to distinguish between groups of persons with regard to internal or external communications on the first level of interception, the IPT found this to be inevitable [7, para. 116 (ii)]. There was also no need for a predefined list of search terms to determine which communications would be further examined, as this would hinder the execution of the warrants and was unrealistic [7, para. 116 (v)]. As the ECtHR had already ruled that there were sufficient safeguards with regard to the supervision by the Interception of Communications Commissioner and the extensive jurisdiction of the IPT itself, the Tribunal was satisfied that for strategic warrants, just as for targeted warrants, there was no need for a judicial pre-authorization [7, para. 116 (vi)].

Secondly, the IPT examined the requirements regarding the duration of the surveillance measures and the procedure concerning the examination, use and storage as well as destruction of the intercepted information [7, para. 117]. These are laid down in Section 15 RIPA, the Code and the arrangements, which satisfied the requirements concerning the quality of the law as not all the details of the procedure needed to be statutory law.

Lastly, the Tribunal came to the question of proportionality, stating that a balance between the interest of national security and the gravity of the interference had to be achieved [7, para. 119]. Highlighting again the Interception of Communications Commissioner and its own jurisdiction, it held that there were adequate and effective measures in place to prevent the abuse of power. Additionally, the rules on the procedure for the issuance of warrants were sufficiently clear to ensure their foreseeability [7, paras. 120 et seq.]. As the ECtHR had already held in *Kennedy* with regard to the interception of internal communications, the safeguards of Section 15 RIPA satisfied the *Weber* requirements as they clearly laid down the duration of and possibilities to extend surveillance measures [7, para. 123]. Even though these could be extended indefinitely, the Secretary of State had to ensure each time that interception was still necessary. Section 15 RIPA also included appropriate safeguards concerning data security, while the Code further defined the persons competent to access the information and ensured that they were destroyed, if no longer necessary. Thus, the Tribunal concluded that with regard to the Tempora programme there was also no violation of Articles 8 and 10 ECHR.

4.4   The Judgment of 6 February 2015

Following up on its pronouncement that, with the disclosures made by the respondents during the initial hearings, the requirements of Article 8(2) ECHR were fulfilled, the Tribunal examined the period before these disclosures in a separate judgment. It found that without the explanations regarding the handling of requests to foreign intelligence services in analogy to Section 8(1) and (4) RIPA, there were no sufficient signposts as to the implementation of this practice [8, paras. 14–21]. Therefore, these provisions were not sufficiently accessible and foreseeable and thus did not meet the requirements of Article 8(2) ECHR. Thus, the exchange of information with foreign intelligence services prior to the disclosures violated Articles 8 and 10 ECHR. Although in this case, the IPT ruled against the government and the GCHQ, both judgments were subject to wide-spread criticism, which will be addressed in the following section.

5   Assessment of the Proceedings Before the Investigatory Powers Tribunal

In the introduction to its judgment of 5 December 2014 the Tribunal sets the scene for the assessment of possible violations of fundamental rights when it states that the relevant actions of the intelligence services are to be regarded in the context of national security [7, para. 6]. It stresses that international terrorism threatens the United Kingdom specifically and that further attacks are very likely to occur.

The provisions of RIPA as a whole are phrased in a very broad manner, which is manifested already in Section 5(2) RIPA, which allows the interception of communications for the far-reaching goals of national security, the economic well-being of the UK and the detection and prevention of serious crime. In order to issue such an interception, the Secretary of State only has to assume, that such a measure will serve one of these aims and is proportionate. With this subjectively phrased criterion, it is questionable, whether the issuance of an interception warrant can even be subject to any form of independent review [24, p. 652]. This gives the Secretary of State considerable discretion in how to interpret the evidence. If instead the provision required that the measure had to objectively serve one of the aims and be proportionate, the discretion of the Secretary of State would be limited and would allow for an independent assessment by a court.

Additionally, as shown above, the issuance of strategic warrants under Section 8(4) RIPA allows for collection of vast amounts of data. It does not only cover the interception of all communications where one of the subscribers is outside the UK, but also includes a comprehensive collection of metadata of any communications. This includes both internal and external communications, as the safeguards clause of Section 16 RIPA, which makes a further examination of information subject to further requirements, applies only to the contents of communications according to Section 20 RIPA. This leaves a loophole for the unfettered interception of metadata, which may be stored if it is likely that it may become useful with regard to the legitimate – and rather broad – aims of Section 5(3) RIPA. While the IPT is right when it states that the collection and use of metadata is a lighter interference than the collection and use of the contents of communications, it has to be stressed that even metadata allow very detailed insights into the life of a person. This contention was shared by the CJEU in its judgment in the case of *Digital Rights Ireland* [23, paras. 47, 54 et seq.]. It found the data retention envisaged by the directive likely to create a feeling of constant surveillance in all citizens due to its massive scale. While the respondents before the IPT contended that the CJEU only invalidated the directive because of a missing link to a threat to public security and insufficient restrictions on access of national authorities, there is more to the judgment than they let on. The requirements established by the CJEU with regard to the handling of the data and data security are indeed derived from the ECtHR's jurisprudence. Yet, the CJEU emphasized the need for the protection of individual communications due to the mass-scale and the particularly grave interference with the right to private life and data protection. It therefore opted for a strict review of the proportionality of the measure.

After the directive had been invalidated, member States were called upon to adapt their national implementation measures. While some national courts, inter alia in Austria, Slovakia, Slovenia and Romania, annulled the national legislation, other member States opted for reform [25, 26]. Amongst the latter group was the UK, where the government chose to fast-track legislation on data retention in a controversial manner [27]. Parliament enacted a new bill on data retention, the Data Retention and Investigatory Powers Act (DRIPA). The bill also included changes to RIPA: under Section 4 DRIPA the legal regime of RIPA is extended extraterritorially, to enable the UK to issue interception warrants to foreign communications service providers which offer their services in the UK [28]. However, after two Members of Parliament applied for judicial review of the act, the High Court in July 2015 ruled that the provisions regarding access to and use of the data were not sufficiently clear and objected to the fact that retention notices were not subjected to judicial or any other independent pre-authorization [29, para. 114]. Thus, the High Court decided that Section 1 DRIPA had to be disapplied after 31 March 2016. However, the judgment deals only with data retention and not with the extension of RIPA and is currently under review in an appeal to the Supreme Court, which referred the case to the CJEU under the preliminary reference procedure of Art. 267 TFEU. There, the case has been fast-tracked and will thus swiftly provide an answer to the questions referred on the measure's compatibility with EU fundamental rights and the CJEU's own judgment in *Digital Rights Ireland* [30].

Both the judgments of the CJEU and the High Court highlight the considerable issues the collection of metadata entails. With its judgment, the High Court has set limits, which have to be applied to similar contexts, such as the even more invasive collection of the contents of communications. This is even more so as the IPT did not even require the advance definition of search terms with regard to the interception of external communications under Section 8(4) RIPA.

The way the Tribunal compares the interception of internal communications under Section 8(1) RIPA and that of external communications under Section 8(4) RIPA is also troubling. In this context, the IPT cites the ECtHR's judgment in *Kennedy* to justify that strategic warrants do not require judicial pre-authorisation. Similarly, it argues with regard to the safeguards of Section 15 RIPA, which in its own reasoning make the surveillance measures lawful, even though they can be extended indefinitely. When it refers to *Kennedy*, the IPT refuses to admit the striking differences between the interception of internal and external communications. While individual warrants are directed against a specifically defined person or premise, this is not the case for strategic warrants [24, p. 652 et seq.]. They are indiscriminate measures with a much broader scope and therefore require more safeguards than the more specific and limited individual warrants.

Furthermore, the Tribunal's assessment of proportionality does not meet the requirements of the ECtHR, which it nonetheless cites. Instead of striking a balance between national security and the individual rights, the IPT is focused solely on the requirements of national security. It merely refers to the safeguards against abuse, i.e. the Interception of Communications Commissioner, its own jurisdiction and Section 15 RIPA, but in no instance does it actually assess the gravity of the interference with the right to privacy.

Concerning the exchange of information with the NSA, the IPT argued that the interference with the claimants' rights was less severe than if the GCHQ itself intercepted the information. Unfortunately, it did not further elaborate this contention, which seems questionable. From a fundamental rights perspective it does not make a difference for the individual whether his or her information is obtained by GCHQ or the NSA, if it ends up in the databases of the GCHQ either way. If anything, this argument sounds as though it was trying to allow GCHQ to escape its fundamental rights obligations by using the NSA for the collection of information.

Yet, the Tribunal's arguments concerning the lawfulness of the exchange of information in analogy to Section 8(4) RIPA is even more troubling. As has been shown, these provisions are also subject to grave concerns regarding their proportionality. While it is fortunate, that the Tribunal at least found the intelligence services' practice to be unlawful until the disclosures of the respondents, the proceedings were not transparent for the public, with the closed hearings of the respondents and even the latter judgment in no way affected their operation of the surveillance measures [31–33].

6 Outlook

6.1 The Proceedings Pending Before the European Court for Human Rights

Shortly after the Snowden revelations, in September 2013, several British advocacy groups and the spokesperson of German advocacy group Chaos Computer Club applied to the ECtHR with an individual complaint based on a violation of Article 8 ECHR [11]. They submit that there is no legal basis for the exchange of information with the NSA and that the legal regime governing strategic warrants is insufficient as it entails mass-scale interception of communications. These warrants are then continuously extended and the notion of national security is too vague. Lastly, the groups allege that the indiscriminate interception of external communications is disproportionate.

In September 2014 another application was filed by the Bureau of Investigative Journalism (BIJ) and one of their reporters, which is based on a violation of Articles 8 and 10 ECHR [12]. The BIJ is a non-profit organisation of journalists, whose high-level investigations have had an international impact. Except for the exchange of information with the NSA, it is of a similar scope to the previous application. However, it focuses on the collection of metadata and external communications.

Aside from substantive questions to the parties, the ECtHR in both proceedings included a question on the exhaustion of domestic remedies [11, para. 10; 12, para. 4]. In order to lodge an application with the ECtHR all domestic remedies have to be exhausted according to Article 35(1) ECHR. Even though neither of the applicants had instigated proceedings before the IPT, the ECtHR is usually generous when it comes to this requirement and takes into account peculiarities of the respective national legal system [17, § 13 para. 23]. Further, the ECtHR points to its own case-law where it has repeatedly held that declarations of incompatibility under Section 4 HRA are not an adequate judicial remedy, as they oblige neither the executive nor the legislature to change the national law [34, paras. 40–44].

After the IPT's judgments, the applicants in these proceedings also lodged a complaint with the ECtHR [35]. The advocacy groups argue that the rules on the exchange of foreign communications under Prism and Upstream are excessively broad and that the Tempora programme does not comply with the minimum statutory requirements set out by the ECtHR. Besides these complaints under Articles 8 and 10 ECHR, they further contend that the IPT wrongly held closed hearings and thus violated the right to a fair hearing under Article 6 ECHR and that the framework for the interception of foreign communications under Section 8(4) RIPA is discriminatory on grounds of nationality and national origin and thus in violation of Article 14 taken in conjunction with Articles 8 and 10 ECHR.

While it is hardly possible to predict the outcome of these proceedings, especially as considerations of proportionality will be paramount, a few points for debate can be identified. The ECtHR, in previous decisions, has repeatedly referred to and taken inspiration from the rights of the European Charter of Fundamental Rights as interpreted by the CJEU, most recently in a case concerning the right to privacy [36, paras. 55 et seq.]. It is not inconceivable that the ECtHR in the cases at hand may draw on the ruling of the CJEU. On the other hand there may be considerable pressure on the ECtHR by the British government, which is generally sceptical of the court's rulings [37]. The Conservative Party even detailed plans to leave the ECHR system [38].[2]

While the strictness of the ECtHR in its proportionality review depends on the legitimate aim it usually awards more discretion when it comes to measures in the interest of national security. However, RIPA relies on the prevention and detection of serious crime as well as the economic well-being. While the latter has now been put in the context of national security by amendments made to Section 5(3) RIPA by Section 3 DRIPA, the ECtHR awards less room for manoeuvre when it comes to reasons other than national security [14, para. 98]. Furthermore, the ECtHR has in the context of searches increased its scrutiny of the national provisions when there was no judicial pre-authorisation for these measures [39, para. 45]. In any case, with the judgments of the IPT the ECtHR has much to review.

---

[2] For a comprehensive assessment of this proposal cf. Greer, S., Slowe, R.: The Conservative's proposal for a British Bill of Rights: Mired in Muddle, Misconception and Misrepresentation, European Human Rights Law Review 4, 370–381 (2015).

6.2   Reform of the RIPA Regime

In the wake of the Snowden revelations there have been several reports evaluating the legal regime on security services: the Intelligence and Security Committee of Parliament conducted its own review. Further, DRIPA foresaw a review of the effectiveness of current legislation and investigating whether there was a need for new or amended legislation, which was conducted by an independent expert, David Anderson QC. Additionally, an independent report performed by the Royal United Services Institute, an independent think tank, was commissioned by then-Deputy Prime Minister Nick Clegg. The reports unanimously concluded that the regulations on the interception of communications were unsatisfactory [40, p. 103; 39, pp. 258 and 285 et seq.; 41, pp. xi and 105 et seq.]. With regard to mass interception of data besides a major overhaul of the system of warrants, all but the ISC called for judicial pre-authorization [41, pp. 108–112]. Concerning the oversight by the IPT, they urged more openness and a domestic appeals chamber [40, p. 116; 39, p. 305; 42, pp. 112 et seq.]. Nevertheless, neither of the reviewers questioned the extensive powers of the intelligence services themselves.

In the meantime, the newly strengthened Conservative government has prepared a draft Investigatory Powers Bill (IPB) [43] and promised a modernized legal regime. Yet, the bill includes even further powers for the intelligence services. The proposal is largely seen as expanding the powers of intelligence services to intercept communication on mass-scale [43, 44]. The interception of external communications as currently governed by Section 8(4) and (5) RIPA is remodelled as Bulk Warrants under Part 6 IPB. Yet, the material scope – except for a slight shift of scope for the purpose of the economic well-being of the UK, which is now only met were it relates to persons outside the UK according to Section 107(2)(a) and (3) IPB – is of the same broad scope as it is under RIPA. The safeguards clauses of Sections 117 and 119 IPB are equally vague and make restrictions subject to their necessity as judged by the Secretary of State. Further, the government did not opt for a judicial pre-authorization of warrants. Instead, they are still issued by the Secretary of State under Section 107 IPB and have to be approved by a Judicial Commissioner according to Section 109 IPB. The standard of review to be applied has been subject to concerns, as the bill does not ensure that the Commissioners apply a strict approach [45]. However, the IPB includes a right to appeal for decisions of the IPT in Section 180 IPB. These appeals are lodged with the Court of Appeal in lieu of specific regulations. As has been demonstrated by the High Court, the general courts may be more aware of the human rights dimensions of cases than the specialised IPT. Thus, this provision is an improvement of the status quo.

Nevertheless, in a recent report, the Intelligence and Security Committee of Parliament voiced serious concerns over the draft Bill, which it found disappointing as it did not cover the powers of the intelligence services, but rather left them scattered in various pieces of legislation [46]. Further, the committee harshly criticised the provisions for an inconsistent protection of privacy and its authorisations for the intelligence services, which were too broad and vague. It concluded that the legislation "suffered from a lack of sufficient time and preparation" [46, p. 2].

7 Conclusions

While the IPT's judgment was lauded by some as a victory of privacy rights, this assessment has to be seen critically. The judicial reconditioning of the Snowden revelations before the Tribunal competent to protect the human rights of individuals against government invasions of privacy has had no lasting effect on the ways the intelligence services operate. Luckily, the ECtHR will have a chance to remedy the failures of the IPT and conduct a proper examination and evaluation of GCHQ's activities. While it is hardly possible to predict the outcome of these proceedings, they have an intrinsic value to themselves: external oversight over a system that has more than once been described as opaque.

Regarding the reviews and the reform process initiated in the United Kingdom itself, caution has to be exercised. It appears as though the consequences of the revelations of mass surveillance are to further tighten the grip of intelligence services on online communications. Any efforts to expand the already over-stretched competences of intelligence services should, in turn, be closely monitored.

Further, the new legislation may also have an impact on the outcome of the proceedings before the ECtHR. It may provide the government with a convenient avenue to escape any criticism: the ECtHR will be concerned only with the compatibility of RIPA with the ECHR. If the court finds a violation of the Convention, the government can point to the new legislation. However, as the assessment of the IPB has shown, that would merely be a distraction, as the new regime of secret surveillance contains no limitation as to the points in question before the ECtHR. Additionally, although the judgments of the court are generally only effective inter partes according to Art. 46(1) ECHR, i.e. it is binding only between the parties involved in the case at hand, it is the function of the court according to Art. 32(1) ECHR to interpret the rights of the Convention. If it finds a violation of the Convention by a certain measure, this extends also to similar measures. Nevertheless, with the now clarified jurisprudence on access to the ECtHR in cases of secret surveillance in *Zakharov*, the court has opened the door for future litigation concerning the IPB as soon as it becomes the law.

References

1. Greenwald, G.: NSA Prism program taps in to user data of Apple, Google and others. The Guardian, 7 June 2013. http://www.theguardian.com/world/2013/jun/06/us-tech-giants-nsa-data?guni=Article:in%20body%20link
2. Hopkins, N.: UK gathering secret intelligence via covert NSA operation. The Guardian, 7 June 2013. http://www.theguardian.com/technology/2013/jun/07/uk-gathering-secret-intelligence-nsa-prism
3. MacAskill, E., Borger, J., Hopkins, N., Davies, N., Ball, J.: GCHQ taps fibre-optic cables for secret access to world's communications. The Guardian, 21 June 2013. http://www.theguardian.com/uk/2013/jun/21/gchq-cables-secret-world-communications-nsa
4. Chrisafis, A.: France 'runs vast electronic spying operation using NSA-style methods'. The Guardian, 6 July 2013. http://www.theguardian.com/world/2013/jul/04/france-electronic-spying-operation-nsa

5. Überwachung: BND leitet massenhaft Metadaten an die NSA weiter. Der Spiegel, 3 August 2013. http://www.spiegel.de/netzwelt/netzpolitik/bnd-leitet-laut-spiegel-massenhaft-metadaten-an-die-nsa-weiter-a-914682.html

6. Mascolo, G., Goetz, J., von Osten, D.: Zusammenarbeit zweier Geheimdienste – Codename "Eikonal". Tagesschau, 3 October 2014. https://www.tagesschau.de/inland/bnd-nsa-datenweitergabe-101.html

7. IPT: Liberty and Others v. GCHQ and Others, Case Nos IPT/13/77/H, IPT/13/92/CH, IPT/13/168-173/H, IPT/13/194/CH, IPT/13/204/CH, Judgment of 5 December 2014

8. IPT: Liberty and Others v. GCHQ and Others, Case Nos IPT/13/77/H, IPT/13/92/CH, IPT/13/168-173/H, IPT/13/194/CH, IPT/13/204/CH, Judgment of 6 February 2015

9. IPT: Liberty and Others v. GCHQ and Others, Case Nos IPT/13/77/H, IPT/13/92/CH, IPT/13/168-173/H, IPT/13/194/CH, IPT/13/204/CH, Order of 6 February 2015

10. IPT: Liberty and Others v. GCHQ and Others, Case Nos IPT/13/77/H, IPT/13/92/CH, IPT/13/168-173/H, IPT/13/194/CH, IPT/13/204/CH, Determination of 22 June 2015

11. ECtHR: Big Brother Watch and others v. the United Kingdom, App. no. 58170/13, Statement of Facts of 9 January 2014 (pending)

12. ECtHR: Bureau of Investigative Journalism and Alice Ross v. the United Kingdom, App. no. 62322/14, Statement of Facts of 5 January 2015 (pending)

13. ECtHR: Zakharov v. Russia, App. No. 47143/06, Judgment of 4 December 2015

14. Marauhn, T., Thorn, J.: Kapitel 16: Privat- und Familienleben. In: Dörr, O., et al. (eds.) EMRK/GG Konkordanzkommentar, vol. I, 2nd edn. Mohr Siebeck, Tübingen (2013)

15. ECtHR: Klass and others v. Germany, App. no. 5029/71, Judgment of 6 September 1978

16. ECtHR: Malone v. the United Kingdom, App. no. 8691/79, Judgment of 2 August 1984

17. Grabenwarter, C., Pabel, K.: Europäische Menschenrechtskonvention, 5th edn. Beck, Munich (2012)

18. ECtHR: Leander v. Sweden, App. no. 9248/81, Judgment of 26 March 1987

19. ECtHR: Bykov v. Russia, App. no. 4378/02, Judgment of 10 March 2009

20. ECtHR: Rotaru v. Romania, App. no. 28341/95, Judgment of 4 May 2000

21. ECtHR: Weber and Saravia v. Germany, App. no. 54934/00, Decision of 29 June 2006

22. ECtHR: Szabo and Vissy v. Hungary, App. no. 37138/14, Judgment of 12 January 2016

23. CJEU: Joined Cases C-293/12 and C-594/12 Digital Rights Ireland and Seitlinger and Others, Judgment of 8 April 2014, EU:C:2014:238

24. Hörnle, J.: How to control interception-does the UK strike the right balance? Comput. Law Secur. Rev. **26**, 649–658 (2010)

25. Vaniaio, N., Miettinen, S.: Telecommunications data retention after Digital Rights Ireland: legislative and judicial reactions in the Member States. Int. J. Law Inf. Technol. **23**, 290–309 (2015). Advance Access

26. Kühling, J., Heitzer, S.: Returning through the National Back Door? The future of data retention after the ECJ judgment on directive 2006/24 in the UK and elsewhere. Eur. Law Rev. **40**, 263–278 (2015)

27. Emergency surveillance bill clears Commons, The Guardian, 16 July 2014. http://www.theguardian.com/world/2014/jul/16/emergency-surveillance-bill-clears-commons

28. Smith, G.: Dissecting DRIP - the emergency Data Retention and Investigatory Powers Bill. Cyberleagle, 12 July 2014. http://cyberleagle.blogspot.co.uk/2014/07/dissecting-emergency-data-retention-and.html

29. High Court of Justice, Queen's Bench Division: R. (on the application of Davis and others) v. Secretary of State for the Home Department and others. Case No: CO/3665/2014, CO/3667/2014, CO/3794/2014, Judgment of 17 July 2015

30. CJEU: Case C-698/15 Davis and Others, Order of 1 February 2016, EU:C:2016:70

31. Privacy International: GCHQ-NSA intelligence sharing unlawful, says UK surveillance tribunal. Press Release, 6 February 2015. https://www.privacyinternational.org/node/482
32. Liberty: GCHQ intercepts communications of human rights groups. Press Release, 22 June 2015. https://www.liberty-human-rights.org.uk/news/press-releases-and-statements/gchq-intercepts-communications-human-rights-groups
33. Wheelhouse, A.: The Legality of Mass Surveillance Operations. Oxford Human Rights Hub Blog, 7 February 2015. http://ohrh.law.ox.ac.uk/the-legality-of-mass-surveillance-operations/
34. ECtHR: Burden v. the United Kingdom, App. no. 13378/05, Judgment of 29 April 2008
35. ECtHR: 10 Human Rights Organisations and Others v. the United Kingdom, App. no. 24960/15, Statement of Facts of 24 November 2015 (pending)
36. ECtHR: Delfi AS v. Estonia, App. no. 64569/09, Judgment of 16 June 2015
37. Watt, N., Mason, R.: Cameron 'committed to breaking link with European court of human rights'. The Guardian, 1 June 2015. http://www.theguardian.com/law/2015/jun/01/david-cameron-european-court-of-human-rights
38. Conservative Party: Protecting Human Rights in the UK, p. 5, London (2014). https://www.conservatives.com/~/media/files/downloadable%20Files/human_rights.pdf
39. ECtHR, Camenzid v. Switzerland, App. no. 21353/93, Judgment of 16 December 1997
40. Intelligence and Security Committee of Parliament: Privacy and Security: A modern and transparent legal framework, London (2015). https://b1cba9b3-a-5e6631fd-s-sites.googlegroups.com/a/independent.gov.uk/isc/files/20150312_ISC_P%2BS%2BRpt%28web%29.pdf?attachauth=ANoY7coGhW2Ehaqy1VRIMKAhsgXIb65gbZ6rLs0Z-yEiA0U_T-MyF1wV0RDdlyhG1CgLsM0h-fG3-7rVVgSsdANXhuNtSXcx_61IPJOEWFSbh0usafUjfcDVtGmGIwNA3vHGC0-ZJoJdXUq6x-tFgC4k8EKt9HqH9OiOd6l1qCfbyM1dpn_JNfQ8RxcskFMz0ndA5qwcxUsuOhuW2LbIBqEQ5B6uFAr9zYvSKu4FLjWV0LjcYOF3TDvig6xDwjMTebxEY3o7t_RD&attredirects=1
41. Anderson, D.: A Question of Trust, London (2015). https://terrorismlegislationreviewer.independent.gov.uk/wp-content/uploads/2015/06/IPR-Report-Print-Version.pdf
42. Royal United Services Institute for Defence and Security Studies: A Democratic Licence to Operate, London (2015). https://www.rusi.org/downloads/assets/ISR-Report-press.pdf
43. Draft Investigatory Powers Bill, November 2015. https://www.gov.uk/government/uploads/system/uploads/attachment_data/file/473770/Draft_Investigatory_Powers_Bill.pdf
44. Wheelhouse, A.: The Investigatory Powers Bill: A (Somewhat) Different Balance Between Privacy and Security. Oxford Human Rights Hub Blog, 25 November 2015. http://ohrh.law.ox.ac.uk/the-investigatory-powers-bill-a-somewhat-different-balance-between-privacy-and-security/
45. Travis, A., MacAskill, E.: Theresa May unveils UK surveillance measures in wake of Snowden claims: The Guardian, 4 November 2015. http://www.theguardian.com/world/2015/nov/04/theresa-may-surveillance-measures-edward-snowden
46. Murphy, C.C., Simonsen, N.: It's time to overhaul the Investigatory Powers Bill. UK Human Rights Blog, 11 February 2016. http://ukhumanrightsblog.com/2016/02/11/its-time-to-overhaul-the-investigatory-powers-bill/
47. Intelligence and Security Committee of Parliament: Report on the draft Investigatory Powers Bill, London (2016). https://b1cba9b3-a-5e6631fd-s-sites.googlegroups.com/a/independent.gov.uk/isc/files/20160209_ISC_Rpt_IPBill%28web%29.pdf?attachauth=ANoY7cpPzZp9EmENG7bQZEi_c310A6r-dV_L-_m7w8jBnmE_H4c8yPpEL5fgJkiGeulmYn8wPnwI27SAgHov7XyAZUnJEKxHFoYiN13baQgUkXIwfp_aC-Us9pM0d0-o_ToLfJkniTRluNbsvvDI–q2vMmbYbegA_muG4gB94Zsb4KY4lrdEQdshu191DnE0C7V9Qlz1dAJrYj4xEQaGxuZ2nly9Sy8bopaSa7in7Fo71KBCdhjVKDhP4lQi_OfJaCTR6vlrhh9&attredirects=0

Automated Log Audits for Privacy Compliance Validation: A Literature Survey

Jenni Reuben$^{(\boxtimes)}$, Leonardo A. Martucci, and Simone Fischer-Hübner

Karlstad University, 651 88 Karlstad, Sweden
{jenni.reuben,leonardo.martucci,simone.fischer-hubner}@kau.se

Abstract. Log audits are the technical means to retrospectively reconstruct and analyze system activities for determining if the system is executed in accordance with the rules. This approach to compliance is referred to as compliance by detection. In the case of privacy adherence validation (or) privacy audits, the rules for compliance are less well defined and more contextual than in the case of traditional security audit. The aim of the paper is to understand the aims, techniques and challenges for realizing privacy compliance by detection. Using systematic literature review as the research tool we described the state-of-art privacy auditing approaches through taxonomies. We present two taxonomies, *(i)* classified in terms of auditing techniques and *(ii)* classified in terms of audit objectives. Following the observation gained from the state-of-the art we discuss challenges and suggest guidelines for utilizing log-based automated privacy audits.

Keywords: Log audit · Privacy violation detection · Privacy compliance · Privacy audits · Automation

1 Introduction

Compliance is a practice to ensure that the implemented practices and the execution of business processes of an organization is in accordance with regulations, legislations, industrial standards or agreed upon commercial contracts and policies. In particular, the practice to ensure the execution of business processes on personal data in accordance with enterprise policies thus data protection regulations is referred to as privacy compliance [17] or privacy audits.

Compliance is a perpetual and an essential practice for an organization, and it takes time, resources and cost [4]. As result of advancement in Information Technology (IT), the task of realizing compliance is increasingly automated [17,20]. However, in an organizational setting automating the businesses processes to comply with regulatory requirements is not straight forward.

S. Fischer-Hübner—This research was funded by A4Cloud and SmartSociety, two research projects of the Seventh Framework Programme for Research of the European Community under grant agreements no. 600854 and no. 317550.

A hierarchical approach is presented in [20] to facilitate compliance automation from the abstract regulatory constraints down to the concrete IT systems level. According to Sackmann et al. [20] there are two approaches to achieve compliance, one is a preventive approach and the other one is a detective approach. In the preventive approach the obligations (constraints derived from data protection laws in case of privacy compliance) are strictly enforced in the IT operations and thus non-compliant events are prevented from occurring. Whereas in the detective approach, activities of the system are monitored and validated against the compliance obligations. In this paper, we focus on the detective approach for achieving privacy compliance.

In the detective approach, compliance adherence is mainly validated through automated audits where the business process executions are recorded and retrospectively analyzed for policy conformance. This approach of realizing compliance demonstrates responsibility and thus accountability, provides flexibility in process executions, helps to validate future obligations, and deters policy violations. The key idea behind the automated audits, which automatically verifies the events that are registered in the logs against specifications is thus similar to intrusion detection methods. However in the context of privacy compliance, privacy principles and concepts, unlike security functions, are less well defined [10]. Hence, intrigued by the idea of privacy compliance verification we aim to synthesize the state-of-the-art auditing techniques that are used to realize privacy compliance by detection.

Research in automatic verification of privacy compliance has been ad hoc and diverse, ranging from well-evaluated proof-of-concepts to theoretical research ideas that propose approaches for validating the data handling practices of an organization. To the best of our knowledge, no scientific review has been done that describes the state-of-the-art in automated audits for privacy compliance validation. We reviewed existing streams of work in this field using the systematic literature review for summarizing the state-of-the-art. Major contributions of this paper are as follows:

- We systematically synthesize the existing technical knowledge of this research domain to provide a consolidated view of the state-of-the-art and explain its conceptual relationships. We present the consolidated view as a taxonomy, which is based on the auditing techniques. (Sect. 3).
- We qualitatively analyze the motivations for log-based automated privacy audits and derive a second taxonomy, which is based on privacy audit objectives (Sect. 4).
- Based upon the insights gained from the above two taxonomies, we conceptualize a set of initial guidelines for utilizing log-based automated privacy audits (Sect. 5).

2   Method

To provide an in-depth overview of the state-of-the-art, we used a systematic literature review process [18]. This process provides methodological rigor in terms of planning, conducting and reporting the literature review.

As the initial step, a research protocol was designed following [18]. The research protocol specifies the objectives of the review, the search strategy to identify relevant literature, and a strategy to classify the primary studies (the identified sources of this review) for evaluation. The following subsections describes each steps in detail.

2.1   Identification of Objects

A thorough and unbiased search for relevant literature is the essence of a systematic literature review. For the scientific literature sources, we used our university library's one-search service - EBSCO discovery service[1] mainly to ensure that disciplines other than information technology were not overlooked. Prior to the search, keywords, free texts and their synonyms were identified from the following objectives.

- What are the technical approaches that have been proposed to validate privacy compliance or to detect privacy non-compliance?
- What are the motivations for performing privacy compliance verification through log audits?
- Could privacy concerns be detected from log audits, if so what are the privacy concerns that can be validated?
- What are the limitations of the current approaches?

Table 1 lists the search strings used for this study. The identified search strings were combined appropriately during the search to locate as many relevant articles as possible. The search process was stopped when the different combination of the search strings were not returning any new results.

The search was performed during week 51 in 2014 and yielded 1723 results in total to be evaluated for relevance.

2.2   Selection of Primary Studies

The articles returned by the search were examined for relevance from the title, abstract, and subject headings following these exclusion criteria

- Exclude if the focus of the proposed approach is clearly not a privacy-compliance by detection.
- Exclude if the focus of the paper is not technical but relates to constitutions, legislation and regulations.

---

[1] EBSCO discovery service is a gateway to access various scholarly databases (with and without full text) in many different disciplines and it also includes electronic resources like e-magazines, e-books and etc. The complete list of resources indexed by the discovery service can be found at [1]. The updated version of the list is not available yet, hence recently added database such as ACM is missing in the out dated list.

Table 1. Search strings

Phrases (Including free texts)	Synonyms
Privacy concerns	
Privacy analysis	privacy audit
Privacy compliance	privacy enforcement
Privacy non compliance	privacy violation
Access logs	
Audit trails	

As a result a total of 25 articles were identified and imported to EndNote[2] - a bibliography management tool. Next, we performed a backward (i.e. searching the citations of the identified articles) and a forward search (i.e. locating the papers that cites the identified articles) on the identified articles to ensure fullest coverage of related work. All the relevant literature resulted from the forward and backward search was further narrowed following a second set of inclusion and exclusion criteria, which are listed below:

– Include the most completed and related version, if there exist several related studies by the same authors or by the same research group.
– Exclude short papers where the technical description of the solutions were not described.
– Exclude if the privacy-compliance auditing was *discussed* in parts of the proposed prototype but clearly was not the main focus, because in most of these cases the verification part is not automated.
– Exclude if the privacy-compliance verification is performed by other means than the log audits.

This step resulted in a reduction in the number of the primary studies. The total number of relevant literature identified and reviewed for this work are 14, full texts of the 14 articles were located and imported to EndNote for further processing.

2.3 Quality Assessment, Classification and Synthesis

As the next step in the process, all the primary studies were carefully analyzed. The aim of the study is to bring together existing but divergent research for two purposes; (1) to give a snapshot of the field revealing the design foundations, which will help future researchers in this field to position their research and (2) to analyze the privacy requirements that are accounted for in the state-of-the-art thus indicating the uncovered privacy requirements. Classification systems and

---

[2] http://endnote.com/, accessed June 10, 2016.

the resulting classification are proven to be an effective strategy for deconstructing the foundations of a domain [19]. The taxonomy[3] focuses on the characteristics of this particular research area and its conceptual relationships rather on the evolutionary relationships. Therefore a broad set of characteristics are extracted from the primary studies to inductively analyze the conceptual relationships. This follows though not rigorously[4] the taxonomy development framework proposed by Nickerson et al. [19], which is based on a three-level indicator model suggested by Bailey et al. [5]. We used particularly the empirical-to-conceptual approach, where the characteristics of each object under study are observed and analyzed for similarities in order to form categories.

After identifying the purpose of the taxonomy, which is to provide a scientific understanding of the state-of-the-art, the meta-characteristics [19] were specified to drive the development of a taxonomy. The meta-characteristic identified for the taxonomy that is presented in Sect. 3 is technical design. Hence the characteristics to be extracted from each primary study are algorithms, inputs and outputs of the algorithms, their performance, scalability and technical limitations. In addition, design principles such as the aim of the solution, system settings, users of the system were extracted, which are helpful to deduce the nature of each category. These extracted characteristics are later qualitatively analyzed for the taxonomy presented in Sect. 4.

3   A Taxonomy of Audit Techniques

Following the approach described in the Subsect. 2.3, seven to eight different characteristics are extracted and observed from each primary study. Some of the characteristics are not clearly determined from the primary studies, hence related abstract notions are identified, simplified and analyzed. In order to develop a taxonomy of technical approaches to privacy-compliance verification, the main criterion that drives the taxonomy development is identified as detection (verification) algorithm, given the events and the privacy specifications. As mentioned earlier, checking the system activities registered in the logs for detecting non compliance is thus similar to Intrusion Detection Systems (IDS), which is evident from the detection algorithms used in the primary studies. The technical architecture of these detection algorithms are analyzed to derive functional dimensions. Within the 14 technical designs, 6 of the solutions specify patterns for detection prior to the verification phase, where five in six solutions define patterns for compliance and one solution defines patterns for non-compliance. The remaining 8 solutions train a classifier to learn the compliant state, which is further used to detect outliers. Evidently, this follows the two primary types of IDS techniques, namely misuse-based IDS and anomaly-based IDS. Further

---

[3] In this paper the words classification and taxonomy are interchangeably used to mean the result of the classification process.

[4] For example, the cycles of our taxonomy revision process was intuitive, there was no ending conditions such as objective and subjective endings were specified to terminate the iteration.

sub dimensions of the taxonomy are derived based on the verifying characteristics of the detection algorithms. Figure 1 depicts the resulting classification,
which consists of 2 dimensions of the technical designs observed from the existing privacy-compliance by detection solutions.

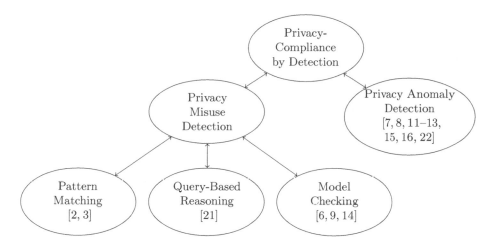

Fig. 1. Technical taxonomy of privacy-compliance by detection solutions.

3.1   Privacy Misuse Detection

As mentioned earlier, the common characteristic of the technical architecture in
this category of solutions is, the privacy misuse patterns (either compliant or non-
compliant) that are used for detection are expressed explicitly. Generally these
patterns are known in advance, and are looked up in the logs for a mismatch
in case of compliant patterns or a match in case of non-compliant patterns
to detect violations. Three different checking approaches are observed in the
technical design of the primary studies within this category, namely, pattern
matching, query-based reasoning, and model checking.

Pattern Matching. The system settings of these detection algorithms are
integrated IT systems offering web-enabled IT services, self-service identity management feature of an application, etc. Individuals release data items while interacting with these systems. The inherent characteristic of these systems is that
individuals can specify privacy preferences that define conditions and obligations
for their data usage. Activities of the system, i.e. every action on the data items,
are recorded in a log file (audit trails) for later review. During the review (audit)
the actions recorded in the logs are matched against the applicable rules in the
privacy preferences.

There are two primary studies which fall under the pattern matching approach, Accorsi [2] and Accorsi et al. [3]. Accorsi [2] proposes a matching approach

based on counterexamples. Prior to the verification step, potential violations are derived from the privacy preferences of individuals. These patterns are later used to find a match in the log view that corresponds to an individual. A violation is detected if a match is identified.

Accorsi et al. [3], propose a novel approach for pattern matching to improve the efficiency of the log audits. In the first step of the audit process, individualized audit trails are transformed into an action tree which is a hierarchical representation of activities based on the structure of the data items. In the second step, the algorithm sequentially processes the rules in the privacy preferences of individuals and searches for a node in the tree that corresponds to the data item referred to in the rule. When such a node is determined, the actions recorded in the node are checked for agreement with the applicable rule in the privacy preference. This process is iterated and at the end of each iteration, matched actions are pruned from the action tree. At the end of the audit, the nodes that remain constitute the sum of violations pertinent to the privacy preferences.

Query-Based Reasoning. The system setting of this solution is very similar to the setting mentioned above, where the individuals can formulate privacy preferences for their data usage. Privacy related events are logged when subjects (processes, softwares, participants) of the system act upon the managed data items. Samavi et al. [21] propose a query based reasoning approach to derive obligations applicable to an access request and to verify the fulfillment of these obligations. They define two ontologies in their framework, namely L2TAP (Linked Data Log to Transparency, Accountability and Privacy) and SCIP (Simple Contextual Integrity Privacy). L2TAP ontology allows logging of events such as changes in the privacy preferences, and information related to access requests and access activities. This ontology provides provenance assertions (when and by whom), which are associated with the activity that triggers the change. SCIP ontology provides semantics for the events logged in L2TAP logs, and uses SPARL queries with RDFS reasoning support for auditing. The first step in the auditing process is to use SPARL queries to identify all the obligations linked to an individual's privacy preferences that match the access requests. In the next step the status (fulfilled, pending, violated) of the linked obligations are identified using SPARL queries to determine the compliance of the access request. In case of multiple obligations that are linked to an access request a series of SPARL queries are used to evaluate the combined effect of these obligations in order to determine the overall compliance of the access request.

Model Checking. The system setting of this approach is enterprise computing solutions and the design objective is to validate compliance of the system in accordance with privacy regulations, or enterprise policies, or data protection directives. These specifications are expressed in logical forms, and the actual usage of personal data recorded in the logs are also represented as models. Given this, a model-checking algorithm verifies whether a given formula is satisfied by the model. The auditing algorithms of three primary studies use the model-checking approach. Garg et al. [14] formalize all the 84 disclosure-related clauses of the Health Insurance Portability and Accountability Act (HIPAA)[5] Privacy Rule using first-order logic. Additionally, in their framework the audit trails are expressed as partial structures. During the audit, the auditing algorithm iteratively checks for a violation, given the policy and the audit trails. It is iterative because sometimes information contained in the logs is insufficient for determining whether a policy is satisfied or not (for e.g. in case of future obligations), hence the algorithm runs iteratively when more information is available. Banescu et al. in [6] formalize the business processes of an enterprise. During the audit, the modeled system events which are generated during the execution of the business process are replayed over the business process model to identify violations, which are later quantified. The events are classified during this process to identify the type of violation in regard to the business process model. Butin et al. [9] adopt a similar approach; they express parts of the EU Data Protection Directive[6] and the audit trails in logical form. For the verification of the state of the logs, its compliance properties are derived and defined from the formalized EU Data Protection Directive. A log trace (audit trails) is compliant if it satisfies all its compliance properties. The audit framework proposed by Butin et al. operates on "privacy friendly" logs and they mathematically proves the correctness of the log analysis that verifies the compliance to the data protection obligations.

3.2 Privacy Anomaly Detection

The common characteristic of the technical architecture of the solutions presented in this category is that the detection is anomaly-based. The system setting of these solutions are similar to system setting of privacy misuse detection solutions, but the design objective is to detect unexpected attempts. The anomaly-based detection systems identify events that deviate from an abnormal profile in the case of supervised method, or from the other items in a dataset in the case of unsupervised method. A combination of statistical, machine learning and data mining techniques are observed in eight primary studies irrespective of the anomaly detection method. Venter et al. [22], Bhattacharya et al. [7], Boxwala et al. [8], Gupta [15] and Heatley et al. [16] use the supervised anomaly detection method. The training set required to train the classifier is built manually for two of the solutions but Bhattacharya et al. [7] use an association rule data mining technique to generate patterns of violations for the training set. Similarly Heatley et al. [16] and Gupta [15] use statistical methods like decision tree induction technique and Latent Dirichlet Allocation (LDA) respectively to build the training set, which contains the "normal" and the "abnormal" behavior. Given the model (training data set), the classifier using statistical techniques such as k-nearest neighbor, Logistic Regression (LR) and Support Vector Machine (SVM) predicts the probability for the access request to be an outlier.

---

[5] http://www.hhs.gov/ocr/privacy/, accessed on June 10, 2016.
[6] http://eur-lex.europa.eu/LexUriServ/LexUriServ.do?uri=CELEX:31995L0046:en:
HTML, accessed on June 10, 2016.

However, Chen et al. [11] present an unsupervised anomaly detection method for system settings where building a clearly labeled training set is difficult. In their approach, the first step is to aggregate the features in the audit trails into community structures using a combination of statistical methods such as graph-based modeling and dimensionality detection. In the second step the deviation probability of the elements from its closest neighbor is determined using the k-nearest neighbor algorithm. Fabbri et al. [13] describe an approach similar to that of Chen et al. for forming aggregated social structures but use the social graph to explain clearly the context of the events in an audit trail. The basis for this is that these explanations are later reviewed by the privacy officers to detect violations. Similarly Duffy [12] defines a framework that combines anomaly detection algorithms such as the one proposed by Chen et al. and two other algorithms (Patient-Flow Anomaly Detection Systems (PFADS) and Specialized Network Anomaly Detection (SNAD)) to provide contextual explanations thus allowing patients and privacy officers to have better understanding of the access logs.

3.3 Implications of Intrusion Detection Approach to Privacy Audits

As illustrated and depicted in Fig. 1, the approaches to validate privacy compliance follows intrusion detection techniques and hence inherit the underlying limitations yet bring intrinsic challenges. For instance, misuse detection algorithms match specific patterns from the audit trails for detecting misuse, under the assumption that all the patterns for validation are known in advance. However relying on well-known patterns degrade the purpose of the validation algorithms. Moreover, the patterns for privacy invasion are difficult to define primarily because privacy invasive incidents are mostly context dependent.

Furthermore, the expressiveness of the compliance requirements as patterns is constrained by the limitations of the formal languages, for instance, purpose(s) need to be explicitly expressed for each data item. In addition, human intervention is generally required for deciding policy violations, and for providing additional semantics besides the information registered in the logs.

Anomaly detection algorithms on the other hand are not concerned with known notable events but with the abnormal system or user behavior. However, in order to detect outliers (abnormality), the classifier in the case of supervised learning method requires a fair amount of training data set to model what is normal for each subject (could be a user, a process, and a software) in a system in order to decide on how probable the activity of a given subject is abnormal. In the case of unsupervised learning though, it is important to model appropriate clusters for detecting outliers that is abnormal from rest of the members in a cluster. Nevertheless, similar to well-known patterns the signals of privacy invasions are challenging to discern because under a slightly different context a system or user behavior would have been legitimate. This may result in many false positives or many false negatives offsetting the purpose of the automation process.

Furthermore, in the literature review we observed that there are more privacy anomaly detection solutions than the privacy misuse detection solutions. This is because, in the case of anomaly-based detection the concept of normality is difficult, if not impossible to transfer from one system setting to another system setting. Although all the solutions in this category target health-care systems, a slightly different condition such as collaborative health-care systems require different training techniques or clustering for modeling expected behaviors.

4   A Taxonomy of Audit Objectives

In Sect. 3 we presented a taxonomy based on the auditing techniques that validate adherence to the privacy compliance requirements. We observe that the utilization of different auditing techniques are highly influenced by the audit objectives. Hence, in addition to the taxonomy of the technical approaches (see Fig. 1), in this section we attempt to conceptualize the state-of-the-art in terms of compliance objectives. Whereby, we provide an analysis of the motivational trends for privacy compliance. There are three compliance objectives deduced from the state-of-the-art for engaging in a log-based automated privacy audits, they are;

- Audit for ex-post obligations
- Audit for permitted exceptions
- Audit for access legitimacy

Audit for Ex-post Obligations. Privacy compliance requirements, which cannot be checked by a policy engine beforehand but are determined after the fact, are realized using automated log audits. Temporal Obligations such as "Delete the stored personal attributes after 2 years" and perpetual obligations such as "Send notice to the end-users every time there is a change in the enterprise policy" indicate after-the-fact compliance actions. To automatically realize these requirements, data handling processes are persistently monitored in the form of audit trails for subsequent actions. The granularity level of the audit trails greatly impact the achievable degree of automation of these requirements.

Audit for Permitted Exceptions. In the health care applications, IT processes such as access control are often lenient to allow for emergency. Herein, patient care and safety outweigh the permission restrictions. However, unauthorized access to patient information arise from the misuse of "break glass policies" may jeopardize the personal integrity of the patients. Therefore, these access exceptions must be supervised regularly in order to handle the risk of misuse. Audit for permitted exceptions helps to both detect and deter violation of these exceptions.

Audit for Access Legitimacy. In service based applications, end-users are allowed to set access preferences to certain data objects that are under the control of the service providers or information fiduciaries such as identity management providers. However, regulation such as the proposed EU General Data Protection Regulation (GDPR)[7] and agreed upon end-user agreements mandate service providers' accountability, i.e. require the service providers to demonstrate the exercised responsibilities instead of just promising that the end-user preferences will be honored. To automate this requirement, related actions of the system are recorded in the logs, compared and verified using the log audits for compliance to the conditions arising from the end-users' privacy access preferences. Further, the log audits that validate compliance to laws and regulations also include access and disclosure compliance. Therefore, the solutions that provide mechanisms for validating compliance in accordance with the laws, and regulations are also included in this category.

Figure 2 shows the categorizations of the primary studies in accordance with the audit objectives listed above.

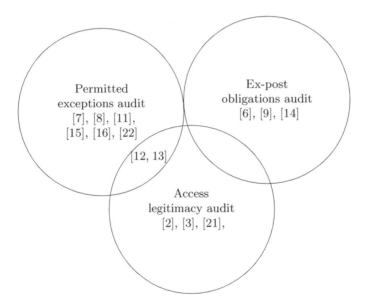

Fig. 2. Three audits objectives in the context of privacy

Taxonomy of audit objectives point out how well each objectives are covered (or not covered yet) by the state-of-the-art. Further, Fig. 3 illustrates the mapping of the privacy audit techniques to the privacy audit objectives.

Pattern matching, and query-based reasoning algorithms provide solutions to determine if the permissions set by the end-users are indeed respected.

---

[7] http://ec.europa.eu/justice/data-protection/document/review2012/com_2012_11_en.pdf, accessed on June 10, 2016.

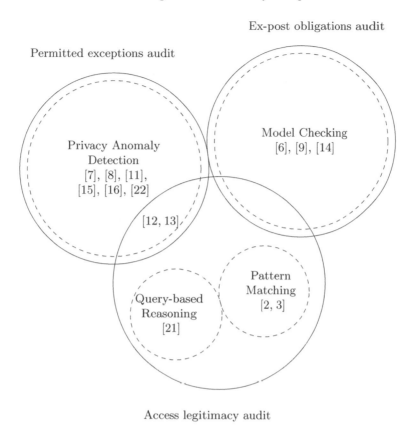

Fig. 3. Privacy audit objectives and respective techniques

From Sect. 3.1, we note that the model checking algorithms present auditing solutions to model the observable state of a system and validate if the system is compliant as expected. Hence, model checking solutions also address accountability requirement for access and disclosure activities.

Further, from our literature review, we observe that privacy anomaly detection mechanisms provide auditing solutions for supervising the risk integrated in the enforceable policies (for e.g. "break glass"). It can be noted that anomaly detection algorithms could as well suitable for access legitimacy audit. However, as mentioned earlier the inherent limitations of anomaly detection algorithms such as high number of false positives and impractical conditions for transferring the state of normality makes the anomaly detection algorithms less reliable. Nonetheless, the practical usefulness of anomaly detection for other privacy audit objectives may be a new potential research direction to investigate further.

5   Guidelines

Compliance by detection approaches are long established IT processes in an organizational setting. However, in the context of privacy compliance requirements there is no one size fit all solution. In this section, we tentatively provide initial guidelines based upon our analysis of the state-of-the-art for aiding implementation of responsible log-based automated privacy audits.

– Any organization providing service to consumers usually processes information or data. An assessment procedure to classify the type of data is an essential point of departure. The classes of data such as private, public, sensitive or nonsensitive are very much context-dependent, i.e. the context of the application domain and various features of the service are need to be considered.
– Depending on the classification of the data and the application domain, applicable regulations, standards, and laws must be reviewed in order to derive the privacy compliance requirements.
– Classify the privacy-compliance by detection requirements into afore mentioned audit objectives. It is important to note that the list of objectives presented in Sect. 4 are the privacy audit directions inferred from the state-of-the-art. There could be different objectives for employing privacy audits depending on the class of the data, classification domain, and jurisdiction.
– Based on the identified privacy audit objectives, employ the respective algorithms as depicted in Fig. 3.

6   Conclusions

We systematically reviewed and classified the existing privacy compliance validation solutions in relation to the auditing techniques and the audit objectives. In this paper we attempt to deconstruct the theoretical foundations of the state-of-the-art in order to explain the conceptual relationships of the existing solutions. Nonetheless, we recognize that the presented taxonomies are itself artifacts hence subject to evaluation. We attempt to conceptualize the presented taxonomies for mutually exclusivity and explanatory, to ensure they are extendible when more objects show up in the future.

Privacy compliance validation plays a very important role for success of any business. Despite the recognition of the importance of compliant to privacy requirements, the state-of-the-art has not matured proportionately with the growing privacy expectations. Furthermore, the feasibility of automating the privacy expectations in order to demonstrate compliance is practically restricted by two factors. First, the degree of expressiveness of regulations, laws, standards, and user-laid preferences in a machine-readable form. Second, the level of granularity of the information logged in the audit trails, and the impractical conditions to automatically log certain system activities such as "informed consent". Hence, as a next step, in our future work, we are interested in studying a privacy-aware log design for privacy compliance validation.

Acknowledgments. This work benefits from the invaluable comments, inputs from Rose-Mharie Åhlfeldt and from the anonymous reviewers.

References

1. Databases in onesearch. http://www.kau.se/sites/default/files/Dokument/sub page/2012/06/databaser_i_onesearch_pdf_18607.pdf
2. Accorsi, R.: Automated privacy audits to complement the notion of control for identity management. In: de Leeuw, E., Fischer-Hübner, S., Tseng, J., Borking, J. (eds.) Policies and Research in Identity Management, vol. 261, pp. 39–48. Springer, US (2008)
3. Accorsi, R., Stocker, T.: Automated privacy audits based on pruning of log data. In: 12th Enterprise Distributed Object Computing Conference Workshops. IEEE (2008)
4. Bace, J., Rozwell, C.: Understanding the Components of Compliance. Research G00137902. Gartner (2006)
5. Bailey, K.: A three-level measurement model. Qual. Quantity **18**(3), 225–245 (1984)
6. Banescu, S., Petković, M., Zannone, N.: Measuring privacy compliance using fitness metrics. In: Barros, A., Gal, A., Kindler, E. (eds.) BPM 2012. LNCS, vol. 7481, pp. 114–119. Springer, Heidelberg (2012)
7. Bhattacharya, J., Dass, R., Kapoor, V., Chakraborti, D., Gupta, S.: Privdam: Privacy Violation Detection and Monitoring Using Data Mining (2005). http://hdl.handle.net/11718/1881
8. Boxwala, A., Kim, J., Grillo, J., Ohno-Machado, L.: Using statistical and machine learning to help institutions detect suspicious access to electronic health records. J. Am. Med. Inform. Assoc. **18**(4), 498–505 (2011)
9. Butin, D., Le Métayer, D.: Log Analysis for Data Protection Accountability (Extended Version). Research report no. 8432, INRIA (2013)
10. Cavoukian, A.: The Security-privacy Paradox: Issues, Misconceptions and Strategies. Technical report, Information Privacy Commission/Ontario and Deloitte & Touche (2003)
11. Chen, Y., Malin, B.: Detection of anomalous insiders in collaborative environments via relational analysis of access logs. In: Proceedings of the 1st ACM Conference on Data and Application Security and Privacy (CODASPY), pp. 63–74. ACM, 21–23 February 2011
12. Duffy, E.: Facilitating Patient and Administrator Analyses of Electronic Health Record Accesses. Master thesis, University of Illinois at Urbana-Champaign (2013)
13. Fabbri, D., LeFevre, K.: Explanation-based auditing. Proc. VLDB Endowment **5**(1), 1–12 (2011)
14. Garg, D., Jia, L., Datta, A.: Policy auditing over incomplete logs: theory, implementation and applications. In: Proceedings of the 18th ACM Conference on Computer and Communications Security (CCS), pp. 151–162. ACM (2011)
15. Gupta, S.: Modeling and Detecting Anomalous Topic Access in EMR Audit logs. Master thesis, University of Illinois at Urbana-Champaign (2013)
16. Heatley, S., Otto, J.: Data mining computer audit logs to detect computer misuse. Int. J. Intell. Syst. Account. Finance Manag. **7**(3), 125–134 (1998)

17. Kahmer, M., Gilliot, M., Muller, G.: Automating privacy compliance with expdt. In: E-Commerce Technology and the 5th IEEE Conference on Enterprise Computing, E-Commerce and E-Services, 10th IEEE International Conference on E-Commerce Technology, pp. 87–94, July 2008
18. Kitchenham, B.: Procedures for performing systematic reviews. Joint Technical report 0400011t.1, Keele University and Empirical Software Engineering National ICT Australia Ltd (2004)
19. Nickerson, R., Varshney, U., Muntermann, J.: A method for taxonomy development and its application in information systems. Eur. J. Inf. Syst. **22**(3), 336–359 (2013)
20. Sackmann, S., Kähmer, M., Gilliot, M., Lowis, L.: A classification model for automating compliance. In: 10th IEEE International Conference on E-Commerce Technology (CEC 2008) / 5th IEEE International Conference on Enterprise Computing, E-Commerce and E-Services (EEE 2008), pp. 79–86 (2008)
21. Samavi, R., Consens, M.P.: L2TAP+SCIP: an audit-based privacy framework leveraging linked data. In: 8th International Conference on Collaborative Computing: Networking, Applications and Worksharing, pp. 719–726. ICST / IEEE (2012)
22. Venter, H.S., Olivier, M.S., Eloff, J.H.: Pids: a privacy intrusion detection system. Internet Res. **14**(5), 360–365 (2004)

Privacy-Preserving Access Control in Publicly Readable Storage Systems

Daniel Bosk$^{(\boxtimes)}$ and Sonja Buchegger

School of Computer Science and Communication,
KTH Royal Institute of Technology, Stockholm, Sweden
{dbosk,buc}@kth.se

Abstract. In this paper, we focus on achieving privacy-preserving access control mechanisms for decentralized storage, primarily intended for an asynchronous message passing setting. We propose two modular constructions, one using a pull strategy and the other a push strategy for sharing data. These models yield different privacy properties and requirements on the underlying system. We achieve hidden policies, hidden credentials and hidden decisions. We additionally achieve what could be called 'hidden policy-updates', meaning that previously-authorized subjects cannot determine if they have been excluded from future updates or not.

Keywords: Privacy · Access control · Cloud storage · Decentralized storage · Hidden policies · Hidden policy-updates · Hidden credentials

1 Introduction

Alice and her friends want to communicate asynchronously. To do this they want to use a publicly available file system and write their messages to different files, which the other party later can read. This is a possible architecture for a decentralized online social network (DOSN). We are interested in enforcing access-control policies in such a public file system which does not have any built-in access control mechanisms. Our approach is to introduce a layer of encryption as a logical reference monitor. Beyond the expected confidentiality, Alice wants some stronger privacy properties as well: her friends should not be able to monitor her activity, e.g. infer with whom else she communicates, even the fact that she communicates with others.

We will present an ideal model of communication and its desired properties in Sect. 2, this is what we want to achieve. Then we will present the building blocks that we will use, and their accompanying assumptions, in Sect. 3. We will also assume a simple file system with no built-in access control. This system is discussed and defined in Sect. 3.1. This includes our adversary model: we will let the adversary control the file system.

Then we give two constructions that implement the functionality using different message-passing models and analyse what properties their primitives must

© IFIP International Federation for Information Processing 2016
Published by Springer International Publishing Switzerland 2016. All Rights Reserved
D. Aspinall et al. (Eds.): Privacy and Identity 2015, IFIP AICT 476, pp. 327–342, 2016.
DOI: 10.1007/978-3-319-41763-9_22

have in Sects. 4 and 5. The two message passing models are called the pull model and the push model. In the pull model Alice's friends pull new messages from Alice, whereas in the push model Alice pushes new messages to her friends' inboxes. The motivation is that the pull model is optimized for Alice and the push model for Alice's friends. In a decentralized file system the pull model yields few connections for Alice, but many for her friends (if they have more friends than Alice). Conversely the push model yields many connections for Alice, but only one for her friends (they check their inbox). In some situations connections can be expensive, cf. establishing many Tor [5] circuits to transfer little data and establishing one circuit to transfer more data.

After presenting our constructions we shortly analyse their algorithmic complexity in Sect. 6. Finally we compare our results to related work in Sect. 7 and conclude by summarizing the main contributions and future work in Sect. 8.

2   The Ideal Communication Model

There are several ways Alice can implement the message passing with her friends. We will start by presenting an ideal model of communication (Definition 1) whose properties Alice wants to achieve. Then we will proceed to the details of two alternative protocols (Definitions 4 and 6) that yields the properties of the ideal model.

Definition 1 (Communication Model). *Let $\mathcal{C}_{p,S}$ be a (p, S)-communication model with a publisher p and a set of subscribers S. Then we have the following operations defined on $\mathcal{C}_{p,S}$:*

- *The publisher first runs $\mathcal{C}_{p,S}[p]$.setup(1^λ) and each subscriber $s \in S$ runs $\mathcal{C}_{p,S}[p]$.setup(1^λ), where λ is the security parameter.*
- *The publisher p uses $\mathcal{C}_{p,S}[p]$.publish(R, m) to publish the message m to the designated recipient set R by making it available to all recipients $r \in R \subseteq S$.*
- *Each subscriber $s \in S$ uses $\mathcal{C}_{p,S}[s]$.get() to get the set M of published messages $m \in M$ for which s was in the recipient set.*

Whenever p, S are clear from the context, we will simply omit them, e.g. $\mathcal{C}[p]$.setup and $\mathcal{C}[s]$.setup.

There are two ways the adversary can gain information. The first is from corrupted subscribers and the second is from the public file system over which the communication model is implemented. Hence the second is not visible in Definition 1, but will be in Definitions 4 and 6.

In our desired scenario, Alice acts as a publisher and her friends as the subscribers. We want the following properties:

Message Privacy. No subscriber $s' \in S$ can use $\mathcal{C}[s]$.get for $s' \neq s$. I.e. no subscriber can read the messages of any other subscriber, we call this property *message privacy*.

Hidden Policies. No subscriber s_i must learn which $s_1, \ldots, s_n \in R$ beyond that $i \in \{1, \ldots, n\}$ and $s_i \in R$ for a given message m. I.e. no subscriber must know who else received a message, we call this property *hidden policy*. Thus if Alice publishes a message, none of her friends know who else received it and none can read the others' received messages to check if they have received the same message.

Hidden Policy-Updates. In addition to the hidden-policy property, we want something we call *hidden policy-updates*. Consider the following example: Bob might become jealous if he realizes that Alice no longer includes him in the recipient set for her messages. As such Bob should only be able to determine that Alice publishes content by being in the recipient set himself.

There are several ways to implement the message-passing protocol for the communication model in Definition 1. We will focus on two alternative protocols, one using the pull model and the other using the push model for communication. The push model is analogous to the subscription of magazines: a subscriber contacts the publisher and signs a subscription, whenever the publisher issues a new magazine it sends a copy to the subscriber's mailbox. The pull model is the converse of the push model. It is analogous to the selling of magazines in kiosks: the publisher issues magazines and the 'subscribers' come to the kiosk and buy them whenever they want. We can see that our ideal communication model allows both a pull and push strategy for implementation. We will describe and analyse the pull construction in Sect. 4 and the push construction in Sect. 5. But first we need to review our needed building blocks.

3   Building Blocks

We will now describe the primitives and our assumptions upon which we will base our constructions. We start with a general file system, which is publicly readable and has no built in access control. We then describe the general cryptographic primitives we need and finish with the ANOBE [9] scheme which we will use for part of our construction.

3.1   A General File System

We will model our system as an abstract file system with the operations append (which includes create) and read. The operations are defined as we intuitively expect: we can create an object, read it and also append to it. The file system itself provides no access control.

Definition 2 (Public File System). *A file $f = (i, m_i)$ consists of the identifier i and the associated content m_i. We define the set of files $F = \{(i, m_i)\}$ together with the following operations to be the public file system $\mathcal{FS}$:*

- *$\mathcal{FS}.\mathsf{append}(i, m_i)$ will set $(i, m) \leftarrow (i, m \,\|\, m')$ for $(i, m) \in F$. If $\{(i', m') \in F \mid i' = i\} = \emptyset$, i.e. the file i does not yet exist, this operation will create it by setting $F \leftarrow F \cup \{(i, m_i)\}$.*
- *$\mathcal{FS}.\mathsf{read}(i) = m_i$ if $(i, m_i) \in F$, otherwise $\mathcal{FS}.\mathsf{read}(i) = \bot$.*

We can see in the definition that anyone can read any object in the file system. Anyone can also create new files and append to existing files.

We will let the adversary Eve operate the file system $\mathcal{FS}$ defined in Definition 2. By this we mean that Eve has access to the internal state of $\mathcal{FS}$ directly, i.e. the set of files F. She can thus read all files (same as everyone else), but she can also do arbitrary searches since she does not have to use $\mathcal{FS}$.read.

Although Eve could potentially also modify or delete the files, we do not treat denial-of-service attacks by Eve deleting the files. However, as we will see in our constructions, modifications (but not deletions) made by Eve will be detected.

Eve cannot distinguish between Alice's and Bob's requests to the operations of $\mathcal{FS}$ — in the definition there is nothing to identify who used any of the operations, so this is consistent with the definition. What she can do, is to record the times at which the operations occurred, since she executes them.

This adversary would correspond to a centralized setting, e.g. having the file system hosted by a cloud operator, or a decentralized setting where the adversary can monitor the network at the file system side.

3.2   Cryptographic Primitives

We will use mainly standard public-key cryptography. We need a public-key encryption scheme and two signature schemes. Although we can use shared-key mechanisms in some places, we will maintain a public-key notation throughout this paper and merely point out in the places where a shared-key scheme would be possible.

We will use a public-key encryption scheme $E = (E.Keygen, E.Enc, E.Dec)$. This scheme must be semantically secure under chosen-ciphertext attacks (IND-CCA) and key-private (AI-CCA) [3], i.e. the ciphertext does not leak under which key it was created. We also need an unforgeable signature scheme $S = (S.Keygen, S.Sign, S.Verify)$.

We additionally need an anonymous and semantically secure (ANO-IND-CCA) [9] broadcast encryption (BE) [6] scheme $BE = (BE.Setup, BE.Keygen, BE.Enc, BE.Dec)$. Let $U = \{1, \ldots, n\}$ be the universe of users. $BE.Setup(1^\lambda, n)$ generates a master public key MPK and master secret key MSK for n users. $BE.Keygen(MPK, MSK, i)$ generates the secret key k_i^{Pri} for user $i \in U$. Then $BE.Enc(MPK, m, R)$ will encrypt a message m to a ciphertext c for the set of users $R \subseteq U$ and $BE.Dec(MPK, k_i^{Pri}, c)$ will return m if $i \in R$. Formally we define ANO-IND-CCA by the following game.

Definition 3 (ANO-IND-CCA [9]). *Let $U = \{1, \ldots, n\}$ be the universe of users and BE be BE scheme. BE scheme is anonymous and adaptively IND-CCA (ANO-IND-CCA) if the adversary has negligible advantage in winning the following game.*

Setup. *The challenger runs $BE.Setup(1^\lambda, n)$, where λ is the security parameter. This generates a master public key which is given to the adversary $\mathcal{A}$.*

Phase 1. *The adversary $\mathcal{A}$ may corrupt any $i \in U$, i.e. request its secret key $k_i =$ BE.Keygen(MPK, MSK, i) through an oracle. Additionally $\mathcal{A}$ has access to a decryption oracle to decrypt arbitrary ciphertexts for any $i \in U$, upon request (c, i) the oracle will return BE.Dec(MPK, k_i, c).*

Challenge. *The adversary chooses messages m_0, m_1 such that $|m_0| = |m_1|$ and recipient sets R_0, R_1 such that $|R_0| = |R_1|$. For all corrupted $i \in U$ we have $i \notin R_0 \cup R_1 \setminus (R_0 \cap R_1)$. If there exists an $i \in R_0 \cap R_1$ we require $m_0 = m_1$. Then $\mathcal{A}$ gives them to the challenger. The challenger randomly chooses $b \in \{0,1\}$ and runs $c^* \leftarrow$ BE.Enc(MPK, m_b, R_b) and gives c^* to the adversary.*

Phase 2. *The adversary may continue to corrupt $i \notin R_0 \cup R_1 \setminus (R_0 \cap R_1)$. $\mathcal{A}$ may corrupt $i \in R_0 \cap R_1$ only if $m_0 = m_1$. The adversary is not allowed to use the decryption oracle on the challenge ciphertext c^*.*

Guess. *$\mathcal{A}$ outputs a bit $\hat{b}$ and wins the game if $\hat{b} = b$.*

We define the adversary's advantage $\mathbf{Adv}_{\mathcal{A},\mathsf{BE}}^{ANO\text{-}IND\text{-}CCA}(1^\lambda) = |\Pr[\hat{b} = b] - \frac{1}{2}|$.

Throughout BE can be any BE scheme with the ANO-IND-CCA property. However, we will use the ANOBE scheme by Libert et al. [9] as an example in our discussion and modify it for one of our constructions. For our description of this scheme, which follows, we need slight variants of the above encryption (E) and signature (S) schemes. We need an encryption scheme $\bar{\mathsf{E}} = (\bar{\mathsf{E}}.\mathsf{Keygen}, \bar{\mathsf{E}}.\mathsf{Enc}, \bar{\mathsf{E}}.\mathsf{Dec})$ which is in addition to key-private also robust (ROB-CCA) [1]. For the signature scheme $\bar{\mathsf{S}} = (\bar{\mathsf{S}}.\mathsf{Keygen}, \bar{\mathsf{S}}.\mathsf{Sign}, \bar{\mathsf{S}}.\mathsf{Verify})$, we only need it to be a strongly-unforgeable one-time signature scheme.

3.3   An Anonymous Broadcast Encryption Scheme

We will now describe the ANOBE scheme by Libert et al. [9]. We will use ANOBE to denote this scheme. The algorithms work as follows. ANOBE.Setup generates a master public key $MPK = \left(\bar{\mathsf{S}}, \{k_i^{\mathsf{Pub}}\}_{i \in U}\right)$ and the master secret key $MSK = \{k_i^{\mathsf{Pri}}\}_{i \in U}$, where $(k_i^{\mathsf{Pub}}, k_i^{\mathsf{Pri}}) \xleftarrow{\$} \bar{\mathsf{E}}.\mathsf{Keygen}(1^\lambda)$. ANOBE.Keygen($MPK, MSK, i$) simply returns k_i^{Pri} from MSK. An overview of the encryption function is given in Fig. 1 and an overview of the decryption function in Fig. 2.

Encryption. We must first generate a one-time signature key-pair (s, v), then we choose a random permutation $\pi \colon R \to R$. Next we must encrypt the message m and the verification key (m, v) for every user $i \in R$ in the recipient set $R \subseteq U$ under their respective public key, $c_i = \bar{\mathsf{E}}.\mathsf{Enc}\left(k_i^{\mathsf{Pub}}, m||v\right)$. We let the ANOBE ciphertext be the tuple (v, C, σ), where $C = (c_{\pi(1)}, \ldots, c_{\pi(|S|)})$ and $\sigma = \bar{\mathsf{S}}.\mathsf{Sign}(s, C)$. Note that the signature does not authenticate the sender, it ties the ciphertext together and is needed for correctness.

Decryption. We now have data which would like to decrypt. We parse it as (v, C, σ). If $\bar{\mathsf{S}}.\mathsf{Verify}(v, C, \sigma) = 0$, we return $\perp$ as the verification failed. For each

---

function ANOBE.Enc(MPK, m, R)   ▷ Recipient set R, m to be encrypted.
  $(s, v) \stackrel{\$}{\leftarrow} \bar{\mathsf{S}}.\mathsf{Keygen}(1^\lambda)$ ▷ Signature key-pair, security parameter λ
  Choose a random permutation $\pi\colon R \to R$.
  for $i \in R$ **do**
    $c_i \leftarrow \bar{\mathsf{E}}.\mathsf{Enc}(k_i^{\mathsf{Pub}}, m \parallel v)$
  $C \leftarrow (c_{\pi(1)}, \ldots, c_{\pi(|S|)})$
  $\sigma \leftarrow \bar{\mathsf{S}}.\mathsf{Sign}(s, C)$
  return (v, C, σ)

Fig. 1. An algorithmic overview of the encryption algorithm in the ANOBE scheme.

---

function ANOBE.Dec($MPK, k^{\mathsf{Pri}}, C_{\mathsf{ANOBE}}$)
  if $\bar{\mathsf{S}}.\mathsf{Verify}(v, C, \sigma) = 0$ **then**
    return $\perp$
  for $c \in C$ **do**
    $M \leftarrow \bar{\mathsf{E}}.\mathsf{Dec}(k^{\mathsf{Pri}}, c)$ ▷ Try to decrypt
    if $M = \perp$ **then**
      return $\perp$
    else if $M = (m, v)$ **then**
      return m
  return $\perp$

Fig. 2. An algorithmic overview of the decryption algorithm in the ANOBE scheme.

c in C: Compute $M = \bar{\mathsf{E}}.\mathsf{Dec}\left(k^{\mathsf{Pri}}, c\right)$. If $M \neq \perp$ and $M = (m, v)$, then return m. Otherwise, try the next c. If there are no more c to try, then return $\perp$.

To decrypt an ANOBE ciphertext, we need a trial-and-error decryption procedure to decide if the ciphertext was indeed intended for us. This is costly as it makes the decryption function complexity $O(|S|)$. Libert et al. [9] presented a tag-hint system along with their ANOBE scheme. The tag-hint system reduced the complexity back to $O(1)$. As this is not relevant for our discussion, we refer the reader to [9] but note that it can be used.

4   Construction and Analysis of the Pull Protocol

In this construction, each publisher has an 'outbox' file in the file system. This is simply a file object with a randomly chosen identifier. The publisher adds new publications to the outbox and subscribers pull new content from the outbox. In our analysis we define the protocol for the pull model as follows.

Definition 4 (Pull Protocol). *Let* BE *be a BE scheme,* S *be a signature scheme and* $\mathcal{FS}$ *be a public file system as defined in* Sect. 3. *We denote by* $\mathcal{C}_{p,S}^{\mathsf{Pull}}$ *the* pull protocol *implementing a* (p, S)-communication model *through the operations in* Fig. 3.

$$
\begin{array}{ll}
\textbf{function } \mathcal{C}^{\mathsf{Pull}}_{p,S}[p].\mathsf{setup}(1^\lambda) & \textbf{function } \mathcal{C}^{\mathsf{Pull}}_{p,S}[s].\mathsf{setup}(1^\lambda) \\
\quad i_p \xleftarrow{\text{\textcent}} \{0,1\}^\lambda & \quad \text{Receive from } p. \\
\quad (s_p, v_p) \xleftarrow{\text{\textcent}} \mathsf{S.Keygen}(1^\lambda) & \\
\quad (MPK, MSK) \xleftarrow{\text{\textcent}} \mathsf{BE.Setup}(1^\lambda, |S|) & \textbf{function } \mathcal{C}^{\mathsf{Pull}}_{p,S}[s].\mathsf{fetch} \\
\quad \textbf{for } s \in S \textbf{ do} & \quad C = \mathcal{FS}.\mathsf{read}(i_p) \\
\qquad k_s^{\mathsf{Pri}} \leftarrow \mathsf{BE.Keygen}(MPK, MSK, s) & \quad M \leftarrow \emptyset \\
\qquad \text{Give } (k_s^{\mathsf{Pri}}, v_p, i_p) \text{ to } s. & \quad \textbf{for } (c, \sigma) \in C \textbf{ do} \\
 & \qquad \textbf{if } \mathsf{S.Verify}(v_p, c, \sigma) \neq 1 \textbf{ then} \\
\textbf{function } \mathcal{C}^{\mathsf{Pull}}_{p,S}[p].\mathsf{publish}(R,m) & \qquad\quad \text{Continue with next.} \\
\quad c \leftarrow \mathsf{BE.Enc}(MPK, R, m) & \qquad m_c \leftarrow \mathsf{BE.Dec}(MPK, k_s^{\mathsf{Pri}}, c) \\
\quad \sigma \leftarrow \mathsf{S.Sign}(s_p, c) & \qquad \textbf{if } m_c \neq \bot \textbf{ then} \\
\quad \mathcal{FS}.\mathsf{append}(i_p, c \parallel \sigma) & \qquad\quad M \leftarrow M \cup \{m_c\} \\
 & \quad \textbf{return } M
\end{array}
$$

Fig. 3. Functions implementing the communication model for the pull protocol. The publisher's interface is to the left and the subscribers' to the right.

When Alice executes $\mathcal{C}^{\mathsf{Pull}}[p].\mathsf{setup}$ she will create all needed keys. She also randomly chooses an identifier. Then each respective secret key, the verification key and identifier are given to all her friends.

When Alice wants to publish a message m to the recipient set $R \subseteq S$, she runs $\mathcal{C}^{\mathsf{Pull}}[p].\mathsf{publish}(R,m)$. This operation creates a BE ciphertext and Alice appends the ciphertext to her outbox file. Each friend can then use $\mathcal{C}^{\mathsf{Pull}}[s].\mathsf{fetch}$ to retrieve the ciphertexts from the file system and decrypt them.

Note that we can have symmetric authentication, e.g. replacing S with a message-authentication code (MAC) scheme, although we use the notation of asymmetric authentication. This would yield different privacy properties, i.e. we remove the non-repudiation which S brings. However, this is not at the centre of our discussion, it just illustrates the modularity of the scheme.

We wanted no recipient to know who else received the message, the ANO-IND-CCA property of the BE scheme gives us exactly this. So we achieve the hidden policy that we wanted.

However, we cannot immediately achieve the hidden policy-update property. Bob can read Alice's outbox, conclude that there are entries which he cannot decrypt and thus he can become jealous. In Fig. 3 we see that Bob can count the number of $\bot$ in the output of $\mathcal{C}^{\mathsf{Pull}}[\cdot].\mathsf{fetch}$. One approach to prevent this is that Alice uses a unique outbox per friend, so Bob has his own outbox. This actually reduces the problem to our push construction, which we will cover later. We will instead analyse a simpler solution for the pull protocol now.

4.1 Changing Recipient Set in the Pull Protocol

We will now propose and analyse a solution to the problem of hidden policy-updates, i.e. Jealous Bob. This solution, however, is based on the intricacies of the ANOBE construction, and thus require us to use ANOBE. In essence, the

ANOBE construction, described in Sect. 3.3, allows us to create a ciphertext which decrypts to different messages.[1] We will use this to encrypt a special message that updates the outbox identifier i_p. Half of the recipients will receive i'_p and the other half will receive i''_p. We summarize this algorithm in Fig. 4. Alice could divide her subscribers into an arbitrary number of parts, even $|S|$ for having each subscriber in their own group. But for simplicity we describe the algorithm for dividing the subscriber set into two parts.

---

function SplitGroup(MPK, S_0, S_1)   ▷ Recipient sets S_0, S_1 such that $S = S_0 \cup S_1$ and $S_0 \cap S_1 = \emptyset$.

    $i_0 \xleftarrow{\$} \{0,1\}^\lambda$, $(s_0, v_0) \xleftarrow{\$} \overline{\mathsf{S}}.\mathsf{Keygen}(1^\lambda)$ ▷ Generate new outbox and key-pair.

    $i_1 \xleftarrow{\$} \{0,1\}^\lambda$, $(s_1, v_1) \xleftarrow{\$} \mathsf{S}.\mathsf{Keygen}(1^\lambda)$ ▷ One per new group.

    $(s, v) \leftarrow \overline{\mathsf{S}}.\mathsf{Keygen}(1^\lambda)$ ▷ One-time signature-verification key-pair.

    Choose a random permutation $\pi \colon S \to S$.

    for $s \in S$ **do**

        if $s \in S_0$ **then**

            $c_s \leftarrow \overline{\mathsf{E}}.\mathsf{Enc}\big(k_s^{\mathsf{Pub}}, i_0 \parallel v_0 \parallel v\big)$

        else   ▷ $s \in S_1$

            $c_s \leftarrow \overline{\mathsf{E}}.\mathsf{Enc}\big(k_s^{\mathsf{Pub}}, i_1 \parallel v_1 \parallel v\big)$

    $C \leftarrow \big(c_{\pi(s)}\big)_{s \in S}$ ▷ Put all subciphertexts in random order.

    $\sigma \leftarrow \overline{\mathsf{S}}.\mathsf{Sign}(s, C)$

    return $(i_0, s_0), (i_1, s_1), (v, C, \sigma)$

Fig. 4. An algorithm splitting a subscriber set S into two new S_0, S_1.

We note that this solution does not hide the fact that Alice updated her policy, we just hide from Bob whether he was excluded or not. When Bob get jealous he goes to Eve to ask her help, this means that we must prevent Eve from learning how Alice changed her policy too — the construction is also secure against this strong adversary.

The property we want from this algorithm is that Bob cannot determine how the subscribers are divided. Thus he cannot know whether he is removed or not. This follows from the ANO-IND-CCA property of the ANOBE scheme. We refer the reader to the proof of Theorem 1 in the full version of [9].

Now we know that Bob cannot distinguish whether everyone in the recipient set received the same message or not. We will add the split-group algorithm (Fig. 4) as an extension to the pull protocol of Definition 4 and we summarize this as the Extended Pull Protocol in the following definition.

---

[1] If this is not possible for BE scheme under consideration, then there is always the possibility to create a new instance. However, this might be more costly, since it requires a separate secure channel. But we are not bound to the ANOBE scheme, it simply provides some extra convenience in this case.

function $C_{p,S}^{\mathsf{Pull}}[p]$.split$(R_0, R_1)$ $\quad (i_0, s_0), (i_1, s_1), C$ $\quad\quad \leftarrow \mathsf{SplitGroup}(MPK, R_0, R_1)$ $\quad \sigma \leftarrow S.\mathsf{Sign}(s_p, C)$ $\quad \mathcal{FS}.\mathsf{append}(i_p, C \,\|\, \sigma)$ $\quad$ **return** $C_{p,R_0}^{\mathsf{Pull}}, C_{p,R_1}^{\mathsf{Pull}}$	**function** $C_{p,S}^{\mathsf{Pull}}[s]$.fetch $\quad C = \mathcal{FS}.\mathsf{read}(i_p)$ $\quad M \leftarrow \emptyset$ $\quad$ **for** $(c \,\|\, \sigma) \in C$ **do** $\quad\quad$ **if** $\bar{S}.\mathsf{Verify}(v_p, c, \sigma) \neq 1$ **then** $\quad\quad\quad$ Continue with next. $\quad\quad m_c = \bar{E}.\mathsf{Dec}(k_s^{\mathsf{Pri}}, c)$ $\quad\quad$ **if** m_c is new identifier **then** $\quad\quad\quad (i_p, v_p) \leftarrow m_c$ $\quad\quad$ **else** $\quad\quad\quad M \leftarrow M \cup \{m_c\}$ $\quad$ **return** M

Fig. 5. The additional and modified interfaces of the Extended Pull Protocol. We assume there exists a coding that can differentiate a file identifier from an ordinary message.

Definition 5 (Extended Pull Protocol). *Let $C_{p,S}^{\mathsf{Pull}}$ be an instance of the Pull Model as in* Definition 4. *Then we define the* Extended Pull Model *to additionally provide the interfaces in* Fig. 5.

Note that the execution of $C_{p,S}^{\mathsf{Pull}}[p]$.split$(R_0, R_1)$ results in two new instances of the pull protocol, namely $C_{p,R_0}^{\mathsf{Pull}}$ and $C_{p,R_1}^{\mathsf{Pull}}$. After this happens, Alice should no longer use $C_{p,S}^{\mathsf{Pull}}$, instead she should only use these two new instances.

We could instead incorporate $C^{Pull}[p]$.split into the $C^{Pull}[p]$.publish interface and let it keep track of the different groups (instances) in the state, this would make it more similar to the definition of the ideal model (Definition 1). However, for presentation purposes, many simpler algorithms are better than fewer that are more complex.

On the subscribers' side, due to the construction of $C_{p,S}^{\mathsf{Pull}}[s]$.fetch, their instance $C_{p,S}^{\mathsf{Pull}}$ is automatically turned into $C_{p,R_i}^{\mathsf{Pull}}$, for whichever $i \in \{0,1\}$ Alice put them in.

4.2 Running Multiple Pull Instances in Parallel

Now it remains for us to convince ourselves that Bob cannot distinguish between different instances of the pull protocol: i.e. Alice posting to two both R_0 and R_1 or Alice posting to R_0 and Carol to R_1.

We will use an information-theoretic argument. We can see that $C_{p_0,S_0}^{\mathsf{Pull}}$ is information-theoretically independent from both $C_{p_1,S_1^0}^{\mathsf{Pull}}$ and $C_{p_1,S_1^1}^{\mathsf{Pull}}$. Although $C_{p_1,S_1^0}^{\mathsf{Pull}}$ and $C_{p_1,S_1^1}^{\mathsf{Pull}}$ are coming from a split, we can see in Fig. 4 that the two instances only depend on the randomly chosen identifiers and verification keys, and the sets of users. The public keys can remain the same, the key-privacy property of $\bar{E}$ will ensure this. It follows that $C_{p_1,S_1^0}^{\mathsf{Pull}}$ is as indistinguishable from $C_{p_1,S_1^1}^{\mathsf{Pull}}$ as $C_{p_0,S_0}^{\mathsf{Pull}}$ is indistinguishable from $C_{p_1,S_1^i}^{\mathsf{Pull}}$, for $i \in \{0,1\}$. Thus Bob's only chance is by distinguishing who received what new outbox in the split message, but this is difficult given the ANO-IND-CCA property.

5   Construction and Analysis of the Push Protocol

The idea of the push model is for each subscriber to have an inbox in the file system — as opposed to the pull model, where the publisher has an outbox. This is simply a file object with a randomly chosen identifier. The publisher then puts all published material in the inbox of each subscriber.

We can see that if we simply put the broadcast ciphertext from the pull protocol in all inboxes, then Eve can relate them since they contain identical ciphertexts. We thus have to make some more modifications. We will use the protocol in the next definition in our analysis.

Definition 6 (Push Protocol). *Let* $\mathsf{E} = (\mathsf{E.Keygen}, \mathsf{E.Enc}, \mathsf{E.Dec})$ *be an AI-CCA encryption scheme,* $\mathsf{S} = (\mathsf{S.Keygen}, \mathsf{S.Sign}, \mathsf{S.Verify})$ *be a strongly unforgeable signature scheme, and* $\mathcal{FS}$ *be a public file system. We denote by* $\mathcal{C}_{p,S}^{\mathsf{Push}}$ *the push model protocol implementing a* (p, S)-*communication model through the operations in* Fig. 6.

When Alice executes $\mathcal{C}^{\mathsf{Push}}[p]$.setup it generates a signature-verification key-pair (s_r, v_r) for every subscriber $r \in S$ and gives the respective verification keys to each subscriber. Each subscriber $r \in S$, when they execute $\mathcal{C}^{\mathsf{Push}}[s]$.setup it generates a public-private key-pair. Additionally they randomly choose a string as an identifier for their inbox. They give the public key and the identifier to Alice.

---

function $\mathcal{C}_{p,S}^{\mathsf{Push}}[p]$.setup$(1^\lambda)$
  for $r \in S$ **do**
    $(s_r, v_r) \xleftarrow{\mathfrak{C}} \mathsf{S.Keygen}(1^\lambda)$
    Give v_r to r.

function $\mathcal{C}_{p,S}^{\mathsf{Push}}[p]$.publish$(R, m)$
  for $r \in R$ **do**
    $c_r \leftarrow \mathsf{E.Enc}(k_r^{\mathsf{Pub}}, m)$
    $\sigma_r \leftarrow \mathsf{S.Sign}(s_p, c_r)$
    $\mathcal{FS}$.append$(i_r, c_r \parallel \sigma_r)$

function $\mathcal{C}_{p,S}^{\mathsf{Push}}[r]$.setup$(1^\lambda)$ $\triangleright\, r \in S$
  $(k_r^{\mathsf{Pub}}, k_r^{\mathsf{Pri}}) \xleftarrow{\mathfrak{C}} \mathsf{E.Keygen}(1^\lambda)$
  $i_r \xleftarrow{\mathfrak{C}} \{0,1\}^\lambda$
  Give $(k_r^{\mathsf{Pub}}, i_r)$ to p.

function $\mathcal{C}_{p,S}^{\mathsf{Push}}[r]$.fetch $\triangleright\, r \in S$
  $C \leftarrow \mathcal{FS}$.read$(i_r)$
  if $C = \perp$ **then**
    return $\emptyset$
  $M \leftarrow \emptyset$
  for $(c, \sigma) \in C$ **do**
    if $\mathsf{S.Verify}(v_r, c, \sigma) \neq 1$ **then**
      Continue with next.
    $m_c \leftarrow \mathsf{E.Dec}(k_r^{\mathsf{Pri}}, c)$
    if $m_c \neq \perp$ **then**
      $M \leftarrow M \cup \{m_c\}$
  return M

Fig. 6. Functions implementing the communication model for the push model protocol. The publisher's interface is to the left and the subscribers' to the right.

When Alice wants to send a message m to a subset $R \subseteq S$ of her subscribers, she uses $\mathcal{C}^{\mathsf{Push}}[p]$ to create a ciphertext c_r with signature σ_r for each recipient $r \in R$. Then she uses $\mathcal{FS}$ to append $c_r \| \sigma_r$ to the file with identifier i_r. The operation $\mathcal{C}^{\mathsf{Pull}}[r].\mathsf{fetch}$ works similarly as in the pull protocol, however, it uses a different file. It starts by reading the inbox from the file system. Then it iterates through the list of entries, decrypting each entry. Each entry, if successfully decrypted, is a new message. It appends the message to the list of messages which it returns upon finishing.

Note that, similarly as for the pull protocol, the authentication scheme S can be symmetric. Here, the encryption scheme E can also be a symmetric-key scheme, provided it is key-private. We can simply let $k^{\mathsf{Pub}} = k^{\mathsf{Pri}}$ and $s = v$ to achieve this. This would yield private group communication with few key exchanges. However, we use the notation of public-key cryptography in our abstraction. This makes the push protocol modular as well.

Before we continue our analysis of what Eve can do against the push protocol, let us first look back at the pull protocol. Imagine that Eve gets access to a publication oracle for an instance of the pull protocol, and remember that she controls the entire file system. It is not hard to convince ourselves that Eve cannot learn anything more from the file system than she can from the ciphertext alone (when playing the ANO-IND-CCA game): each publication just appends the new ciphertext to the same file in the file system — no matter how she changes the recipient set.

Let us now look at what Eve can do in the push protocol. Here she can actually learn information by observing the file system. Whenever a message is published she learns which inboxes are used to get messages from the publisher, thus she can relate several inboxes. Hence, the security analysis of this protocol is only interesting when the protocol is run in parallel.

5.1   Running Multiple Push Instances in Parallel

There is one issue we must consider before continuing our discussion of the security of the push protocol. For the security discussion to make sense we must first, as for the pull protocol, convince ourselves that Eve cannot distinguish between parallel instances of the push protocol. Thereafter we can continue our discussion of the security of the push protocol run in parallel.

We will give an information-theoretic argument for the indistinguishability. Each encryption in Fig. 6 depends on the following: the public key of the recipient, the signature key for the authentication, and the message. Both the public key and the signature key is unique per recipient and instance. It follows that two encryptions of the same message are equally likely done within the same instance as in two different instances. This follows from the security of the encryption scheme E. Thus, Eve's only chance is to decide from the ciphertexts that they contain the same message, but since E provides IND-CCA security this is possible only with negligible advantage.

Now we know that it makes sense to talk of the security when running parallel instances. Assume that we run n instances of the push protocol in parallel. It is not too difficult for Eve to distinguish which inboxes are related. Eventually one instance will publish when no other instance is publishing. Then that instance can be distinguished from others when publishing at the same time, hence Eve can learn more and more over time — even without using anything like the publication oracle mentioned earlier. To deal with this problem, we will introduce a mix-net.

Definition 7 (Mix-Net). *Let $m_1, \ldots, m_k$ be messages from senders $1, \ldots, k$. A mix-net is a functionality $\mathcal{M}$ such that on inputs $m_1, \ldots, m_k$ the outputs $\mathcal{M}[1](m_1), \ldots, \mathcal{M}[k](m_k)$ are unlinkable to its senders. More specifically $\Pr[i \mid \mathcal{M}[i](m_i)] = \Pr[i] = \frac{1}{k}$.*

We note that by definition the mix-net will not output anything until the last input slot has received input.

We will now assume that the calls to $\mathcal{FS}$ in the push protocol (Fig. 6) are replaced with $\mathcal{M}_w[\cdot](\mathcal{FS}.append(\cdot, \cdot))$ and $\mathcal{M}_r[\cdot](\mathcal{FS}.read(\cdot))$, where $\mathcal{M}_w$ and $\mathcal{M}_r$ are two mix-nets for writing and reading operations, respectively. The input slots are unique to each instance of the push protocol, instance i has input slot $\mathcal{M}[i](\cdot)$.

Remember that the inbox identifier is randomly chosen, this means that the probability for an inbox being used by two instances is low ($\approx 1/2^{\lambda/2}$). Without the mix-net Eve can also distinguish which inboxes are related by looking at the distribution of messages in the files in the file system. It is unlikely in practice that the behaviour of all publishers will be uniform, so Eve will eventually learn the related inboxes. However, due to the assumed mix-net, it will enforce a uniform number of messages, n messages in yield n messages out. There are mix-nets that add dummy messages to improve throughput — which will be needed for efficiency reasons — but we refer to that literature for a discussion on its security.

Another technique to distort the distribution is that each subscriber can reuse the inbox across instances for different publishers — this is actually desirable for the push protocol also for efficiency reasons, the subscriber has only *one inbox for all* publishers. However, this allows the publisher to determine that a subscriber subscribes to other publishers, i.e. a scenario related to Jealous Bob, but this time a Jealous Alice. This in turn can be solved by adding noise to each inbox, thus making real messages indistinguishable from noise. A more efficient solution would be for Bob to share an inbox with an *unknown* other subscriber. Bob can pick an inbox which already contains messages and use the same identifier. This would make fetching new messages less efficient, but will reduce the amount of noise needed.

Finally we note that if Eve did not control the entire file system, she would not be able to relate inboxes that are not in the part she controls. She would be able to read them, but the accuracy of her timing attacks would be reduced to how often she could read the files to detect change. She could still do the message distribution attacks though. This change of the adversary takes us from a potentially centralized setting to a distributed setting where there is no network wide adversary, but an adversary controlling only a part of the network of the file system nodes.

6   Algorithmic Complexity

We will now summarize the algorithmic complexity for our constructions. The performance is interesting to evaluate from two perspectives: the publisher's (Alice in all examples) and the subscriber's (Bob in all examples). From the publisher's perspective, it is interesting to investigate the needed space for key storage, communication complexity for publication and time complexity for encryption of new material. From the subscriber's perspective, the complexity of key-storage size and the time-complexity of aggregating the newest published messages are the most interesting aspects. An overview of the results is presented in Table 1.

Table 1. The storage, communication and time complexities in the two models. S is the set of all subscribers, R is the set of recipients of a message. All values are $O(\cdot)$.

Publisher	Pull	Push	Subscriber	Pull	Push
Key-storage size	$|S|$	$|S|$	Key-storage size	1	1
Ciphertext size	$|R|$	$|R|$	Ciphertext size	$|R|$	1
Encryption	1	$|R|$	Decryption	1	1
Communication	1	$|R|$	Communication	1	1

The space complexity for the key management is the same for both the pull and push protocols. If we have $|S|$ subscribers, then we need to exchange and store $O(|S|)$ keys: we need one public key per friend.

The space complexity for the ciphertexts are $O(|R|)$ for both models. However, the pull protocol is slightly more space efficient since we need less signatures. In the push protocol we require one signature per ciphertext, i.e. $O(|R|)$, whereas for the pull protocol we only need one per message.

The time complexity for encryption depends on the underlying schemes. But we can see that in the push protocol we get a factor $|R|$ to that of the encryption scheme, whereas we have a constant factor in the pull protocol. The time complexity for decryption on the other hand has a constant factor for both models.

Finally, we look at the communication complexity for the different protocols, which differ slightly. If we look at one single instance, then we get a constant number of connections for the subscribers. However, most subscribers will have to pull from several publishers, this is the argued benefit of push model of communication — there is only one inbox to read.

7   Related Work

Harbach et al. [7] identified three desirable and (conjectured sufficient) properties for a privacy-preserving AC mechanism: hidden policies, hidden credentials, and hidden decisions. The work in [7] focused on fully homomorphic encryption and is thus not directly feasible for our purposes. However, the properties are still relevant in our setting.

Hidden policies means that the access policy remains hidden from anyone but the owner and the subjects learn at most if they have access or not. This is the same definition as we used above, and we arguably achieve this property in both of our constructions. Furthermore, we also achieve what we call 'hidden policy-updates' as well (Jealous Bob), which prevents previously-authorized subjects from determining whether they are no longer authorized to access newer versions.

Hidden credentials means that the subject never has to reveal the access credentials to anyone. In our case this is a cryptographic key, and as a consequence we allow the subject to anonymously read the ciphertext from the storage node. This means that the storage node cannot track which subjects are requesting access to which objects.

Hidden decisions means that no-one but the subject must learn the outcome of an access request. This means that no-one should learn whether or not a subject could decrypt the ciphertext or not. However, if everyone only requests ciphertexts that they know they can decrypt (which is the most efficient strategy), then the storage operator can easily guess the decision. Most constructions probably suffer from this, including ours. This decision together with non-anonymized users would allow the storage operator to infer parts of the policy, hence breaking the hidden policy property. To prevent this subjects could also request ciphertexts they cannot decrypt (dummy requests of PIR). However, anonymous requests makes this a less relevant problem.

There is also related work in the DOSN community. There are several proposals available for DOSNs, e.g. DECENT [8], Cachet [10] and Persona [2]. The AC mechanisms in these proposals focus on providing confidentiality for the data. E.g. Persona uses KP-ABE to implement the AC mechanism and unfortunately, this yields lacking privacy: as this is not policy-hiding, anyone can read the AC policies and see who may access what data. There are also general cryptographic AC schemes that focus on achieving policy-hiding ciphertexts, see the section of related work in [7]. E.g. Bodriagov et al. [4] adapted PE for the AC mechanism in DOSNs. Works in this area that have employed policy-hiding schemes for DOSNs have also focused on solving the problem of re-encryption of old data upon group changes. We do not solve this problem, but rather contribute the insight that it would violate our desired privacy properties. So besides being more efficient in some cases, less efficient in others, they do not require the same properties.

8   Conclusions

We achieve privacy-preserving access control enforcement in a public file system lacking built-in access control. We presented two alternatives: the pull and the push protocols. Both implements the model of a publisher distributing a message to a set of subscribers.

The pull protocol achieves strong privacy properties. It essentially inherits the ANO-IND-CCA property of its underlying BE scheme. The subscribers cannot learn who the other subscribers are even if they control the network of the file system or the whole file system. Further, if the publisher wishes to exclude any of the subscribers from future publications, then all subscribers learn that there was a policy update but no one learns what changed — not even those excluded!

The push model for communication is an interesting case. Conceptually, the only difference between the push and pull models is that we distribute the message, instead of everyone fetching it. This seems to yield better privacy properties at first glance, but it turns out that we had to make considerable changes before we could get any security for the push protocol. Hence the security guarantees are much weaker, we have to make some trade-offs. One alternative is that the adversary can only control a part of the file system, or monitor only part of the network, this would make Eve's timing attacks more difficult. Eve can still compute the distributions of messages over the inboxes and relate them, so we need some techniques to make this estimation more difficult. But it is difficult to achieve any guarantees against the distribution attacks, we have to resolve to techniques like differential privacy. However, there are benefits: unlike in the pull protocol, when the subscriber wants to make a policy update, none of the subscribers will even be notified that there has been a policy update — let alone determine if they have been excluded.

As was pointed out in Sect. 7, we do not treat group management (i.e. revoking the credentials for subjects) as is done in other schemes. If the publisher excludes a subscriber, it is only from future publications — not from past! In fact, we can conclude from our treatment above that such functionality would actually violate the privacy properties. Even if possible, any subject could have made a copy anyway, i.e. it is the problem of removing something from the Web. However, other group changes are easily done, the most expensive one is to give a new subscriber access to old publications — this requires re-encrypting or resending all publications.

An interesting future direction would be to explore Eve's limitations in the push protocol in more detail. For example, under what conditions can Eve estimate the message distributions over the inboxes, according to what distributions should the subscribers add noise? This would help us design an efficient scheme that can distort the distributions and guarantee security.

Both protocols are modular enough to provide better deniability, e.g. using a MAC scheme for authentication of messages would remove the non-repudiation property. To let all subscribers, and not only the publisher, publish messages. Another interesting direction would be the opposite: stronger accountability. An example of desired accountability would be that Bob wants to verify that Carol received the same message, if Alice told him that she sent a copy to Carol as well. Due to the privacy properties this is not possible in the current protocols.

Acknowledgements. This work was inspired by some work with Benjamin Greschbach and work of Oleksandr Bodriagov and Gunnar Kreitz. We would like to thank the Swedish Foundation for Strategic Research for grant SSF FFL09-0086 and the Swedish Research Council for grant VR 2009-3793, which funded this work. We would also like to thank the anonymous reviewers and especially Anja Lehmann for valuable feedback.

References

1. Abdalla, M., Bellare, M., Neven, G.: Robust encryption. In: Micciancio, D. (ed.) TCC 2010. LNCS, vol. 5978, pp. 480–497. Springer, Heidelberg (2010)
2. Baden, R., Bender, A., Spring, N., Bhattacharjee, B., Starin, D.: Persona: an online social network with user-defined privacy. In: SIGCOMM (2009)
3. Bellare, M., Boldyreva, A., Desai, A., Pointcheval, D.: Key-privacy in public-key encryption. In: Boyd, C. (ed.) ASIACRYPT 2001. LNCS, vol. 2248, p. 566. Springer, Heidelberg (2001)
4. Bodriagov, O., Kreitz, G., Buchegger, S.: Access control in decentralized online social networks: applying a policy-hiding cryptographic scheme and evaluating its performance. PERCOM Workshops **2014**, 622–628 (2014)
5. Dingledine, R., Mathewson, N., Syverson, P.F.: Tor: the second-generation onion router. In: USENIX Security Symposium, pp. 303–320 (2004)
6. Fiat, A., Naor, M.: Broadcast encryption. CRYPTO 1993. LNCS, vol. 773, pp. 480–491. Springer, Heidelberg (1994)
7. Harbach, M., Fahl, S., Brenner, M., Muders, T., Smith, M.: Towards privacy preserving access control with hidden policies, hidden credentials and hidden decisions. In: Privacy, Security and Trust (PST), pp. 17–24 (2012)
8. Jahid, S., Nilizadeh, S., Mittal, P., Borisov, N., Kapadia, A.: DECENT: a decentralized architecture for enforcing privacy in online social networks. PERCOM Workshops **2012**, 326–332 (2012)
9. Libert, B., Paterson, K.G., Quaglia, E.A.: Anonymous broadcast encryption: adaptive security and efficient constructions in the standard model. In: Fischlin, M., Buchmann, J., Manulis, M. (eds.) PKC 2012. LNCS, vol. 7293, pp. 206–224. Springer, Heidelberg (2012)
10. Nilizadeh, S., Jahid, S., Mittal, P., Borisov, N., Kapadia, A.: Cachet: a decentralized architecture for privacy preserving social networking with caching. In: Proceedings of the 8th International Conference on Emerging Networking Experiments and Technologies, pp. 337–348 (2012)

Ontology-Based Obfuscation
and Anonymisation for Privacy
A Case Study on Healthcare

Leonardo H. Iwaya[1]([✉]), Fausto Giunchiglia[2], Leonardo A. Martucci[1],
Alethia Hume[2], Simone Fischer-Hübner[1], and Ronald Chenu-Abente[2]

[1] Karlstad University, Karlstad, Sweden
{leonardo.iwaya,leonardo.martucci,simone.fischer-hubner}@kau.se
[2] Trento University, Trento, Italy
{fausto,hume,chenu}@disi.unitn.it

Abstract. Healthcare Information Systems typically fall into the group
of systems in which the need of data sharing conflicts with the privacy.
A myriad of these systems have to, however, constantly communicate
among each other. One of the ways to address the dilemma between data
sharing and privacy is to use data obfuscation by lowering data accuracy
to guarantee patient's privacy while retaining its usefulness. Even though
many obfuscation methods are able to handle numerical values, the obfuscation of non-numerical values (e.g., textual information) is not as trivial, yet extremely important to preserve data utility along the process. In
this paper, we preliminary investigate how to exploit ontologies to create obfuscation mechanism for releasing personal and electronic health
records (PHR and EHR) to selected audiences with different degrees of
obfuscation. Data minimisation and access control should be supported
to enforce different actors, e.g., doctors, nurses and managers, will get
access to no more information than needed for their tasks. Besides that,
ontology-based obfuscation can also be used for the particular case of data
anonymisation. In such case, the obfuscation has to comply with a specific
criteria to provide anonymity, so that the data set could be safely released.
This research contributes to: state the problems in the area; review related
privacy and data protection legal requirements; discuss ontology-based
obfuscation and anonymisation methods; and define relevant healthcare
use cases. As a result, we present the early concept of our Ontology-based
Data Sharing Service (O-DSS) that enforces patient's privacy by means
of obfuscation and anonymisation functions.

1 Introduction

In today's Information Society, people are surrounded by information technology in their everyday life. Providers of information services often record and

This research was funded by SMARTSOCIETY, a research project of the Seventh
Framework Programme for Research of the European Community under grant agreement no. 600854.

Published by Springer International Publishing Switzerland 2016. All Rights Reserved
D. Aspinall et al. (Eds.): Privacy and Identity 2015, IFIP AICT 476, pp. 343–358, 2016.
DOI: 10.1007/978-3-319-41763-9_23

categorize people, or data subjects, into *profiles*. Profiles consist of personal data that is managed, shared and modified by different information systems; often without the individual's consent [4]. To protect the subject's rights over their personal data, security and privacy are imperative in the design of solutions that handle sensitive information. Security is commonly addressed by means of the principles of confidentiality, integrity, and availability. Privacy, in turn, stands for fundamental rights and freedoms of subjects to have their right to privacy with regards to the manipulation and processing of personal data [1].

Among current technologies, Healthcare Information Systems (HIS) are frequent target of information security and privacy researches. The reasons are manifold. HIS are essential and widely-deployed systems that manage highly sensitive data; providers have to comply with security/privacy regulations; and, data breaches might cause expensive penalties and damage to the company's reputation. Notwithstanding, the patient's records have to be shared among multiple healthcare service providers, either for primary and secondary purposes. For instance, Electronic Health Records (EHR) might be distributed, within affiliated hospitals and medical centers (i.e., inter-institutional EHR). In this case, medical data is exchanged for primary use, i.e., *meaningful use* for patient's treatment, with an implied trusted domain and confidentiality among medical staff. However, EHR are also increasingly being used for secondary purposes, such as release of data for governmental health programs and research [5]. EHR can also be integrated to Personal Health Records (PHR)(e.g., HealthVault[1] and PatientsLikeMe[2]), and consecutively linked to all sorts of patient-centered and patient-controlled information systems (e.g., mobile healthcare). These multiple data flows add further concern regarding security and privacy.

One way, that we focus in this paper, to cope with the dilemma between data sharing and data privacy refers to the use of abstractions; in particular the use of obfuscation and anonymisation. In our research we are considering the concept of abstraction as a broader field – that remains to be understood. By abstraction we mean, the process of mapping a problem representation onto a new one, preserving certain desirable properties and reducing its complexity [8]. Particular cases of abstraction studied here are obfuscation and anonymisation.

By obfuscation we mean, to lower individual data item accuracy in a systematic, controlled, and statistically rigorous way [2]. By anonymisation, we intent to protect privacy by making a number of data transformations so that individuals whom the data describe remain anonymous[3]. In this case, data transformations are essentially obfuscation functions that can achieve anonymity. Anonymity, in turn, is a property of an individual that cannot be identified within a set of individuals, the *anonymity set* [15]. The anonymisation process can have variable degrees of robustness [19], depending on how likely is to: (1) single out an individual in the dataset; (2) link records concerning the same individual; or, (3) infer the value of one attribute based on other values. Therefore, we claim

---

[1] Microsoft HealthVault (www.healthvault.com).

[2] PatientsLikeMe (www.patientslikeme.com).

[3] Anonymous: someone unknown; not distinct; or, lacking individual characteristics.

that anonymisation is a special case of obfuscation; and accordingly, obfuscation is a special case of abstraction.

In this paper, we aim to investigate the problem of data obfuscation and its particular case of anonymisation, through the use of a privacy-enhancing ontology-based obfuscation mechanism for releasing PHR and EHR to selected audiences with different degrees of obfuscation. Data minimisation and access control are supported, as different actors, e.g., doctors, nurses and managers, will need to get access to the just amount of information needed for their tasks. In addition, an ontology-based obfuscation can be used to decrease the semantic loss, i.e., maintain a high degree of utility of the anonymised data. This research contributes to: stating the problems in the area; reviewing privacy and data protection legal requirements; discussing ontology-based obfuscation and anonymisation methods; and defining relevant healthcare use cases. As a result, we present the early concept of our Ontology-based Data Sharing Service (O-DSS) that enforces patient's privacy by means of obfuscation and anonymisation functions.

This paper is organized as follows. In Sect. 2 we briefly motivate this research with respect to the legal aspects of privacy and data protection regulations and legislations around HIS. In Sect. 3 we provide a summary of the relevant terminology, existing methods for data obfuscation and anonymisation, and related work on ontology-based approaches. In Sect. 4 we introduce a preliminary design of our privacy-preserving O-DSS. In Sect. 5 we discuss the research future work, and in Sect. 6 we present our conclusions.

2   Data Protection Regulations and Legislation

The European legal privacy framework that we will in this section refer to is based on the EU Data Protection Directive 95/46/EC [1] and the upcoming General EU Data Protection Regulation (GDPR) [6], which was approved by the European Council in June 2015 and is expected to replace the national laws implementing the Directive in the near future (probably in 2016).

For the Health Care section, there is no specific harmonized EU data protection legislation, as this is rather regulated by different national legislation that takes consideration of the national different heath care practices.

Still, the general rules of the Directive and soon of the GDPR will apply unless there are overriding (national or EU) legal rules.

Of particular importance for motivating our work is the general privacy principle of data minimisation included in the Data Protection Directive and Regulation, for instance cf. Art. 5 (c), (e) GDPR: Personal data should be: *"(c) adequate, relevant, and limited to the minimum necessary in relation to the purposes for which they are processed"*; *"they shall only be processed if, and as long as, the purposes could not be fulfilled by processing information that does not involve personal data (data minimisation)"*; and *"(e) kept in a form which permits direct or indirect identification of data subjects for no longer than is necessary for the purposes for which the personal data are processed"*;

Furthermore, the Art 23 of the GDPR requires that the data controller should follow a *Data Protection by Design and by Default* approach by implementing *"technical and organisational measures appropriate to the processing activity being carried out and its objectives, such as data minimisation and pseudonymisation..."*.

Besides the European framework, in the United States the Health Insurance Portability and Accountability Act of 1996 (HIPAA), is also another well-known example of regulatory mechanism for privacy. Some of the most traditional methods (e.g., k-anonymity) as well as the HIPAA's standards for anonymisation/de-identification are discussed in Sect. 3.

3   Background and Related Work

According to [8], the process of abstraction relates to the process of separating, extracting from a representation another "abstract" representation, which consists of a *brief sketch* of the original representation. Therefore, the same authors were able to informally define abstraction as: *the process of mapping a representation of a problem onto a new representation, which helps to deal with the problem in the original search space by preserving certain desirable properties, and, is simpler to handle.* This concept was originally define in the field of artificial intelligence, in which abstraction refers to reasoning. Likewise, the objective of obfuscation also incorporates the very same elements. Obfuscation is a reasonable transformation of the data that preserves certain properties (e.g., semantics, analytics, statistics), and typically entails generalization. That is why we also define obfuscation (and anonymisation) as special cases of this broader theory of abstraction.

For this research, we are particularly interested in abstractions that can be supported by ontology-based knowledge representations to either obfuscate or anonymise values. In addition, we also consider practical aspects of the healthcare field, such as: clinical vocabularies and ontologies that are employed in the data structures used in EHR. This and other concepts that are grounding our work are explained and briefly discussed in this section.

3.1   EHR's Data Elements

Medical standards for EHR vary from one country to another, but the Health Level Seven (HL7) and Comite Europeen de Normalization – Technical Committee (CEN TC) 215 are probably the most renowned ones. The HL7 group develops the most widely messaging standard for healthcare in United States. The CEN CT 215 operates in 19 European member states and is the main healthcare IT standards in Europe. The work of such organizations is important to achieve interoperability among HIS, which for EHR refers to the definition of clinical vocabularies, message exchange formats, and EHR ontologies. In the present research, however, we are only interested in how to exploit the structured vocabularies and ontologies during the anonymisation process.

In brief, clinical vocabularies or standard vocabularies are used to agree upon the use of medical terminologies when writing in a patient record. All the terms are usually encoded in order to facilitate data exchange, comparison, or aggregation among HIS. Some established examples are the International Classification of Disease (ICD[4]) and the Systematized Nomenclature of Medicine - Clinical Terms (SNOMED-CT). Nevertheless, data elements inside EHR may also be in free-form text, for example, clinician's notes. Any anonymisation method for EHR needs therefore to cope with structured data elements as well as form-free running text.

3.2   Conventional Anonymisation Methods

The k-anonymity, formulated by Sweeney [17], was one of the first and well-known formal methods that address the issue of data anonymisation. In a more formal definition, the initial scenario consists of a data holder that held a collection of person-specific, field structured data; and wants to share a version of this data with researchers. The data holder considers the following problem [17]: *"How can the data holder release a version of its data with scientific guarantees that the individuals who are the subjects of the private data cannot be re-identified while data remain practically useful?"* The solution is the k-anonymity property, which means that the information for each person contained in the released data cannot be distinguished from at least $k - 1$ individuals whose information also appear in the released data. In brief, anonymised data with k-anonymity property guarantee an anonymity set size of $k - 1$.

To do so, the program receives as input a table with n rows and m columns, in which each row of the table represents a person-specific record of the population and the entries in various rows should not be unique. The algorithm than applies two different methods to achieve k-anonymity:

- Suppression, certain values have to be simply replaced by an asterisk '*'. For instance, person direct *identifiers* should be omitted (e.g., name, address, phone, personal numbers).
- Generalization, individual values of attributes are replaced by broader category. For instance, an attribute 'age' can be replaced by a range of values, i.e., age '21' by '≥20'.

The k-anonymity offers a straightforward and to some extent effective method, but the approach is still susceptible to homogeneity and background knowledge attacks, leading researchers to the design of improved version, such as l-diversity [11] and t-closeness [10]. All these methods are, however, somewhat naive when dealing with non-numerical values and are unable to maintain enough semantic coherence after anonymisation [12]. To cope with semantics, many authors proposed different ontology-based anonymisation methods, further explained in the next section.

---

[4] http://www.who.int/classifications/icd/en/.

Besides the formal methods for data anonymisation, we could also consider heuristic-based strategies. For instance, with respect to the HIPAA Privacy Rule [14], the EHR can be de-identified using the *"Safe Harbor"* standard. In this case, a number of 18 types of identifiers that compose the Protected Health Information (PHI) should be removed. Safe Harbor is a very simple approach, but it does not provide any scientific guarantees for anonymity sets nor protection to re-identification attacks [3]. Fortunately, the HIPAA Privacy Rule also considers a second standard called *"Expert Determination"*, which means the application of statistical or scientific principles to reduce re-identification to a very small risk.

3.3   Ontology-Based Approaches

An ontology is a method for knowledge representation, which uses a formal, explicit and machine readable structure of concepts hierarchically interconnected by a semantic network [7]. These powerful data structures enable knowledge organization, sharing, and emulation of cognitive processes and/or common understandings of specific domains. We are particularly interested in the concept of semantic obfuscation of ontology-based systems that can be used to restrict the release of information according to the audience. A few ontology-based privacy-preserving mechanisms were recently proposed. In this section, we made an effort to summarize and briefly evaluate the findings of these studies.

Access Control and Context Obfuscation. In a more generic approach, the work of [18] proposes a *context obfuscation* mechanism for pervasive networking and context-aware programs. The system allows the users to set different privacy preferences and stipulate rules to control the access of context information. In brief, all the attributes related to an user can have different access control settings for information, depending on the context, requesters, and use purposes. Besides the privacy preferences, the user can also define granularity levels of access, which is based on ontological structures that can capture the granularity relationship between instances of an object type.

For example, when the patient Alice wants to give to her doctor Bob access to her attribute Diagnosis, she configures her privacy preferences as follows:

```
privacy_pref_list.add_rule(
    consumer = Bob,
    attribute = Diagnosis,
    purpose = Treatment,
    allow = True )
```

In addition, Alice can set the generalization level $l \in \mathbb{Z}$ that should be applied to the attribute. The higher the level, the higher the generalization level would be, i.e., going upwards in the ontology (for instance, see Fig. 5).

```
generalization_pref_list.add_rule(
   consumer = Bob,
   attribute = Diagnosis,
   level = 0 )
```

This context obfuscation mechanism was already used in [16], to provide a privacy-preserving and granular access control to PHR. The authors, however, are still missing the link with real ontologies and medical vocabularies, which could greatly improve the obfuscation quality in real HIS systems.

Ontology-Based Anonymisation. An ontology-based data set anonymisation with categorical (i.e., textual) values is proposed by Martínez et al. [12, 13]. They aim at preserving data semantics of anonymised values. The proposal relies on a set of heuristics to optimize obfuscation, and ensure scalability in cases of heterogeneous data sets and wide ontologies. In addition, their algorithm also employs k-anonymity to provide a minimum set of privacy guarantees. To do so, the solution relies of the measurement of the semantic similarity, i.e., to quantify the taxonomical resemblance of compared terms based on a knowledge base. Therefore, it is possible to semantically compare, rank and group the most similar record values. Subsequently, the method aggregates values in a group, which refers to the process of replacing the values in several records by a single one, summarizing and making them indistinguishable (i.e., k-anonymity set). This operation performed by means of the author's proposal of a centroid calculus for multi-variate non-numerical data, to obtain accurate centroids in a group (for further details we refer the reader to [12, 13]). Their use case [13] provides a more concrete example of EHR anonymisation, including many categorical values from SNOMED CT, which makes the method's applicability more realistic.

3.4 Ontology-Based Identity Management and Access Control

In [9], the authors introduce the concept of a privacy-enhanced Peer Manager, in which the original idea was designed to preserve privacy in collective adaptive systems. The Peer Manager works as an user-centered identity management platform that keeps user's information private. This framework was built upon the privacy policy language PPL (PrimeLife Policy Language), with which every user can control his personal information by imposing access and usage control restrictions. As a privacy-enhancing structure, this platform instead of directly allowing access to peer's information, creates a *Profile* structure that are sent as replies to queries. The created Profile, in turn, reveals only partial or obfuscated information about the Entities. In essence, the Peer Manager never discloses the Entities' original data, but derived Profiles previously defined by the users. Besides, if compared to [18], the Peer Manager supports a far more general and robust approach for access control and obfuscation.

3.5 Putting Things Together

The approaches discussed here employ obfuscation in different scenarios yet with similar goals. In summary, we aim to integrate the proposals [13,18] into the Peer Manager [9] obfuscation functions, and thus, demonstrate how it can be applied to healthcare systems (e.g., EHR and PHR) using real medical ontologies.

4 Obfuscation and Anonymisation for HIS

Health information is, in general, managed by systems for primary purposes, i.e., the provisioning of health care to the benefit of the patient. It is noteworthy, however, that aforementioned requirements are still valid, such as trusted medical environment, with implied confidentiality among healthcare workers. The medical institutions usually are the data custodians in case of EHR, and thus, any data breach is the institution's responsability. Security mechanisms in the EHR should provide confidentiality, integrity, availability, and make personnel accountable for unauthorized data release, by means of logging and auditing tools.

Nevertheless, health care services also use the health information for secondary purposes, such as general public health monitoring, evaluation of healthcare programs, and research. In the case of a secondary use, data should be subject to *de-identification* or *anonymisation*, such as the aforementioned Safe Harbor and Expert Determination standards from HIPAA. In this section we explain how obfuscation and anonymisation can be used in the healthcare context.

4.1 Ontology-Based Data Sharing Service

We propose an ontology-based data sharing service (O–DSS) to mediate access to healthcare data sets. Many HIS applications fit in this scenario. In this preliminary research we focus on Semantic Obfuscation (SO) and Data Anonymisation (DA) for standard HIS, such as EHR and PHR. In brief, we consider the following use cases and their information flows:

1. Primary Use
   - EHR → O–DSS (SO) → privacy-preserving patient treatment (hospital and clinics).
   - PHR → O–DSS (SO) → patient's granular control of own health.
   - EHR ∪ PHR → O–DSS (SO) → reminder or alert systems for family or caregivers.
2. Secondary Use
   - EHR ∪ PHR → O–DSS (SO + DA) → medical research repository.
   - EHR ∪ PHR → O–DSS (SO + DA) → nationwide HIS network.

Each information flow refers to a different branch of this use case (examples of flows 1, 2, and 4 are depicted in Fig. 1). Therefore, the SO and DA techniques should deal with different requirements, according to the target application of the data. In what follows, we provide further details of each use case.

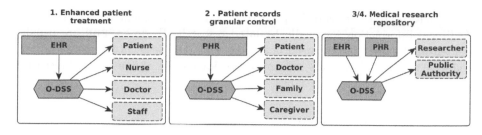

Fig. 1. A healthcare use case for ontology-based obfuscation for HIS. The dashed boxes are the data requesters $r \in R$, and EHR and PHR are the data providers $p \in P$. The ontology-based data sharing service obfuscates data from p that is communicated to r.

UC1: Privacy-Preserving Patient Treatment. Patient's data can be accessed by clinicians, nurses, secretaries, and accountants for many purposes inside the hospital. All the employees are making meaningful use of the data, and therefore, they are under an implied confidentiality agreement. Furthermore, medical institutions also are allowed to share EHR among affiliated institutions and healthcare services – still, the institution is liable for the data's confidentiality. In such cases, it is more important to enforce access control and, in a privacy-preserving perspective, apply data minimisation whenever possible to reduce risks of data leakage.

UC2: Patient's Granular Control of E/PHR. PHR are being increasingly used by patients to track their own daily activities (e.g., wellness and fitness applications), or to have an interface to their EHR (e.g., patient web portals or dashboards). In particular, if patients transfer their data to private services (non-medical) that support the management of health records (e.g., Microsoft HealthVault), than, the medical institutions might not be liable for the secrecy of released data. This user-centered applications encourage patients to have more control of their own health, and also, provide means to granularly share PHR with other healthcare services, social networks, family, and so on. In this case, we consider that patient consents with the data release, but mechanisms should provide the patient with granular control in the form of selective disclosure and obfuscation options in dependence on the different data consumers.

UC3: Reminder or Alert Systems. Reminder systems are commonly used for drug treatment compliance, and can be linked to EHR, to provide reminders to out-patients or chronic patients. Some alert mechanisms also exist, providing EHR access to family members and caregivers in case of emergencies. As presented in Fig. 1, the data flows might come from EHR or PHR, since there are private non-medical services that support this applications. This use case has privacy requirements that are similar to UC2, since the user can have directly configure access control settings.

UC4: Medical Research Repository. EHR are frequently used as source of clinical information for medical-related research. To do so, EHR are usually de-identified and/or anonymised before releasing the data, in which cases there would be no need of patient's consent; exceptional cases of non-medical research, e.g., marketing or financial studies.

UC5: Nationwide HIS Network. Similarly to UC4, more ambitious projects aim to create nationwide HIS networks, that would interconnect EHR systems within a country (i.e., primary use), or even, medical repositories for research (i.e., secondary use) – also knows as translational research information system (TRIS). For instance, in [5], the authors examine the privacy issues on building a database integrating clinical information from an EHR systems with a DNA repository.

4.2   So and DA Functions

The O–DSS provides two fundamental functions: semantic obfuscation (SO) and data anonymisation (DA). The SO function is specially grounded on the proposals: peer profiling [9] and context obfuscation [18]. That is, we aim to partially show or obfuscate the record (i.e., to provide data minimisation instead of anonymisation), based on the concept of Peer Manager for access control, and also, exploit the medical ontologies for data obfuscation.

The DA is grounded on k-anonymity [17] and improved techniques presented in [12,13]. Figure 2 illustrates how the O–DSS manages the data flows to provide SO and DA. Besides, in Figs. 3 and 4, O–DSS is placed into context in line with aforementioned use cases.

Primary Use and Semantic Obfuscation. In the case of primary use, the semantic obfuscation (SO) acts as a data minimization mechanism. The objective is to restrict the amount of health information that should be disclosed for a

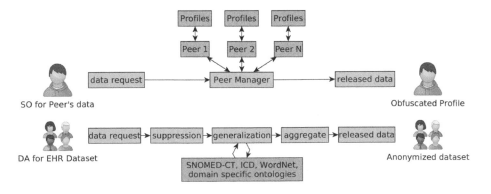

Fig. 2. O–DSS processes for SO and DA.

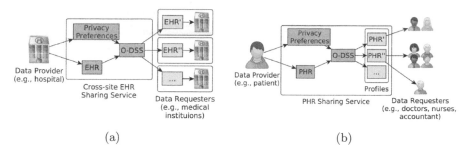

Fig. 3. Data release/sharing for (a) cross-institutional patient treatment and (b) user-centered (ontology-based) obfuscation and granular access control for PHR.

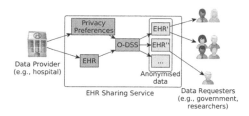

Fig. 4. Data release/sharing to create research repositories.

specific task (e.g., visualize a patient record or check a doctor's schedule) and to a specific person or role (e.g., a nurse) to the required minimum. Healthcare Personnel from different Departments will have different access right: nurses will only have access to EHR of patients that they are treating; psychiatric diagnoses, might only be seen by psychiatrists, but not by other treating doctors (who may however see that a psychiatric diagnosis exists); and, values about blood infection/HIV would be read by all Healthcare Personnel for employee's security reasons.

We define two sets of actors: data *providers* (P), i.e. the data subject (patient, PHR user) and data *requesters* (R), where R makes queries to P about specific health information.

Alice $\in P$ is first registering with the Peer Manager that acts as a data controller and enforces the *Alice*'s privacy preferences on her behalf. The Peer Manager provides *Alice* with a set of PPL policies for different peer profiles representing partial identities that the Peer Manager should manage on *Alice*'s behalf. *Alice* can either choose from this set of policies or construct her own policies for profile. For enabling that *Alice* can determine different semantic obfuscations for different "audiences", PPL is extended with obligations to apply different obfuscation operations at different granularity along a specified ontology hierarchy in dependence of different data requesters or roles of data requester (that correspond to different "downstream controllers" in PPL terminology). *Alice* is sending his profiles together with the PPL policies that should apply for these profiles to the Peer Manager.

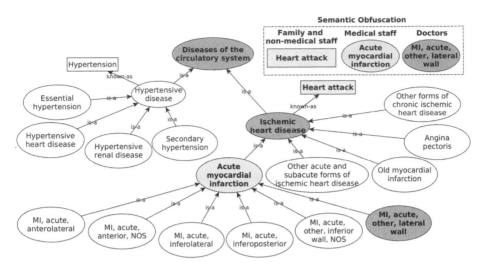

Fig. 5. Example of ontology-based obfuscation.

Once when $Bob \in R$ makes queries to *Alice* about specific health information, following the approach in [9], the request has to be mapped into a profile of *Alice* $\in P$ that will be returned to *Bob*. Hence, before replying, the Peer Manager would check the access rights that *Alice* has given to *Bob*, i.e., the profile that *Alice* has decided to reveal to *Bob* for a given task and purpose (according to the PPL policy that *Alice* has defined or chosen for that profile). Furthermore, if the access conditions are fulfilled, i.e. data is to be forwarded to a so-called downstream controller (*Bob*), the obfuscation obligations that were defined in the policy for the event of data forwarding are first triggered by the Peer Manager: Within the revealed profile (i.e., an attribute-based description of *Alice*), the ontology-based semantic obfuscation is applied to each attribute, allowing *Alice* to obfuscate its data with different granularity levels (i.e., different semantic level) according to the obfuscation obligations defined in the profile's PPL policy for downstream controller *Bob* (or for his role). Thus, as shown in Fig. 6, the Peer Manager follows the PPL obligations, e.g., executing the obfuscation functions accordingly.

Different attributes with different types of values will require appropriate ontologies/mechanisms to obfuscate them. The Fig. 5 shows an example of how the ontology-based obfuscation can be used on an attribute describing diagnosis of a patient in order to abstract the information revealed to different requesters (namely, family member, medical staff, or doctor). Another way to perform semantic obfuscation in a patient's profile is by revealing different sub-sets of attributes (i.e., complete obfuscation of some attributes). For instance, a doctor would be able to retrieve the list of prescribed medications from a patient while a hospital accountant would only see the aggregate drug cost. Hence, *Bob*'s access rights determine the accuracy of how data is accessible, i.e. the level of achieved obfuscation.

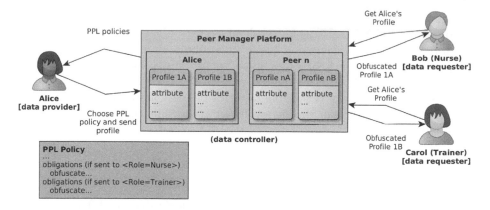

Fig. 6. Obfuscation process with Peer Manager and PPL.

Some important distinctions from the work of [18], we did not emphasize the use of *context*, which would allow *Alice* to further refine her privacy preferences based on her location and current activity. Nonetheless, our proposal considers that the SO function should exploit real medical vocabularies, such as ICD-10 and SNOMED-CT, instead of using *ad-hoc* or domain specific ontologies. Moreover, we integrate our mechanism with the Peer Manager [9], which provides a more sophisticated access control model.

Secondary Use and Data Anonymisation. If an entire data set of health information has to be shared for a secondary purpose with a data processor, such as a public health organization, an ontology-based semantic obfuscation/anonymisation can maximize data utility by preserving the data semantics while eliminating personal information from the data set to the degree required, i.e., the mandatory data anonymisation (DA) process. The data consumer is usually a third party, such as a research institution or a public service that need the data for secondary purpose (see Fig. 4).

Also in this case the general notion of abstracting the information of profiles, as proposed in [9], can be applied. The main difference is that a data consumer is now asking for the whole set of, for instance, patients profiles. Before replying, the peer manager should be able to find/compute a profile for each peer (i.e., patient) in the data set such that certain level of anonymity is guaranteed. For example, if the peer agreed to reveal information for a secondary purpose provided that k-anonymity is guaranteed, then the anonymisation process has to be applied (i.e., follow PPL obligations) to attributes of profiles until such requirement is achieved. Considering again the example from Fig. 5 and the attribute describing the diagnosis on each peer's profile, the anonymisation process needs to select the level of detail to be included in the revealed profiles such that a given patient's record can not be re-identified by their diagnosis. For these cases, the ontology is important to improve the data utility during the mandatory data anonymisation (DA) process. Here we adopt the solution presented in [13], that enables k-anonymisation of structured non-numerical medical retaining semantics by using SNOMED-CT as knowledge base.

Moreover, by exploiting real medical vocabularies in the ontology-based obfuscation the approach becomes more robust and usable in real scenarios dealing with E/PHR. Another important feature to highlight is that a solution designed in this way is scalable in terms of the underlying ontology being used, i.e., the ontology can change, evolve or grow while the above approach is still applicable.

5   Future Work

Currently, we have mainly positioned how ontologies-based obfuscation and anonymisation can be used in HIS; by addressing legal requirements, reviewing many of the existing methods and putting them into the context of HIS. We also show how SO and DA can be used together with the Peer Manager and PPL. Notwithstanding, we noticed that concepts could be refined, and the link between theory of abstraction and obfuscation can be further formalized. In a broader sense, we aim to understand how the areas the privacy and the ontology areas could cooperate, in order to support data privacy.

Apart from that, future work has many challenges that remain to be addressed. Currently, we are not discussing the usability issues for setting all the privacy preferences for SO and DA. In addition, regarding obfuscation, the problem of inferences by correlations (e.g., infer the patient's original disease given the list of drugs/medical procedures) is still open. And for DA, we are considering mainly k-anonymity (i.e., anonymisation by generalization), but other methods based on randomization (e.g., noise addition, differential privacy) are also worthy considering. A complete solution would make use of many different DA methods.

6   Conclusions

This paper presented the use of a privacy-preserving ontology-based obfuscation mechanism intended to obfuscate health information either for primary or secondary use. In the case of primary use, minimization of personal data means that an actor gets no more information than needed and with an appropriate semantic level. For secondary use, the proposed mechanism can minimize the semantic loss of data, such that a high degree of utility is maintained, while data is anonymised to the specified DA requirements. Additionally, we described five use cases to illustrate the O–DSS, and we discussed how it can be integrated with the existing Peer Manager. Obfuscation capabilities were expected in the PrimeLife and Smart Society (i.e., Peer Manager) projects, but there were no clear examples on how to use them. The obfuscation functions can be implemented by extending the obligations in the PPL policy, defined between data requester and data controller, and thus, allowing SO and DA over the attributes.

Acknowledgments. The authors gratefully acknowledge Hans Hedbom for his assistance with PrimeLife Policy Language and reviews that helped to improve the manuscript. Furthermore, the authors also thank Rose-Mharie Åhlfeldt, anonymous reviewers and participants of IFIP Summer School (2015), whose comments and suggestions greatly contribute to enhance and clarify our work.

References

1. Directive 95/46/EC of the European Parliament and of the Council of 24 October 1995 on the protection of individuals with regard to the processing of personal data and on the free movement of such data. Official J. L **281**, 0031–0050 (1995). http://eur-lex.europa.eu/LexUriServ/LexUriServ.do?uri=CELEX:31995L0046:EN:HTML

2. Bakken, D.E., Parameswaran, R., Blough, D.M., Franz, A.A., Palmer, T.J.: Data obfuscation: anonymity and desensitization of usable data sets. IEEE Secur. Priv. **6**, 34–41 (2004)

3. Benitez, K., Malin, B.: Evaluating re-identification risks with respect to the hipaa privacy rule. J. Am. Med. Inform. Assoc. **17**(2), 169–177 (2010)

4. Camenisch, J., Sommer, D., Fischer-Hübner, S., Hansen, M., Krasemann, H., Lacoste, G., Leenes, R., Tseng, J., et al.: Privacy and identity management for everyone. In: Proceedings of the 2005 Workshop on Digital Identity Management, pp. 20–27. ACM (2005)

5. El Emam, K.: Methods for the de-identification of electronic health records for genomic research. Genome Med. **3**(4), 25 (2011). http://genomemedicine.com/content/3/4/25

6. EU Commission: Proposal for a Regulation of the European Parliament and of the Council on the protection of individuals with regard to the processing of personal data and on the free movement of such data (General Data Protection Regulation) (2015). http://data.consilium.europa.eu/doc/document/ST-9565-2015-INIT/en/pdf

7. Fensel, D.: Ontologies. Springer, Heidelberg (2001)

8. Giunchiglia, F., Walsh, T.: A theory of abstraction. Artif. Intell. **57**(2), 323–389 (1992)

9. Hartswood, M., Jirotka, M., Chenu-Abente, R., Hume, A., Giunchiglia, F., Martucci, L.A., Fischer-Hübner, S.: Privacy for peer profiling in collective adaptive systems. In: Camenisch, J., Fischer-Hübner, S., Hansen, M. (eds.) Privacy and Identity 2014. IFIP AICT, vol. 457, pp. 237–252. Springer, Heidelberg (2015). doi:10.1007/978-3-319-18621-4_16

10. Li, N., Li, T., Venkatasubramanian, S.: t-closeness: privacy beyond k-anonymity and l-diversity. In: IEEE 23rd International Conference on Data Engineering, 2007. ICDE 2007, pp. 106–115, April 2007

11. Machanavajjhala, A., Kifer, D., Gehrke, J., Venkitasubramaniam, M.: L-diversity: privacy beyond k-anonymity. ACM Trans. Knowl. Discov. Data **1**(1) (2007). http://doi.acm.org/10.1145/1217299.1217302

12. Martínez, S., Sánchez, D., Valls, A.: Ontology-based anonymization of categorical values. In: Torra, V., Narukawa, Y., Daumas, M. (eds.) MDAI 2010. LNCS, vol. 6408, pp. 243–254. Springer, Heidelberg (2010)

13. Martínez, S., Sánchez, D., Valls, A.: A semantic framework to protect the privacy of electronic health records with non-numerical attributes. J. Biomed. Inform. **46**(2), 294–303 (2013)

14. OCR: Guidance Regarding Methods for De-identification of Protected Health Information in Accordance with the Health Insurance Portability and Accountability Act (HIPAA) Privacy Rule. Office for Civil Rights (2012). http://www.hhs.gov/sites/default/files/ocr/privacy/hipaa/understanding/coveredentities/De-identification/hhs_deid_guidance.pdf

15. Pfitzmann, A., Hansen, M.: A terminology for talking about privacy by data minimization: anonymity, unlinkability, undetectability, unobservability, pseudonymity, and identity management (August 2010). http://dud.inf.tu-dresden.de/literatur/Anon_Terminology_v0.34.pdf, http://dud.inf.tu-dresden.de/literatur/Anon_Terminology_v0.34.pdf. v0.34

16. Rahman, F., Addo, I.D., Ahamed, S.I.: PriSN: a privacy protection framework for healthcare social networking sites. In: Proceedings of the 2014 Conference on Research in Adaptive and Convergent Systems, pp. 66–71. RACS 2014. ACM, New York (2014). http://doi.acm.org/10.1145/2663761.2664199

17. Sweeney, L.: k-anonymity: a model for protecting privacy. Int. J. Uncertainty Fuzziness Knowl.-Based Syst. **10**(5), 557–570 (2002)

18. Wishart, R., Henricksen, K., Indulska, J.: Context obfuscation for privacy via ontological descriptions. In: Strang, T., Linnhoff-Popien, C. (eds.) LoCA 2005. LNCS, vol. 3479, pp. 276–288. Springer, Heidelberg (2005)

19. WP29: Opinion 05/2014 on anonymisation techniques, April 2014. http://ec.europa.eu/justice/data-protection/article-29/documentation/opinion-recommendation/files/2014/wp216_en.pdf

Author Index